Finds from the Frontier:
Material Culture in the 4th–5th Centuries

Finds from the Frontier:
Material Culture in the 4th–5th Centuries

Edited by Rob Collins and Lindsay Allason-Jones

CBA Research Report 162
Council for British Archaeology
2010

Published 2010 by the Council for British Archaeology
St Mary's House, 66 Bootham, York YO30 7BZ

ISBN 978-1-902771-81-6
British Library Cataloguing in Publication Data
A catalogue for this book is available from the British Library

Typeset by Archétype Informatique, www.archetype-it.com
Cover designed by BP Design, York
Printed and bound by The Charlesworth Group

Front cover illustrations: Milecastle near Steel Rigg on Hadrian's Wall (Sophie Cringle); fragment of Late Roman plate with polychrome mosaic insets from Quarry Farm, Ingleby Barwick (Jeff Veitch, © Durham University)

Back cover illustrations: (top) Crambeck parchment ware sherd from York (© York Archaeological Trust); (bottom left) replica of gold crossbow brooch from Erickstanebrae, Dumfries & Galloway (© National Museums of Scotland); (bottom right) flask from Scorton, near Catterick (Jennifer Jones, © Durham University)

Contents

List of figures

List of colour plates (between pages 16 and 17)

List of tables

Acknowledgements

The authors would like to thank all those who participated in the original conference for their contributions to the discussions and their useful and insightful comments.

We also wish to acknowledge the assistance of:
Pat Harrison (Newcastle University)
Catrina Appleby (CBA)

This publication would not have been possible without the generous financial support of the Society for the Promotion of Roman Studies, the Cumberland and Westmorland Antiquarian and Archaeological Society, the Society of Antiquaries of Newcastle upon Tyne, and Hadrian's Wall Heritage Ltd.

List of Contributors

Lindsay Allason-Jones, Newcastle University

Paul Bidwell, Tyne and Wear Archives and Museums

Richard Brickstock, Durham University

Rob Collins, Newcastle University/Portable Antiquities Scheme

Hilary Cool, Barbican Research Associates

Jon Coulston, University of St Andrews

Alexandra Croom, Tyne and Wear Archives and Museums

Mark Hassall, University College of London

Fraser Hunter, National Museums of Scotland

Jacqui Huntley, English Heritage

Colm O'Brien, Sunderland University

Jennifer Price, Durham University

Brian K Roberts, Durham University

Sue Stallibrass, University of Liverpool

Tony Wilmott, English Heritage

Summary

Finds from the Frontier brings together the papers given at a conference held at Newcastle upon Tyne in 2008. The aim of the original conference was to elucidate the life of the 4th-century *limitanei* of Britain through their material culture. The period had traditionally been seen as one of declining standards in the Roman military and materially poorer than during the Principate. The papers consider whether the artefacts that were left behind justify this stance and largely come to the conclusion that, on the contrary, the period was rich in artefacts that have much to tell us about the late frontier.

The geographic focus of the volume is the broader frontier and is not limited to the traditional line of Hadrian's Wall itself. 'Frontier' can be taken as shorthand for 'frontier zone' in many cases throughout the volume, and includes the area between the Humber-Mersey line and the Forth-Clyde line. This region, corresponding to central Britain, includes a number of well-known civilian settlements as well as the traditional military installations more commonly associated with the frontier. The area also looks north of the Wall, to encompass sites such as Traprain Law as well as the 'outpost forts'.

Throughout the volume a number of sites have provided key assemblages for interpretation, usually those that have been the focus of modern excavation or re-assessment. Along the Wall corridor, these sites are South Shields, Housesteads, Vindolanda, Birdoswald, and Carlisle; to the south of the Wall are Binchester, Piercebridge, Catterick, and York. The most important aspect of these key sites, other than the fact that they are all fort sites, is that a clear understanding of the stratigraphy, with generally clear dating evidence provided for phases of structural activity, has unequivocally identified the later material, some of which would have passed for 2nd or 3rd century material if found or discussed without context.

Several of the papers in this volume have addressed logistical aspects of the military economy. Ceramics, coins, glass, and environmental evidence, for example, indicate a shift in the supply and dietary economy in the late frontier. These shifts must be considered with reference to the geographic origins of objects and aspects of cultural practice. Other papers, such as those considering dress accessories and military equipment, interpret the material in a social framework. More than one contributor has noted that particular changes in the various classes of artefact occur in the second half of the 4th century, many of them in the last quarter of the 4th century.

Unlike many works on later Roman Britain, this volume concludes with chapters on the material culture and landscape of the early post-Roman frontier zone and offers suggestions for future research for scholars of both the late Roman and Early Medieval periods.

Sommaire

Finds from the Frontier regroupe les contributions à un colloque réuni à Newcastle upon Tyne en 2008. L'objectif de cette réunion était d'examiner le mode de vie des *limitanei* au 4ème siècle apr. J.-C. en Grande-Bretagne à travers les vestiges de leur culture matérielle. Cette époque a longtemps été perçue comme une période de déclin dans l'armée romaine, matériellement plus pauvre que durant l'époque du Principat. Les articles contenus dans ce volume considèrent si une telle position est justifiée à la lueur des vestiges matériels et concluent que, tout au contraire, l'époque se caractérise par une abondance d'objets riches en information sur cette zone frontalière tardive.

L'aire géographique est une zone frontalière assez large qui ne se limite pas à la frontière linéaire traditionnelle que représente le Mur d'Hadrien. Dans les articles du volume le terme 'frontière' décrit une zone frontalière qui comprend la région entre les fleuves Humber, Mersey, Clyde et Forth. Cette région située au centre de la Grande-Bretagne contient plusieurs habitats civils bien connus en plus des établissements militaires traditionnellement associés à la défense des frontières. La zone au nord du Mur d'Hadrien est également considérée, tenant en compte des sites tels Traprain Law et les 'avant-postes'.

Plusieurs sites, la plupart ceux qui ont fait l'objet de mises au point ou de fouilles méthodiques récentes, ont fournit un ensemble de mobilier de première importance pour l'interprétation. Ce sont les sites de South Shields, Housesteads, Vindolanda, Birdoswald et Carlisle le long du Mur d'Hadrien, et Binchester, Piercebridge, Catterick et York au sud.

L'aspect le plus important de ces sites-clefs, outre le fait qu'ils étaient tous fortifiés, réside dans le fait qu'ils ont livré des ensembles tardifs indisputables qui auraient pu passer pour du mobilier datant du 2ème ou du 3ème siècle apr. J.-C. s'ils avaient été découverts hors contexte. En effet ce sont la lecture de la stratigraphie ainsi que les dates fournies par les phases structurelles qui ont permis cette identification.

Plusieurs auteurs se penchent sur les aspects logistiques de l'économie militaire. L'étude de la céramique, de la numismatique ou des vestiges biologiques, par exemple, indique qu'un changement dans le ravitaillement et dans l'alimentation s'est produit pendant cette phase tardive. Ces changements sont à mettre en relation avec l'aire d'origine des objets et avec certain aspects liés à la pratique culturelle. D'autres contributions, telles celles qui considèrent les accessoires vestimentaires et l'équipement militaire, interprètent les données sous leur aspect social. Enfin plus d'un auteur remarque que c'est à partir du milieu du 4ème siècle apr. J.-C mais surtout au cours du dernier quart du 4ème siècle apr. J.-C que des changements particuliers se discernent dans diverses classes d'objets.

A l'encontre d'autres ouvrages concernant l'époque romaine tardive en Grande-Bretagne, ce volume conclut avec un examen de la culture matérielle et le paysage du début de l'époque post-romaine dans cette zone frontalière et formule certains thèmes de recherche à poursuivre en archéologie de l'Antiquité tardive et du haut Moyen-âge.

Zusammenfassung

Finds from the Frontier enthält die Referate einer Tagung, die in Newcastle upon Tyne in 2008 stattfand. Die Ziehlsetzung der Tagung war das tägliche Leben der limitanei des 4. Jahrhunderts n.Chr. durch ihre materiellen Überresten ins Licht zu bringen. Dieses Jahrhundert war traditionell als eine Epoche abnehmender Lebensbedingungen im römischen Militär angesehen, eine Zeit der Verarmung im Vergleich zum Prinzipat. Die Artikel behandeln die Frage, ob die hintergelassenen Artefakte solch einen Standpunkt begründen; die Autoren kommen im Gegenteil weitgehend zum Schluß, dass es eine Fülle von Artefakten gibt, die vieles über eine späte Grenzregion auszusagen haben.

Das Grenzgebiet, das in diesem Band betrachtet wird, ist nicht nur auf die traditionelle Linie der Hadriansmauer beschränkt. Der Begriff 'Grenze' wird in manchen Fällen in dieser Sammelarbeit als Kurzschrift für 'Grenzgebiet' benutzt und schließt die Gebiete zwishen den Flüssen Humber, Mersey, Clyde und Forth ein. Diese Gegend, die im Zentrum von Großbritannien liegt, enthält mehrere bekannte Zivilsiedlungen sowie die üblichen militärishen Anlagen die normalerweise mit der Grenze in Zusammenhang stehen. Die Zonen nördlich der Mauer, mit Fundorten wie Traprain Law und befestigte 'Außenposten', werden auch berücksichtigt.

Mehrere Fundorte haben bedeutende Sammlungen geliefert: im Allgemeinen sind es neuere Ausgrabungen oder Auswertungen. Entlang des Korridors der Hadriansmauer sind es die Anlagen von South Shields, Housesteads, Vindolanda Birdoswald und Carlisle, und südlich der Mauer Binchester, Piercebridge, Catterick und York. Die wichtigsten Eigenschaften dieser entscheidenden Fundorte, abgesehen von der Tatsache, dass sie alle befestigt waren, sind eine klare Einsicht in die stratigraphische Folge der Fundstätten und generell gut datierte Bauphasen. Es war deswegen möglich späteres Material, das sonst außerhalb Kontext als Funde des 2. oder 3. Jahrhunderts gelten könnte, eindeutig zu identifizieren.

Logistische Aspekte der militärischen Wirtschaft werden in mehreren Artikeln in diesem Band besprochen. Eine Auswertung der Töpferei, Münzen, Glas oder Umwelt, zum Beispiel, zeigt, dass die Versorgung und die Ernährungsweise an der Grenze sich in spätantiker Zeit verändert hat. Diese Veränderungen muss man in Zusammenhang mit den Herkunft der Artefakte sowie mit kulturell verschiedenen Bräuchen stellen.

Einige andere Beiträge, wie diejenige die Kleidungszubehör und militärische Ausrüstung auswerten, interpretieren die Befunde im Rahmen einer Überlegung über soziale Bedingungen. Mehr als einer bemerkt, dass bestimmte Veränderungen in den verschiedenen Artefaktklassen in der zweiten Hälfte des 4. Jahrhunderts und besonders im letzten Viertel des 4. Jahrhunderts vorkamen.

Im Gegensatz zu anderen Sammelbänden über Britannien in der Römerzeit enthält dieser Band auch Schlußkapitel, die die materielle Kultur und die Landschaft des nachrömischen Grenzgebietes behandeln. Der Band schließt mit Empfehlungen für zukünftige Forschungsrichtungen in der Archäologie der spätrömischen sowie der frühmittelalertlichen Perioden.

Foreword *Rob Collins and Lindsay Allason-Jones*

This volume is the result of a conference hosted by the (then) Museum of Antiquities at Newcastle University in March 2008. It would be fair to say that before the conference, there was some apprehension on the part of many of the speakers about the amount of material they had available which they felt was relevant to the period. The conference, however, could be largely described as an 'eye-opener' for the audience and the speakers alike. There was more material available for study than many had realised, and each paper generated questions and comments from conference delegates. The success of the conference, and the general dearth in the literature about the late frontier in Britain, led inevitably to this publication. The following volume is not, however, a straight report on conference proceedings. As editors, we have encouraged the contributors to provide a coherent statement of the existing evidence as well as provide their interpretation of that evidence. In this manner, we hope that the volume can introduce dedicated scholars and interested amateurs alike to the quantity and quality of material found in the late frontier.

Throughout the volume, '4th century' can often be taken to mean the 'long' 4th century, in the manner of modern academic usage where other historical periods do not fit into neat century divisions (eg the 'long' 19th century which covers the period from the French Revolution to the outbreak of the First World War). In Roman Britain, there were serious military, economic, and social implications as a result of the break-away 'empire' of Carausius and Allectus (AD 286–96), its suppression by the Tetrarchy, and the subsequent northern campaigns of Constantius Chlorus. Along Hadrian's Wall, this is clear from archaeologically attested reorganisations at Birdoswald, South Shields, and elsewhere (*RIB* 1912; Bidwell and Speak 1994, 33–43). The split from legitimate, centrally based imperial government by the end of the first decade of the 5th century likewise affected economy and society, particularly in the frontier zone where the military was explicitly linked with the state. Thus it makes some good sense to consider artefacts over a period that begins in the later 3rd century and continues into the early 5th century and beyond, focusing on the northern frontier, but also taking account of developments in the rest of Britain and in the wider Roman empire.

The geographic focus of the volume is the broader frontier and is not limited to the traditional line of Hadrian's Wall itself. 'Frontier' can be taken as shorthand for 'frontier zone' in many cases throughout the volume, and includes the area between the Humber-Mersey line and the Forth-Clyde line. This region, geographically corresponding to central Britain, includes a number of well-known civilian settlements as well as the traditional military installations more commonly associated with the frontier. The area also looks north of the Wall, to encompass sites such as Traprain Law as well as the 'outpost forts'.

An aspect that should be remembered, particularly in reference to the late 4th and 5th centuries, is the difficulty that archaeologists face when dating the post-Roman period. Post-Roman occupation tends to be less intensive in nature, and particularly vulnerable to disturbance, agricultural or otherwise. In rural areas or places where occupation is not continuous from the Roman period to the medieval period or later, the late 4th and 5th centuries are thus stratigraphically closest to the surface and therefore more susceptible to damage and intrusion from both animal and human activity, and this considerably biases the archaeological record when compared with the rest of the Roman period. Furthermore, dating the 5th and 6th centuries, particularly when imported artefacts are absent, can be difficult. Often, dating archaeological strata to these centuries is based on a *terminus post quem* (TPQ) provided by the latest Roman coins or ceramics, or a *terminus ante quem* (TAQ) provided by distinctive Anglo-Saxon, Viking, or medieval artefacts. There were considerable changes in the material culture of these centuries, as will be seen in this volume, and advancing our understanding of these changes has been a consistent challenge.

Despite this, the authors who contributed to this volume are to be congratulated for their efforts. We have included a number of catalogues of different classes of evidence, providing much needed updates to older material or creating new resources. There are also papers that provide excellent typological overviews of material typical of the 4th century not found elsewhere. The papers advance our understanding of the period, highlighting changes in the material culture, and offer insights into a dynamic frontier society at the end of the Roman period and beyond.

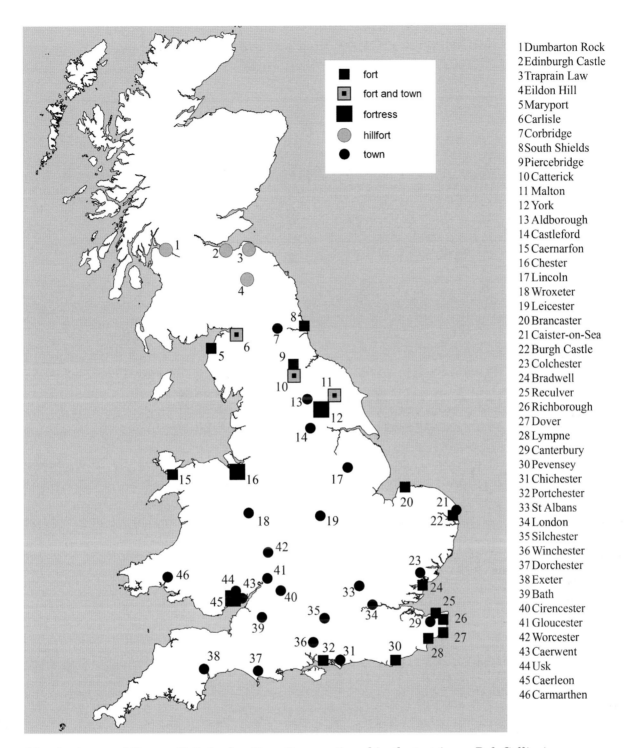

1 Dumbarton Rock
2 Edinburgh Castle
3 Traprain Law
4 Eildon Hill
5 Maryport
6 Carlisle
7 Corbridge
8 South Shields
9 Piercebridge
10 Catterick
11 Malton
12 York
13 Aldborough
14 Castleford
15 Caernarfon
16 Chester
17 Lincoln
18 Wroxeter
19 Leicester
20 Brancaster
21 Caister-on-Sea
22 Burgh Castle
23 Colchester
24 Bradwell
25 Reculver
26 Richborough
27 Dover
28 Lympne
29 Canterbury
30 Pevensey
31 Chichester
32 Portchester
33 St Albans
34 London
35 Silchester
36 Winchester
37 Dorchester
38 Exeter
39 Bath
40 Cirencester
41 Gloucester
42 Worcester
43 Caerwent
44 Usk
45 Caerleon
46 Carmarthen

Map 1   A map of Roman Britain, locating sites mentioned in the text (map: Rob Collins)

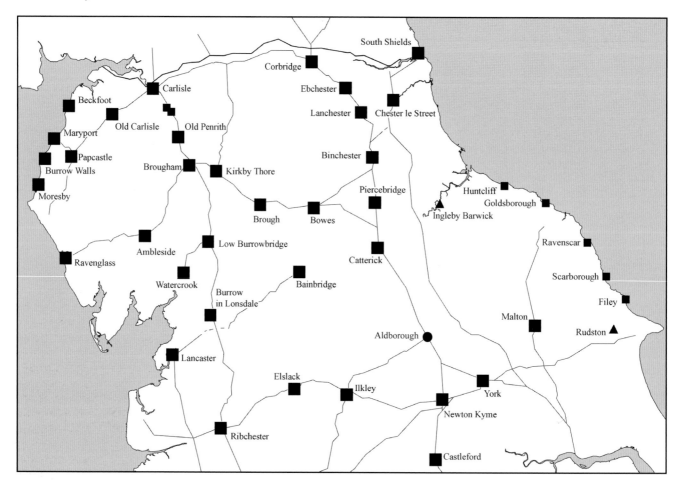

Map 2   *A map of northern England, locating military installations and towns with military installations (squares), towns (circles), and villas (triangles), as well as the Roman road network in the region (map: Rob Collins)*

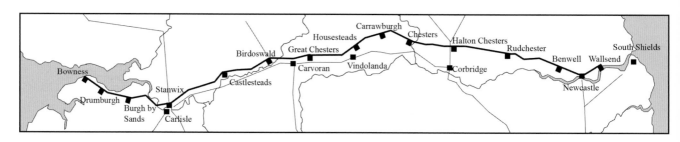

Map 3   *A map locating the forts along Hadrian's Wall and the Stanegate (map: Rob Collins)*

1   A different life *H E M Cool*

'This late period is generally seen as one of declining standards in the Roman military and materially poorer than previous centuries.'

Original conference abstract

'It's life Jim, but not as we know it.'

Dr McCoy to Captain Kirk, *Star Trek*

A number of difficulties must be faced when exploring finds from 4th-century frontiers, and most of them do not reside in the objects themselves but rather in the way we approach them. The finds sit in museums and stores quietly waiting to be asked to tell their stories; but we generally ask them the wrong questions and do not pay attention to the answers they try to give. The first quotation at the head of the paper encapsulates the problem nicely. Within its original context it appeared somewhat apologetic as though the period and its finds were not really of sufficient standing to justify a conference. We see in the phraseology, consciously or not, the shadow of Gibbon's *Decline and Fall of the Roman Empire*. Gibbon wrote on the first page of his work that AD 98–180 was the happy period when the Roman Empire 'comprehended the fairest part of the earth, and the most civilised portion of mankind'. Against such a background how can what

happened in the 4th century be anything other than a decline? It is the aim of this paper to look at the assumptions underlying this concept of a decline as far as the finds go, and then to go on to consider whether seeing finds from the frontier as a special case is a sensible decision.

Different but not poorer

To any finds specialist the idea that the 4th century was materially poorer than the earlier periods is a strange one, as 4th-century assemblages tend to be as large as, if not larger than, what had gone before on similar types of sites. What cannot be doubted though, is that the nature of the finds had changed greatly by the 4th century, and it is probably this that allows the idea of relative poverty to emerge. This can be explored by considering the Roman soldier and his trappings. To most people, the mental image that springs to mind will be that of a 1st- or 2nd-century legionary dressed in *lorica segmentata* (Fig 1.1). Generations of school children grew up seeing a model of just such a soldier as part of museum displays (eg Potter 1983, fig 31), and these days it is the style most favoured by military re-

Fig 1.1 A scene from Trajan's column showing legionaries in lorica segmentata *(picture: MJ Baxter)*

1

Table 1.1   A comparison of the functional profile of assemblages from five military sites

	Castleford		Caerleon		Caister		Portchester		Birdoswald	
	No	**%**	**No**	**%**	**No**	**%**	**No**	**%**	**No**	**%**
Personal	14	28	*18	12	63	43	36	62	20	43
Toilet	1	2	1	1	1	1	1	2	3	7
Textiles	5	10	–	–	8	6	4	7	6	13
Household	–	–	8	5	12	8	3	5	–	–
Recreation	4	8	*3	2	10	7	–	–	7	15
Weights etc	–	–	1	1	2	1	–	–	1	2
Writing	1	2	1	1	1	1	2	3	–	–
Transport	1	2	3	2	2	1	–	–	–	–
Tools	6	12	5	3	15	10	6	10	3	7
Fasteners	7	14	70	45	20	14	3	5	2	4
Agriculture	–	–	3	2	1	1	1	2	–	–
Military	12	24	43	28	9	6	2	3	4	9
Total	51		156		145		58		46	

*see Appendix 1.1 for the problems of quantifying these categories

enactment societies. Of the six re-enactment groups which appear to be active in Britain currently, four favour this period compared with one for the 3rd century and one for the 4th century and beyond.[1] What doesn't automatically spring to mind is the 4th-century soldier who, with his flashy belt equipment, would have been just as obviously a military man to his contemporaries (see Coulston, this volume). To a certain extent we can be excused for the bias towards the early period as a similar thing was happening in the 4th century as well. Whilst the Tetrarchs might have been happy to be portrayed as idealised late 3rd-century soldiers, as in the porphyry group now built into the south-west external façade of San Marco at Venice (Plate 1; also Elsner 1998, pl 29), the Arch of Constantine at Rome looks further back. This monument, built to celebrate the emperor's *decennalia* in AD 315, includes a considerable number of relief scenes re-used from earlier monuments (Cameron 2006, 24, fig 4; Elsner 1998, 187–8, pl 126). The propaganda aim was to place Constantine's victories squarely within the context of those of his illustrious predecessors, but the casual viewer, then as now, would have come away with the impression that proper soldiers wore *lorica segmentata,* which by then had not been the case for well over half a century (Bishop 2002, 91, fig 10.1).

This association in our minds between the military and *lorica segmentata* is important for it was a type of armour with many fiddly fittings which appear to have been in constant need of repair and renewal (Bishop 2002). Consequently, excavations on any 1st- or 2nd-century site with military, especially legionary, involvement will generally produce these fittings to a greater or lesser degree (see for example Catterick – Lentowicz 2002, 62 nos 169–77; Cramond – Holmes *et al* 2003, 103 nos 1–9). The

impact such fittings can have on assemblages of small finds from military sites can be seen from an inspection of Tables 1.1 and 1.2. These summarise five assemblages that are all undoubtedly military given their contexts. The first is a midden deposit dated to the mid- to late 70s from the campaigning fort at Castleford. The second is material associated with the Phase IV barracks (mid-2nd to mid- to late 3rd century) at the Roman Gates site within the legionary fortress at Caerleon. Next follow two assemblages from within Saxon Shore forts (Caister-on-Sea and Portchester) which may both be dated to the middle years of the 4th century. Finally there is a group of material from occupation within the fort at Birdoswald dating to the second half of the 4th century (see Appendix 1.1 for details).

These assemblages have been chosen to give a chronological progression, and, as can be seen from Table 1.1, the two earliest ones have a noticeably different profile from the 4th-century ones. At both Castleford and Caerleon obviously military items account for approximately one-quarter of the total assemblage. This is not the case among the 4th-century assemblages, which are all dominated by personal ornaments with the numbers of obviously military items being negligible.

In Table 1.2 the personal ornaments and military equipment categories for the five sites are presented in more detail. (The very small numbers of hobnails and the single ear-ring have been omitted.) The military material has been divided into fittings from armour (plate, scale, and chain), belt and baldrick fittings, and the 'other' category consisting of weapons, apron mounts, etc. In the personal ornaments the beads have been divided between large beads (overwhelmingly melon beads) and small beads of types that are known to have been used as parts of bead strings such as necklaces and

Table 1.2 A detailed comparison of the personal ornaments and military items in Table 1.1

	Castleford		Caerleon		Caister		Portchester		Birdoswald	
	No	**%**	**No**	**%**	**No**	**%**	**No**	**%**	**No**	**%**
Armour fittings	5	10	19	12	–	–	–	–	–	–
Belt etc fittings	–	–	11	7	4	3	–	–	3	7
Other military	7	14	13	8	5	3	2	3	1	2
Brooches	9	18	6	4	6	4	1	2	5	11
Finger ring	1	2	1	1	1	1	–	–	1	2
Large beads	4	8	1	1	–	–	–	–	–	–
Small beads	–	–	1	1	4	3	–	–	8	17
Hairpins	–	–	3	2	30	21	17	29	2	4
Bracelets	–	–	4	3	23	16	18	31	3	7
Total	51	–	156	–	145	–	58	–	46	–

bracelets. In the personal ornaments brooches, finger rings, and large beads may be considered gender neutral. Bracelets, hairpins, and bead strings, by contrast, are overwhelmingly female items, judged by both associations in graves and in the literary sources.

This table shows that in the archaeological record what may be termed the 'visibility' of different groups of people changes with time. In the 1st and 2nd centuries, it is the soldier that dominates military assemblages, overwhelmingly with parts of his armour. In the 4th century changes in women's fashions of adornment make females the most conspicuous group, in military as in civilian contexts. By then the wearing of bead strings had become ubiquitous amongst all sections of society, as opposed to being primarily associated with the women associated with the military when they first appeared in any numbers from the late 2nd century (Brewer 1986, 149–51, nos 9–73; Cool 2004, 385–90). Bracelet fashions had also changed, with the preference being to wear many slender bracelets at a time. Like the earlier *lorica segmentata*, both the bead strings and the bracelets were easily broken, heightening the visibility of females in the small finds assemblages. Unless we consider that males should always be more visible, these tables are not telling us about declining standards and material poverty. What they are telling us is that uniform and jewellery fashions were now different from what they had been earlier.

Similar major changes can be seen in many other categories of finds evidence. To take the most obvious within pottery, the vessels on the table go from being dominated by a standard range of glossy bright orange imported *terra sigillata* to indigenous wares in a variety of hues. The colour-coated wares of the Nene Valley industry that played a major role in pottery supply in the late Roman period (Tyers 1996, 173–5) ranged from black to red/brown and were matt rather than glossy (Anderson 1980, 38).

It is noticeable that the Romano-British fine ware industries did not provide the smaller cup forms that the *terra sigillata* industries had. While not all of the samian cups would have been used for drinking, it is clear that some were (Biddulph 2008). It is also clear that from the later 2nd century the glass industries provided the main source of small drinking vessels (Cool 2006, 149). It is a matter of taste as to whether a table furnished with black pottery and colourless glass should be seen as a decline compared to one with bright orange pottery. In the mid-1st century, Petronius has the multi-millionaire Trimalchio say that he prefers drinking out of glass to other materials but the problem is it breaks (*Satyricon* XV.50). By the 4th century even quite humble people could enjoy the experience, judging by the distribution of the glass fragments. Should the fact that they had glass rather than samian cups be looked on as impoverishment or enrichment? Probably only archaeologists would think the former.

By the 4th century the world was very different from what it had been in the 2nd, and it was a difference that permeated all aspects of life from the individual's relationship with the state to the way he conducted his private life. Within the former category the extension of Roman citizenship by Caracalla in AD 212 did away with one of the major social differentiations of the Roman world, that between citizen and non-citizen. Given that Roman law was carefully graded to deal with disputes between these two groups (Salway 1981, 525), this in itself would have been a major disruption to what had gone before (Mattingly 2006, 337). Within a military milieu, of course, it removed a major difference between legionary and auxiliary troops. Equally, local administration was very different in the 4th century, with the burden of tax collection falling heavily on the local elites and the consequent efforts to avoid this (White 2007, 53). In the personal domain burial customs had changed markedly from a predominantly cremation rite to one of inhumation, and from one where grave and pyre goods were not exceptional to one where they increasingly were (Philpott 1991, 225). Similarly, there can be no doubt that the changing religious environment had an effect on how people conducted their lives. The advent of Christianity within these shores often focuses on explicitly Christian artefacts such as the Water Newton treasure, the earliest surviving liturgical plate from anywhere in the empire (Hartley *et al* 2006, 210–22). On a less spectacular but probably more fundamental level, it may be that the strictures of the early Church fathers were influencing aspects of diet and appearance (Cool 2006, 238–42). We need to study our 4th-century finds against their social context, and it is neither appropriate nor relevant to judge them against a perceived 2nd-century golden age.

Where's the frontier?

Having established that a 4th-century assemblage will be fundamentally different from what had gone before, and that soldiers will not form so conspicuous an element of even military assemblages, does it make sense to think of the frontier as having its own distinctive material culture? In the 2nd and 3rd century the way of exploring this is easy: one can just look at the evidence of Hadrian's Wall and its associated establishments and compare that with what is going on elsewhere, both in the north and more widely. Differences rapidly emerge. We can note, as just one slightly frivolous example, that the Wall population was drinking wine that would have tasted different from that consumed in other areas. The amphora evidence suggests much of the country was being supplied by Gallic wine producers whereas such amphorae are seriously under-represented on the Wall sites, presumably because much was being supplied in barrels from other producers (for references see Cool 2006, 134–5).

By the 4th century though, the simple and long-established equation in the minds of most people that Hadrian's Wall equals *the* frontier no longer works. This often attracts less attention than it should. In most works on Roman Britain, whilst acknowledgement is generally made that different frontiers grew up in the later period with the establishment of the Saxon Shore defences, relatively little attention is paid to them. This is well illustrated in the current standard work on Roman Britain where the 1st- to 3rd-century military community attracts five times the space that the 4th-century one does (Mattingly 2006, 87–252). The possibility that frontier assemblages can be found elsewhere in Britain will be considered further below; first we will consider what, if anything, is distinctive about the assemblages from the Wall area.

Wine again provides a useful point of entry as the Campanian black sand amphorae of the mid-3rd- to mid-4th-century map an interesting distribution. They seem to arrive at the port at South Shields

and be distributed from there (Fig 1.2A). The distribution is very much a north-eastern one, along the Wall as far as Vindolanda and down into Yorkshire via Dere Street with the only outlier being noted at a site in Gloucestershire (see Williams 1994, 219; other references in Cool 2006, 135).[2] This north-eastern distribution is repeated in other distinctive forms of 4th-century material culture like the large composite bone and jet hairpins (Fig 1.2B; Cool and Mason 2008, fig 11.3).

It is also within this area that the distinctive 4th-century belt equipment occurs. Unlike the earlier periods, belt equipment is not the exclusive possession of soldiers in the 4th century (Swift 2000b, 2), but it was an element of their uniform. Elsewhere in this volume (see Coulston) it is noted how rare these fittings are in general on the Wall, but they have been found at Vindolanda (Bidwell 1985, 122, no 28, fig 41) and South Shields (Allason-Jones and Miket 1984, 192, nos 3.611, 614–15). Further south in this north-eastern area belt fittings such as these are regular, if not particularly common, features of 4th-century assemblages, for example at Beadlam (Neal 1996, 45–9, nos 2 and 4, fig 31), Catterick (Cool 2002a, 32), Piercebridge (Cool and Mason 2008, fig 11.10 no 260) and Malton (propeller belt stiffener; unpublished excavations by MAP). Taken all together this evidence suggests that in the 4th century there is a major difference between the western and eastern parts of the Wall and their hinterlands. Other aspects of life also mirror this. In animal husbandry, for example, it has been suggested that there was significant variation between animal bone assemblages east and west of the Pennines (Stallibrass 2000, 74).

When looking for the location of 4th-century and later frontiers in Britain, the distribution of prick spurs is a useful tool (Fig 1.3). At the outset it needs to be said that spurs are rare, not just within Britain but within the rest of the empire too. The standard work on Roman military equipment mentions them only twice, once in a Republican and once in a 4th-century context (Bishop and Coulston 2006, 69, 227). Clearly the Roman cavalry rarely felt the need for them. The first work to consider Romano-British spurs considered them very rare but defined two types, one of which was distinctly Romano-British (Shortt 1959, 69), and it is this type we are considering (Fig 1.3 for illustrations). It was in use in the late 4th century and beyond, and an increasing number are coming to light both from excavation and via the Portable Antiquities Scheme. The input from that scheme is important as, even though coverage is not uniform, it provides a check on whether a distribution map is giving a good approximation of where items were actually used as opposed to where field workers have been active. In Figure 1.3, for example, it can be seen that Lincolnshire is well supplied with the type whereas Norfolk is not. Given that both counties have seen considerable metal detecting activity over the years, with a long and honourable record of reporting such

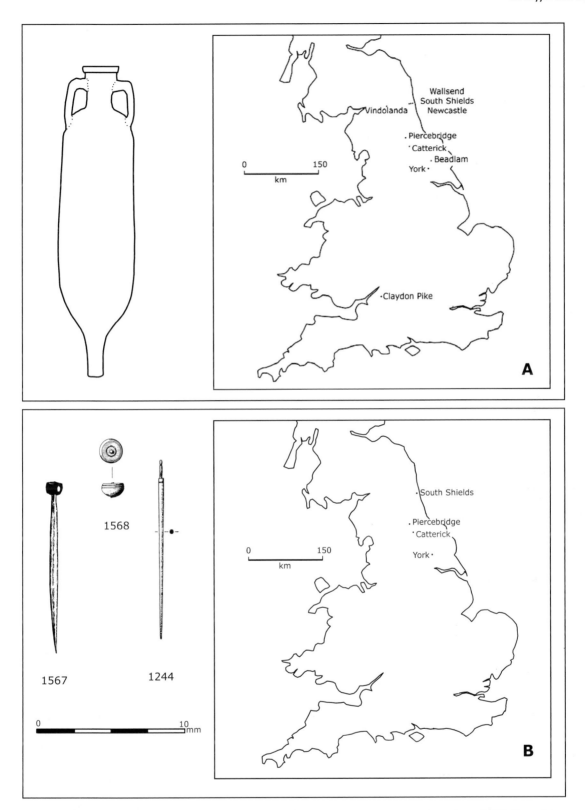

Fig 1.2 Regional distributions of artefacts associated with the eastern end of Hadrian's Wall and its hinterland: A, Campanian almond-lipped black sand amphora of the mid-3rd to mid-4th century; B, Composite bone and jet hairpins of the 4th century, illustrated examples from Piercebridge (Cool and Mason 2008)

finds for recording, it is likely that this is reflecting use patterns.

The status of these spurs has long been equivocal: were they items of military uniform or were they used by civilians? The confusion arose because of the very varied types of sites they came from, including villas and towns as well as military establishments. The first author to reconsider them recently concluded his paper with the words 'while these spurs could be associated with the Roman army, the lack of real

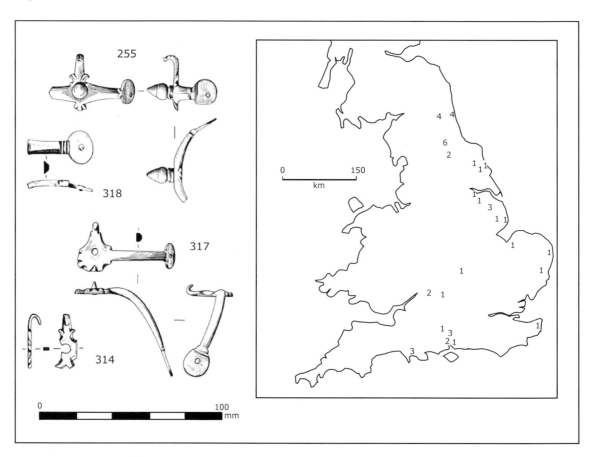

Fig 1.3   The distribution of late 4th-century prick spurs. Source Worrell 2004b with additions from Piercebridge, Winchester Library excavations (unpublished, Oxford Archaeology) and the Portable Antiquities Database (reference numbers NARC-D98096, NMS-588B84). Illustrated examples from Piercebridge (Cool and Mason 2008)

military associations means that they could also be related to the chase' (Leahy 1996, 240). It is implicit that the 'real military associations' referred to are cavalry forts within the northern frontier area. Other authors who have considered them, myself included, have been equally puzzled; but we have probably all been guilty of not considering these items against their proper chronological and social background. The 'real military associations' referred to are irrelevant for these items, given that they pre-date the period when the spurs were in use, and much more attention needs to be paid to why spurs suddenly appear in the archaeological record.

One of the features of the late Roman period was the pressure on the frontiers and the consequent settlement of communities of people who had previously been considered barbarians within the empire (Mattingly 2006, 225–30). These communities brought with them their own costumes and equipment which influenced and transformed many aspects of life for the long-established inhabitants of the empire, the bead-string necklaces referred to in the first part of this paper being a good example. It seems likely that the appearance of spurs was one aspect of this phenomenon. It is noticeable that spurs form part of the goods in elite graves in the 3rd and 4th centuries beyond the frontiers,

such as at Gommern in Germany and Garwolin in Poland (Aillagon 2008, 662, 683). The famous Stilicho diptych, an ivory hinged panel depicting Stilicho with his wife and son (Fig 1.4 and Frontispiece; Aillagon 2008, 244, cat III.7) also provides some insights. At the time it was made in *c* AD 400, Stilicho was the most powerful man in the western empire, acting as regent for the child emperors. He is depicted as a soldier with shield, spear, and a sword with its attendant belt and strap fittings. His cloak is fastened by a crossbow brooch on his right shoulder. The brooch has often attracted attention as showing that crossbows were appropriate for the socially elite (Swift 2000b, 3–4 for references), but his feet have attracted less notice (other than Swift 2000a, 212, suggesting they show a new shoe form). What can be seen are bands going around the back and over the front of the ankle. The angle of his left foot shows that they meet on the inside of the foot in a roundel, with possibly another band going down to the instep. I would argue that this arrangement is more likely to depict spur straps than shoe decoration as the roundel would be the attachment disc on the metal spur around the back of the foot for the leather ankle straps. It does not appear to be a sensible part of a shoe.[3] If the interpretation of these details is correct, the association with the

Fig 1.4 Drawing of the figure of Stilicho from the Stilicho diptych. Note the straps and roundel fitting on his left foot

2000b, 69–77). Subsequent analysis of the individuals' teeth has shown that though some were indeed incomers they were not all coming from the same place (Evans *et al* 2006). Probably their ethnicity counted for much less than their status as military men, and the individual with the spurs was likely to have held considerable power and authority in the community. By the late 4th century when this burial took place, 'Roman' officers and gentlemen would no doubt have looked very alien and barbaric to a time-travelling 2nd-century visitor, but presumably quite normal to their 4th-century contemporaries.

With the likely military associations of the spurs established, we can return to the distribution map (Fig 1.3), and consider what it tells us about frontiers. It is a predominantly coastal distribution, with many examples coming from sites either on or close to the eastern seaboard or the major inlets, such as the Humber estuary or the Wash. This is a type of distribution which fits with the threat of raiding that provoked the building of the Saxon Shore defences, and indeed several spurs have been found in either the forts belonging to the system (Caister-on-Sea, Richborough) or the coastal fortlets associated with it further north (Filey). As Worrell (2004b) first pointed out, there are two distinct clusterings, one in the north-east to which the eastern Hadrian's Wall and its hinterland belongs; and one in the south-central area with most examples having been found in Hampshire but with others in Dorset, Gloucestershire and Oxfordshire.

The southern area is particularly interesting as it borders and in some cases includes part of the West Country, an area which, judged by the small finds normally thought to signify 4th-century soldiers and other officials (crossbow brooches and belt fittings), appears to be the most overtly militarised in the country. Belt equipment is extremely common. Cirencester appears to be the centre of the largest concentration of such equipment in Britain (Swift 2000a, 185), and there is evidence that it was being manufactured in the town (Paddock 1998, 306). The work that will set out this evidence remains unpublished, but it is certainly the case that such material is a regular feature of mid-4th-century and later assemblages on both urban and rural sites in the area (see material cited in Cool 2007, 348; see also Leech 1982, 115, no 38, fig 82, 252, no 157, fig 123; Viner 1998, 213, nos 13.9–10, fig 102). There is also evidence that regional styles of belt equipment evolved which were not in use elsewhere (Swift 2000a, 2). Crossbow brooches occur regularly though not in similar numbers to the belt equipment. Though the eastern part of the country may have more crossbow brooches in absolute numbers, it is the west and especially the south-west that has the higher concentration of gold and gilded examples (compare Swift 2000a, figs 13, 15). What are we to make of all this, given that the West Country is not traditionally seen as a military stronghold or frontier area? Recently White has made a case for there having been a second coastal command in

sword, shield, and spear unequivocally says that spurs were part of military costume. What is especially important to note here is that Stilicho was half Vandal and what we seem to have is a coming together of 'Roman' and 'barbarian' elite military fashions.

Against such a background, the probability that our spurs formed part of the uniform of senior officers is high, and it is probably as one of these officers that we should interpret the individual buried with a gilded crossbow brooch with the inscription VTOR FELIX (*good luck to the user*) and VENE VIVAS (*live well*) on either side of the bow, silver belt fittings and a pair of spurs, who was uncovered during the most recent excavations at the Lankhills School cemetery at Winchester. (The excavations were conducted by Oxford Archaeology and the group of finds is currently being studied by the author. Illustrations of it in an unconserved state, prior to the discovery of the inscription, can be seen in Booth 2007.) Lankhills has produced more graves with males buried with crossbow brooches and belt equipment than any other cemetery in Britain, but this is the only burial which has both spurs and an inscribed brooch (Clarke 1979, and unpublished excavations). The debate as to who these people were is ongoing. The original author of the report on the earlier excavations believed they were incomers from the Danubian provinces. Subsequent study, placing the grave goods in context, suggested that the patterns of deposition had parallels in that area as did some of the items themselves, but that other elements such as the bracelets were often British forms (Swift the 4th century that protected the west, just as the *Comes litoris Saxonici* was responsible for the east (White 2007, 59). Whilst this might explain some of this concentration, and the Severn estuary would indeed provide as much a gateway to rich areas of the diocese of *Britannia* as the Humber estuary did, it scarcely explains the all-pervasive nature of these finds.

It is clear from the amount of late Antonine to Severan military equipment in southern England that the presence of soldiers was far from unusual there. Mike Bishop long ago suggested that this should be seen as reflecting dispersed military units in towns carrying out policing and other duties, as is seen in other provinces (Bishop 1991). I have gone as far as to suggest that some of the distribution in Gloucestershire could reflect the settlement of retired soldiers returning home (Cool 2007, 348). The extent of the 4th-century belt equipment, crossbow brooch, and occasional spur evidence in the West Country seems to go far beyond this pattern. So we are left wondering: are we looking at an unexpected militarisation of an area not previously thought of as a frontier; are we looking at an area overburdened by state officials who were also entitled to wear the military belt; or are we looking at a fashion statement amongst a possibly militarised elite. The West Country was populated throughout the Roman period by people who favoured regional types of ornamentation and who consumed things in large quantities compared with many other areas of Roman Britain. Is the liking for belt equipment and the development of local styles just one aspect of this? Against that explanation though, the possibility that Lincolnshire was heavily militarised in the 4th century has also been suggested by Leahy (1996, 240), and that too is another area not normally considered as a centre of military activity.

Such questions raise fundamental doubts about where the frontiers were in the 4th century and how we identify them. The certainties of the 1st and 2nd centuries, when it was relatively easy to spot military sites, is long gone by then. For an installation of the earlier date, even if the defences of a fort have not been located, the pottery or glass vessel assemblages, the brooch assemblages, and quite often the grain and animal bone assemblages will mark out the community living there as military. This is not so obviously the case in the 4th century. Traditionally the 4th-century military disposition has been seen as a dichotomy between the low-grade frontier troops (the *limitanei*) and the field army (the *comitatenses*). It would be gratifying if we could make the equation that belt equipment, crossbow brooches, and spurs equals *comitatenses* and the lack of these things in what appear to be military establishments, such as those on the western side of Hadrian's Wall, equals *limitanei*. As we have seen, however, such equations are not easy to make. It would be satisfying if we could take as a starting point that because Hadrian's Wall was something

that could be interpreted as a fixed frontier in the earlier centuries, it remained so in the 4th century and so its inhabitants and their material culture could be viewed as patterns of what *limitanei* would have had access to. The ease with which differences can be drawn between the western and the eastern parts of Hadrian's Wall and its hinterland, both in the material culture and the types of units listed there in the *Notitia Dignitatum* (Mattingly 2006, 239), suggests it is far from being that simple. To the eyes of a 4th-century beholder the difference between the units of the frontier armies and those of the field army may well have been stunningly obvious – by the cut and fabric of the cloaks, the colour of the tunics, for example. For us, dealing with a tiny sub-set of their possessions, it is not so easy or so obvious.

I would argue that currently we are a long way from understanding what is going on in the 4th-century in Britain, and so the concept of frontier finds as a category in themselves is not at present one that can be made with any ease. Within Romano-British studies, there is a tendency to see Hadrian's Wall as a separate self-contained entity. It is easy to see why this view has grown up. In part it comes from the long-established tendency of people who work in the area of Roman military studies to see their study area as somehow separate from the wider Roman world (Alston 1995, 3; Gardner 2007, 29). Hadrian's Wall falls into an even more specialised sub-discipline: the world of frontier studies, the fascination of which is illustrated by activities as diverse as conferences such as the *Limes* and the urge to make the extant frontiers into a unified Unesco World Heritage Site. I would suggest that if the 4th-century finds from the Wall are going to be used to cast light on its inhabitants, they have to be placed much more within the context of what is going on elsewhere in Britain, both to the north and the south, than is currently done.

It is extremely important to understand what is happening in the 4th century not only for its own sake, but also because it provides the key to understanding the 5th century and beyond. It will enable us to go beyond the frequently sterile discussions about the 'end of Roman Britain' that often owe more to an author's ideology than their engagement with the evidence. I have written elsewhere that the patterns in material culture that can be detected at the end of the 4th century and into the 5th are just parts of trajectories that have their origins a century or more earlier and which in some cases continue for a century or more beyond (Cool 2000a; 2003; 2006, 223–35). In the 5th-century Roman north we can certainly see occupation continuing within forts and other defended sites sometimes associated with refortifications or the modification of existing fortifications (Wilmott 1997, 224–31; Cool and Mason 2008, 308). The argument is that these sites became the centres for local militias or war bands. Given the possible 4th-century militarisation seen in such unlikely areas as the West

Country and Lincolnshire, possibly this too was not such a break with the past as might at first be suspected.

We stand at the beginning of a very interesting period in the study of the 4th century, both in the northern frontier area and elsewhere, but to get the best value out of our work we need to do a number of things. It is necessary to set the patterns we find against the changed social and political background that existed in the 4th century so that we can better understand them. We need to reintegrate the study of the Hadrian's Wall area with the wider currents of thought about what is happening contemporaneously in the rest of Britain. Such an approach cannot fail to benefit all the areas. And finally we must never forget the words of the immortal Dr McCoy quoted at the head of this paper, which might perhaps be rephrased for this journey as 'It's Roman Jim; it's just not the 2nd century'.

Appendix 1.1

The assemblages have excluded structural ironwork and quern fragments. Functional attributions generally follow Crummy 1983, though it should be noted that all belt and buckle fittings have been placed in the military category and ferrules have been assigned to the fasteners and fittings.

Castleford

The midden is discussed in Abramson *et al* 1999, 47, Trench 14 Phase 1c. The finds discussed are derived from Cool and Philo 1998. For the precise catalogue numbers see Cool and Philo 1998, 37, contexts 108, 112, 172, 177 and 178. Part of the midden was waterlogged and this preserved organic material, but these items have been excluded from Tables 1.1 and 1.2 to allow comparison with the other, non-waterlogged assemblages.

Caerleon

The phase is discussed in Evans and Metcalf 1992, 65–71, and the finds are those assigned to Phase IV in the specialist reports. It should be noted that the contexts of 21 frit melon beads and 19 glass gaming counters were not stated in the report (*ibid* 184–

5). This means that in Table 1.1 the totals for the personal ornaments and recreational categories are probably understated and in Table 1.2 that for large beads is as well. Both types of finds were going out of use during the earlier part of the period under consideration.

Caister-on-Sea

This is the material from the refuse in the E squares on the rampart and the rubbish associated with building 1 (see Darling and Gurney 1993, 13, 16–28, 250). For the precise catalogue numbers see Cool 2000a, 56–7.

Portchester

The material is derived from the pits dated to the second quarter of the 4th century and to the middle occupation (Cunliffe 1975, 43–4, 78). For the precise catalogue numbers see Cool 2000a, 57.

Birdoswald

The assemblage is derived from the deposits on the relaid floor of Building 197 and those associated with the Period 5 collapse of the west end of Building 198 and the backfilling of the sub-floor (Wilmott 1997, 208–9). For the precise catalogue numbers see Cool 2000a, 56.

Notes

1 Source: http://www.larp.com/legioxx/index.html – checked 4 August 2008. 1st- to 2nd-century groups – Ermine Street Guard, Leg II Augusta, Leg XIIII Gemina, the Antonine Guard; 3rd-century group – Quinta; 4th-century and later – Comitatus.

2 See also http://ads.ahds.ac.uk/catalogue/archive/amphora_ahrb_2005/index.cfm – search for Campanian almond-rim type).

3 I am most grateful to my friend Quita Mould for sharing her boundless knowledge about shoes with me in relation to the discussion of Stilicho's feet, though naturally she is not responsible for the conclusions I have drawn.

2　The late Roman frontier: a structural background　*Tony Wilmott*

Ten years ago, at the Roman Archaeology Conference held at Durham in 1999, Pete Wilson and I organised a session on the Late Roman Transition in the North of Britain (Wilmott and Wilson 2000). The session brought together excavators, specialists in the areas of finds study, ceramics, and environmental studies, and academics with an interest in the topic. The discussions generated were wide ranging and stimulating. It became very clear that the end of the northern frontier was not a straightforward matter, and that the varied and small-scale evidence from a number of sites did not tell a consistent story. This volume of papers demonstrates the continued interest and engagement of scholars in the period, in particular in its material culture. This contribution, however, will revisit some of the structural and stratigraphic evidence in order to present a wider background for the studies which follow.

The study of the Roman frontier in northern Britain has been pursued for over 400 years, and this study has naturally followed agendas that have changed through time. It was only in the early 20th century, for instance, that Hadrian's authorship of the Wall was finally proven. The problem-oriented work of the 1920s and 1930s was aimed largely towards morphological questions and aspects of the construction of the Wall. Alongside these efforts, excavations within a number of the Wall's installations, notably on Milecastle 48 in 1911, began to develop the concept of Wall-Periods, which were proposed in their final form following the 1929 Birdoswald excavation (Richmond and Birley 1930) – the first in any Wall fort to be conducted 'with special regard to stratification'. The Periods were, it was thought, connected firmly to historical events, and this is reflected in their description as Hadrianic, Severan, Constantinian, and Theodosian. The last Wall-Period, the Theodosian, consisted of rebuilding work dated to the later 4th century, which was thought to be the result of reconstruction following the great Barbarian Conspiracy of AD 367. At Birdoswald this period included the reuse of two inscriptions which were held to help date the previous two Wall-Periods. The system of Periods became the basis of most interpretation on Hadrian's Wall for several decades.

Since the mid-1970s, a great deal of work has demonstrated that the history of the Wall is far more complex than the Wall-Period idea allowed. Though major trends can be discerned, the attribution of these to particular and very specific imperial actions has long been unacceptable. The influence of the Wall-Period concept casts a long shadow, however, and I refer to it here because Ken Dark (1992) postulated a final 'Wall-Period', namely a coordinated sub-Roman re-defence of the frontier.

In recent years, large-scale excavation has taken place at South Shields, Wallsend, Vindolanda, Birdoswald, and Carlisle. These excavations, together with smaller-scale work in and around Newcastle and at the western end of the Wall, have opened up new questions about the frontier. Completely new chapters are being written. Most importantly for us today, the excavation of large areas, combined with a rejection of established preconceptions, has allowed previously invisible or unconsidered evidence for the very latest periods of occupation to be investigated (Wilmott 2000; Collins 2009).

To examine the end of the Wall, it is necessary briefly to review the later Roman phases. From the little evidence we have, by the end of the 3rd century the civil settlements had declined to the point of abandonment at Vindolanda and Housesteads. The decline in these settlements must reflect a major change in the economic life and organisation of the fort settlement, though what might have caused this disruption is not clear, at least partly because the original function of the *vici* within the Roman settlement landscape is not clearly understood either. It should be stressed that excavations on the *vici* of the Wall have been very few, while the work of Alan Biggins and David Taylor has demonstrated that the *vici* were far more extensive than previously imagined. There can be no certainty that the phenomenon of abandonment was a general pattern, though at Vindolanda, as John Casey (1985) has shown, it is convincingly demonstrated by the disparities in the coin assemblages between fort and *vicus*. Whatever the case, *vicus* abandonment has been associated in the past with a change in barrack accommodation. The early unitary barracks within the forts were altered in the early to mid-3rd century. At Housesteads, Great Chesters, and Wallsend, these single buildings placed under one roof with a longitudinal ridge were transformed into a series of small buildings individually roofed and known, perhaps unfortunately, as chalets (Fig 2.1A). It was originally thought that these little buildings, each with its own separate building history, represented 'married quarters', and that the finds assemblages reflected strong evidence for a female presence (Daniels 1980). The conclusion that the families of soldiers in the *vici* moved to safety behind the fort walls followed. The implication of this interpretation of the chalets was that there must have been a drastic reduction in garrison size. If each building accommodated a soldier and his family, whereas it had previously been used by eight men, such an interpretation would imply a reduction to 10% of the 2nd-century unit strength. This was apparently supported by evidence from

A

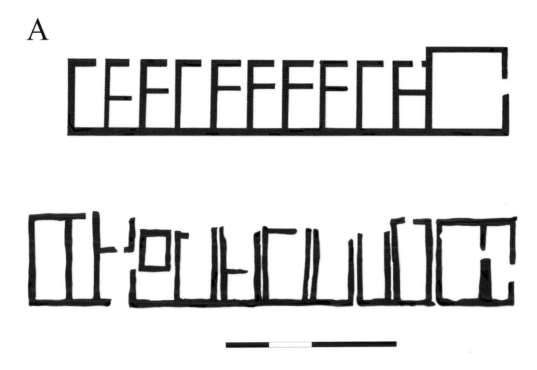

B

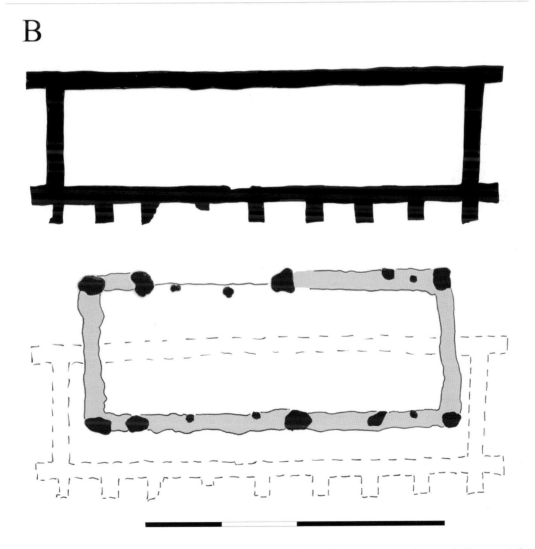

Fig 2.1 A, The typical Hadrianic barrack (top) compared with the chalet-style barrack (bottom), both at Housesteads; B, The plan of a horreum *from Birdoswald (top) compared with the plan of the timber hall (bottom) that replaced it in the 5th century. All scales 20m (drawing: Rob Collins)*

elsewhere. Units of only 100 or so certainly existed in the reign of Diocletian: one North African cohort mustered only 164; and the fort at Eining (Germany) was about one-tenth the size of its early predecessor, prompting Simon James (1984) to postulate a commensurate reduction in garrison. Doubt now attends these interpretations. The completion of work on the Housesteads finds and broader study, particularly by Lindsay Allason-Jones (1995; 2009), proves that the association of chalets with female objects is not actually strong at all (eg needles are not exclusively feminine artefacts). Recent work, particularly by Paul Bidwell (1991), first at Vindolanda (Bidwell 1985) and then South Shields (Bidwell and Speak 1994), has cast further doubt on the idea of northern fort garrisons as attenuated, tiny units. In these forts, again from the later 3rd century, at the same time as the chalets at Housesteads, barracks of a wholly new kind were built. These were similar to the 2nd-century barracks, but reduced the numbers of *contubernia* from ten to five or six. This type of barrack reflects the presence of fewer, differently organised troops, it is true, but it is a far cry from 100 or so soldiers with families. It reflects the continuation of traditional Roman military organisation. A current argument exists as to whether the chalets and reduced barracks are different aspects of the same organisation or whether there is a difference in status between wall forts with chalets, and hinterland forts with the new barracks (Hodgson and Bidwell 2004).

Another class of fort building which also seems to have been altered in the late 3rd and early 4th century was the *praetorium*. Certainly at South Shields, a courtyard house was constructed from scratch in the south-east corner of the fort (Plate 2). Nick Hodgson (1996) has clearly shown that this was a building with Mediterranean antecedents, exceptional even for the towns of Roman Britain. It had a clear formal hierarchy of rooms, culminating in a *triclinium* with couch positions indicated by flagstone areas in the *opus signinum* floors. As Hodgson points out, the design of the house suggests the social status and sophistication that is expected of the commander of a typical frontier garrison, even in the early 4th century. In fact, the plan is entirely consistent with the role of a commander such as Flavius Abinnaeus, who commanded a unit at Dionysias in Egypt at the same time as the South Shields house was built. The Abinnaeus archives reveal a *patronus* in the true sense – someone who interacted with the civilian world in a variety of ways and who thus acted as a local representative of the power of Rome. He even acted as a judge in cases beyond his official jurisdiction (Bell *et al* 1962).

The South Shields house is not alone; in the contemporary new-built fort at Piercebridge, a lavish courtyard house was built in a corner (Cool and Mason 2008). Elsewhere, earlier *praetoria* were altered and extended. Though the excavations tend to be of early date, and limited, this can probably be seen on the Wall at Housesteads, Chesters, and possibly Birdoswald, as well as at Chester-le-Street and Ilkley south of the Wall. It is certainly true at Vindolanda, Piercebridge, and Binchester, where new large and elaborate commander's residences were built. These buildings suggest that many garrisons were local centres of power, presided over by highly influential officers.

This work shows that the northern frontier was not (as a traditional view had it, eg Luttwak 1976, 170–3) composed of small moribund garrisons of soldier farmers, but a flourishing and functioning specimen of the late Roman military frontier world, clearly recognisable elsewhere in the empire. It is true that the garrisons of *limitanei* were static, and legal marriages led to the acquisition of stable lifestyles, families, and roots. By the 3rd century at the latest, local recruitment in Britain was supplying the normal needs of the auxiliary units in the island, and ethnically and culturally these units would have had much in common with the inhabitants of the surrounding areas within the frontier zone (Dobson and Mann 1973). In AD 313, it was mandated that soldiering would be a hereditary occupation and up to AD 372 the sons of soldiers drew rations. The *limitanei* received pay and supplies, and they should not be thought of as soldier-farmers, or as a peasant militia. Though it is generally thought that such troops were poorly paid and supplied, they were probably better off than their 3rd-century predecessors (see Brickstock, this volume). There is no evidence for the working of land by soldiers in their own interest, even in the eastern empire, until AD 443 (Isaac 1988, 139–47). These soldiers were commanded by influential and high-ranking officers, and a number of commanders' residences were improved to accommodate these men.

On the British frontier the appearance of the system changed radically by the end of the 4th century, beginning in the mid-4th century. There are three key stratigraphic sequences for this change in the northern frontier area. The best of these remains the sequence at Birdoswald (Wilmott 1997, 203–22), and one of the main reasons for this is that the sequence is stratigraphically sealed. In fact there are two stratigraphic sequences on the excavated site: the first runs from the Hadrianic construction of the Turf Wall to phases of timber construction on the remains of the stone buildings of the fort, and the second begins in around the 13th century and continues to the 20th. The only stratigraphic rupture comes between these phases. There is therefore a break between two periods of continuous occupation at Birdoswald, but this break comes after an extended sequence of occupation, continuing well after the latest Roman coins and pottery.

It is important to stress that continuous occupation does not mean unchanged occupation. Major change is attested within the framework of continuity. From the 2nd to the mid-4th century one can recognise a Roman auxiliary fort, containing the suite of structures which one might expect of such an installation. These structures, one can be reasonably certain, continued to be used in similar ways. The beginning of radical change at Birdoswald comes when the large granaries change function, or cease to be used. The first evidence for this was found in the south granary, where the floor was removed, the ventilated sub-floor infilled, and the flagstones replaced. The intact survival of this floor, and the fact that the sealed fill deposit was entirely scanned by metal detector meant that all dating evidence was recovered. The coin sequence stopped c AD 348, and contained no coins of the *Fel Temp Reparatio* type at all. This was despite the fact that elsewhere in the near vicinity of the building such coins continued to be lost. We can regard this deposit as a sealed and well-dated event. In the north granary, the collapse of the roof was followed by a phase during which the building was used as a stone quarry, and for piecemeal refuse disposal. The Severan inscription in the building excavated in 1929 probably came from this operation. Again the deposits filling the sub-floor were 100% sampled. The coinage here was a virtually complementary group to the south granary group, beginning around the AD 340s, containing *Fel Temp Rep* issues, and running on until the reign of Valens. In the south granary, occupation and reflooring culminated in the placing of a sequence of stone hearths at the west end, around which were dropped a worn Theodosian silver coin, a black glass ring, and a gold earring – objects of high status remarkable for this site.

In this sequence we see that the pattern of development is strikingly similar to that summarised by Tainter (1988, 21), in his description of the use of architecture following social and economic collapse:

Little new construction [is undertaken], and that which is attempted concentrates on adapting existing buildings ..., public space [will be] turned to private. People may reside in upper storey rooms as lower ones deteriorate. Monuments are often mined as easy sources of building materials. When a building starts to collapse the residents simply move to another ... Palaces and centralised storage facilities may be abandoned, along with centralised redistribution of goods and foodstuffs ...

It seems likely that the granaries were disused because the garrison did not need central, large-scale storage. It implies the end of a system of large-scale military supply, possibly in favour of low-level piecemeal requisitioning and taxation direct to the army in kind. In the vicinity of Abinnaeus' fort at Dionysias in Egypt, though the collection of supplies under the *annona* was technically the responsibility of civilian officials, it was in practice the troops who exacted the tax, and tax registers survive among the documentation (Bell *et al* 1962). On the Wall, it is difficult to see where the civilian part of the system was located – especially if the *vici* were deserted. It seems natural that supply was exacted on the spot, and that any disputes would be settled by the commander, as happened in Egypt.

The subsequent sequence in the north granary is of two successive timber buildings. The *terminus post quem* for these is represented by the coinage of Valens, though if these buildings are the functional successors of the reused granary, the interpretation I prefer for reasons I will come on to rests with the Theodosian coin. The first timber phase is founded on the north granary, with posts on the wall tops, and a new stone floor laid, sealing the earlier rubbish deposits. Its successor was built partly on the north granary and partly on the *via principalis* (Fig 2.1B). Structurally the building was supported by paired posts, implying timber-framed construction. Although the structure was surface-built on stone pads, leaving a minimal archaeological trace, its maximum external dimensions of 23m x 8.6m show that it was a substantial and important structure. This building was deliberately shifted away from the walls of the Roman building in order to create a new spatial relationship with the west gate. This spatial change is important in any consideration of the significance of the building. The granary had been built to respect a dual-portal gate. When the south portal was blocked in the early 3rd century, the road between the north portal and the granary wall was dead ground. The second large timber building deliberately occupied this dead ground, and was placed alongside the road from the new portal. The building would have been the first thing a visitor saw on entering the fort enclosure. In addition to these principal timber buildings, each phase featured smaller service buildings placed upon the surface of the intervallum road.

This sequence of structures is effectively undated, except for the fact that they all have a *terminus post quem* provided by the latest Roman pottery and coins. If the timber buildings were the functional successors of the reused granary, their *terminus post quem* rests with the Theodosian coin of c AD 395. If one suggests a beginning around AD 420, how long could they then carry on? Both buildings were substantial, the first possibly, the second almost certainly, framed, and surface-built on stone walls or pads, avoiding the ground-level rot which would affect ground-fast posts. A long life can be suggested for both phases. I have suggested an average chronology of 50 years per structure, allowing a tentative end in the first quarter of the sixth century. Longer chronologies are certainly also possible.

In the reused south granary, the position of the hearth, together with the high-status nature of the finds around it, might indicate that this was the place set aside for the use of the commander. In plan, the long narrow building with a hearth at one end is highly reminiscent of the halls of the post-Roman British and Anglo-Saxon periods. It seems likely that if this analogy is correct, the granary was the only building within the fort whose shape and size would lend itself to such a function. The only alternative might be the *principia*, though this might either have been too specialised in its plan, which was designed for the military system of the

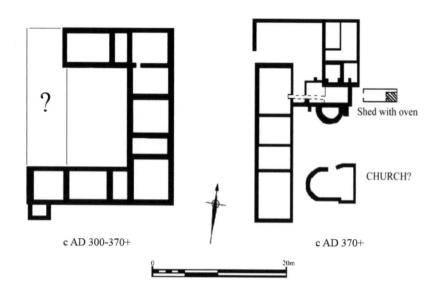

Fig 2.2   *The* praetorium *at Vindolanda, showing the probable church in the latest phase* (© *Vindolanda Trust*)

2nd century, or previously altered to serve other functions. The *principia* forecourt at South Shields, for example, appears to have been partially transformed into a Christian church by the end of the 4th century (Bidwell and Speak 1994, 103–5). If the hall interpretation is correct for the granary, it follows that the two successive timber buildings were its functional successors. The most useful *comparanda* to the second building are certainly the halls of the post-Roman, British population of northern and western Britain at South Cadbury (Alcock 1995) and at Doon Hill. The successive Doon Hill buildings are generally interpreted as timber halls which would have been the residence of a royal official, noble, or chieftain, taken over as a royal lodging during progresses, though these excavations have yet to be published. At Cadbury Castle, the analogous building was the principal structure of its phase, interpreted as 'the feasting hall of whatever noble warrior lived at Cadbury with his war-band' (Alcock 1987a, 182).

A further element in the late timber structures at Birdoswald was a timber portal which was post-built outside the gatehouse. This would allow for gates to be hung opening outwards and closing inwards, as opposed to the Roman gates which opened inwards, and were thus less defensible.

A precisely similar arrangement was also provided at the west gate at South Shields (Bidwell and Speak 1994, 143). The gate replacement at South Shields is also the culmination of a long late Roman sequence, and therefore has a relative date. After a coin of AD 388–402 was deposited in the final road metalling through the gate, a ditch was cut through the road, cutting off direct access. After a period of natural silting, the ditch was filled with rubble from the gate. The installation of the timber gate and establishment of an inhumation cemetery followed.

The evidence from South Shields, however, is not of structural continuity like Birdoswald, but of dislocation. In the courtyard house, two skeletons with identical injuries were found buried. Some time had elapsed between death and burial, and radiocarbon dating suggested a date of death in the early to mid-5th century (Hodgson 1999, 82). How these two pieces of evidence fit together is not clear. The burials might signal the end of occupation on the site, and a violent end at that. Perhaps South Shields fell victim to its geographical position as the eastern seaboard became unsafe, and these burials were the victims of raiders from across the North Sea, or those who circumvented the Wall by sea from the north. If the principal danger in the late 4th century came from the sea, then the contrast which we now see between our best two sequences in the Wall zone is explained by the relative security of sites in the centre of the Wall zone.

Among the hinterland forts, Binchester (Ferris and Jones 2000), like Birdoswald, shows a long sequence. Here a new and elaborate *praetorium* was built in the early to mid-4th century. Subsequently, *c* AD 370, a large bath house was added to the *praetorium* and then enlarged (Plate 3). Some time after that, the building was divided by unmortared rubble walls, and the *praefurnium* to the bath became choked with debris after a number of rebuildings. Later still, one of the rooms in the building was used as a smithy, while another room became a slaughterhouse, and a midden developed over the *praefurnium*. Subsequently, the midden was levelled, and a flagstone floor laid over it. This was associated with a timber building, and fragments of sawn antler attest to its use as a workshop. The collapse of the vault of the bath house was cut by a grave containing grave goods which included an 'Anglian' brooch of a type dated to the mid-6th century. Here a break in the stratigraphic sequence is followed by an Anglo-Saxon cemetery in the centre of the fort and the robbing of stone, possibly for the 'Saxon' church at nearby Escomb.

Elsewhere on the frontier, structural activity that probably relates to the late 4th and 5th century has been found in the shape of earthwork redefences at Birdoswald, Vindolanda, and Housesteads, the last mentioned including a timber tower. Recently, evidence for Christianity has been found, in particular in the form of three possible churches at Vindolanda (Fig 2.2), Housesteads, and (tenuously) Birdoswald, and another at South Shields. These supplement two apparent long cists (one adjacent to the Housesteads possible church), the well-known Brigomaglos stone from Vindolanda, and a second Class I inscribed stone from Castlesteads in demonstrating the possibility of an ongoing Christian milieu for the continued occupation of the Wall zone (Wilmott 2000).

The contents of this volume enhance knowledge of the artefactual evidence for the periods under review. They build upon the papers published in 2000 (Cool 2000a; Brickstock 2000a; Evans 2000). It might be noted at this point that the study of artefacts, and the reappraisal of such evidence, is a more accessible source from which to review the period than further structural and stratigraphic data, as the latter are reliant upon the expensive excavation of further sequences, assuming that excavated sites yield good sequences of the correct periods.

The north Britons of the 4th and 5th centuries were in the recent past held to be archaeologically invisible, and the soldiers of the Wall to have 'disappeared into the soil from which they sprang' (Breeze and Dobson 1987, 384). The brief foregoing summary does, I hope, demonstrate that this is not the case, but comprehending the small body of data which we have is still far from simple. It is possible, however, to arrive at a tenuous model for the development of the period. The late Roman frontier was consistent with that of other provinces. The units were smaller, but were still functioning as military units. The commanders' residences suggest an increase in the status of commanders, who possibly gained roles in the wider civilian arena, as did Flavius Abinnaeus in Egypt. This may have led to the forts being recognised as having an informal (or formal) administrative *territorium*. The end of the 4th century and beginning of the 5th certainly marks a major change which can be seen archaeologically, particularly in the end of pottery distribution and the monetised economy. The stratigraphic sequences which extend and develop beyond this threshold contain evidence for the response to this change. Material culture may, as Cool (2000a) argues, be developing in a 'natural' cycle of development, though this cycle shows signs of major simplification in contrast to the varied material culture that had gone before. This trend, as Esmonde-Cleary (2000) argues, seems to be curtailed by the apparent economic dislocation. If an apparent trend to simplification of the material culture was disrupted, this seems to be an indication of the depth of the dislocation, by which all Roman artefacts in the later sequences were 'terminally residual'.

If this change had such an impact on material culture, economy, and industry, then similar drastic effects upon building styles might also be expected, and this is certainly seen at Birdoswald, where the timber buildings were the context for social and administrative changes. Ken Dark (1992; 2000b) has suggested that the finds of the 5th and 6th centuries on the Wall represent a 'fifth Wall period'; a deliberate reoccupation of the frontier by a sub-Roman structure descended from the command of the *Dux Britanniarum*. This is to go far beyond the capacity of the evidence, and begs questions on the communications system and the 5th-century status of York, the centre of that command. It also fails to account for the capacity of settlements to change, and to wax and wane over a period of two centuries. I prefer a model similar to that advanced by Tainter (1988), where previously collaborating units develop in their own right at a lower or local level of administration, and may even become competitors. In a sense, this complicates the evidence, as each site must then be regarded on its own merits rather than as a part of a continuing larger system. This is clear when comparing Birdoswald and South Shields. A certain amount of common development took place, for example similar alterations were made to the south-west gate at South Shields as to the west gate at Birdoswald, but occupation seems to have ended in the early to mid-5th century. Development at South Shields may have been cut short due to a violent event at that date, while at Bridoswald development continued beyond that date.

Evidence for early post-Roman occupation in forts of the other north-west provinces is as rare as in Britain. The only possible example known to this writer is at Alzey, where timber-built long buildings succeed to stone structures in the third phase of a sequence which begins with the construction of the fort under Valentinian (Oldenstein 1986). The excavator interprets this as a mid-5th-century military reoccupation. Holder (1982, 103) has compared Britain to other provinces, such as Spain and Noricum, where no combined effort was made against invaders by populations or garrisons, concluding that 'with no concerted effort in time of trouble individual units would have been destroyed ... [or] faded away over a period of time'. Esmonde-Cleary (1989, 142) cites the account in the *Vita Sancti Severini* of the *limitanei* of Noricum Ripense in AD 452; pay had ceased, troops sent to get pay had been killed by barbarians, and consequently only a few very small formations were left. He suggests the same pattern for the British northern frontier. The situation in Noricum is represented by Pauli (1980, 50) in terms of a 'decimated populace [dwelling] in congested quarters in the forts', presumably having taken refuge there. These attitudes rely on the *limitanei* maintaining a 'Roman' and 'military' role, and the double assumption firstly that this would make them automatic victims of barbarian assault and secondly that there were 'barbarians' around who were bent on aggression. There is another model for the response of such units which is provided by Procopius and cited by Casey (1993b, 73), in which

> Roman soldiers ... stationed on the frontiers of Gaul to serve as guards gave themselves, together with their military standards, and the land which they had been guarding for the Romans to the Aborychi and the Germans; and they handed down to their offspring all the customs of their fathers .... For even at the present day they are clearly recognised as belonging to the legions to which they were assigned in ancient times, and they carry their own standards when they enter battle ... And they preserve the dress of the Romans in every particular, even as regarding their shoes.

James (1988, 84) has seen the key to Frankish success in the Gallo-Roman acceptance of them as the heirs of Rome. Just from these few historical sources, it is clear that there was a patchwork of responses to the crisis of the 5th century in the West, and it cannot be expected that the response of *limitanei* in one province, or in one locality, would necessarily mirror that of another. Unlike the majority of the frontiers of north-west Europe, Hadrian's Wall was not overrun quickly either by Pictish or Anglian incomers. This is clearly demonstrated by the successful existence in the north and west of the former diocese of Brittonic polities which did not fall under Anglian control until the 6th century (Dark 1994). Birdoswald is located well within this area of survival.

In 1993, John Casey (1993a; 1993b) set the agenda for studies in these matters, arguing that as official supply failed in the early 5th century, so the residual garrison may have continued to extract a customary levy from the agricultural population in return for armed protection in a relationship which combined symbiosis and coercion. It would make sense for the area under the power of the commander as *patronus* to develop into a region more directly or possessively controlled and protected by an individual fort as larger social and administrative structures broke down. It may be that as the situation developed the unit might become a self-sustaining community around a hereditary commander, perhaps receiving personal oaths of allegiance in the manner of the late Roman *bucellarii*. This is an institution which Whittaker (1993) has seen as key to the transition from the late empire to the Early Medieval Germanic kingdoms. This would also be consistent with the style of the buildings at Birdoswald. The central hall with surrounding service buildings closely resembles the feasting hall of a powerful individual surrounded by a warband so familiar to us from the *Gododdin* or *Beowulf*. Though these phenomena are often seen as implying the reassertion of Celtic social custom by the later 5th century, Ken Dark (1994) has suggested that all of the elements of sub-Roman 'heroic' society were in fact present in Roman Britain. The concept of kingship was not alien in the late Roman world. The post-Roman hall is paralleled by late Roman aisled buildings, and occasions were marked by feasts. Panegyric writing was common, and late Roman aristocrats had bands of retainers. Arguably, these factors are consistent with the continuity of *Romanitas*.

Birdoswald, in a strong position with a cliff on one side, a marsh on the other and surrounded by walls, was probably one of a patchwork of defended places which continued or began at this time to the north and south of the Roman Wall. It may have possessed additional legitimacy based upon its Roman antecedents. It is this kind of evidence which will need to be addressed in order to insert detail into the change in orientation of the northern British frontier from east–west in the 4th century to the 5th-century north–south frontier between the vestiges of sub-Roman Britain to the west, and the growing Anglian presence in the east.

Plate 1   The Tetrarchs, San Marco, Venice (M J Baxter)

Plate 2 The reconstructed praetorium *courtyard at South Shields (picture: Rob Collins)*

Plate 3 The praetorium *bath house at Binchester (picture: Rob Collins)*

Plate 4   The Staffordshire Moorlands pan; max D 94mm (picture: S Laidlaw, © PAS)

a

b

c

Plate 5, a–c   Fragments of late Roman plate with polychrome mosaic insets from Quarry Farm, Ingleby Barwick; max W (a) 47mm (picture: Jeff Veitch, © Durham University)

Plate 7 Crambeck parchment ware sherd from York, probably depicting a soldier; max H 83mm (© York Archaeological Trust)

Plate 6 Flask from Scorton, near Catterick (picture: Jennifer Jones, © Durham University)

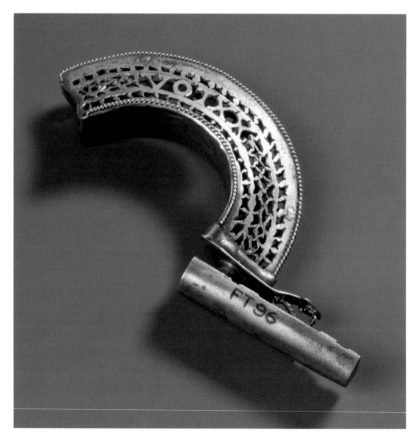

Plate 8 The gold crossbow brooch from Erickstanebrae, Dumfries & Galloway; L 94mm (replica; © National Museums of Scotland)

3   The written record and the late Roman frontier   *Mark Hassall*

Introduction

Late 3rd- and early 4th-century inscriptions from the frontier zone in general and Hadrian's Wall in particular are surprisingly rare. The latest dated inscriptions from sites on Hadrian's Wall are the famous 'building' record (*RIB* 1912) found at Birdoswald and dedicated to the period AD 297–305 by the mention of the tetrarchs (the emperor Diocletian and his three colleagues), and a more or less contemporary inscription from Chesters. The latter is a dedication to Jupiter Dolichenus and can be precisely dated to the end of the 3rd century in AD 286 (Tomlin and Hassall 2005, 480–1, no 8). There is also a late tombstone from Carlisle of Flavius Antigonus Papias, a Greek (*RIB* 955) whom, it has been argued, is Christian on the basis of a feigned(?) lack of concern about the precise age of the deceased who lived 'more or less 60 years' (*vixit annos plus minus* LX). If this is correct then it should probably date to the 4th century, after Constantine's formal recognition of Christianity in AD 313, although the mere fact that the deceased's religious affiliations are ambiguous means that even if it is Christian it could be earlier than that date. A second tombstone from Carvoran (*RIB* 1828) may also be Christian. It records that Aurelia Aia lived for 33 years 'without any stain' (*sine ulla macula*), and this too has been taken to be a Christian formula.

Taking the frontier to include the system of fortlets on the Yorkshire coast, then the honour of being the latest inscription will probably go to another building record (*RIB* 721) from the installation at Ravenscar (Fig 3.1). The creation of this system of fortlets is usually attributed to Count Theodosius as part of the defensive measures taken in AD 369 after the Barbarian Conspiracy of AD 367 when Nectaridus, Count of the Coastal District (the Saxon Shore), was killed and Fullofaudes, the Duke in charge of the northern military district, including Hadrian's Wall, was ambushed and captured (Ammianus Marcellinus XXVII, 8). In the passage recording the Roman response (XXVIII, 3), Ammianus describes how Theodosius, having recovered the military situation, protected the frontiers with watch posts and garrisons (*vigiliis et praetenturis*), and both the words used here and the language of the Ravenscar inscription with its mention of a tower and fort (*turrem et castrum*), accord with the actual plan of the fortlets with their lofty towers set in a small, rectangular, defended enclosure for the garrisons (*praetenturae*). The rounded corners of these latter are furnished with token bastions whose actual military effectiveness may be doubted since they do not project beyond the line of the adjacent walls and would not enable archers or soldiers armed with *manuballistae* who were stationed on them to provide enfilading fire.

Milestones

Apart from these four inscriptions there is a group of over a dozen 3rd- or early 4th-century milestones from the Wall hinterland. One of the most interesting is also the earliest, a milestone from Langwathby in Cumbria dated to AD 222/223, so considerably earlier than the period under discussion. It was set up by the *Civitas Carvetiorum* and names the emperor Severus Alexander (Tomlin and Hassall 2005, 482, no 11). An earlier find from Brougham (Wright 1965, 224, no 11), also set up by the *Civitas Carvetiorum* in honour of the Gallic usurper Postumus (AD 258–68), fits better into the general chronological horizon. These two inscriptions will be cited below in another context. A third milestone found at Gallows Hill, a mile south of Carlisle (*RIB* 2291), carries three inscriptions of which the primary text (*RIB* 2291) names Carausius (AD 286–93). The remainder include mentions of Diocletian, his colleague Maximian, and their immediate successors (*RIB* 2288, 2292, 2293, 2297, 2301 (3) and (4), 2302, 2303, 2310, and 2311). The suggestion has been made (Sauer 2007) that these, and others of similar date from elsewhere in the province, were not so much records of work carried out on particular stretches of road, the ostensible reason for their erection, as instruments of propaganda in a period of political instability, drawing the attention of passers-by to the particular emperor or usurper named at the expense of his rivals.

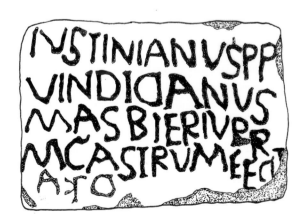

Fig 3.1   The building inscription from Ravenscar, RIB *721 (drawing: Rob Collins)*

Corvées and civitates

Possibly the most significant group of inscriptions from the frontier region, if also the most enigmatic, is the series of building inscriptions from the Wall itself, detailing work done by *corvées* from three southern *civitates* – the Durotriges Lendinienses, the Dumnonii, and the Catuvellauni – as well as three other inscriptions recording work on *pedaturae* (specific lengths measured in feet) carried out on the initiative of individuals such as Vindomorucus, attested on a building inscription found at Drumburgh (*RIB* 2053). In the early 1940s C E Stevens suggested that these recorded work undertaken during the general reconstruction of the frontier by Count Theodosius (Stevens 1940, 148; 1941, 359). Building work on the Wall by the southern *civitates* would, in the present writer's opinion, suit a late Roman context well, for this was the age when *civitates* throughout the empire were expected to carry out unpleasant tasks, referred to in the legal literature as *sordida munera*, which included, among other things, the repair of military roads, the manufacture of arms, and the rebuilding of fortifications, as a law of AD 441 specifically indicates (Jones 1964, 205, 452). Compare the work on road building undertaken by the *Civitas Carvetiorum* as recorded on the inscriptions from Langwathby and Brougham mentioned above. Other milestones from the province also record work done on roads by the *civitates*, eg the *Res Publica Belgarum* in AD 238–44 (*RIB* 2222); the *Res Publica Lindensis* in AD 253–59 (*RIB* 2240); and the *Res Publica Civitatis Dobunorum*, AD 283–84 (*RIB* 2250). All are of a broadly similar 3rd-century date and not earlier. However, that works of this kind and even co-operative efforts like the work on the Wall could be undertaken by civilian authorities at a much earlier period is shown, for example, by the construction of the bridge at Alcantara near Carceres in the province of Lusitania (Portugal), which was built in AD 106 (*ILS* 287 and 287a). Indeed, dates earlier than the 4th century have been suggested for the *civitates* inscriptions from the Wall. In a recent survey Michael Fulford proposed that 'all the named *civitates* [stones] are associated with the initial construction of the stone Wall and the replacement of the turf wall in stone, and that they belong to the 2nd century, before the division of Britain into Inferior and Superior' (Fulford 2006, 68). Roger Tomlin also prefers an early date and in discussing a very fragmentary building inscription perhaps set up by the [*C(ivitas) Durot*]*rac(um)*, found in association with the north mound of the Vallum at Cawfields (Wright 1960, 237, no 10; Tomlin *et al* forthcoming), concludes that this stone and the other *civitas* building inscriptions relate to the original construction of the Vallum in the Hadrianic period. Formally, it would be impossible to disprove the views of either Fulford or Tomlin; nevertheless, I can think of no other overtly military work of 2nd-century date from any frontier of the empire which was undertaken by civilians.

For Britain, the two 3rd-century milestones cited above provide some sort of parallel, showing as they do one civilian authority, the *Civitas Carvetiorum*, engaged in large-scale engineering works in that period, though it is of course not impossible that the *civitates* undertook this sort of work earlier but that their participation is simply not mentioned on the inscriptions.

Place-names

The dramatic discovery in 2003 of an enamelled bowl, the so-called Staffordshire Moorlands pan (Plate 4; Worrell 2004a, 326; Tomlin and Hassall 2004, 344–5), bearing an inscription which includes the names of the four westernmost Wall forts, though itself probably not of late Roman date, has given new certainty to the identification of the names of the forts which are listed with the units in garrison in Chapter 40 of the *Notitia Dignitatum*. In particular, the presence of the second fort listed, COGGABATA (= *Notitia Dignitatum* ch 40, line 48 CONGAVATA), which is missing from the forts listed on the two analogous inscribed vessels, the Rudge Cup and the Amiens *patera*, confirms that this is a genuine place-name and there is no longer any doubt about the normally proposed identification of the place with Drumburgh. Apart from the evidence of these inscribed vessels, the identification of the Wall forts with those listed in the *Notitia* is aided by the occurrence at various sites of inscriptions naming units given in that document, even though the inscriptions themselves are of 3rd- rather than 4th-century date. For a recent attempt to make sense of the fort names listed in the *Notitia* in the Wall hinterland and on the Cumbrian coast see Hassall 2004.

Conclusion

From the survey given above, it is apparent that epigraphy plays only a small part in our understanding of the Wall, its garrison, and its hinterland in the 4th century. Neverthless, inscriptions of an earlier date, notably the list of forts named on the Staffordshire Moorlands pan and its analogues, and the inscriptions that name the 3rd-century Wall garrisons, are crucial in helping to elucidate the evidence of that vitally important 4th- or early 5th-century document, the *Notitia Dignitatum*. One *desideratum* would be to settle once and for all the date of the *civitas* inscriptions, for these are of great intrinsic interest in showing civilian involvement in a major military project, something that would be unusual before the 4th century. Here Fulford has rightly drawn attention to the significance of the recently discovered Langwathby milestone attesting to work done by the *Civitas* of the Carvetii on road building in AD 222–23. This really does suggest that the *civitas* inscriptions on the Wall could be of Severan date and this is the date at which I have argued the western end of the Wall was converted from turf to stone (Hassall 1984). If this were indeed the case, and they do not belong to a 4th-century context, then apart from the assist-ance inscriptions provide to the identification of the place-names mentioned in the *Notitia*, the signifi-cance of epigraphy for the later phase of the frontier would be almost negligible!

4   The supply and use of pottery on Hadrian's Wall in the 4th century AD   *Paul Bidwell and Alexandra Croom*[1]

Introduction

The systematic study of late Roman pottery on Hadrian's Wall began almost a century ago with the publication of the excavations at Milecastle 48, Poltross Burn (Gibson and Simpson 1911). Less than twenty years later, the 1929 excavations at Birdoswald established the general range of pottery-types in use in the late 4th century. They came from a limited range of sources and represented many of the same types that occurred at the Yorkshire coastal fortlets. Grey wares, parchment ware (vessels in a yellowish-white fabric with decoration in red paint) and an oxidised fabric, sometimes with decoration in white paint (used for

bowls of rounded profile with flanges, ultimately derived from the samian Dr 38), were all supplied from the kilns at Crambeck in East Yorkshire. Vessels in calcite-gritted ware, mainly cooking pots but also dishes and bowls, were equally common; they were also from East Yorkshire, although probably not from the same sources as the grey wares and fine wares (Evans 2000, 40; Monaghan 1997, 1033). More recently, it has been recognised that the later 4th-century pottery used on the Wall and in its hinterland included lid-seated cooking pots made in a grey heavily gritted fabric, a type which first appeared in the later 3rd century. The only other pottery of significance during this period was from the Nene Valley and consisted of colour-

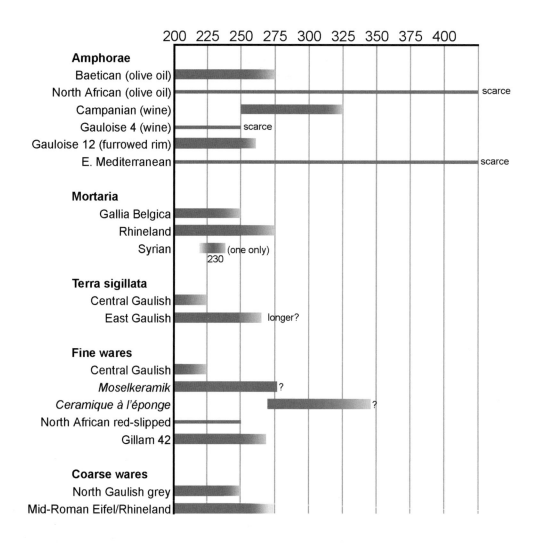

Fig 4.1   Importation of pottery to Hadrian's Wall and northern Britain during the period AD 200–425

coated ware versions of coarse ware forms (flanged bowls, dishes, and jars), 'Castor' boxes, beakers, and flagons.

Much less was known in the 1920s and 1930s about later Roman pottery supply before the late 4th century, and a clearer picture only began to develop following the open-area excavation of forts on and near the Wall that began in the 1970s. Large gaps in the picture still remain and other areas are hazy. The main purpose of this contribution is to set out what is known about the transformation of a complex system of pottery supply in the late 3rd century – with variations not only between the Wall and different parts of its hinterland but also between the western, central and eastern sectors of the Wall – into what at first sight might seem to be almost a monopoly, controlled by the East Yorkshire potters, which operated across northern Britain beyond the Mersey and Humber.

One aspect of the pottery supply that all these areas had in common in the late 3rd or early 4th century was the almost complete cessation of importation from Gaul, Germany, and the Mediterranean at a date when pottery from these sources, though not in large quantities, was still reaching southern Britain (Fig 4.1). The only imports in northern Britain after the early 4th century were amphorae from North Africa and the Eastern Mediterranean, which occur in very small numbers, and also Italian amphorae which were imported from *c* AD 250 and continued to arrive in the early to mid-4th century.

The main types of pottery available on Hadrian's Wall during the 4th century AD

Gillam's type-series (first published as Gillam 1957a, its last revision being Gillam 1970) is still essential to the study of Roman pottery in northern Britain. Table 4.1 lists all the main Gillam types found on the Wall in the 4th century, together with the dates ascribed to them, and also provides a concordance to the type-series for East Yorkshire wares published in Corder and Birley (1937). Finally, a new series of dates is given for the types, based for the most part on recent research summarised in the following sections. However, a few details need to be examined here. The type examples for the rouletted beakers Gillam Types 56 and 58 (Table 4.1, no 8), described as being normally colour-coated ware, are probably both in Crambeck reduced ware; Type 58 is definitely reduced ware, while the original published description for Type 56 reads 'blue-grey, polished; white fracture' (Birley 1930a, 194, no 46). The carinated bowl, Type 178, dated AD 290–350, is now known to have been made in the Holme-on-Spalding-Moor industries from at least the mid-3rd century (Creighton 1999, 162; table 5.15, type B03a), but is occasionally found in Crambeck reduced ware (Fig 4.7, no 43). The segmental bowl, Type 299, dated AD 370–400 in the first edition

(Gillam 1957a) was subsequently identified as a type made in the Midlands, where it occurs in early 3rd-century deposits.

Table 4.2 lists additional forms from the East Yorkshire industries not originally noted in Gillam, some of which appear in very small numbers. The calcite-gritted ware forms have all been identified on Hadrian's Wall, but as yet not all of the Crambeck wares have been noted. However, relatively few large late assemblages have been published from Wall sites, and it is likely that many of these forms are represented in unpublished groups, along with other types not listed.

Gillam's dating of East Yorkshire wares

The earliest occurrence of East Yorkshire grey wares known to Gillam was in the strongroom of the outpost fort of Bewcastle, the coins from which established a *terminus post quem* of *c* AD 273 for its filling (Richmond *et al* 1938, fig 23, no 20, and pp 232–4 for the coins). The contents of the strongroom were regarded as a destruction deposit resulting from a barbarian incursion in AD 296, the possibility of which is now generally discounted (Frere 1967, 343). Scepticism has also been expressed as to whether the deposit had any connection with the destruction of the fort at whatever date (Austen 1991, 48–9). Neither of these more recent views have much effect on the dating of the strongroom deposit. A persuasive case has been made for the abandonment of the outpost forts in AD 312 or 314 (Casey and Savage 1980; Casey 1991b; a single Huntcliff-type found unstratified in the fort baths is not necessarily evidence for anything except casual, short-lived occupation in the later 4th century; Gillam *et al* 1993, fig 21, no 46). The date of the strongroom deposit lies somewhere between *c* AD 273 and AD 312/314 and probably towards the earlier part of that period, for after the strongroom was filled the shrine above was rebuilt.

The absence of Crambeck parchment ware, Huntcliff-type cooking pots and most of the grey ware types at Bewcastle was used as evidence for their late 4th-century date. Until the early 1980s the fort was thought to have been held until shortly after AD 367 and 'the absence of the distinctive later fourth-century types, as discovered at Birdoswald in 1929' was evident (Richmond *et al* 1938, 203). The late types at Birdoswald came from levels of Period IV, dated to after AD 364 because of the presence of a coin of Valentinian in the previous level (Richmond and Birley 1930). The end of Period III was connected with the destruction of AD 367; much of the Period IV pottery, that is, 'the distinctive later fourth-century types', came from Building IVa, a cook-house that had been 'looted and burned' in a destruction subsequent to that supposedly of AD 367 (*ibid*, 170–1). Cooking pots of Huntcliff-type were found in a deposit ('III/IV') that spanned Periods III and IV ('the deposit

Table 4.1   Occurrences and dating of the main pottery types found on Hadrian's Wall during the 4th century

Cat no	Fabric and form	Type	Gillam's dating	C&B	revised dating
Calcite-gritted ware (Fig 4.2)					
1	Cooking pot with curved rim	160–1	300–370		300–370
2	Cooking pot, Huntcliff-type, plain	162	360–400		360–400+
3	Cooking pot, Huntcliff-type, grooves on body	163	360–400		360–400+
4	Plain-rimmed dish (not included in Gillam as a separate type)				300–400+
	Knobbed rim variant with internal bead				300?–400+
	Flat rimmed	332	340–400		340?–400
Crambeck grey wares (CRA RE) (Figs 4.2 and 4.3)					
5	Jar with countersunk-lug handles	40	290–400	3	270–400
		41	320–400	3a	320–400
6	Flagon, not included in Gillam's types			14	270?–400
	Wide-mouthed variant			14a	270?–400
	Pinched-neck			15	270?–400
7	Beaker, not included in Gillam's types			11	270–400
8	Rouletted beaker	43	350–400	12	270–400
		56	300–400		270–400
		58	300–400		270–400
	Pentice-moulded			12a	270–400
9	Wide-mouthed jar or bowl	190	350–400	4	270–400
10	Bowl imitating, or reminiscent of samian Dr 38	203–4	360–400	5a	270–400
11	Flanged bowl	229	350–400	1	270–400
12	Flanged bowl with internal wavy line	231–2	370–400	1b	370–400
13	Flanged dish	315	350–400	1a	350–400
14	Dish with groove below the rim	320–1	350–400	2a	270–400
15	Dish with plain rim	333	350–400	2	270–400
16	Segmental bowl, knobbed rim often with internal bead, not included in Gillam's types			10a	?
17	Bowl with everted rim, not included in Gillam's types			13	270–400
	Variant with long neck			13a	270–400
	Variant with rounded rim			13b	270–400
Oxidised ware, often with decoration in white paint					
18	Bowl imitating, or reminiscent of, samian Dr 38	203	360–400	5	early C4?–400
Crambeck white ware (CRA WH) and parchment ware (CRA PA) (Fig 4.3)					
19	Wall-sided mortarium	288	360–400	7	370–400
	with painted decoration	289	370–400		370–400
20	Mortarium with double-flanged rim, often with painted decoration	290	370–400	8	370–400
21	Bowl imitating, or reminiscent of, samian Dr 38, with painted decoration	207–8	370–400	5b	370–400
22	Segmental bowl, vertical rim with two grooves, often painted	297	370–400	9	370–400
23	Segmental bowl, knobbed rim often with internal bead, painted	298	370–400	10	370–400
24	The earliest mortarium-type in Crambeck white ware is not included in Gillam's types			6	300–400
Late gritty grey ware (Fig 4.4)					
25	Lid-seated jar	153	290–370		270–400+
Nene Valley ('Castor') ware, late colour-coated types (Fig 4.5)					
26	Narrow-mouthed jar, representing all containers including jars (the type specimen needs re-examining to check its fabric identification)	35	350–400		350–400
27	Beaker-style flagon	62	300–350		350–400
	Beaker	57	300–400		270–370
28	Bowl imitating, or reminiscent of, samian Dr 38	206	360–400		360–400
29	Flanged bowl	230	360–400		360–400
30	Dish, inturned wall	334	350–400		360–400
31	Dish	335	360–400		360–400

Key
C&B Corder and Birley 1937

Table 4.2 Additional types from the East Yorkshire industries

Cat no	Fabric and form
Calcite-gritted ware (Fig 4.6)	
32	Cooking pot with simple everted rim
33	Cooking pot with defined shoulder
34	Flagon
35	Tankard Unpublished examples from Carlisle and Corbridge
36	Lug-handled jar everted rim lid-seated (370–400+) A body sherd from South Shields comes from a mid-4th century context (Dore 1983, fig 33, no 309)
37	Wide-mouthed bowl everted rim lid-seated (370–400+)
38	Flanged bowl One example found in a late 3rd- or early 4th-century context
Crambeck reduced ware (CRA RE) (Fig 4.7)	
39	Narrow-necked jar, possibly a form of Corder and Birley 1937 type 14
40	Narrow-mouthed jar. Can have frilled cordon
41	Cooking pot
42	Grey ware version of Corder and Birley 1937 type 9, usually found in parchment ware
43	Biconical bowl
44	Colander, a variant on Corder and Birley 1937 type 13. Bowls and/or jars with holes only in the flat base are also known (Malton: Bidwell and Croom 1997, fig 37, no 417; Crambeck kilns: Corder 1928, pl VII, nos 189), as are cheese-presses (Vindolanda: Bidwell 1985, MF fig 12, no 118)
45	Flagon or jar with moulded decoration. Face pots and smith pots are also known (Corder and Birley 1937, pl 3.3; Catterick: Evans 2002, fig 137, no SS48, Bell and Evans 2002, fig 193, no DBS5)
Crambeck parchment ware (CRA PA) (Fig 4.8)	
46	Small flagon
47	Beaker
48	Funnel-necked beaker
49	Cup
50	Parchment ware version of Corder and Birley 1937 type 13, usually found in reduced ware
51	Bowl, variant on Corder and Birley 1937 type 7, without exterior groove
52	Bowl, possibly based on Oxfordshire ware type P24 (Young 1977)
53	Dish
54	Bowl with flange and bead
55	Colander, a variant on Corder and Birley 1937 type 13
56	Face pot
57	Flagon with moulded face mask

may be assigned exclusively to the fourth century, and the bulk of it to the second half of the century'; *ibid*, 189); the other late types were apparently not present in this deposit. Gillam's dating of Huntcliff-type cooking pots from *c* AD 360, a decade before the emergence of Crambeck parchment ware, stems from their presence in the 'III/IV' deposit at Birdoswald. Bewcastle and Birdoswald thus provided Gillam with the primary evidence for the dating of 4th-century pottery on Hadrian's Wall. Although destruction events, now given little credence, were invoked to explain the origins of the

relevant deposits, those at Birdoswald were dated independently by coins and still provide a valid framework for the chronology of the pottery.

When Gillam published his *Types*, the two decades since the publication of Birdoswald in 1938 had yielded little new information. The only real advance had been the excavation of the Carrawburgh *mithraeum* in 1950 where, in levels of Period III, products of the Throlam and Norton kilns were identified (Richmond and Gillam 1951, fig 11, nos 44 – the illustrated example of Gillam Type 189 – and 45, as well as a cooking pot of Type 161 in calcite-gritted ware; *ibid*, fig 11, no 43, Gillam's Type example). The last three decades, however, have seen the recovery of much new information, which alters some of Gillam's dating.

The earliest appearance of East Yorkshire wares on Hadrian's Wall

Calcite-gritted ware is known at South Shields in securely stratified contexts dating from the early 3rd century (Bidwell and Speak 1994, table 8.10; unpublished, East Quadrant, *c* AD 205/207–222/235, 0.02% by weight of the entire assemblage of 77.40kg). At Vindolanda, in the excavations in the north-east part of the fort, its earliest occurrences were in Period 4 construction deposits, dating to *c* AD 235 (Bidwell 1985, table VII, 1.6% by weight in an assemblage of 3.8kg). These occurrences of the ware are so rare and the quantities involved so small that only a single unidentifiable rim fragment is included amongst the sherds. In a context at South Shields (22802) dated from AD 222/235 to the late 3rd or early 4th century there is a straight, sharply everted rim in calcite-gritted ware, an example of so-called Knapton ware (Corder and Kirk 1932, 96–9) which was current in East Yorkshire during the 3rd century, and indeed much earlier. Further examples were found in unstratified contexts at Vindolanda. Gillam's Type 156, dated AD 230–280, appears to be Knapton ware; of the three examples he cites, one from Corbridge is from a 3rd-century deposit and the others are unstratified.

Analysis of pottery fabrics has shown that the calcite-gritted ware production site at Knapton did not produce the late 4th-century Huntcliff-type jars and other vessels, which were perhaps made near the east end of the Vale of Pickering (Evans 2000, 40). This new production site may have been the first to produce the jars with a curved everted rim (Gillam Type 161; Fig 4.2, no 1). An example was found at Bewcastle (Hodgson and Richmond 1938, fig 27, no 40) which shows that the type had appeared by the early 4th century. It later developed into the Huntcliff-type jar (Fig 4.2, nos 2–3).

Gillam's dating of the reduced wares (in 'smooth lead-grey' fabric) implies that he believed that the Crambeck industry started in earnest in AD 350/360, but that there were small quantities of earlier 'proto-Crambeck' ware (Gillam 1973, 61), which presumably included the countersunk lug-handled jars Type 40 from the Bewcastle strongroom (described as being of the smooth lead-grey fabric) dated AD 290–400, and Type 41 (from the Corder and Birley 1937 Crambeck type series) dated AD 320–400. Excavations in recent decades at Bewcastle, Vindolanda, and South Shields have produced many more examples of East Yorkshire grey wares stratified in late 3rd- or early 4th-century deposits, showing that most of the Crambeck reduced ware range was available from the start:

Pedestalled beaker (Fig 4.2, no 7): at Vindolanda a complete pedestalled beaker was found in an occupation level of Period 4B (*c* AD 250/60–275/300; Bidwell 1985, fig 71, no 139); a rim, probably also from a pedestalled beaker, was found in Period 4B construction levels (*c* AD 250–60; *ibid*, fig 69, no 104). The latter was apparently in Crambeck fabric (cf *ibid*, 179) and, if correctly identified, provides an earlier date than that from Bewcastle for the appearance of the ware in the Wall zone. A base from another beaker was also found in a Period 5 construction layer (*c* AD 275–300; *ibid*, 199).

Type 40, jars with counter-sunk lug handles (Fig 4.2, nos 5.1 and 5.2): Vindolanda (Bidwell 1985, 199, *c* AD 275–300); South Shields (unpublished, several examples).

Type 190, wide-mouthed bowls or jars (Fig 4.3, no 9): Vindolanda (Bidwell 1985, fig 72, no 157, no earlier than *c* AD 250 and under levels of *c* AD 275–300); South Shields, unpublished.

Type 203–4, bowls imitating, or reminiscent of, samian Dr 38 (reduced ware equivalent of Fig 4.3, no 21): Bewcastle (Austen 1991, fig 13, no 110).

Type 299, flanged bowls (Fig 4.3, no 11): Bewcastle (Austen 1991, fig 13, nos 111–12; Gillam *et al* 1993, fig 21, nos 47–50); South Shields (Bidwell and Speak 1994, fig 8.12, no 127, late 3rd or early 4th century, and numerous unpublished examples).

Types 320–1, dishes with groove below the rim (Fig 4.3, no 14): Bewcastle (Austen 1991, fig 13, no 124); South Shields (several unpublished examples).

Type 333, dish (Fig 4.3, no 15): Bewcastle (Gillam *et al* 1993, fig 20, no 17); South Shields (Bidwell and Speak 1994, fig 8.9, no 46, AD 222–35 to late 3rd or early 4th century, and several unpublished examples).

Narrow-mouthed jar (Fig 4.7, no 40): Vindolanda (Bidwell 1985, fig 73, no 176, *c* AD 275–300).

Fig 4.2 (opposite)   Pottery from the East Yorkshire industries: nos 1–3 calcite-gritted wares, 4–8 Crambeck reduced wares. 1, Malton (after Bidwell & Croom 1997). 2, Dalton Parlours (after Sumpter 1990). 3, Milecastle 48 (after Gillam 1970). 4, South Shields (after Bidwell & Speak 1994). 5.1, Corder & Birley 1937 type 3, South Shields (after Dore & Gillam 1979). 5.2, Corder and Birley 1937 type 3a, Scarborough (after Hull 1932). 6, Corder & Birley 1937 type 14a, Newcastle (after Bidwell & Croom 2002; the handle has been restored); type 14 (not illustrated) has the same rim form but has a very narrow mouth and neck. Both types can be found both with or without handles. Pinched-necked flagons (type 15) and spouted flagons (Corder 1928, pl VII, nos 183–7) are also known. 7, Corder & Birley 1937 type 11, South Shields (after Dore & Gillam 1979); decoration can consist of two grooves on the body or burnished lattice or line decoration, or be absent altogether. 8, Corder & Birley 1937 type 12, South Shields (after Dore & Gillam 1979)

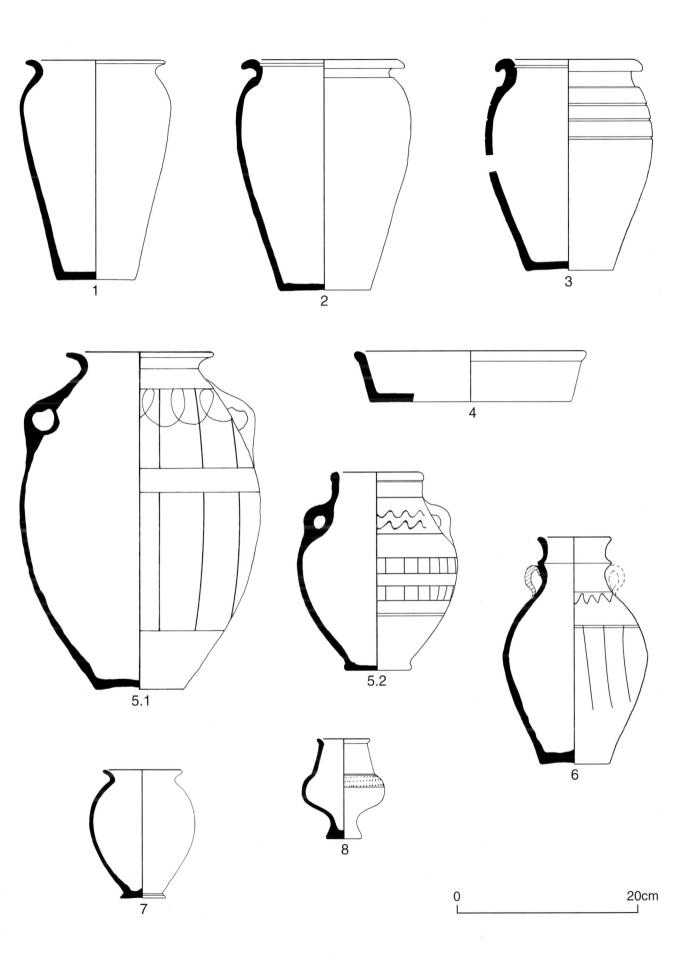

The only Crambeck mortarium datable to this period is Type 6 (Corder and Birley 1937) which was not included in Gillam's *Types* (Fig 4.3, no 24). Absent from the coastal fortlets and other late deposits, it was dated by Gillam to 'a period before the Picts' War of AD 367, but as it was made at Crambeck, not long before' (Gillam 1957b, 257, no 13). K Hartley (1995, 310) placed the emergence of Crambeck Type 6 mortaria 'perhaps as early as AD 280/300' because examples are found in such large quantities that production limited to a short period around the middle of the 4th century seemed unlikely. At York Minster, for example, there were 60 Crambeck Type 6 mortaria and 78 of the later Types 5, 7 and 8 (*ibid*, table 13). There are no stratified mortaria that substantiate this early dating. This might well be because the type emerged at the beginning of the 4th century, too late to have occurred in the late 3rd-century deposits at Vindolanda and the Period 6 demolition/Period 7 construction deposits at South Shields.

East Yorkshire wares on Hadrian's Wall from the early to mid-4th century

There are no substantial, well-dated groups of East Yorkshire wares from Hadrian's Wall and its vicinity later than the occupation of Bewcastle (ending in AD 312/314) or earlier than those that used to be regarded as of Wall Period IV, which are usually associated with coins of the Houses of Valentinian or Theodosius. At the beginning of this half-century period Crambeck reduced ware and much smaller quantities of calcite-gritted ware were finding their way to Hadrian's Wall. By the end of this period these wares predominated. A group from the lower filling of a well at Rudston, probably deposited between AD 295 and 330, shows that, in East Yorkshire also, grey wares were far more common than calcite-gritted ware (Rigby 1980, 73). A higher deposit in the well, associated with Valentinianic coins of AD 364 or later, contained much more calcite-gritted ware than other East Yorkshire fabrics, a pattern typical of late 4th-century deposits on Hadrian's Wall.

In 1967 a jar in calcite-gritted ware was found at Cridling Stubbs, Womersley, south-east of Castleford; it contained a hoard of 3300 coins which was closed in AD 345 or 346 (Pirie 1968, 127–9). The vessel is perhaps an early version of the Huntcliff-type jar: its drawing seems to show a groove on the inside of the rim and there is an offset below the rim on its exterior, but its pear-shaped profile is not typical. Efforts to locate the jar to check on these details have so far proved unsuccessful. It is perhaps a transitional type and evidence that the Huntcliff-type was emerging in the mid-4th century. That would not necessarily mean that the type immediately appeared on Hadrian's Wall in large quantities. There is as yet no reason to reject the date of *c* AD 360 for the fully developed version.

In the absence of groups of the relevant date on Hadrian's Wall, another approach can be taken. If East Yorkshire wares did not predominate until the 360s or 370s, what would the main sources of supply have been during the preceding half-century? For much of the 3rd century the main sources of coarse wares in the central and eastern sectors of the Wall were near the Thames estuary; most of the BB2 and Thameside types and fabrics can all be paralleled amongst material from the kilns at Mucking, Grays, Orsett, and Tilbury, on or near the north bank of the Thames in Essex. In 1994 it was proposed that these wares continued to arrive on Hadrian's Wall until the last two decades of the 3rd century (Bidwell and Speak 1994, 224). At that time a distinctive late product of these kilns, the conical flanged bowl, was thought to have been absent from Hadrian's Wall, but a few examples are now known at Newcastle,

Fig 4.3 (opposite)   Pottery from the East Yorkshire industries: 9–17 Crambeck reduced wares; 19–24 Crambeck parchment wares. 9, Corder & Birley 1937 type 4, Crambeck (after Corder & Birley 1937); this is a wide category, with a variety of possible rim and shoulder types. 11, Corder & Birley 1937 type 1, Newcastle (after Bidwell & Croom 2002). 12, Corder & Birley 1937 type 1b, Milecastle 9 (after Gillam 1970); examples can also have two internal lines. 13, Corder & Birley 1937 type 1a, Piercebridge (after Hird 2008). 14, Corder & Birley 1937 type 2a, South Shields (after Dore & Gillam 1979). 15, Corder & Birley 1937 type 2, South Shields (after Dore & Gillam 1979). 17, Corder & Birley 1937 type 13, South Shields (after Bidwell & Speak 1994); type 13a has a long neck and can be rouletted on the body (not illustrated), while type 13b has a rounded rim (not illustrated). 19, Corder & Birley 1937 type 7, Dalton Parlours (after Sumpter 1990); can be found as both bowl and mortarium. 20, Corder & Birley 1937 type 8, York (after Monaghan 1997); this type appears to have been only been made as a mortarium. 21, Corder & Birley 1937 type 5b, South Shields (unpublished, context 6200); can also be found as a mortarium, but these are rare (Corder & Birley 1937, 30; cf Malton: Swan 2002, fig 20, no 269), further the height of the wall above the flange can be tall or short, straight or curved, and with groove or without (cf Corder 1928, pl II, no 24; Dore & Gillam 1979, fig 41, no 228). 22, Corder & Birley 1937 type 9, Newcastle (after Bidwell & Croom 2002); this type is occasionally found as a mortarium (cf York: Swan 2002, fig 20, no 278). 23, Corder & Birley 1937 type 10, Corbridge (after Gillam 1970, no 298); the type includes a large variety of rim forms: the grey ware version, type 10a, appears to be rare on the northern frontier. 24, Corder & Birley 1937 type 6, York (after Hartley 1995); the number of grooves on the rim can vary, and some examples also have an incised wavy line on the flange (see Hartley 1995 for sub-types)

Wallsend, and South Shields (Bidwell and Croom 2002, fig 15.8, nos 79–80; fig 15.10, no 116). The type copied a BB1 form which did not emerge until after *c* AD 270 (Holbrook and Bidwell 1991, 98–9). Another significant find was made at South Shields in the Period 7 barrack immediately to the north-east of the courtyard house. Buried in the *contubernia* passages was a series of complete pots, their rims flush with the floor (a practice also known in earlier barracks at South Shields); one was a Thameside jar and the others included BB1, calcite-gritted, and Dales-type jars. The barrack was built in *c* AD

286–318, but the vessel in question was not inserted into the passage floor until the internal partitions were renewed, an event which was unlikely to have occurred before the early 4th century.

It is likely therefore that pottery from the Thames estuary continued to arrive on Hadrian's Wall for some time after *c* AD 300. The only other major source of pottery for the Wall in the early 4th century was the BB1 industry of south-east Dorset. At the eastern end of the Wall BB1 played an important part in the pottery supply from the Hadrianic period until well into the second half of

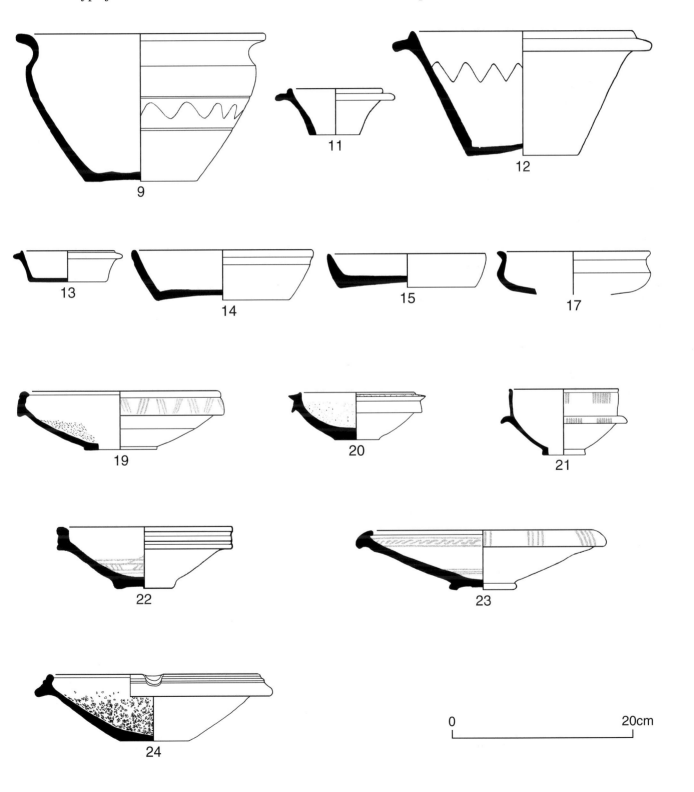

the 2nd century, as recent unpublished excavations at South Shields and Wallsend demonstrate. In a series of large earlier 3rd-century groups at these two sites, BB1 is present in only tiny quantities (eg South Shields, south-east corner, Period 4 demolition to Period 5A/6B demolition, *c* AD 207–09 to AD 222–35: BB1 = 1.34% by weight and 2.58% by EVEs; Wallsend, Buddle Street midden, second quarter of the 3rd century: BB1 = 1.04% by weight and 2.4% by EVEs). In the 4th century it began to be imported in quantity again: in two published groups from South Shields, with a very broad dating from the late 3rd to the late 4th century, it represents 8% and 8.7% by EVEs and 6.7% and 5.6% by weight (Bidwell and Speak 1994, table 8.10). These groups are dominated by late 4th-century pottery and in most contexts the BB1 will have been occurring residually (see below), which suggests that in the earlier 4th century BB1 had a substantial share of the pottery supply. At Vindolanda in the central sector BB1, scarce in the early 3rd century, had become common by the end of the century (Bidwell 1985, table VII). At the western end of the Wall the BB1 industries were major suppliers from the Hadrianic period until the end of its importation in the second half of the 4th century.

Other coarse wares certainly reached the eastern sector of Hadrian's Wall in the 4th century, for example, Dales ware and Dales-type vessels, and double lid-seated jars in heavily gritted and, very occasionally, shell-tempered wares (see Fig 4.4; Bidwell and Speak 1994, 232). At Vindolanda and South Shields they appear in varying quantities in late 3rd- and 4th-century groups, ranging from less than 1% to 13–15% (Bidwell 1985, table VII; Bidwell and Speak 1994, table 8.10). There is no clear pattern in their occurrence but this type of pottery was certainly of importance at some stages during the period in question.

Using this fragmentary information, it is possible to offer a hypothetical reconstruction of the pottery supply to the eastern sector of the Wall in the 4th century before the East Yorkshire kilns came to dominate the market:

First quarter of the 4th century: the Thameside kilns continued as the main source of pottery, supplemented by smaller quantities of BB1 and East Yorkshire grey wares, Dales ware and Dales-type vessels, and double lid-seated jars in gritty and shell-tempered wares. Calcite-gritted wares remained scarce.

Second (and third?) quarter of the 4th century: supplies from the Thameside kilns came to an end early in this period, if not a little before, and the gap was largely filled by increasing quantities of BB1 and East Yorkshire grey wares and the other types of pottery noted above.

This reconstruction is perhaps also valid for the central sector of the Wall. Groups at Vindolanda certainly demonstrate the importance of BB1 during the later 3rd century and through much of the 4th century (Bidwell 1985, table VII).

East Yorkshire wares on Hadrian's Wall in the late 4th century

From the end of the 1920s the influx of pottery from what was thought to have been a single source at Crambeck (this was before calcite-gritted ware was identified as the product of a separate industry) was associated with Wall Period IV, which followed the Picts' War of AD 367. The key deposits were at the Yorkshire coastal fortlets and at Birdoswald. On the basis of the coin finds the former were long thought to have been built by Count Theodosius as part of his restoration of the frontier in AD 369 (Craster 1932, 253). More recent opinion now favours a connection with the policies of Magnus Maximus and a construction date of *c* AD 383 (Casey 1979, 75); the considerable wear displayed by the Valentinianic coinage (of AD 364–78) from Carr Naze, Filey, strongly supports this later dating (Brickstock 2000b, 137). The relevant deposits at Birdoswald have already been discussed above. The important point to note is that 'the distinctive later fourth-century types' came from the destruction of the Period IV cook-house which had been 'looted then burnt' (Richmond and Birley 1930, 170, 176) and therefore that the pottery was associated with the end of the Period IV occupation, at least in that part of the fort. Gillam surely had this in mind when he fixed on the date of AD 370 for the introduction of Crambeck parchment ware and other late types: AD 370 was the date at which the types first appeared on Hadrian's Wall and not the date at which they became prevalent, although Gillam was clear that they rapidly captured the market (Gillam 1973, 61). The introduction of the Huntcliff-type jars was dated a decade earlier because of their occurrence in a deposit which spanned Periods III and IV, as noted above.

Gillam's two key deposits therefore belong to the very end of the Roman period in northern England. Many later 4th-century pottery groups have been recovered since Gillam published his *Types*. They need to be examined in order to see whether they conform to Gillam's conclusions about the dating of the latest types. In most instances the dating depends on coin finds, and it is possible to separate out those deposits where the latest stratified coins are of the period AD 364–78 (Coin Period 19), or the latest coins from the site as a whole are of that period.

Hadrian's Wall forts

Huntcliff-type jars and Crambeck parchment ware were absent from Period 5 occupation and demolition at Vindolanda (*c* AD 275/300–370: Bidwell 1985, 201). At South Shields there are no overall rebuildings after the beginning of Period 7; Period 8 consists of a series of modifications in various parts of the fort, characterised by changes to room arrangements in barracks, courtyard house and *principia,* the filling of hypocaust basements and channels, and the laying of crude surfaces of reused facing stones both in room interiors and over streets. Some of the paving in the courtyard house was laid at a date after AD 375 on coin evidence. The only relevant published sequence is from the defensive ditches beyond the south-west gate where the deposits preceding Period 8 contained no late types (Bidwell and Speak 1994, 138). The earliest contexts for Huntcliff-type jars amongst the unpublished pottery are a number of deposits dating to before the laying of the paving (contexts 5249, 5251, 9662, and possibly also 5877). Period 8 construction also produced further Huntcliff-type rims (3157, 5210) and a Crambeck parchment ware bowl (3034).

Milecastles

Three milecastles (nos 9, 35 and 51) have produced coins of Valentinian and Valens, although pottery has only been published from two of them. Huntcliff-type jars were found at Milecastle 9, Chapel House (Birley 1930b, pl LIII, nos 70–2), and in some quantity from Milecastle 35 (Dore 1984, 112), where the coin of Valens (of AD 374; Casey 1984a, no 20) showed slight wear; Crambeck parchment ware and the late Nene Valley types were absent. Huntcliff-type jars and an oxidised Crambeck bowl are known from milefortlet 5, Cardurnock (Simpson and Hodgson 1947, fig 11, nos 20–4; fig 11, no 40), where no coins were recovered (or at least none was published). Milecastle 48, Poltross Burn, produced Huntcliff-type jars and a Crambeck parchment ware bowl of Gillam Type 207 (his type specimen; Gibson and Simpson 1911, pl 18, no 330), which is the only example of this ware published from a milecastle; the latest coin was an issue of AD 317–24, but only ten coins were recovered. At Milecastle 50, High House, where the latest of eight coins were dated to AD 309–13 and 309–14, no late pottery types were recovered (Simpson 1913, 336–70).

Forts in north-west England

The most useful evidence is from Ribchester (Edwards and Webster 1985) and Watercrook (Potter 1976; 1979) which have produced 304 and 100 coins respectively. Neither fort has produced coins later than AD 378. Huntcliff-type jars are present at both forts, but only in small quantities; the other late types are absent. Ravenglass and Ambleside have Huntcliff-type jars and Crambeck parchment ware, and the latter fort has also produced late Nene Valley types. Few coins have been published from these forts: 37 legible coins from Ravenglass, the latest a coin of Valens (AD 364–67), 'although its condition would suggest that its loss should be placed after 370' (a *solidus* of Theodosius was found nearby at Muncaster Castle), and 13 legible coins

from Ambleside, the latest of which is also a coin of Valens (AD 364–78) (Shotter 1993, 68).

Brough-on-Humber

The coin-list from this town and possible late Roman naval base consists of 518 coins. After the mid-4th century there was a marked fall in the supply of coinage; there are eight coins of the House of Valentinian, and only one later issue, a coin of Magnus Maximus (AD 383–88). Huntcliff-type jars, Crambeck parchment ware and late Nene Valley colour-coated types were present but only in very small quantities, about 1% of the total number of sherds found (Wacher 1969, 205); this was taken as an indication of 'the lack of strength in the post-370 occupation at Brough'.

The villas at Rudston (Humberside) and Dalton Parlours (West Yorkshire)

Amongst the 42 coins from Rudston, the three latest issues were Valentinianic and were found in the upper filling of a well along with Huntcliff-type jars and Crambeck parchment ware (a segmental bowl, a bowl with vertical grooved rim, and a small flanged bowl: Rigby 1980, 81, nos 289, 291). It was stated that 'there is a notable absence of the latest Crambeck parchment ware mortaria, types 7 and 8, [and] there are no platters, dishes or jars in Nene Valley colour-coated ware' (*ibid*, 94); accordingly, it was thought that occupation had come to an end before the building of the coastal fortlets.

There were 87 coins from Dalton Parlours, a series ending abruptly with a single Valentinianic issue, suggesting that occupation did not continue much beyond *c* AD 370. Substantial numbers of Huntcliff-type jars and Crambeck parchment ware vessels were found on the site, but apparently no late Nene Valley colour-coated ware (Sumpter 1990, 145).

This evidence suggests that by AD 378 at the latest, Huntcliff-type jars were well established and appearing in increasing quantities. Several of the sites with Valentinianic coinage produce at least some Crambeck parchment ware, but its intermittent appearances suggest a date of introduction towards the middle or end of the period AD 364–78 (Bidwell 2005, 20).

Developments in the supply of Crambeck reduced and calcite-gritted wares

During the later 4th century and beyond, the quantities of Crambeck reduced ware declined while supply of calcite-gritted ware increased. This reflects the increasing use of cooking pots and jars and a corresponding diminution in demand for bowls and dishes, or at least those made in pottery rather than

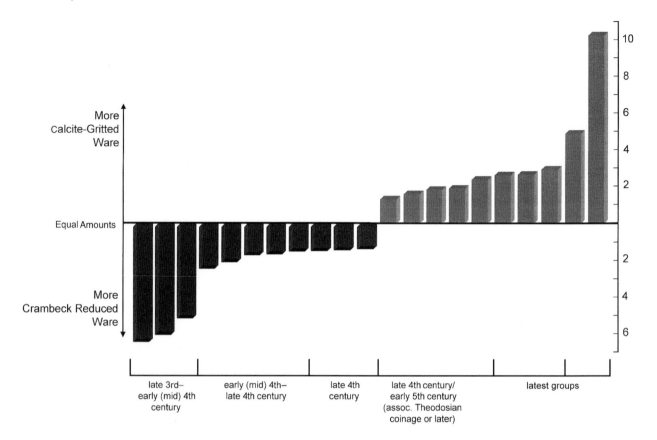

Table 4.3   The ratio between Crambeck reduced ware and calcite-gritted ware from the late 3rd to the early 5th century

metal or wood (Evans 1993). Table 4.3, which shows the changing quantities of the two wares, is based on 21 groups spanning the period from the late 3rd century to some unknown date after the end of the 4th century. It effectively shows the transition from use of a wide range of specialised pottery types, with varying functions in storing, preparing and serving food and drink, to a narrow selection of types which was entirely dominated by jars and cooking pots. Put more broadly, it shows how a long-established tradition of Roman provincial pottery use, ultimately derived from Mediterranean societies, gave way to a reliance on basic and probably multi-purpose types. At the end of the Roman period in northern Britain, the trend was towards the same sort of pottery use which is found in the Iron Age and through much of the medieval period (cf Evans 1993, 109).

The pottery groups in Table 4.3 are arranged in sequence according to the increasing amounts of calcite-gritted ware which occur in them. They also fall into six chronological series which reflect these increases. It must be emphasised that the series do not all consist of groups with similar dating evidence. For example, coins have to be used for dating with great care, and the south granary group at Birdoswald is in Series F, the latest in the sequence, even though coins associated with the group only provide a *terminus post quem* of *c* AD 350 (see Bidwell 2005 for arguments that all the coins are residual). There are other factors, in addition to datable objects, which

will indicate the broad contemporaneity of groups. No coins were associated with the important group of pottery recovered in 1952 at Thornborough Farm, Catterick, but it came from a building, now known to have been within the later Roman fort, which had been altered 'not perhaps before AD 370', following which 'rough repairs' were made to the floor of one of its rooms (Gillam 1957b, 240). The pottery was from the latest occupation level, from a layer of fallen plaster which sealed that level, and from topsoil and late unsealed deposits (two late Roman military buckles were found on the floor of Room I). How long the building continued in occupation is uncertain, although the excavator thought it likely to have been many years after 400. Despite the lack of associated closely datable objects, the position of the pottery group in the sequence of occupation means that it sits very comfortably alongside the pottery from the Scarborough coastal fortlet (the ratios of Crambeck reduced ware to calcite-gritted ware at Catterick are 1:2.67 and at Scarborough 1:2.64, both based on estimates of the number of vessels represented).

Another important consideration is the size of the groups used to compile the table. The smaller the group, the more likely it is to be unrepresentative of the wider contemporary pottery supply. However, quite large groups might be misleading if they include large amounts of residual pottery. In Table 4.3 groups with a total weight less than 5kg have been excluded, but our preference is for groups

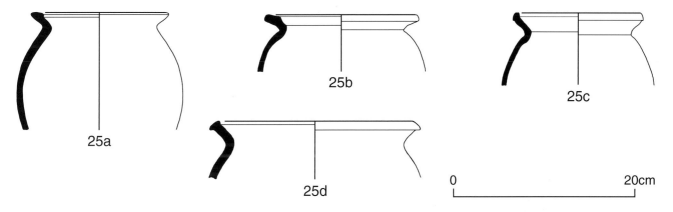

Fig 4.4   Selection of rim types in heavily gritted wares: 25a, South Shields (after Dore & Gillam 1979); 25b–d, Piercebridge (after Hird 2008)

which weigh at least 25kg. The south granary group at Birdoswald, already discussed above, is a possible illustration of how misleading small groups might be. After the Carr Naze coastal fortlet at Filey, the Birdoswald group has the widest variation in the ratio of Crambeck reduced ware to calcite-gritted ware, 1:4.9, but the group weighs only 7.57kg. However, there is twice as much Crambeck reduced ware as BB1, probably occurring residually, in the group than the sum of the other two wares, and it is doubtful whether the group provides a reliable indicator of the quantities in use when it was deposited as filling of the granary basement.

Publication of the full commentary on the groups used in Table 4.3 will appear soon. The detailed statistics are already available on the Hadrian's Wall Ceramic Database (www.twmuseums.org.uk/archaeology/ceramic%20database/introduction.html). The table is published here to establish one important point: that the ratios of Crambeck reduced and calcite-gritted wares continued to change from the last quarter of the 4th century, which seems to have been the tipping point when calcite-gritted ware began to predominate, and into the 5th century. The trajectory of change had far to go, as pottery use not only continued well into the 5th century but also underwent a series of changes. More generally, the table is meant to provide a framework for assessing the date of larger groups, although its full potential, together with its problems and pitfalls, will not be apparent until the commentary is published.

Heavily gritted wares

From the late 3rd century a hard, mid- to dark-grey ware with abundant large inclusions, usually of quartz, was used for the production of jars and cooking pots with flat-topped, cupped or double lid-seated rims (Fig 4.4; Gillam Type 153 is one of the many different rim forms found in this ware). The ware was used for hand-made and wheel-thrown vessels, and there seems to have been a number of

different production sites, including Catterick (Bell and Evans 2002, fabric R5). Distribution was apparently concentrated along Dere Street up to the Wall, and therefore it never had the same geographic spread as the East Yorkshire industries across the whole of the north (Croom *et al* 2008). Although the types in this ware seem to have developed from those current in the 3rd century, it is most common during the first half of the 4th century. Fabric R5 at Catterick, for example, was principally made in the early and mid-4th century (Bell and Evans 2002, 453). Production probably continued until the end of the century, but the ware as a whole became less common. It made up 25–35% of the coarse wares in the first half of the 4th century at Catterick Bridge, but only 15–16% by the end of the century (*ibid*, 452–3), and a maximum of 7% in the very late deposit found in the 1952 excavations at Thornborough Farm, inside the fort (Gillam 1957b, table 1). At Piercebridge it made up 18.6% in the mainly mid-4th-century fill of the outer ditch and only 3% in the very late 4th/early 5th-century fill of the inner ditch (Croom *et al* 2008), and only 1.7% of the very late 4th-century pottery at Newcastle (Bidwell and Croom 2002, table 15.9). As the ware was only used in the manufacture of jars and cooking pots, it was not in competition with Crambeck reduced ware (which did not produce them), but with the calcite-gritted ware industry.

Late Nene Valley ware and Oxfordshire ware
(Fig 4.5)

The east coast trade in coarse wares petered out in the early 4th century, but limited quantities of Nene Valley fine wares (and initially some mortaria from the same source) continued to reach the north until a very late date, probably by overland routes (Evans 2000, 40; Swan 2002, 71). Changes in the Nene Valley industries in the late 3rd or early 4th century resulted in a decline in the production of the beakers, jugs and boxes that had previously

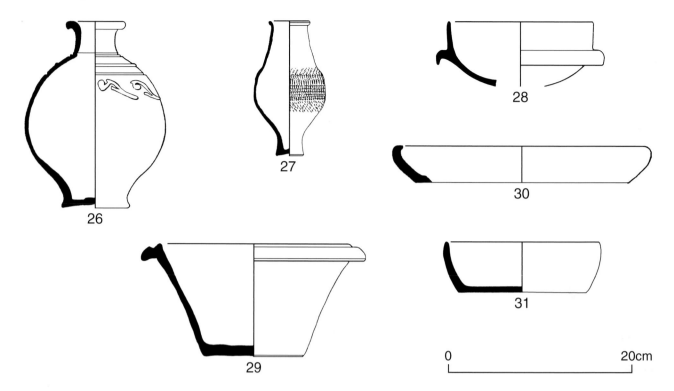

Fig 4.5   Late Nene Valley ware. 26, Birdoswald (after Gillam 1970). 27, Catterick (after Evans 2002). 28, South Shields (after Bidwell & Speak 1994). 29, Catterick (after Cooper 2002). 30, Newcastle (after Bidwell & Croom 2002). 31, South Shields (unpublished, context 3201)

been the mainstay of the industry, and by the middle of the 4th century at the latest production consisted of mainly bowls, dishes and jars (Perrin 1999, 87).

Although plain-rimmed dishes were probably made in small numbers from the late 2nd century onwards, most appear to be 4th-century in date (*ibid*, 101) and there are only a few possible examples in the north dating to the 2nd or 3rd centuries (Evans 2002, 280). The 4th-century examples of the dishes, as well as hemispherical and conical flanged bowls and jars, are frequently found associated with pottery dated to AD 370 or later. On the Catterick Bypass and the Catterick Bridge sites, Nene Valley coarse ware forms were found with Corder and Birley 1937 type 1b bowls in Crambeck reduced ware (Evans 2002, fig 132, nos G5.1, G5.2, G5.5, G5.10; 260, no G5.30 (not illustrated); Bell and Evans 2002, 452). At Birdoswald a conical flanged bowl was associated with Crambeck parchment ware (Hird 1997, fig 167, nos 174, 182) and at South Shields another such bowl came from the same context as a type 1b bowl (Bidwell and Speak 1994, fig 8.10, nos 77–8). At South Shields and Vindolanda more examples of the coarse ware forms were found in ploughsoil and unstratified contexts than were found stratified, suggesting they were most common at the very end of the Roman period (Bidwell and Speak 1994, 225).

A few red colour-coated bowls in Oxfordshire ware have been recorded at South Shields, Corbridge, Birdoswald, and Carlisle. A bowl from Newcastle

is a type which can be dated to *c* AD 340 or later (Bidwell and Croom 2002, fig 15.9, no 97) and another from Corbridge can be dated to *c* AD 350 or later (Young 1977, 309). A stamp-decorated Dr 45 imitation from Corbridge dated to *c* AD 360–400 (Gillam 1957a, Type 287) suggests that examples of the ware continued to reach the Wall in the later 4th century.

Summary of the main sources of pottery supply in the 4th century

In the eastern and central sectors of Hadrian's Wall, during the last quarter of the 3rd century and possibly from the later part of the third quarter of that century, Dales ware, heavily gritted jars with lid-seatings, Crambeck grey wares and Crambeck Type 6 mortaria, in addition to mortaria from Cantley or Catterick, make their first appearance. Calcite-gritted ware, previously very rare on the Wall, begins to appear in small but significant quantities, and BB1 reappears in rather larger quantities. Thames-estuary wares and BB2 still dominate the pottery supply, grey ware cooking pots and jars were probably still arriving from Yorkshire kilns such as those at Norton, and established sources of specialist wares continue (Mancetter-Hartshill mortaria and colour-coated wares and mortaria from the Lower Nene Valley).

By the end of the first quarter of the 4th century, Thames-estuary and BB2 wares were no longer

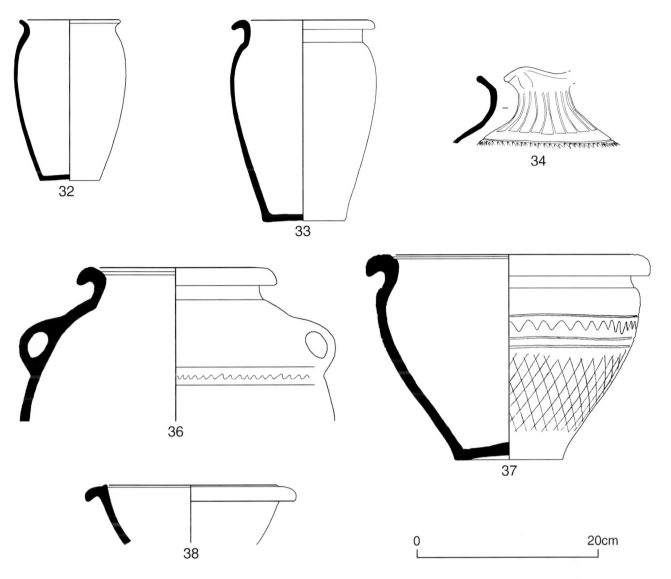

Fig 4.6   Additional calcite-gritted ware types. 32, Malton (after Bidwell & Croom 1997). 33, Watercrook (after Lockwood 1979). 34, York (after Monaghan 1997); a complete example is known from Corbridge and a handle from South Shields (both unpublished). 36, Seamer (after Mitchelson 1951). 37, Castle Howard (after Hull 1932). 38, South Shields (after Bidwell & Speak 1994, late 3rd- or early 4th-century context)

reaching northern Britain. Dales ware is never very common and would only have supplied a small percentage of the cooking pots or jars in use. At the eastern end of Hadrian's Wall and in north-eastern England, BB1 rarely makes up more than 10% of any late Roman assemblage, of which only about half of the vessels are cooking pots. The main types of cooking pots and jars were in calcite- and heavily gritted fabrics, the former also used for a few other, much rarer types, the early chronology of which is unclear, and the latter used exclusively for lid-seated jars of several types. Heavily gritted wares seem to have been more common at sites such as Piercebridge and Catterick. The only significant alternatives to the bowls and dishes supplied from the Thames estuary were BB1 and Crambeck reduced ware. The latter certainly shows a dominance in late

4th-century groups which had probably been established very soon after supply from the area of the Thames estuary failed.

Figures from Vindolanda and Birdoswald show that in the later 3rd and earlier 4th centuries BB1 occurred in much larger quantities in the central sector than farther east. At these sites, heavily gritted wares are well represented, but how much calcite-gritted ware was in use during this period is uncertain. At the west end of Hadrian's Wall and in north-west England, BB1 had been the principal coarse ware in use since the later 2nd century, a position that was maintained until well into the 4th century. It is uncertain when mortaria from Mancetter-Hartshill, the Lower Nene Valley and Cantley-Catterick no longer reached Hadrian's Wall, although it is usually assumed to have been in *c* AD

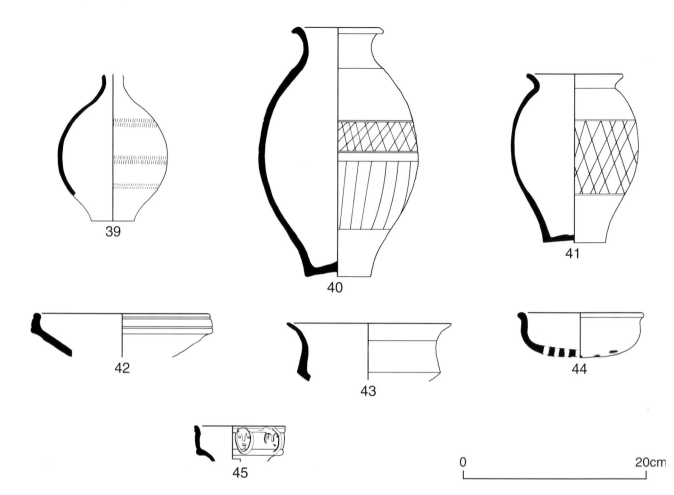

Fig 4.7 Additional Crambeck reduced ware types. 39, Malton (after Bidwell & Croom 1997). 40, Chester-le-Street (unpublished, Sunderland Museum). 41, Malton (after Bidwell & Croom 1997). 42, Malton (after Bidwell & Croom 1997). 43, Vindolanda (after Bidwell 1985, microfiche); the form was used by Yorkshire industries such as Norton and Hasholme from the first half of the 3rd century, and is occasionally found in the Crambeck fabric. 44, Catterick (after Evans 2002). 45, Malton (after Bidwell & Croom 1997)

350, before the full range of Crambeck mortaria appeared.

By the time Huntcliff-type jars and Crambeck parchment ware were introduced, in *c* AD 360 and 370, BB1 is thought to have disappeared. Later groups can shed little light on the end of BB1 in the North: it is impossible to be certain whether the ware in these groups is occurring residually. Its absence from the coastal fortlets probably means little, as it is rare in East Yorkshire (eg as at Rudston: Rigby 1980, 93). More significant is the general recession in the distribution of the ware throughout all but south-west Britain from the mid-4th century, a trend which can be assumed to have affected the frontier in northern Britain (Tyers 1996, 185; for a late Roman decline in BB1 in London, a possible entrepot for the export of the ware to the east end of the Wall, see Symonds and Tomber 1991, fig 2; for a decline at York after *c* AD 300, see Monaghan 1997, 891, fig 320; information from north-west England is lacking).

In the last quarter of the 4th century, in addition to calcite-gritted and Crambeck wares, jars in heavily gritted fabrics and colour-coated wares from the Nene Valley were still reaching the Wall. There are no clear indications of the date at which their importation or production came to an end.

Some questions

The picture of the pottery supply at the beginning of the 4th century which emerges in the previous sections is complex, with a wide range of types arriving from sources in southern Britain while a number of minor industries were active in north-east England and Yorkshire, and perhaps in north-west England, although these last did not survive much longer. It has been suggested that the drastic simplification which had taken place by the end of the 4th century was imposed as a result of a military contract obtained by the East Yorkshire potters (Evans 1989, 78–9). However, even at this late date, those potters had not achieved a complete monopoly in northern Britain. At Catterick there was a small industry producing parchment ware, bowls in oxidised ware

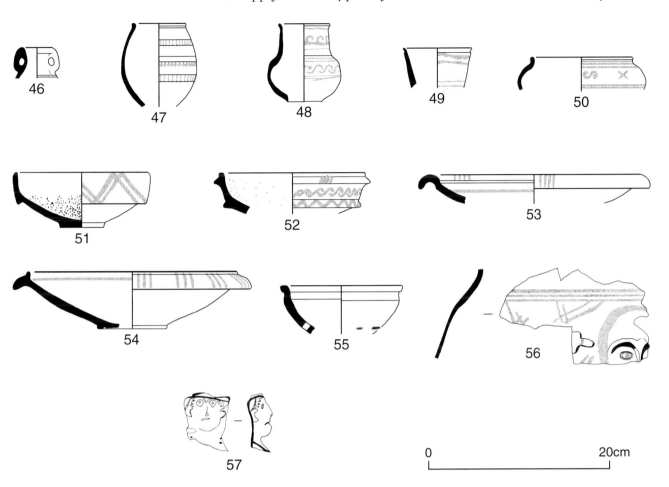

Fig 4.8 Additional Crambeck parchment ware types. 46, Catterick (after Evans 2002). 47, South Shields (after Dore & Gillam 1979); everted rim beakers are also known (Malton: Bidwell & Croom 1997, fig 35, no 377). 48, York (after Monaghan 1997). 49, York (after Monaghan 1997). 50, Piercebridge (after Hird 2008). 51, Piercebridge (after Hird 2008). 52, South Shields (after Dore & Gillam 1979). 53, South Shields (after Dore & Gillam 1979). 54, Catterick (after Bell & Evans 2002). 55, Piercebridge (after Hird 2008). 56, Malton (after Braithwaite 1997). 57, Crambe kiln (King & Moore 1989, fig 2, no 1)

with decoration in white paint, and grey wares; its products were distributed locally with outliers only at Binchester, Piercebridge, and York (Evans 2002, 270–5, figs 138–40; Bell and Evans 2002, 455–6, fig 210). A kiln at Bainesse Farm produced close imitations of late BB1 (Busby *et al* 1996). Catterick is also probably a source of later 3rd- and 4th-century mortaria and jars in heavily gritted ware which reached Hadrian's Wall.

New data make it possible to suggest that supply from other potteries contracted because of successful competition from East Yorkshire, and perhaps also because of wider economic factors, rather than because of the imposition of a contract (cf Swan 2002, 73). More than 30 years on, Gillam's description of the 'east-Yorkshire trickle [that] became a flood' in the late 4th century now seems to exaggerate the contrast between the earlier and later supply of the ware (Gillam 1973, 61). By the beginning of the 4th century East Yorkshire products were of much more importance than Gillam recognised. There are scarcely any groups of the early to mid-4th century, but a steady growth in the distribution and quanti-

ties of East Yorkshire wares is an attractive (though unproven) hypothesis. The introduction of Huntcliff-type jars and, about a decade later, of Crambeck parchment ware could be seen as a standardisation of production and the introduction of a more expensive ware, which resulted from control of the northern pottery supply. How pottery and other goods were distributed is indicated by the discovery of market areas of 4th-century date in the forts at Newcastle (Bidwell and Snape 2002, 275–80) and Carlisle (information from D Shotter and the late V Swan). At Newcastle finds in larger quantities than usual of 'native' or local traditional ware in 4th-century levels indicate trade with the population in the landscape outside the forts and probably beyond the Wall (Bidwell and Croom 2002, 169–70). Nothing is known of the basis of this trade, and north of the Tees Valley late Roman pottery occurs at very few non-military sites.

Systems of supply are central to other questions about late Roman pottery in northern Britain. Swan (2002, 73) has shown that the supra-regional dominance of the East Yorkshire industries reflects a similar pattern in the rest of Roman Britain. A comparison with other frontier areas would be very instructive. The wide distribution on the Lower Rhine and in northern Gaul of lid-seated jars in Mayen ware, a heavily gritted fabric, is an obvious parallel to the prevalence of Huntcliff-type and other lid-seated jars in northern Britain. Another question worth investigating is whether imported wares in other frontier zones show the same dramatic falling-away, in comparison with imports in adjacent civil zones, that occurred in Britain. More work is needed on the origins of the Crambeck industry, including further excavation of the kilns and their associated structures. The antecedents of some of the types are a matter of controversy (Swan 2002, 73), and the topic needs re-examination. Scarcely anything is known about the production sites of calcite-gritted ware, and perhaps even a limited programme of field-walking would produce useful results.

The date at which production of East Yorkshire wares came to an end is a question which requires investigation into 5th-century rather than 4th-century pottery supply. However, for Evans (2000) the near monopoly that the East Yorkshire potters achieved, supposedly through a contract to supply the army, meant that when the monetary economy failed, the distribution system likewise failed and pottery use rapidly came to an end. If during the 4th century the growth of the East Yorkshire industries had been much more gradual, the distribution of its products might have become firmly embedded in the structure of frontier society and able to survive a change in the basis of economic exchange. Understanding of pottery supply in the 5th century depends on our knowledge of what happened in north Britain during the 4th century.

Notes

1   The research for this article was partly based on work carried out for the Hadrian's Wall Ceramic Database, funded by the North East Regional Museums Hub (www.twmuseums.org.uk/archaeology/ceramic%20database/introduction.html).

5 Late Roman glass vessels in the Hadrian's Wall frontier region *Jennifer Price*[1]

Introduction

The glass vessels found in late Roman Britain were markedly different from those known in the 1st to 3rd centuries AD, in their forms and in the colour and quality of the glass used to make them. By *c* AD 300, the prismatic bottles that were a major part of nearly every later 1st- to 3rd-century assemblage in the province had disappeared, and the use of jars, flasks and unguent bottles was in decline. As a rule, these were not replaced by other forms of containers,

with the result that fewer vessels were in circulation and they had a more limited range of functions. Tablewares therefore became very prominent, particularly those produced for consuming and serving liquid. Open forms of tablewares, principally drinking vessels and bowls (Fig 5.1), dominated late Romano-British glass assemblages; closed vessels such as jugs and bottles (Fig 5.2) were present as a minor element. These changes were noted and illustrated in the study of glass from excavations at Colchester (Cool and Price 1995, 211–23) and, using

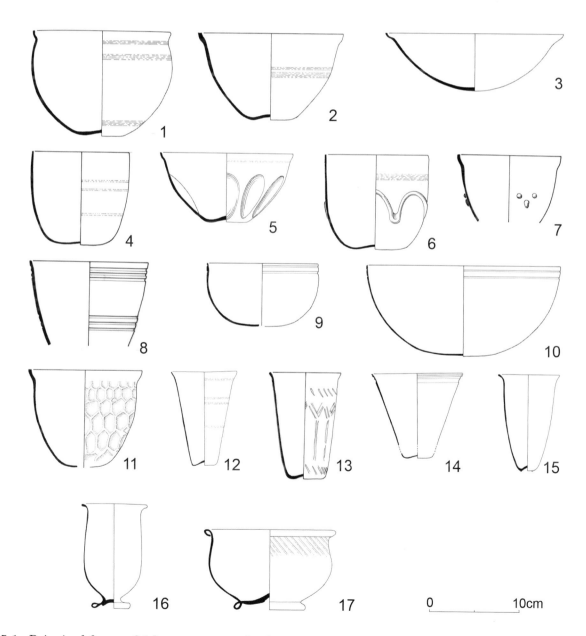

Fig 5.1   Principal forms of 4th-century cups, beakers, and bowls in northern Britain

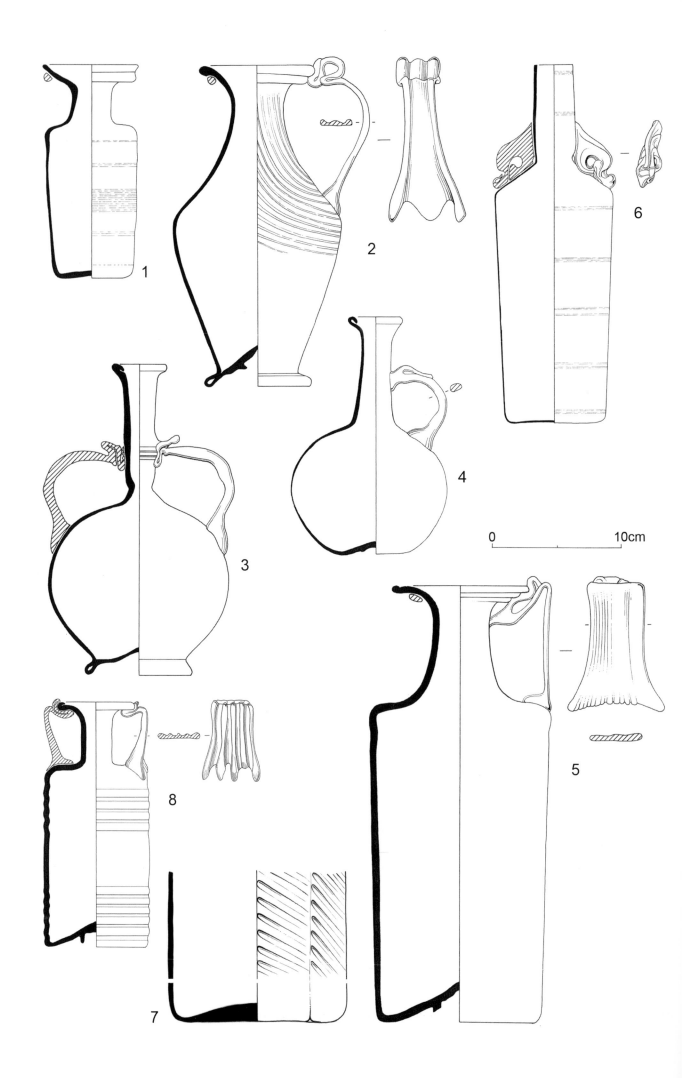

different methods of counting, Cool (2006, last eight rows of table 19.1) and Price (2000a, fig 2) have shown similar results at late Roman military, rural, and urban settlements in many parts of Britain.

By the 4th century, most vessels were made in pale greenish, greenish colourless, yellowish-green or bluish-green glass which was often blown very thinly and of poor quality, being full of bubbles and black specks. In the later 4th century glass in distinctly stronger shades of green and yellowish-green appeared, but it was still of poor quality. Some fine pieces of tableware were made in colourless glass with few impurities but glass of this quality was rather uncommon. Strongly coloured glass was sometimes applied as decoration, but complete coloured vessels were rare (Cool 1995; Price 2000b).

The dominant forms of drinking vessels were thin-walled convex cups (Fig 5.1, nos 4, 6; Price and Cottam 1998, 117–19) and conical beakers (Fig 5.1, no 12; *ibid*, 121–3). The majority of these, and the convex bowls (Fig 5.1, nos 1, 3; *ibid*, 124–9), had cracked-off, unsmoothed rims and little decoration except for faint horizontal abraded lines, though some had applied trails and blobs or mould-blown patterns. From the middle of the 4th century onwards, shallow bowls with cracked-off rims and indented sides (Fig 5.1, no 5; *ibid*, 128–9), drinking vessels with fire-rounded rims (Fig 5.1, nos 15–16; *ibid*, 129–31), and bowls with tubular rims, sometimes with ribbed decoration on the body (Fig 5.1, no 17; *ibid*, 131–3) were also made. Drinking vessels and bowls in glass of finer quality, often with complex cut decoration, are found in small numbers for much of the century.

The majority of the closed forms, principally jugs and bottles, are assumed to be tableware for serving liquids. The majority of jugs either have funnel mouths, biconical bodies with spiral ribbing and high folded base rings (Fig 5.2, no 2; Price and Cottam 1998, 163–5), or rolled rims, convex bodies and concave bases or folded base rings (Fig 5.2, nos 3–4; *ibid*, 165–8). Nearly all the bottles have cylindrical bodies, often with abraded lines, and either funnel mouths and angular ribbon handles (Fig 5.2, no 5; *ibid*, 204–5) or vertical rims, cylindrical necks and dolphin-shaped handles (Fig 5.2, no 6; *ibid*, 206–7), though a version of the last with a hexagonal ribbed body (Fig 5.2, no 7; *ibid*, 208–9) is also known. Very few of the 4th-century vessels in Britain appear to have been designed to contain and transport liquid. One such bottle form has been recognised, often known as a Frontinus bottle from the inscriptions found on many of the bases, with a wide rim, narrow neck, angular handles and a thin-walled, mould-blown cylindrical body with corrugations at the top and bottom (Fig 5.2, no 8; *ibid*, 209–11; Price 2005). These bottles were made in various sizes, and the largest held nearly two litres of liquid. Unguent bottles have rarely been found

in settlements, although some long pipette-shaped examples are known from late Roman burials (Price and Cottam 1998, 187–8; Cool 2002b).

Most of the information about late Roman vessel glass in Britain comes from settlements, as little was deposited in burials. This shows that glass vessels were used almost exclusively for drinking and for serving food and liquid, with a little evidence for the transport of small quantities of commodities in glass containers. It is also apparent that glass was not used to the same extent or in the same ways by every section of the population, or in every region. Considerable quantities of both ordinary and high-quality tableware have been recorded at many of the wealthy rural residences, as at Barnsley Park and Frocester Court in Gloucestershire and Beadlam, North Yorkshire (Price 1982; Price 2000a; Price and Cottam 1996), some military and urban settlements, and at shrines such as Uley, Gloucestershire (Price 1993), while others have produced little or none. It is noteworthy, for example, that rich assemblages of late Roman glass came from the fort at Caister-on-Sea, Norfolk (Price and Cool 1993), the town at Dorchester, Dorset (Cool and Price 1993, 154–7), and the suburban settlement at Towcester, Northamptonshire (Price and Cool 1983), whereas little was noted in the fort at Caernarvon, Gwynedd (Allen 1993, 219), or Exeter, Devon (Charlesworth 1979, 224; Allen 1991, 220), London (Shepherd 2000, 127) or parts of Colchester (Cool and Price 1995, 231–2). Vessels are generally very rare in rural settlements other than those of high status, though the late 4th- to 5th-century settlement at site XII, Overton Down, Wiltshire, produced a group of drinking vessels and bowls (Fowler 2000, 104–5).

At this period, a small proportion of the glass in Britain is similar to vessels known from distant areas of the Roman world, and these may have come from Italy and the western Mediterranean provinces, or from further afield in the eastern Mediterranean region. Nearly all of the Romano-British forms, however, are closely comparable with the ones found in the adjacent areas of the Continent such as north and western France or the lower and middle Rhineland, where a greater quantity and wider range of vessels has survived. Very many of the forms are characteristic of the north-west provinces and there is little doubt that they were made in the region; late Roman workshops have been found in Germany, as in the Hambach Forest, west of Köln (Brüggler 2006), and in northern France, as at Lavoye, Ste-Menehould (Foy and Nenna 2001, 58) and elsewhere. It is also probable that glass workshops operated in Britain in the 4th century, although no certain physical evidence for the structures has been recognised. Much of the ordinary vessel glass found at Romano-British sites may have been produced close to where it was used, perhaps by itinerant craftsmen, and some of the vessel forms

Fig 5.2 (opposite)   Principal forms of 4th-century flasks, jugs, and bottles in northern Britain

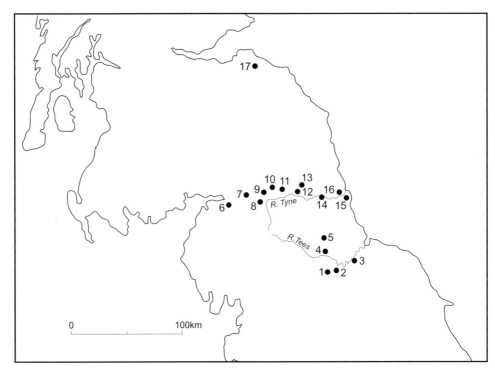

Fig 5.3   Sites in the northern frontier region: 1, Catterick; 2, Scorton; 3, Quarry Farm, Ingleby Barwick; 4, Piercebridge; 5, Binchester; 6, Carlisle; 7, Birdoswald; 8, Vindolanda; 9, Housesteads; 10, Carrawburgh; 11, Chesters; 12, Corbridge; 13, Halton Chesters; 14, Newcastle; 15, South Shields; 16, Wallsend; 17, Traprain Law

of the later 4th century do not seem to occur in other provinces. A small amount of evidence for glassblowing found at Binchester (see below) may suggest some military involvement in glassworking at this period in the northern frontier region.

Glass vessels in the northern frontier region

Late Roman vessel glass, almost always in a very fragmentary state, has been found in varying quantities in many of the settlements in the northern frontier region (Fig 5.3). The majority of these are military or civil establishments on or near to Hadrian's Wall and in the hinterland to the south of the Wall, but the hillfort at Traprain Law, to the north of the Wall, and the villa at Quarry Farm, Ingleby Barwick, and the cemetery at Scorton near Catterick have also been included.

The military settlements on or close to the line of

Hadrian's Wall, particularly those in the western and central sectors, have produced a limited quantity and range of late Roman vessels, and the glass of this period accounts for only a very small percentage of the total amount of Romano-British glass found at each site (Table 5.1). Most are ordinary drinking vessels and bowls with little decoration except abraded lines, with few pieces of tableware of high quality or vessels for serving or transporting liquid.

There was a military base and a town at Carlisle in the 4th century, but glass vessels of the period are very scarce. Some excavations, such as Castle Street (Cool and Price 1991) and the Botchergate, Rickergate, and Millennium sites (information from Chris Howard-Davis), did not produce any fragments, and others had very little. Four vessels, a cup or beaker with a blue blob, a conical beaker with abraded lines, a shallow indented bowl, and a funnel-mouthed jug, were identified at Annetwell Street, two cups, one

Table 5.1   4th-century vessel fragments from five forts on or near to Hadrian's Wall

Site	No of 4th-century AD fragments	Total no of Romano-British fragments	% of 4th-century AD fragments
CARLISLE Blackfriars	19	1108	1.7
BIRDOSWALD	22	474	4.65
VINDOLANDA	10	635	1.57
HALTON CHESTERS	4	200	2.0
NEWCASTLE	15	184	8.15

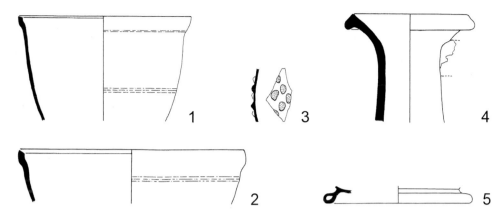

Fig 5.4 Vessel fragments from Blackfriars Street, Carlisle (after Price 1990)

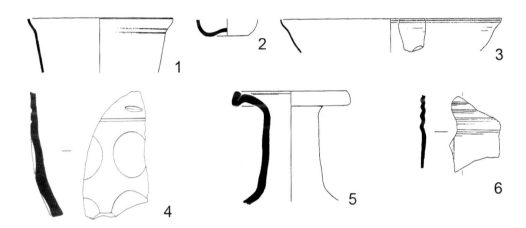

Fig 5.5 Vessel fragments from Birdoswald (after Price and Cottam 1997)

with a row of blue blobs, and a corrugated bottle came from the Northern Lanes, and a cup with abraded lines and a beaker with a fire-rounded rim from the Southern Lanes (all unpublished). A slightly larger group of nine vessels, seven drinking vessels with abraded lines, self-coloured trails, and coloured blobs, and two jugs (Fig 5.4) was found at Blackfriars Street (Price 1990, 177–9, mf 2/79–80, nos 72–78, fig 164). The shallow indented bowl and the beaker with fire-rounded rim indicate that glass vessels were present in the later 4th century, but there is no evidence for any vessels of higher quality and the total of eighteen vessels suggests that glass did not feature as an item of everyday use in late Roman Carlisle.

A military unit was based at the fort at Birdoswald in the early–mid-4th century, and occupation to the end of the 4th century is evidenced by coins, pottery, and other finds (Wilmott 1997, 201–9). Eight glass vessels of this period were recorded (Price and Cottam 1997, 344–6, 348, 352–5, nos 12, 71–6, figs 248–9; see Fig 5.5). Six were drinking vessels, five of which, a convex cup with abraded lines, three conical beakers, and a shallow bowl with indents, were ordinary vessels, and one, a colourless thick-

walled convex bowl with two rows of large facets was of higher quality. Convex bowls with comparable rows of large facets are known in the Rhineland (eg Fremersdorf 1967, 76–7, pl 46), but they are rare in Britain. The two closed vessels were a jug or bottle with a rim and neck similar to the one from Black-friars Street, Carlisle, and a small bluish-green corrugated bottle. Other very similar small corru-gated bottles are known on the northern frontier, at Vindolanda (Fig 5.6, no 4, and unpublished), and Coventina's Well at Carrawburgh (Fig 5.7, Carraw-burgh 1).

The fort at Vindolanda was also occupied by a military unit during the 4th century. Excavations in the north-east corner of the second stone fort (Bidwell 1985) produced seven late Roman glass vessels (Price 1985, 210–11, 213, nos 31–5, 51, figs 77–8; see Fig 5.6). Six were cups and bowls, including three conical beakers, two shallow indented bowls, and a mould-blown convex cup or bowl with hexagonal design, and one was a small bluish-green corru-gated bottle of the kind also found at Birdoswald. Three of the vessels were quite unusual. Mould-blown bowls with hexagons are not very common in

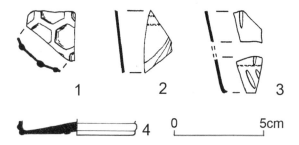

Fig 5.6   Vessel fragments from Vindolanda (after Price 1985)

Britain. They have been noted at urban and rural settlements in southern Britain (Price and Cottam 1995, Fowler 2000, 104, fig 6.23, 1–9), but are rare on the northern frontier, apart from this example and two pieces at South Shields. Two of the conical beakers are also uncommon. One, made in nearly colourless glass and decorated with linear- and short narrow facet-cutting is comparable with finds from South Shields, Traprain Law, and Binchester, while the other, which has a diagonal band of opaque white streaks, has not been recognised elsewhere in the north but has a few parallels in late contexts in southern Britain, as at Clausentum, Southampton (Harden 1958, 49, no 28, fig 13), and Gloucester (Price 1983, 170, no 19, fig 98). The shallow indented bowl, the beaker with opaque white streaks and perhaps the mould-blown bowl show that some glass

was used in the later 4th century. More recently, excavations in the *praetorium* at Vindolanda have produced an extensive range of late Roman vessel glass, including a bowl with a figured scene and other cups and bowls of high quality, and more has come from the east granary and elsewhere in the fort and the *vicus* (unpublished, information from Robin Birley).

No late Roman vessel glass from the fort at Housesteads has yet been published, and little is known about it. Six drinking vessels and bowls have been identified in the Corbridge Museum, five from the fort and one from the *vicus*. The fort group includes a shallow bowl from the commanding officer's house, a conical beaker and two convex cups, one with dark blue blobs and the other with heavy wheel-cut lines, from the barracks in the north-eastern corner of the fort excavated by the late Charles Daniels (information from Denise Allen), and a convex fragment, probably a cup, from near the north wall. A more elaborately decorated shallow convex bowl with abraded lines and vertical facets came from Building VIII in the *vicus*.

Three fragments of 4th-century glass are known from Carrawburgh. A cup or bowl with a group of three blue blobs was noted by Charlesworth (1959, 50), a small corrugated bottle came from Coventina's Well (Fig 5.7, Carrawburgh 1; Allason-Jones and Mackay 1985, 39, no 133), and a high folded base, probably from a jug, was found recently in field-walking (PAS record NCL-F44B96).

The late Roman vessel glass found when the fort

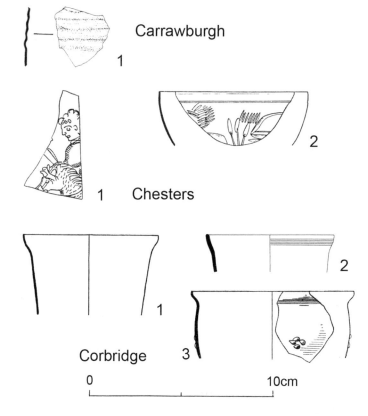

Fig 5.7   Vessel fragments from Carrawburgh, Chesters, and Corbridge (after Charlesworth 1959; Allason-Jones and McKay 1985; Allen 1988)

at Chesters was investigated in the 19th century is now held in the Clayton Collection at Chesters and the Corbridge Museum. Summary information about some finds was published by Budge (1907), and pieces from two bowls with figured scenes were illustrated by Charlesworth (1959, 46, fig 7, 1–2; Fig 5.7, Chesters 1–2). Four conical beakers, three bowls, a colourless flask or jug with a large funnel mouth, and a bottle with dolphin-handles and cylindrical body have been identified as coming from Chesters, though more may have been found, as many of the glass fragments in the Clayton Collection now lack exact provenances.

The bowls are noteworthy. One probably had a tubular rim and belonged to the group of vessels appearing in Britain in the mid- to late 4th century, and the other two are colourless with different styles of figured decoration. The horse and rider fragment, showing part of a hunting scene, was incised freehand with a sharp point, a form of decoration named the Wint Hill style after a nearly complete shallow bowl found in north Somerset (Harden 1960). The second fragment, showing a head and plants, probably part of a harvesting scene, was cut on a wheel, using massed broad shallow grooves and short narrow facets to form the figures, in the *parallele schliff-fürchen* style (Fremersdorf 1967). Both styles of cutting are known on vessels of the mid-4th century from other sites in Britain, often being found at high-status rural settlements (see Price 1995 for the distribution of finds of these groups), and they are also found elsewhere in the north-west and western provinces, particularly in the Rhineland (Harden 1960; Fremersdorf 1967, 159–71, pls 205–28, 179–89, pls 246–70). Fragments of bowls with freehand incised scenes have also been recorded at South Shields and Binchester, and in the *praetorium* at Vindolanda, but no other examples similar to the small bowl with the head and rushes have been found in the region, although another style of figured cutting is known at Traprain Law and Binchester.

Despite extensive excavation of the civil and military settlements at Corbridge during the past century, very little 4th-century glass has been recorded (Fig 5.7, Corbridge 1–3). Rim fragments of conical beakers and a convex cup with dark green blobs were noted by Charlesworth (1959, 50, figs 7.8, 8.2), and a rim fragment from a cup or beaker came from the excavations between 1947 and 1980 (Allen 1988, 290, no 17, fig 131). A few other pieces are also known. Fragments of four conical beakers on display in Corbridge Museum may be the vessels noted by Charlesworth, but three others have been identified, a conical beaker, a thick-walled convex cup, and a bottle or jug with a large funnel mouth, the last two being made in the dark yellowish-green glass characteristic of the later 4th century. This very small number of vessels, a minimum of eight cups and beakers and one closed vessel, suggests strongly that, as in Carlisle, glass vessels were rarely used in late Roman Corbridge.

A little more general information about late Roman glass in the central sector of Hadrian's Wall comes from the Clayton Collection, where material now without exact provenance is known to be from work at Chesters, Carrawburgh, Housesteads and other Wall sites. Most are drinking vessels and bowls which duplicate the finds from known Wall settlements. They include two cups with blue blobs and two nearly colourless conical beakers with shallow linear- and facet-cutting similar to the piece from Vindolanda already mentioned. Four jugs and cylindrical bottles were also present.

Halton Chesters is another Wall fort where little late Roman glass has been found. Two convex cups and a bottle with dolphin-shaped handles were recorded in the excavations in the south-west area of the fort and western extension directed by the late John Gillam in 1960–61 (information from the late John Dore).

Newcastle upon Tyne produced a little more material. The fort was occupied for much of the 4th century, and the coin evidence suggests that a market may have operated in and around the *principia* in the mid- to later 4th century (Bidwell and Snape 2002, 275–80). The glass of this period came from ordinary convex cups and conical beakers, accounting for more than 8% of the Roman vessel glass fragments from the site, a higher proportion than from Wall forts further to the west.

For the most part the late Roman levels at Wallsend have not survived, and there is little information about the 4th-century occupation of the fort (Hodgson 2003). Only one fragment, a shallow convex bowl with abraded lines, was recorded (Worrell 2003, 196, 198–9, fig 137.9).

The fort at South Shields has been extensively excavated since the late 19th century. It was replanned at the end of the 3rd or beginning of the 4th century and occupied throughout that century (Hodgson 1999). A much larger quantity of late Roman glass has been found there than at any of the other forts in the vicinity of Hadrian's Wall. Numerous ordinary convex cups and conical beakers, two mould-blown cups or bowls with hexagonal designs, a fragment from a shallow colourless bowl with a freehand incised scene, and a cylindrical corrugated bottle came from the early excavations. Recent work by Tyne and Wear Museums Archaeology has found late Roman glass in more than 150 contexts of 4th- to 5th-century date (unpublished, information from Alex Croom and Nick Hodgson).

The courtyard house, built in the south-east corner of the fort at the end of the 3rd century and occupied as a high-status residence throughout the 4th century (Hodgson 1996), has produced more than 170 finds of late Roman vessel glass in contemporary and residual contexts. As elsewhere, most of the vessels were ordinary convex cups, conical beakers and shallow indented bowls, though some cups had trailed decoration, and some conical beakers were nearly colourless with linear- and facet-cut patterns. The presence in the building of several colourless

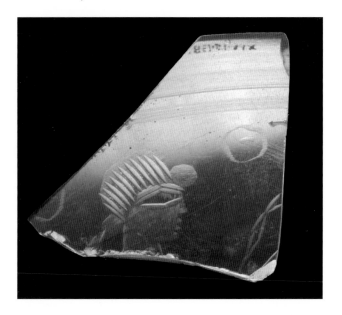

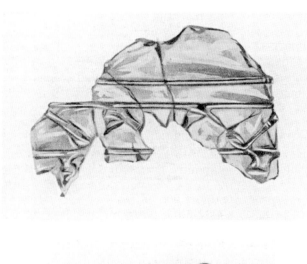

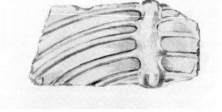

Fig 5.8   a (left), Bowl fragment with figured cutting from Traprain Law (photograph: National Museums of Scotland); b (top right) and c (bottom right), vessel fragments with zig-zag and vertical pinched trails from Traprain Law (after Cree 1923)

convex bowls with deep facet-cut designs provides clear evidence for the use of these vessels in the 4th century. Bowls of this kind have also been noted at Catterick (Fig 5.10, no 1) and other forts in the south of the study area, but not elsewhere in the vicinity of the Wall, except at Birdoswald (Fig 5.5, no 4), and in the *praetorium* at Vindolanda. Jugs or bottles and a cylindrical corrugated bottle were also present.

To the north of Hadrian's Wall, the only site which has produced more than one or two fragments of 4th-century vessel glass is Traprain Law, a hilltop settlement with an exceptionally rich assemblage of late Roman material (Hunter 2007a, 36, and this volume). In his doctoral thesis, Dominic Ingemark identified 52 glass fragments from approximately 20 vessels of this period (Ingemark 2003, 275–6), and others are present among the groups of miscellaneous fragments (*ibid*, 181–91). As elsewhere, most of the vessels are drinking vessels and bowls, many of ordinary quality. They include nine convex cups, two conical beakers with abraded lines and five conical beakers or cups with fire-rounded rims (*ibid*, 85–6), two cups with coloured blobs (*ibid*, 96–7), a colourless bowl with figured cutting (Fig 5.8a; *ibid*, 91–3), a beaker and a convex vessel with unusual trailed decoration (Fig 5.8b–c; *ibid*, 100–3), and two convex cups or bowls with scratched decoration (*ibid*, 93). Few vessels for serving liquids were identified; the yellowish-green glass of a chain handle from a jug suggests that it was made in the 4th century but the form of the jug itself is not known (*ibid*, 132), and another late Roman jug with a D-sectioned handle (*ibid*, 187, Q2) was also present. In the context of the northern frontier region, the range and diversity of the late Roman glass at Traprain is remarkable. A noteworthy quantity of glass of the late 4th century

is present, and there is also some evidence for the use of vessel glass in the late 5th or 6th century.

In addition to the ordinary drinking vessels, the assemblage contains four unusual vessels from three different traditions of production. The first is a colourless convex bowl with figured cutting of excellent quality. One of the three fragments, showing a probably female head facing right and part of a curved feature, perhaps a hoop, has often been published (eg Curle and Cree 1916, fig 27; Curle 1932, fig 6; Charlesworth 1959, pl 1.5; Price 2000b, pl 3, Hunter 2007a, fig 16; Fig 5.8a). Short, fine wheel cuts define the head, details of the face and other features, small and very shallow oval marks indicate areas of flesh, and fine abraded lines are used for the background motifs behind and in front of the head. The lozenge-shaped eye is a characteristic of the style of cutting. There is little evidence for close dating of vessels in this style in Britain and the pieces known are generally very fragmentary, apart from a bowl found in a pit at Colliton Park, Dorchester (Drew and Selby 1939, 5–6, pl 3; Fremersdorf 1967, 177, pls 242–3; Harden 1969, 64, fig 8). Elsewhere, however, several vessels are known in later 4th-century contexts. Complete pieces are known from burials in northern France (Painter 1971) and the Rhineland (Fremersdorf 1967, 171–9, pls 230–41, 244–5). For a long time, these vessels were thought to have originated in the Rhineland, but it is now clear that they are widely distributed, particularly in the western provinces, with a marked concentration of finds in Rome (eg Sagui 1996; Paolucci 2002), and it seems likely that they were made there.

The second of the unusual vessels is a cylindrical beaker with two horizontal trails enclosing a zig-

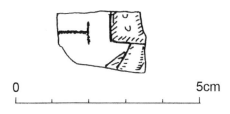

0   5cm

Fig 5.9   Vessel fragment with scratched letter and figure from Binchester (Jennifer Price)

zag trail on the upper body, and at least two vertical pinched trails extending down the body (Fig 5.8b; published upside down in Cree 1923, fig 21; Curle 1932, fig 43). Fragments with similar trails have come from late contexts at settlements in southern Britain, such as Frocester Court (Price 2000a, 110–12, nos 29–30, fig 7.3) and Overton Down (Fowler 2000, fig 6.23, no 24), but they are not otherwise known in the northern frontier region. The Traprain vessel may be a claw beaker, as it is similar in some details to a claw beaker from Mucking, Essex, thought to date from the early 5th century (Harden *et al* 1987, 257–8, no 146; Evison 2008, no 57, fig 10, col pl 2) and to others of late 4th-century date found in the Rhineland and northern France (Follman-Schultz 1995). Evidence for the claws, however, has not survived and the fragment is also closely comparable with the tall beakers with bands of horizontal and zig-zag trails and scored vertical and serpentine trails found in late Roman burials in northern France (Cabart 2008, 46, no 20, fig 10). Although the exact form has not been established, there is no doubt that the vessel came from northern France or the Rhine area in the late 4th century or a little later.

The last two are from pale greenish and bluish-green convex vessels with scratched rings and other curved and linear motifs which were probably made in the Mediterranean region in the late 5th or 6th century. Glass decorated in this manner has been recorded at five other sites in Britain. One, a fragmentary conical bowl with three horizontal bands of scratched decoration, is said to come from an Anglo-Saxon burial at Holme Pierrepont, Nottinghamshire (Price 2000b, 24–6, fig 9.3, pl 7; Evison 2008, 47 no 6, fig 1, pl 1), and the others have been found in settlements in south-west England and south-west Scotland, at Trethurgy (Price 2004, 88, 92, no 2, fig 51), Tintagel (Campbell 2007b, 226–7), Cadbury-Congesbury (Price 1992, 134, 139, nos 10–11, fig 97), and Whithorn (Campbell 1997, 300, fig 10.4, 1–5). Imported ceramics from the Mediterranean and western France have also been found in these and other late 5th- and 6th-century settlements in western Britain (Campbell 2007a, 56–8).

To the south of Hadrian's Wall, 4th-century glass vessels have come from three military settlements: Binchester, on the River Wear; Piercebridge, on the River Tees; and Catterick, on the River Swale. The commanding officer's house in the fort at Binchester

was rebuilt in the late 3rd century, further building took place in the middle of the 4th century, and the building was occupied into the 5th century (Ferris and Jones 2000; Ferris and Jones forthcoming). Late Roman vessel glass was found in greater quantity here than at any other settlement in the northern frontier region (Price and Worrell forthcoming). More than 15% of the Romano-British vessel glass belonged to this period (232+ out of 1503 fragments), and nearly 60 vessels were identified. The majority of the vessels were open vessels, including 20 beakers, 16 cups and 9 bowls, with a smaller number of closed vessels, including one flask as well as 6 jugs and 7 bottles. As elsewhere, most of the drinking vessels and bowls were quite ordinary, though some were of higher quality. There were three nearly colourless beakers with linear- and facet-cutting, similar to pieces already noted at Vindolanda and other forts along the Wall, and one decorated with figured cutting in the same style as the Traprain Law bowl. Colourless bowls with rows of circular facets similar to the examples from South Shields, Piercebridge, and Catterick were also present, as well as fragments from three shallow bowls with freehand incised scenes similar to the pieces from Chesters and South Shields. The largest piece shows a letter, probably I, from the inscription below the rim (Frere and Tomlin 1991, no 2419.56; Fig 5.9) and the legs of a figure wearing a short garment with spots similar to one worn by the rider on the hare hunt bowl from Wint Hill (Harden 1960, 48–51, figs 1–2, 5–6). No indented bowls were noted, but there was some evidence for the use of drinking vessels in the later 4th century. Two of the beakers had fire-rounded rims, and a bowl with a cracked-off rim was thick walled and made in the strong greenish glass of this period.

Among the closed forms, an unusual early 4th-century form of flask with an indented body similar to one from the Butt Road cemetery in Colchester (Cool and Price 1995, 155, no 2, 1188–9, fig 9.8) was recognised. Most of the jugs had funnel mouths, biconical bodies with optic blown ribs, or rolled rims, but one with an unusual discoid body may have come from a jug with a pouring spout, similar to one from Pear Wood, Brockley Hill (Harden 1975), and others found in northern France (eg Dilly and Mahéo 1997, 87, no 100, pl 9). Two of the cylindrical bottles had dolphin-shaped handles.

Most late Roman tableware forms known in Britain were found at Binchester and the assemblage is unusual in being broadly comparable in richness and variety with the glass from the settlement in earlier periods; more examples of late Roman jugs were recorded than from the 2nd- to 3rd-century phases of occupation. There is also a little evidence for glass vessels being blown in the fort in the 4th century, as moiles, the surplus part of the blown gather left on the end of the blowing iron after the vessel was finished, and some other glassworking waste, were found. As yet, these finds are unique in the region, although it is possible that

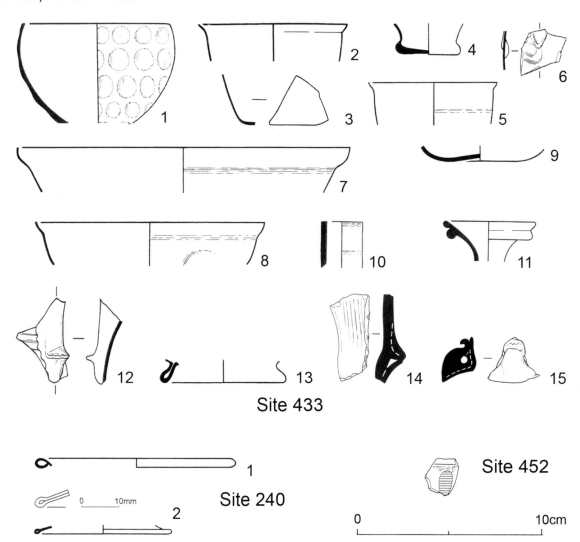

Fig 5.10   Vessel fragments from Catterick (after Cool et al 2002)

vessels could also have been blown in other military settlements or in towns.

At Piercebridge, the area of the fort was occupied in the 4th century (Cool and Mason 2008, 297–308), and nearly 8% of the Roman vessel fragments (100 out of 1265) belonged to this period (Cool and Price 2008). Most were ordinary drinking vessels, some with looped trails and blue blobs, and bowls, including two colourless bowls with rows of facets of the kind already noted from South Shields and Binchester. As at Binchester, there was a notably wide range of closed forms. They included vessels, probably jugs or bottles, with funnel mouths, a small globular jug, a flask or bottle with vertical rim and cylindrical neck with abraded lines, and dolphin-handled bottles with cylindrical and mould-blown ribbed hexagonal bodies. A base fragment from a dark blue vessel, comparable in colour with a miniature jug in a 4th-century burial in York (Harden 1962, 140, pl 67, H 12, fig 58), may also belong to this period. Some vessels, such as the small globular jug, the hexagonal-bodied bottle, and the dark blue jug, are quite unusual and have not otherwise been noted in the northern frontier region, and the presence of

vessels such as the beakers with fire-rounded rims, shallow indented bowls and small globular jugs show that glass vessels were being used in the later 4th century.

The defences of the late fort and town at Catterick were constructed in the later 3rd or early 4th century, and both settlements were inhabited throughout the 4th century (Wilson 2002, 446–66; Wilson 2003a, 259–61). Late Roman vessel glass was found in four areas (Fig 5.10; Cool *et al* 2002). The central part of the town (site 433) produced 36 fragments from at least 21 vessels (out of 328 fragments from at least 90 vessels from the site). The twelve open vessels were principally ordinary conical beakers and convex cups, two with looped trails, and shallow convex bowls with indents, although one piece of higher quality, a colourless bowl with rows of circular facets similar to finds already noted from South Shields, Binchester, and Piercebridge was identified. Nine closed vessels were recorded, a higher proportion than at most sites in the northern frontier region, though comparable with the finds at Binchester and Piercebridge. They included jugs with optic-blown diagonal ribs and high tubular base-rings, bottles,

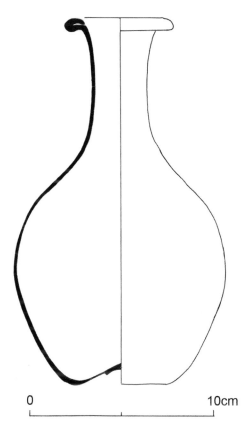

Fig 5.11   Flask from Scorton (Yvonne Beadnell)

0   10cm

or perhaps flasks, with either funnel mouths or vertical rims and cylindrical necks, and bottles with angular ribbon handles or dolphin-shaped handles. Elsewhere, a cup with a blue blob came from the fort (site 452), and two areas to the north and east of the main settlement produced small amounts of late Roman vessel glass. A probable jug with high tubular base-ring was found on site 434, and three vessels, a bowl with tubular rim, a probable jug with high tubular base-ring, and a cylindrical bottle, came from Catterick Bridge (site 240).

Given the extent of the excavations in and around the walled settlement and the evidence for urban life in Catterick in the 4th century, this total of approximately 26 late Roman vessels is curiously small. The presence of shallow indented bowls and the small bowl with a tubular rim shows that some vessels were in use in the later 4th century, but there is little evidence either for high-quality table-wares or for commodities reaching the settlement in glass containers.

The last sites are rather different from the ones considered so far, and the glass vessels fall outside the range recorded elsewhere in the region. The villa complex at Quarry Farm, Ingleby Barwick, on the south bank of the River Tees (Archaeological Services University of Durham forthcoming) is one of several rural settlements of high status recognised in the lower Tees valley in recent years and the only one to produce any 4th-century glass. Three body fragments from a large and very shallow dish sagged over a former and ground and polished on both surfaces

were found in unstratified deposits. The dish was made in almost colourless glass, with thin sections of polychrome floral canes and curving strips set into the upper surface to form a design with groups of flowers and stems and wavy bands of bright colour (Plate 5a–c). This is a spectacular piece of tableware which was perhaps intended for display rather than for serving food. The form and techniques of production are unparalleled in 4th-century Britain, apart from a minute fragment found in a Romano-British settlement at Vineyards Farm in Gloucestershire (Price 1991, 71–3, no 1, fig 25), and do not seem to be recorded elsewhere in the western provinces. A group of sagged and ground shallow dishes and bowls in strongly coloured and colourless glass with canes fused into the inside surface to form Nilotic and other scenes, with birds, flowers, lotus buds and reeds was identified by Grose (1989, 197, 208, no 227). He assigned them tentatively to the late Hellenistic or early Roman period, but also noted that finds from the Kharga Oasis and elsewhere in Egypt suggested that they might be of Egyptian origin and late Roman date. Numerous pieces of similar bowls from Douch and Ain et-Turba in the Kharga Oasis have since been published (Nenna 2002, 157, figs 10–11; Hill and Nenna 2003, 88 (group 5), fig 1.4; Nenna 2003, 94, fig 1.3), and there is now little doubt they were made in Egypt and used in the 4th to early 5th century.

The only glass vessel from a funerary context in the study area was found in a small cemetery with fifteen late Roman inhumation burials at Hollow Banks Quarry, Scorton, to the north-east of Catterick (Speed forthcoming). The vessel, a pale bluish-green flask with rolled rim, ovoid body and concave base with pontil scar (Fig 5.11, Plate 6), came from Grave 7, which contained an adult male buried fully clothed in a wooden coffin, with a crossbow brooch on his right shoulder and a belt buckle near his left hip. The flask was found near the feet, with two complete Nene Valley pottery vessels, a beaker, and a dish. It is a simple and undecorated vessel of ordinary quality which held about 0.80–0.85 litres of liquid and presumably functioned as a serving vessel in the burial, though it was probably made as a container to transport liquid rather than as an item of tableware. Despite its ordinariness, the Scorton flask seems to be unique in Britain, but it is closely comparable with numerous vessels known from 4th-century burials in northern France, particularly Normandy and Picardy (eg Sennequier 1985, 112–15, nos 183–9; Dilly and Mahéo 1997, 87–8, nos 104–7, 109, 116–7, pl 9), and probably came to Britain from this region.

Discussion

In any interpretation of the information presented here, it is necessary to remember that the vessel glass now available for study is only an unquantifiable part of what was actually present in the settlements of the Hadrian's Wall frontier region in the 4th century. Glass fragments and other finds of this period often do not survive, or are unstratified, because the late Roman levels of many settlements have been damaged by post-Roman agriculture, building or industrial activity. In extreme cases, as at Wallsend, most of the 4th-century levels have disappeared. The activities of early investigators, who often did not collect and record all the broken odds and ends they found, have also diminished the amount of material available for study.

Another practice very likely to have affected the survival of glass in particular is the deliberate collection and removal of broken vessels and windows for recycling. This material, which is known as cullet, was sought after by glass workshops in the Roman world for melting and forming into new vessels and objects, and the extreme fragmentation of the majority of 4th-century vessels in the northern frontier region suggests that systematic collection did take place at the time.

Most late Roman vessel glass in the northern frontier region has been found in the military bases along the Wall and in the southern hinterland, and the greatest quantity and variety of glass, including some decorated tablewares, has come from the residences of officers. The assemblage from the courtyard house at South Shields illustrates the range of glass in a late Roman military building of high status in the region. It is dominated by drinking vessels, some dating from the late 4th century, with a little evidence for glass vessels for serving or transporting liquid. Some tablewares are of high quality, but there are no exceptional vessels. The *praetorium* at Vindolanda has produced a rather similar group of vessels, including a bowl with figured cutting, and a very wide range of vessel forms, including various jugs and bottles, are known from the residence of the commanding officer at Binchester. By contrast, the commanding officer's house at Housesteads contained almost no late Roman glass but it is unclear whether the building was a high-status residence during the 4th century.

Little glass, apart from ordinary drinking vessels or bowls, has been found in other areas of the forts. This is particularly noticeable along Hadrian's Wall, where only eleven jugs and bottles and five containers were noted, but the forts of the southern hinterland had a slightly wider range of glass, including some serving vessels.

With the exception of the hilltop settlement at Traprain Law, which was situated outside the frontier but in close contact with the Roman world and with access to glass from a variety of sources, the remaining settlements in the region also have very little glass. Glass vessels appear to have been virtually unknown to the population of the urban settlements. Almost none came from Carlisle and Corbridge, although they seem to have been thriving regional communities in the 4th century, receiving goods from elsewhere and presumably hosting markets and fairs similar to that recognised in the fort at Newcastle, and only a little more was found at Catterick, which is widely recognised as a flourishing late Roman town. The rural population also seems to have had little acquaintance with 4th-century vessel glass.

One reason for this may have been the cost. Comparatively little is known about the cost of glass vessels in the Roman world, but information dating from the beginning of the 4th century is found in the section on glass vessels (16.1–16.6) in the Edict of Maximum Prices published by Diocletian in Antioch in AD 301 (Erim and Reynolds 1973, 103; Giacchero 1974; see also Barag 1987, 113–16; Stern 1999, 460–6). Section 16.1–16.6 lists three categories of glass (glass; glass cups and smooth vessels; window glass) in two qualities (Alexandrian and Judaean), priced by weight in pounds. The first category is thought to be raw glass for glassworkers to melt and form into vessels, costing 24 *denarii* for Alexandrian quality and 13 *denarii* for Judaean greenish quality; the second presumably refers to undecorated vessels, costing 30 *denarii* for Alexandrian quality and 20 *denarii* for Judaean quality. These figures show that much of the value lay in the glass itself, as the skills involved in forming ordinary vessels added only 25–33% to the basic cost, and that glass vessels were sold by weight, rather than by the piece. It is uncertain to what extent the Edict was relevant to the north-western provinces, but it is noteworthy that vessels of ordinary quality, particularly drinking cups, were often blown very thin, which would have kept the cost down if they were sold by weight. Section 16 of the Edict also listed some more expensive kinds of glass, again sold by weight. Only traces of lines 7a–9 have survived, but they seem to refer to three kinds of glass costing 40, 30, and 20 *denarii* per pound respectively, the last two being coloured (Giacchero 1974, 170–1; Barag 2005, 184).

The 4th-century glass vessels in the frontier region vary in quality but all are likely to have been more expensive than their ceramic counterparts. Comparisons of the prices of 4th-century glass and pottery tablewares are difficult to establish since the information about pottery vessels has not been found, but a section on ceramic materials in the Edict of Maximum Prices (15.88–15.101) includes an entry (15.98) for pottery containers with a capacity of 2 *sextarii* (1.094 litres) costing 2 *denarii*, which allows a rough calculation to be made. The Scorton flask, the only intact glass container in the study area, holds 0.85 litre and weighs 188g (ie 57.4% of a Roman pound of 327.45g). If this vessel is accepted as a smooth vessel of Judaean quality, it would have cost around 11.5 *denarii*, which is nearly six times as expensive as the pottery container which held nearly 25% more. If this calculation is valid, the rarity of 4th-century glass containers for commodities is understandable, and even ordinary thin-walled glass vessels costing around 4–5 *denarii* (assuming 4–5 to the pound at 20 *denarii*) may have been beyond the means of many of the people living in the region.

Nothing is known about how glass vessels reached the region or how they were acquired. It has been suggested that simple vessels could have been blown locally in markets and fairs by independent craftsmen, or in forts with the support of the military authorities. It might be thought sensible to produce cheap vessels as close as possible to the market for which they were intended, to reduce the risk of breakage and the cost of packing and transport, but there is little evidence that glass blowing took place in the region in the 4th century, except at Binchester, and even ordinary vessels may have been produced in workshops elsewhere in Britain.

As we have seen, the categories of glass listed in section 16.1–16.9 of the Edict of Maximum Prices were all priced by weight, but it is also possible that some glass tablewares were sold as individual pieces, particularly where much of the value was added by the skills of craftsmen other than the glassworkers. One such group of craftsmen would have been the glass cutters, who are known to have worked independently in the late Roman world. Disputes between glassworkers (*vitriarii*) and glass cutters (*diatretarii*) were recorded by Ulpian in the 3rd century (*Digest* 9.2.27, 29; cited in Trowbridge 1928, 110, 119), and both groups were included in the lists of craftsmen exempted from military service in the 4th–5th centuries (*Codex Theodosianus* 13.4.2).

Two groups of 4th-century beakers, cups, and bowls with cut decoration have been identified in the northern frontier region. Facet- and linear-cut beakers and bowls could have been produced in Britain, though it is more probable that they came from production centres elsewhere in the northwestern provinces, such as the Rhineland, and they may have been supplied directly from there, or purchased in markets or shops on the northern frontier, or arrived in the region as personal possessions.

Cut tablewares of very high quality were much rarer; only nine pieces with figured cutting have been noted in the region. Vessels of this kind were decorated with a wide variety of biblical, mythological, hunting, marine or other scenes. They were presumably commissioned from specialist *ateliers* and are rather unlikely to have been purchased locally. Their use appears to have been confined to army officers and other individuals of high status posted to, or based in, the frontier region, who may have purchased or perhaps acquired them through mechanisms outside the ordinary course of commerce, such as gift exchange.

Gift giving, by emperors and other powerful Romans, of precious metals, precious stones, clothing, equipment, and other desirable objects is well attested in the late Roman world. Such ceremonies often took place to commemorate anniversaries, family celebrations, political appointments, imperial posts, and other events. The practice helped to define and support the structure of late Roman society and to cement relations with leaders of social groups beyond the frontiers (see discussions in Painter 1989; 1993; Guest 2005, 22–6). The possibility that some glass vessels of high quality may also have been part of the hierarchy of late Roman gift giving has been considered by Painter (1989; 1993, 113), and more recently by De Tommaso (2000), Paolucci (2002) and others.

It is thus possible that the bowls at Vindolanda, Chesters, and South Shields, and the bowls and beaker at Binchester were gifts to army officers or government officials, while the bowl at Traprain Law could have been a diplomatic gift. It is noteworthy that a bowl fragment cut in the same style as the Traprain piece which was found in the Basilica Hilariana on the Caelian Hill in Rome may have been made as a commemorative gift in AD 391. The surviving piece, which was covered with gold-leaf, shows part of a central male figure and a juvenile bust, and part of an inscription mentioning Symacchus as consul, probably the Q Aurelius Symacchus who was *consul ordinarius* in AD 391 and his son, probably Q Fabius Memmius Symacchus (Paolucci 2002, 67–8; Oliver 2005, 749).

The Egyptian polychrome mosaic bowl with floral designs from Quarry Farm, Ingleby Barwick, was also of great luxury, and must have been an extraordinary and exotic vessel in the northern frontier region, either as an official gift or a cherished personal possession. The flask from Scorton near Catterick was also associated with a military or government official who died there and was buried in his uniform.

It is not surprising that army officers and government officials of high status appointed to posts on the northern frontier were the principal users of late Roman glass vessels in the region, but the decline in the use of glass vessels among other social groups, such as the soldiers, townspeople and rural communities, is very sharp. This may have occurred because the vessels had become too expensive or were difficult to come by, or they may have been irrelevant to societies which had lost, or had never acquired, the habit of using glass vessels. Whatever the causes, very few late 4th-century glass vessels are found in the frontier region except in the houses of senior officers, and only at Traprain Law is there a suggestion that they continued in use after the early 5th century.

Notes

1   I wish to thank my colleagues in the Department of Archaeology, Durham University, for helping me to produce this paper: Yvonne Beadnell for drawing the map and figures, and Jeff Veitch and Jenny Jones for providing the images of the Quarry Farm polychrome fragments and the Scorton flask. I am also very grateful to Denise Allen, Robin Birley, Richard Brickstock, Rob Collins, Hilary Cool, Alex Croom, the late John Dore, Nick Hodgson, Christine Howard-Davis, Fraser Hunter, Dominic Ingemark, and Georgina Plowright for access to and information about unpublished material.

6 Military equipment of the 'long' 4th century on Hadrian's Wall   *J C N Coulston*

Introduction

The organisation, numbers, and survival of troops in the northern frontier is not just a problem concerning the 'end' of Roman Britain, but one which relates to the upheavals of the later 3rd century, the campaigns of Constantius I, the supposed *barbarica conspiratio* and its Theodosian aftermath, and the movement of troops by British usurpers and central government into and out of the British provinces until the early 5th century. The disposition of troops in northern Britain under the *comes Britanniae* and along Hadrian's Wall under the *dux Britanniarum*, is presented in the *Notitia Dignitatum*, supposedly dating to the early 5th century (*Occidentalis* VII.153–6, 199–205, XL.17–56). One tile-stamp from Chester-le-Street may directly corroborate the *numerus vigilum* in the same location as in the manuscript (*Oc.* XL.24; Bishop 1993, 67, fig 16), whilst the specific units correspond quite closely to known 3rd-century garrisons. There has been some scholarly disbelief that such a list was fully up to date or realistically reflected such a late situation, and a long-held opinion has been that frontier formations were massively reduced in manpower and internal organisation from the later 3rd century onwards (Mann 1974; 1991; Hassall 1976; Daniels 1980; Welsby 1982, 133–45; Holder 1982, 97–103; James 1984; Breeze and Dobson 1985, 17–18, fig 11; 2000, 230–46; Esmonde Cleary 1989, 56–63; Casey 1993a and 1993b; Mattingly 2006, 238–47). Reinterpretation of Tetrarchic barracks at a number of Wall sites has modified this view so that formations at this time are not now seen as quite such shadows of their former establishments (Hodgson and Bidwell 2004; in general see Duncan-Jones 1978; MacMullen 1980; Treadgold 1995; Coello 1996; Elton 1996, 89–101; Nicasie 1998, 67–74). In addition, the marked distribution of military artefacts away from the frontier, in Yorkshire and further south in England, has raised questions about the nature of military service and of military presences across the late provinces. Such distributions may reflect long-established trends (Bishop 1991), or newer developments such as the militarisation of bureaucracy under the Tetrarchy; the presence of military units, including barbarian mercenaries, throughout the provinces; or the late development of local militias by towns and bodyguard forces of *bucellarii* by the landed elite (Liebeschuetz 1986; Welch 1993; Whittaker 1993; Laycock 2008, 113–34).

In a volume dedicated to late Roman finds from Hadrian's Wall it would be helpful to present military equipment artefacts as a contribution to discussion of these military historical questions.

Throughout the present paper, as with the rest of the volume, the 4th century is taken to mean the 'long' 4th century, considering military equipment over a period which runs from the later 3rd to the early 5th century, focusing on the northern frontier, but with developments in Britain as a whole and in the wider Roman Empire taken into consideration.

Roman military equipment studies are based upon a range of species of source material. Artefactual discoveries are a crucial element, but they are necessarily supplemented by ancient iconography and both literary and sub-literary evidence. Every class of information has its advantages and disadvantages. Site formation and depositional processes are an essential element of artefactual interpretation. The genre and production context of pictorial representations of soldiers and their equipment inform the viewer about reliability and stylisation. Written sources likewise require situating within their proper genre if they are to be employed in any reliable manner. These three areas of evidence are all incomplete and selective, and are further affected by temporal and geographical biases.

Discussion of military equipment in use in the later period of Roman occupation in Britain is hampered by particular source limitations. With the dubious exception of the British listings of unit titulature in the *Notitia Dignitatum*, written sources are almost entirely absent (see Hassall, this volume). Apart from milestones, epigraphy declines rapidly in the British provinces through the later 3rd and 4th centuries. It disappears entirely in the contexts of army construction activities after the Tetrarchy, and in personal commemoration somewhat earlier in the 3rd century. There are very few 4th-century figural military gravestones from anywhere in the Roman Empire (Éspérandieu 1907–66, no 1780, 3940–43, 4043, 5496; Franzoni 1987, nos 12-7 and 20-3; Boppert 1992, no 18; Bishop and Coulston 2006, fig 133), and none known at present from Britain. In partial compensation, the army bursts into vivid colour in other genres of representation, starting with 3rd-century religious frescoes and principally expanding into 4th-century catacomb paintings (Bishop and Coulston 2006, 17–18). From Britain there is potentially one piece of late military iconography in the form of a *dipinto* on a sherd of 4th-century Crambeck parchment ware from York (Plate 7). This very basically depicts a figure with a small head, a triangular torso and a triangular tunic skirt. The figure's right arm is upraised and holds what appears to be a sword. That the painter intended a military subject is suggested by a line across the waist which projects out on both sides, perhaps to emphasise a military waist belt (Monaghan 1997).

The dearth of literature, epigraphy and sculpture thus places particular emphasis on the recovery and identification of military equipment artefacts. Yet here too there are problems peculiar to the late period. Away from the Saxon Shore there are few military sites which were created *de novo* during the long 4th century, so the focused periods of short occupation and clear abandonment events seen on Julio-Claudian, Flavian, Antonine and Severan installations are absent. Moreover, the latest occupation levels of military sites may be the most vulnerable to post-Roman disturbance, and in any case the nature of site continuity into sub-Roman phases may be unclear. Finds may also not have been recorded by proper context (if a secure one was present) during excavations until comparatively recently. On the Continent one very important mechanism allowing 4th-century equipment to be preserved is through inhumation in a funerary rite generally associated with Germanic groups, the so-called *Laetengräber* (Böhner 1963; Sommer 1984, 88–93; Schulze-Dörlamm 1985). The practice was Germanic but the deposited belts and weapons were for the most part items of Roman manufacture and decoration. Exceptionally, some specialised shafted and bladed weapons were Germanic in design (see below). However, very few graves containing late Roman military equipment have been found in Britain, notably Grave 376 at Winchester Lankhills, with fittings *in situ* from a waist belt worn by the deceased (Clarke 1979, 267–69, fig 33, pl XIVb); a full set of belt plates from the east Roman cemetery of London (Barber and Bowsher 2000, 206–8, B538.4, fig 105); and Grave 1 at Dorchester-on-Thames, Dyke Hills (Bullinger 1969, pl LVIII; Esmonde Cleary 1989, 55–6). No such examples have yet been found along the northern frontier. 'Depot' hoards have been found on continental 4th-century sites, notably the large helmet collections at Intercisa in Hungary (Klumbach 1973, 103–9, pls 45–57) and at Koblenz in the German Rhineland. The latter was found in 1988 and has just been fully published (Miks 2008). The finds from the Housesteads *principia* will be considered in this context below.

There are numerous small finds of 4th-century military equipment fittings from Britain, many made by metal detectorists in England away from the northern frontier. Significant discoveries have also been made in excavations of late military installations, notably at Burgh Castle and Richborough along the Saxon Shore, and at Caernarfon in North Wales, demonstrating that troops in Britain shared in continental developments, even to the extent of some helmets having borne Christian insignia. In the northern British frontier zone there have also been interesting finds of equipment artefacts (see Appendix for Catalogue) and these are the subject of the present paper.

It might also be helpful at this point to characterise the military equipment of the 'long' 4th-century Roman army. One element in particular has caught the attention of modern scholars, the existence of state arms 'factories' (*fabricae*), first established in cities behind the frontiers in the Tetrarchic period, and presented in their fullest form in the pages of the *Notitia Dignitatum* (James 1988; Bishop and Coulston 2006, 238–40). Their prime purpose was to produce specific types of equipment (armour, horse armour, shields, swords, spears, bows and arrows, and artillery) for the expanding Tetrarchic army, and thereafter for formations in the field armies which were not tied to specific bases. They were not a replacement for the normal practice of manufacture and supply at frontier installations. The latter continued to produce metalwork, as in the legionary fortress *principia* at Novae in Bulgaria (see below). The *fabricae* provided an additional tier of manufacture and assembling. None was located in Britain or was even really required for the small number of field army formations stationed in the British provinces, although a *gynaecium* producing clothing was located at Venta in southern Britain (*Notitia Dignitatum*, Oc. XI.60). They were probably concentrations of numerous small workshops rather than 'factories' in the industrial revolution sense of single large buildings with production line methods, but may have had large-scale storage facilities. However, *fabricae* were probably influential in the adoption and spread of helmet designs specifically associated with the long 4th century, and likely also to have provided the mechanism by which high-value items were manufactured as a form of military pay and special reward (eg gilded silver sheathed helmets and shield-bosses, bullion belt fittings and brooches, silver plate).

Finds of military equipment from the frontier region will be examined under the discrete headings of clothing and belts, armour, weaponry, equine equipment, and other miscellaneous items. All the objects have been recovered through the course of archaeological excavation or as chance discoveries by leisure metal-detector users. In the case of the former, the artefacts may be identifiably 'late' by virtue of their form or decoration (Appels and Laycock 2007), but many objects are not intrinsically datable. For example, some forms of spearheads found along Hadrian's Wall are as likely to belong to the 3rd century as to the 4th; for these a dated archaeological context is essential. There is also a bias imposed by materials. Iron finds are less visually identifiable in the excavation process than copper-alloy artefacts, more prone to oxidation and corrosion, more difficult and costly to conserve, and thus less represented in research. Copper-alloy belt fittings, to take one functional category, can often be examined as soon as they come out of the ground and are definable by characteristic forms, resulting in far more attention being paid to them in the modern literature and an enhanced prominence in scholarly perceptions. Late Roman belts are concomitantly represented and studied, whilst iron weaponry is poorly represented in the surviving record and in modern research.

Clothing and belt sets in the long 4th century

Clothing and footwear were issued by the state to late Roman soldiers as part of their pay and economic support. A pattern of dress developed from the late 2nd century onwards for all soldiers across the army: long-sleeved tunics worn with a pair of long, tightly cut trousers, and the rectangular military cloak (*sagum*) which was fastened at the wearer's right shoulder with a brooch. In the now more common polychrome representations of soldiers in 4th-century artworks, the trousers are usually practical dark colours, cloaks always the brown of undyed wool, and tunics almost invariably white with purple borders and other decoration. Characteristic of the long 4th century were round appliqué panels of tapestry weave (*orbiculi*) decorating the skirts and shoulders of tunics, and the edges of cloaks, reflecting in their geometric patterns the ornament of metalwork plates on contemporary belts (James 2000; Bishop and Coulston 2006, 224–5).

Shoes were depicted in both open and closed forms, but this probably varied with climate and region, with a closed upper being preferable away from the Mediterranean region. During the 4th century, hobnails were less often driven into the soles of shoes, reducing the archaeological visibility of military footwear (Bishop and Coulston 2006, 225; see also Allason-Jones, this volume). Given the need for soldiers to march over great distances, this may imply that each soldier needed more shoes over the course of his service, or perhaps long marches were less frequent, particularly for the more sedentary formations of frontier troops. Unfortunately, no military clothing or footwear has been found in 4th-century deposits in northern Britain. However, crossbow brooches do appear in the iconography of late Roman soldiers, and they occur in the northern frontier and north of the Wall (see Collins, this volume; Snape 1993, 20–3, 52–5; Swift 2000b, 42–50, pl 17; Bishop and Coulston 2006, 224, fig 133). They are widespread in the northern continental frontier provinces, but were not a common export to Free Germany (Swift 2000b, figs 13, 55, 59). The richest examples fall within the category of bullion gifts that include belts, helmets, and shield-bosses (cf *Historia Augusta, Claudius* 14.5–14.10).

Military waist belts were worn over the tunic or over armour, and much is known about their metalwork. This is partly because of the 'Germanic' inhumation rite which preserved not only full sets of belt fittings, but also the relative positions of fittings on the belt when worn by the deceased at deposition (Bullinger 1969, fig 62). The belts themselves were generally very broad, with large plates and vertically aligned 'stiffeners' applied to prevent the belt from curling over with wear. Propeller-shaped stiffeners are a particularly characteristic form of the period. A much narrower strap was passed through a commensurately narrow buckle to fasten the belt. Strap terminals were attached to reduce splitting and fraying, and these occur in a discrete series of forms, including amphorae, hearts, and lancets, and vary from undecorated through to elaborate, chip-carved examples. Buckles are generally D-shaped, kidney-shaped, or rectangular, with little or no decoration, or can be highly ornamented with zoomorphic motifs. Additional mounts, such as rings-with-rosettes, are also common, presumably used to suspend small items such as knives, toiletry tools, amulets, and purses (Bullinger 1969; Sommer 1984; Bishop and Coulston 2006, 218–24). These belts represented a smooth development from 3rd-century forms and were neither a new departure nor a foreign intrusion into military equipment practice. They were the next phase of the use of waist belts (early '*baltei*', late '*cingula*') to advertise the wealth and status of soldiers in a manner which started in the 1st century BC and continued through into the 6th century AD, and beyond. Indeed, while clothing and footwear fashions evolved, such belts were the constant visual (and aural) identifier of military service, in conjunction with the open wearing of swords (Bishop 1992; Coulston 2004, 141–2; Bishop and Coulston 2006, 253–4).

The largest category in the catalogue of military equipment from the northern British frontier is that of buckles and associated belt fittings. Zoomorphic and 'simple' buckles have received attention from a number of scholars, along with strap ends and belt mounts (Hawkes and Dunning 1961; Hawkes 1974; Simpson 1976a and 1976b; Böhme 1986; Swift 2000b; Leahy 2007; Appels and Laycock 2007, 168–279; Laycock 2008, 113–28). In general, late belt fittings are found in Britain, Spain, northern Gaul, and along the Rhine and Danube frontiers. As for other late Roman military finds, dating of belt accessories has been based on the excavation of inhumation cemeteries. Some types are fairly uniform throughout the western empire, but regional variation in buckles increased through the 4th century until by the 5th century there were distinct regional and local types (Sommer 1984; Swift 2000b). Indeed, notable stylistic differences between British buckles and continental examples suggest that British manufacturers operated with predictable independence of centralised state factories in the late 4th and 5th centuries (Ager 2007, 142).

In Britain there have been numerous surveys of these buckles and belt accessories, and the forthcoming work by Mark Corney and Nick Griffiths is expected to provide the fullest treatment of the British data. Until such time as that study is available, the British evidence may be defined through the Hawkes and Dunning typology of zoomorphic buckles, and through Simpson's typology of 'simple' or non-zoomorphic buckles (Hawkes and Dunning 1961; Simpson 1976a).

A recent survey of the zoomorphic buckles in Britain has also examined the differentiated distributions south of the Tees and east of the Severn estuaries, with Gloucestershire, Lincolnshire, and East Anglia exhibiting the most marked concentrations (Leahy 2007). Particularly notable is the

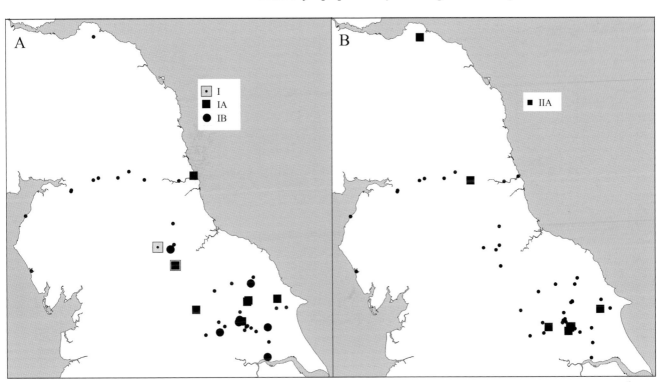

Fig 6.1   A, the distribution of zoomorphic type I buckles; B, the distribution of zoomorphic type II buckles. The small circles indicate sites with other forms of belt equipment (map: Rob Collins)

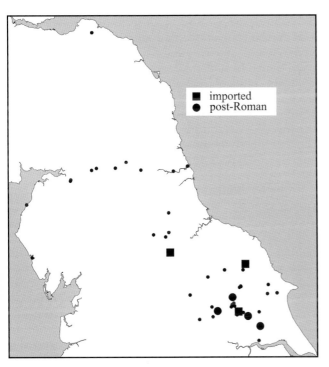

Fig 6.2   The distribution of imported and post-Roman zoomorphic buckles in northern England. The small circles indicate sites with other forms of belt equipment (map: Rob Collins)

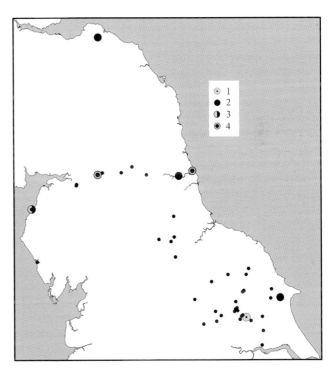

Fig 6.3 The distribution of non-zoomorphic buckle types in the frontier zone, following Simpson 1976a. The small circles indicate sites with other forms of belt equipment (map: Rob Collins)

comparative paucity of zoomorphic buckles from the military areas of northern England and the Saxon Shore. Laycock has argued that this distribution can be further distinguished by different styles of

British-made zoomorphic buckles with more focused distributions corresponding with known tribal zones/*civitates*, namely the Dobunni, Catuvellauni/Trinovantes, Iceni, and Corieltauvi (Laycock 2008,

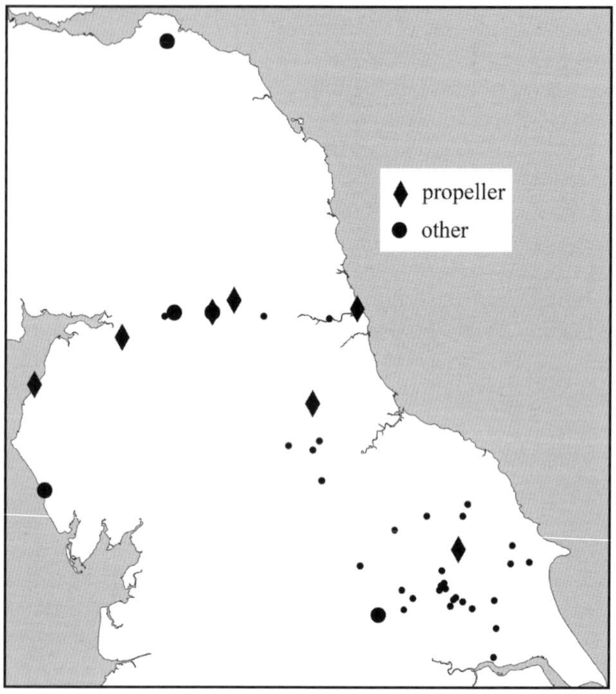

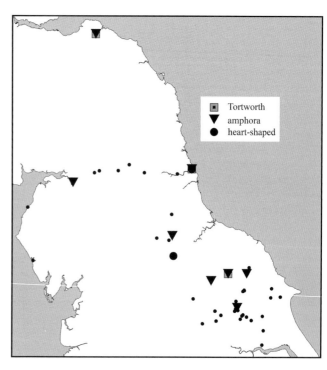

Fig 6.4   The distribution of belt mounts in the frontier zone. The small circles indicate sites with other forms of belt equipment (map: Rob Collins)

Fig 6.5   The distribution of different types of strap ends in the frontier. The small circles indicate sites with other forms of belt equipment (map: Rob Collins)

118–34). There is some overlap in the distributions of these different buckle styles, but the concentrations led Laycock to link the metalwork with local militias in a compelling interpretation. Only a handful of buckles along the frontier have these distinctive stylistic elements.

Previous studies of zoomorphic buckles have exaggerated the paucity of evidence from north of the Humber. Figures 6.1–6.5 provide a series of distribution maps of all belt fittings in the frontier region. North Yorkshire and the East Riding have the majority of the zoomorphic buckles (Figs 6.1–6.2), but this is exacerbated by PAS (Portable Antiquity Scheme) recorded finds, with 60% of the zoomorphic buckles from PAS records, and another 20% made up of non-PAS metal-detector finds (Stuart Laycock, pers comm). The importance of these metal-detected finds in dominating a northern distribution must be qualified because there is a bias in prospecting activities. North Yorkshire is more extensively and intensively searched by hobby metal detectorists than any other northern county, so County Durham, Lancashire, Cumbria, and Northumberland are under-represented (Rob Collins, pers comm). Nevertheless, Hadrian's Wall has received more attention from archaeologists than the Roman sites of Yorkshire, and comparatively few buckles have been discovered along the Wall, even if more belt accessories have been found in this region than previous studies have indicated.

Other belt fittings from the Hadrian's Wall region include heart-shaped and amphora terminals for the narrow straps which passed through the buckles (Fig

6.5). These are well-recognised finds across Britain and on the Continent (Sommer 1984, 49–56; Appels and Laycock 2007, 248–52). An amphora terminal from South Shields (Allason-Jones and Miket 1984, no 3.611) is nicely paralleled by an example in lead from Stanwix (Fig 6.6; Collingwood 1931a, no 75) which is clearly a master for the process of casting copper-alloy terminals, and which may be added to the small body of masters and failed castings which survive for late Roman belt fittings (Sommer 1984, fig 1).

Propeller belt appliqués form another small but varied group of finds, also well attested in Britain and on the Continent (Bullinger 1969, 36–7, figs 8, 55, 57, 60, pls III, XIV, XXVII–XXXII, LII, LXV; Sommer 1984, 4–6, figs f, h, pls 29, 32, 34, maps 2–3; Appels and Laycock 2007, 268–75). Plain examples have been recovered at Vindolanda and Maryport (Fig 6.7C); single axial-ribbed at Maryport (Fig 6.7C); and double axial-ribbed at South Shields (Allason-Jones and Miket 1984, no 3.888; Bidwell 1985, fig 41.28; Webster 1986, 63–5, fig 7.41). To judge from their dimensions, the four stiffeners from Maryport represent fittings from at least three different belts. The two, more elaborate, single-ribbed examples have carinated tooling along their ribs, and each is decorated with four circular projections around the central 'hub'. The latter features are also seen on an example from Carrawburgh which is the most ornate representative of the class from the frontier region (Breeze 1972, fig 16.166). The four projections and the 'blades' of the propeller are decorated with dots in incised circles, the axial double rib has beaded

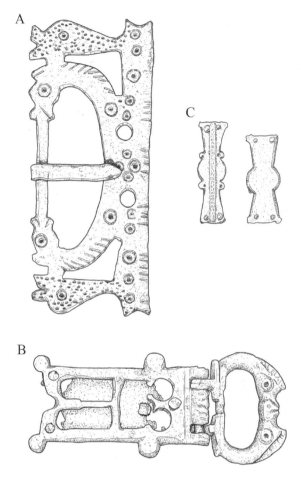

Fig 6.7 A, the imported dragon buckle from Catterick; B, the zoomorphic buckle from Corbridge; C, two variants of propeller-shaped stiffeners from Maryport (drawing: Rob Collins)

Fig 6.6 A lead amphora-shaped strap end mould-maker from the fort at Stanwix (© Tullie House Museum)

decoration, and the 'hub' has triangular projections. The ends of the blades have curvilinear profiles. Close parallels for all these features in combination may be found on pieces from Neuß and Trier in Germany, and Amiens in France, which belong to the type defined by Sommer as '*Propeller mit violinförmigen Mittelstück*'. Their general distribution favours northern Gaul and the Rhineland, with very few along the Danube and none in Free Germany (Sommer 1984, figs f.1, 10, h.1, map 3).

When the distribution is looked at in more detail, however, some interesting patterns emerge (and here the writer is especially grateful to Rob Collins and Lindsay Allason-Jones for sharing their observations). First, there is a notable absence of evidence from most of Cumbria, Lancashire, and Greater Merseyside. This may be due to some bias in excavations and metal detecting, but crossbow brooches are known from these areas (Collins, this volume, Fig 7.4). Considered in terms of the actual numbers of buckles and belt accessories found per site, known Roman military installations generally have a higher number, whereas most of the sites in Yorkshire are single finds. To some extent, this introduces the overriding advantage of excavated (as opposed to metal-detected) finds, namely, context. Some of the examples in the Catalogue are included due to their context (cf Appels and Laycock 2007). For example, the sites along the Wall include only three zoomorphic buckles, two from South Shields and one from Corbridge (Fig 6.7B), two non-zoomorphic buckles of Simpson types, and a number of undiagnostic buckles datable by context. Strap ends and mounts are also represented. In fact, the diversity of accessories is greatest along the Wall. It is further notable that belt mounts are only known from Roman military sites (Fig 6.4), and Simpson-type buckles and strap ends are considerably more limited in number and distribution than the zoomorphic buckles (Fig 6.3).

A number of belt accessories were found in the Traprain Law Hoard but recent analysis of the objects dates them to the mid-5th century and attributes their form and production to a continental, perhaps even Danubian, tradition (Painter 2006). Thus, these objects were most likely imported. While this is interesting, the present paper is not the place to explore the significance and implications of the Traprain Hoard. However, it is worth noting how different the belt fittings are from examples found along the frontier. Another imported buckle was found at Catterick (Fig 6.7A), although this is not necessarily later in date than the first decade of the 5th century. Three examples of zoomorphic buckles of a type dated by Hawkes and Dunning to the 5th century were found at Market Weighton, Barton-le-Willows, and Nunburnholme (see Catalogue). The imported buckles and the 5th-century types are from the southeastern area of the frontier zone.

Armour in the long 4th century

Armour consisted of cuirasses, throat armour (gorgets and coifs), limb armour (*ocreae* and *manicae*), helmets and shields. Body armour tended to be scale or ring-mail cuirasses, with manuscript illuminations further showing greaves and segmented metal limb-defences (Coulston 1990; Elton 1996, 110–15; Bishop and Coulston 2006, 208). There is little evidence to support the traditional view that armour provision for Roman troops declined in the late period, and much to suggest that in the Roman East at least infantry and cavalry armour actually became more protective. Formations of heavily armoured cavalry (*catafracti* and *clibanarii*) proliferated and one, the *equites catafractarii iuniores*, was present in Britain under the command of the *comes Britanniarum* (*Notitia Dignitatum*, Oc. VII.200). Late helmets were of relatively simple construction compared to techniques employed in the 1st to 3rd centuries AD, and consisted of a multi-part bowl dominated by a fore-and-aft ridge piece, a separate neck guard, and two cheek-pieces, all of iron. Generally these were edge-laced to a leather lining, so no hinges were necessary. Incomplete representative examples of the type have been found at the Saxon Shore forts of Burgh Castle in Norfolk (Johnson 1980b) and Richborough in Kent (Lyne 1994). Numerous continental examples consisted of an iron helmet covered with a decorated, gilded silver sheath. Some were represented by the sheath alone where water conditions had completed corroded away the iron elements, or where the sheath was retained for its bullion value alone (Klumbach 1973; Bishop and Coulston 2006, 210–16; Miks 2008). T-shaped nasal guards are also a very recognisable artefactual element, and recently it has been demonstrated that labels bearing a *chi-rho* formed insignia on the front of helmet crests, an example likewise recognised at Richborough (Lyne 1994, fig 2.7; Bishop and Coulston 2006, 214; Miks 2008, 52–3).

There are few 4th-century shield fittings from Roman sites in Britain, but continental funerary depositions provide good evidence, as do polychrome artworks, such as painted shield-leathers from Egypt and the illustrated *Notitia Dignitatum* manuscripts (Berger 1981; Grigg 1983; Bishop and Coulston 2006, 216–18). The shield board tended to be oval or circular in shape, fashioned from wooden planks and covered with leather in the manner of oval, 3rd-century examples from Dura-Europos in Syria (James 2004, 160–2, 176–82). Iconography and the occasional archaeological discovery have indicated that both the outside and inside of shields were intricately painted. Artefacts suggest that bosses continued to be domed, but that pointed-conical *umbones* of Germanic form gained some currency. The normal metal grip within the boss, with or without a horizontal bar across the back of the board, is also attested, but from the 3rd century it seems that shield structures were strengthened and rims protected by stitched and shrink-fit strips of rawhide. The sections of riveted, copper-alloy edging strips characteristic of 1st- to 2nd-century shields are entirely absent from 3rd- to 5th-century contexts. A single shield grip of late 3rd- to 4th-century date was found at Vindolanda (Bidwell 1985, fig 47.2).

Weaponry in the long 4th century

Weapons were produced in a variety of forms for a range of tactical purposes. Personal armaments consisted of bladed weapons, shafted weapons and other missile weapons.

Long swords were the primary type of bladed weapon in the later empire, generally termed 'spathae' (Bishop and Coulston 2006, 202–5; Miks 2007, 77–140). These varied in length, but had smooth or ribbed grips with narrow guards and pommels. Sculptural depictions suggest that swords were predominantly worn on the hip suspended from the waist-belt or from a narrow, supplementary belt, rather than hung from a baldric as in the 1st- to 3rd-century manner. Sadly, the often fragmentary nature of swords in the archaeological record means that they are also difficult to date without contextual information. Knives were also worn on the belt, but there is no evidence that the traditional double-edged Roman military *pugio* was used past the 3rd century. Evidence from burials, however, suggests that this was replaced with a single-edged knife (Bishop and Coulston 2006, 205).

There are very few examples of bladed weapons found on the late British frontier. A sword was found at Vindolanda in a late 3rd- to 4th-century context (Bidwell 1985, fig 46.1), and there is a possible sword guard and bone pommel from Birdoswald excavated in later contexts (Summerfield 1997a, nos 275–6). Other sword accessories include a zoomorphic chape from Skirpenbeck (PAS LVPL-917677) and a thin leather strap with 23 silver studs from the Traprain Hoard that may have functioned as a sword belt. A narrow-waisted bone scabbard slide from Great Chesters is difficult to date by context (Allason-Jones 1996b, fig 13.7). Although the form does occur at German frontier sites of the mid- to third quarter of the 3rd century, it is also seen on the Venice Tetrarchs sculpture (Oldenstein 1976, nos 64–5; Bishop and Coulston 2006, figs 99.5, 129). Some late knife forms are found in the frontier. One example from Watercrook has a separate plate at the base of the blade (Potter 1979, fig 89.117), and an example from Vindolanda is large and similar in form to examples from late burials at Winchester Lankhills (Clarke 1979). Knives are not particularly rare finds, even in 4th-century contexts, but what makes these latter two examples exceptional is their larger size and (in the Watercrook example) the baseplate on the blade.

The 4th-century army used both conventional single-handed axes and throwing axes (*franciscae*), with the latter probably introduced by Germanic barbarian recruitment (Dahlmos 1977; Kieferling 1994). While such weapons are attested by both archaeological discoveries and artistic representations, it is unclear how commonly they were employed by regular Roman soldiers (Bishop and Coulston 2006, 205). In the archaeological record, fragmentary examples may have belonged to axes used as tools or employed as weapons, complicating identification. There is an axe-head from Housesteads which exhibits the same curving front-edge profile as other late axe finds in Britain, notably one from the military base at Richborough in Kent, although the type is not entirely chronologically diagnostic (Manning 1976, no 55; cf Bushe-Fox 1949, pl LXI.341–42).

Spear-heads and javelin-heads from 4th-century contexts retain the range of dimensions and head-types seen in previous periods, although a leaf-shaped head is the most prevalent (Cunliffe 1975, figs 124, 171, 175, 177–8; Mould *et al* 2002, fig 270.3, 5–8; Bishop and Coulston 2006, 200–2). New types of heads were adopted through the 3rd century into the 4th. One such type was socketed and had a barbed head on a long iron shank. This may be a developmental continuation of the *pilum* or *spiculum* (*Epitoma Rei Militaris* 2.15, 3.14), influential upon, and perhaps in turn influenced back by barbarian heavy javelins (also known as the '*ango*' in the Early Mediaeval Germanic contexts, von Schnurbein 1974). A few of the weapons on the northern frontier are stylistically late types that can be attributed to the 3rd–4th century on the basis of their form. The longest example is a barbed head from Carvoran (549mm), with others having been found at Housesteads, South Shields, Old Penrith, and Catterick (Richmond 1940; Cowan 1948; Swanton 1973, 22–3, figs 3–5; Manning 1976, nos 21–3; Scott 1980, 339, fig 24.4; Allason-Jones and Miket 1984, no 5.90; Austen 1991, 187; Mould *et al* 2002, 82, fig 270.9–10). The barbing recalls the form of some Republican *pila* (Polybius 6.22; Bishop and Coulston 2006, fig 23.12–13), but is paralleled by 3rd-century

votive spearheads from Scandinavian sacred lakes, particularly Illerup Ådel Types 5–8 (Ilkjær 1990, pls 154–217). This might be taken with ceramic evidence to suggest the presence of Germanic troops at Housesteads, Carvoran and elsewhere in the 3rd century, and possibly into the 4th (Jobey 1979). Similar links may be made for shafted weapon heads found at Richborough (Bushe-Fox 1949, pls LVIII.284, LIX.289; cf Ilkjær 1990, pls 220–31).

A new form of specifically long 4th-century date has a small barbed head on an iron shank, weighted with a lead, truncated biconical jacket and socketed to a wooden shaft (Bishop and Coulston 2006, 200). The length of the wooden element is a matter of debate, and one not really resolved by reconstruction or experimentation (Eagle 1989). Related weapons are depicted with long shafts and flights in the *De Rebus Bellicis* manuscript (Hassall and Ireland 1979, pl IX), while they are also recorded as having been carried in groups on the backs of shields, implying rather more 'pub' dart proportions (Vegetius, *Epitoma Rei Militaris* 1.17). The ancient terms *plumbata*, *mattiobarbulus* or *martiobarbulus* may be attributed to this javelin form. It seems to have been a weapon especially associated with two *legiones* operating under Diocletian in the Danubian theatre, but Vegetius makes it clear that these were common weapons (*ibid* 1.17, 2.16, 3.14, 4.29), and they have a wide incidence as an easily recognisable arte fact class all along the northern frontiers of the late Roman Empire. Britain is particularly well represented by examples found at Burgh Castle, Kenchester, and Richborough in southern England; Caerwent, Caernarfon, and Wroxeter in Wales and the Marches; and at Catterick and Doncaster in the north; but not yet along Hadrian's Wall (Bushe-Fox 1949, pl LIX.295–6; Wacher 1971, fig 26.4–5; Buckland and Dolby 1971, 275–6; Barker 1979; Sherlock 1979; Scott 1980, 339; Casey and Davies 1993, fig 10.12.275–79; Mould *et al* 2002, fig 270.9–10; White 2007, fig 23; cf Appels and Laycock 2007, 282–3). The term *lanceae* was used for light javelins and these may have been a lighter weapon than the heavier *spicula* and *plumbatae* (Bishop and Coulston 2006, 43, 76, 78, 202, 226, 269), but it is clear with much Roman weapons terminology that names evolved, changed, and migrated over time with little technical exactitude.

All the other shafted-weapon heads from northern British sites are attributable to the 4th century not by form, but by context, belonging as they do to long-lasting, generic types. These are the most widespread and typical weapons to be found, and they would also be the most numerous in the Catalogue were it not for the arrowhead hoard from Housesteads (see below). Conical shafted-weapon butts are generally distinguishable only by diameter of socket. As with heads, even this is not a straightforward feature, given that wooden shafts may have been stepped so that the outer circumferences of the sockets were flush with the shaft (cf Engelhardt 1867, pls II–III;

Jørgensen and Vang Petersen 2003, figs 31, 39). It is worth pointing out that there are also five examples of 'door-knob' form, socketed, copper-alloy spear butts from the frontier region. Two from North Yorkshire were found by metal-detector users; one from Vindolanda and two from Traprain Law were excavated finds (see Catalogue). A mould for the production of the type has also been found at Traprain Law (not in the Catalogue) and the form seems to have been of native North British and/or Irish manufacture. Occasional examples have also been found in southern Britain (see Hunter, this volume).

The practice of late Roman archery is represented across the empire by numerous finds of arrowheads and the range of forms (trilobate, barbed, lozenge, bodkin) and attachments (socketed, tanged) continued into the 4th century (Coulston 1985, 264–70; Zanier 1988). Examples come from several northern British sites, most spectacularly from Housesteads. A hoard of more than 800 heads was found during Bosanquet's explorations of the fort *principia*. The excavator opined that arrows had been stored in bundles on shelves in the last occupation phase of a room in the rear range (Bosanquet 1904, 224–45, 290–1, figs 16, 21; Manning 1976, nos 35–44). These arrowheads are flat, barbed, and tanged, some with wood from the shaftments still surviving. Other examples of this type are found in the frontier and on the Saxon Shore at Richborough (Breeze 1972, fig 15.147; Bushe-Fox 1949, pl LIX.294, 302). Given the simplicity of form, such objects must be found in a clear context to allow secure dating. Socketed forms of arrowheads have also been found in 4th-century contexts, for example at Catterick (Mould *et al* 2002, 83, fig 271.18; cf Manning 1976, nos 33–4).

Of course the form of arrowhead cannot suggest the type of bow in use. Wooden self-bows of the Scandinavian-Germanic archery tradition would leave very little archaeological evidence in normal preservation circumstances (Pauli-Jensen 2007). Similarly, the wood, sinew and horn of eastern composite bows would have left little trace. However, the bone or antler laths used to prevent the flexing of composite bow ears and handle, and to act as levers for the powerful stave limbs, are a readily identifiable artefact class (Coulston 1985, 224–34, 245–59; Bishop and Coulston 2006, 88, 134–6, 205–6). None has yet been found in a securely dated 4th-century context in Britain.

Formations of specialist archers were present in most provinces throughout the Roman period, and archery equipment was available for general training and for mural defence throughout the army of the Principate. However, since specialist regiments were largely drawn from the eastern empire, there were fewer in the north-western provinces and only one is directly attested for Britain throughout the Roman occupation. However, whilst *cohors I Hamiorum*, at Carvoran on Hadrian's Wall and at Bar Hill on the Antonine Wall, is conspicuously absent from the *Notitia Dignitatum*, the *equites Suri* under the command of the *comes Britanniarum* may very well have consisted of eastern horse-archers, to judge from its title (*Notitia Dignitatum, Oc.* VII.204). Following one model, it may be that specialised materials, particularly horn, were distributed from the east through Pavia to supply composite bows for field army units (Coulston 1985, 290). If the same assumptions may be used for bows and arrows as have been made for the other equipment production processes beyond the centralised late *fabricae*, then composite bows were also normally being constructed in Britain in the long 4th century, just as they had been in the 3rd century, as evidenced by unfinished laths in the legionary workshops at Caerleon and Corbridge (Nash-Williams 1932, 94–6, fig 42; Coulston 1985, 226–29; Chapman 2005, 43–8).

Other missile-weapons were used in the late Roman army, such as the *arcuballista*, sling, and staff-sling, though these do not survive in the archaeological record. Biconical, lead and ceramic sling-bullets are attested, but few have yet been found in the northern frontier of Britain in 4th-century contexts, apart from a group of lead shot at Vindolanda (Greep 1987, 199). Additional to these personal weapons, artillery continued to be used through the 4th century. As yet, no characteristic washers, field-frames, cross-struts or other diagnostic metal fittings have been recognised from late artillery weapons in Britain, even though such machines are attested in the earlier Roman period (Hanson *et al* 2007, fig 10.29.31–2, pls 10.4–5; cf Gudea and Baatz 1974; Bishop and Coulston 2006, 206–8). More common earlier finds are the pyramidal iron heads from artillery bolts, but the only evidence for the presence of artillery along the late British frontier is a dubious late bolt-head found at Vindolanda (Bidwell 1985, fig 49.34; cf Cunliffe 1975, fig 124.170). Even if the latter is an artillery projectile and is not a residual item, this is not strong evidence for the frontier army continuing to support and deploy these technically demanding torsion weapons. In earlier periods artillery was generally confined to use by legionary troops, with the uncertain exception of the 3rd-century *ballis(tarium)* epigraphically attested in the outpost fort at High Rochester in Northumberland (*RIB* 1281). From the Tetrarchic period, if not before, specialists such as light infantry *lancearii*, *sagittarii*, *ballistarii* and *equites legionis*, who were hitherto integral to the legionary organisation, seem to have been separated out into independent formations, as they appear in the *Notitia Dignitatum* (Casey 1991a; Tomlin 2000; Speidel 2000; Coulston 2002, 5). This may have made it more difficult to sustain the technology outside the field armies.

Equestrian equipment

Few items associated with cavalry are known from the late period, although tack must have existed for the cavalry formations listed in the *Notitia Digni-*

tatum (*Oc.* VII.199–205; XL.19–21, 35, 37–8, 45, 47, 54–5). Heavy cavalry units (*catafractarii*) may have fielded armoured horses (*Oc.* VII.200: *equites catafractarii iuniores*), and horses for riding required bits, saddle fittings, junctions, buckles, and other metallic fittings.

A number of spurs have been found at sites along and behind the Wall frontier, with numerous examples from Corbridge, South Shields, and Piercebridge (see Fig 1.3, though note this does not include the Maryport example). Spurs are not particularly common finds (see Cool, this volume) and while they are not an exclusively military class of artefact, and do not have a strictly military distribution, these objects probably functioned as a form of social identification. Roman cavalry seemed to operate adequately with and without spurs in previous centuries (Junkelmann 1992, 98–101). Cool speculates that they were a fusion of Roman soldier and barbarian elite, and it may be that they were indicators of social and/or military rank.

Other equipment

The standards and musical instruments which were integral to military life have not impacted on the northern British archaeological record. Other tools and objects would have been used by soldiers. For example, tools for digging, building and foraging were necessary for the collection of food and maintenance of buildings and roads. A tool hoard of the 4th or 5th century was recently found at the villa at Quarry House Farm at Ingleby Barwick outside Middlesbrough (Hunter forthcoming b); although it may not have been military *per se*, it may be indicative of tool forms in use by the army at the time. While it is certainly inadvisable to make unsupported assumptions about the quality and equipment of late Roman frontier troops, their supposed lack of mobility has not yet been qualified by finds of contemporary tent leathers. Examples from Birdoswald, Carlisle, Newstead, Papcastle, and Catterick do not postdate the 2nd century (van Driel-Murray 1990; Hooley *et al* 2002, 339–44).

Discussion

The 'depot' find of arrowheads at Housesteads has fuelled some confused discussion of *principia* having normally functioned as weapons stores (*armamentaria*). This has been further compounded by the discovery in the *principia* of the legionary fortress at Lambaesis (Algeria) of stocks of sling missiles, together with finds of inscriptions using the term *armamentarium*. Actually, all such inscriptions at Lambaesis, including others incorporated in one of the gates, were in secondary use and reveal nothing about the original functions of the main headquarters building (Cagnat 1913, 493–97; MacMullen 1963, 26; Mann 1992; Blagg 2000, 139–40; Bishop

and Coulston 2006, 263–5). The finds in the fort at Housesteads should be considered in the light of late reuse of other buildings for radically different purposes from those for which they were originally intended (Collins 2009). Similarly, evidence was found for working in copper alloy in the latest phase of the *principia* of the legionary fortress at Novae in Bulgaria. Here is represented the final phase of occupation after the installation had ceased to function as a fortress accommodating a full principate-type legion (Sarnowski 1985).

The significance of dated contexts in the identification of military equipment must be reiterated, given the basic functional shape of many weapons, and the biases in preservation rates of different materials (for example, iron and copper alloy). In the case of late Roman artefacts, these are in upper occupation levels that are more likely to have been removed or damaged by post-Roman activities, further biasing the existing archaeological record and degrading the contextual date. A number of artefacts known from 4th-century contexts were not included in the Catalogue, for example 'early' or generic forms of sword chapes. However, it is worth mentioning openwork, D-shaped buckles. Examples were found in 'good' 4th-century contexts at a number of sites, for example Birdoswald, Newcastle, and Piercebridge (see Catalogue). These buckles are typically dated to the 3rd century, but their occurrence in contexts at sites that generally lack other 3rd-century material raises an interesting possibility of a more conservative military metalworking tradition in the northern frontier. This putative conservatism may be further suggested by the small number of zoomorphic buckles, and the restriction of imported buckles and 5th-century types to Yorkshire, south of the frontier area proper.

An alternative interpretation to the discrepant distributions (bearing in mind Cool's suggestion in this volume that we cannot be confident of the actual location of 4th-century frontiers in Britain) may be a more thorough organisation of, and attention to, recycling material on the frontier. Belt fittings, weaponry, and other military objects all contributed to a physical display of social identity, but these were also important functional objects for soldiers. When such objects failed, or were left behind at an owner's death, they were perhaps more likely to have been reused or recycled in a military community than in a non-military context. Outside a highly militarised zone like the frontier, such objects would perhaps have become more personalised and less institutional, although this is to make some sweeping assumptions about the nature of late military institutional society. The mechanism of veteran retirement and settlement south of the frontier area may have occasioned deposition of material in Yorkshire and the southern counties of Britain.

A specific class of equipment which is particularly rare in Britain generally, not just along the northern frontier, is the military belt with large buckle and stiffening plates bearing rich, chip-carved decoration. There are a few plates from Richborough and odd metal-detector finds (Lyne 1999, nos 96–8; Appels and Laycock 2007, 240–1, 262–3). These are most commonly found on the Continent in weapons-graves. There are none of these burials in the northern region, and few elsewhere in Britain. Indeed, the three British burials with belts (London, Winchester, Dorchester-on-Thames) did not include weapons, and only one had a full suite of large, chip-carved plates (London). It might tentatively be suggested that the latter were the equipment of *comitatenses* in the small British field army.

Overall, the corpus of 4th-century military equipment from Hadrian's Wall may seem meagre. In part this is due to the absence of spectacular finds like the 2nd-century Corbridge Hoard, or dismantlement deposits, such as the 1st- and 2nd-century Newstead pits. One Koblenz or Intercisa style 'depot' find of helmets would transform the situation. However, some tentative conclusions may be drawn. One is that the army in north Britain was abreast of continental trends in belt design, as demonstrated by the propeller stiffeners, and in new weapon forms, as represented by the Catterick *plumbatae*. Moreover, the occurrence and distribution of belt fittings in the frontier are greater than previous studies have suggested. The lack of such finds north of Hadrian's Wall (bearing in mind the always notable exception of Traprain Law) may be judged significant when compared with the incidence of Roman belt fittings outside the Rhine frontier in Germany (Swift 2000b, figs 17, 28–9, 42, 62; Bishop and Coulston 2006, fig 140). To this extent, Hadrian's Wall may have been a 'real' boundary, at least in relation to Roman military metalwork, and Roman soldiers were still supplied with, and manufactured, military equipment, at least until the government apparatus and provincial economy collapsed completely.

Appendix 6.1: Catalogue of military equipment from the frontier
Rob Collins and Lindsay Allason-Jones

This catalogue was compiled with the generous assistance of and information provided by a number of individuals as experts, collection curators and/or authors of unpublished reports: Liz Andrews-Wilson (PAS); Katherine Bearcock (York Museums Trust, Yorkshire Museum); Ian Caruana; Hilary Cool (Barbican Research Associates); Fraser Hunter (National Museums Scotland); Kevin Leahy (PAS); Stuart Laycock; Tim Padley (Tullie House Museum); and Georgina Plowright (Corbridge and Chesters Museums).

Abbreviations

PAS   Portable Antiquities Scheme Database
UKDFD   UK Detector Finds Database
YM   Yorkshire Museum

Buckles and belt accessories

Banks East turret 52a, Cumbria
1. Buckle, Simpson Group IV variant with long rectangular plate (copper alloy)
    Allason-Jones 1988, 216, no 4
Barmby Moor, North Yorkshire
2. Buckle, zoomorphic type IIA (copper alloy)
    PAS LVPL-616B18
Barton-le-Willows, North Yorkshire
3. Buckle, zoomorphic type IIIB (copper alloy)
    PAS YORYM-4F4C23
Beadlam, North Yorkshire
4. Strap end, Tortworth type with nail cleaner terminal and incised fish (copper alloy)
    Neal 1996, 45, no 2, fig 31
5. Strap end, type VA (copper alloy)
    Neal 1996, 49, no 4, fig 31
Binchester, Durham
6. Mount, propeller-shaped stiffener (copper alloy)
    Bevan forthcoming a, no 109
Birdoswald, Cumbria
7. Buckle plate (copper alloy)
    Summerfield 1997a, 309, no 249
8. Mount, openwork pelta (copper alloy)
    Summerfield 1997a, 311, no 270
Boroughbridge, North Yorkshire
9. Buckle, zoomorphic type IA (copper alloy)
    Laycock records
Brantingham, East Yorkshire
10. Buckle, zoomorphic type IB (copper alloy)
    PAS YORYMB277
Buttercrambe with Bossall, North Yorkshire
11. Buckle, zoomorphic type IB (copper alloy)
    PAS LVPL-7E3EB0
12. Strap end, amphora-shaped (copper alloy)
    PAS LVPL-91B063
Byland with Wass, North Yorkshire
13. Strap end, amphora-shaped (copper alloy)
    PAS SWYOR-7632E7
Carlisle, Cumbria
14. Mount, propeller-shaped stiffener (copper alloy)
    Ian Caruana, pers comm
Carrawburgh, Northumberland
15. Belt mount, propeller-shaped stiffener (copper alloy)
    Breeze 1972, 137, fig 16, 166
    Catterick, North Yorkshire
16. Buckle, zoomorphic type IA (copper alloy)
    Hawkes and Dunning 1961, no 2, fig 13d
17. Buckle, zoomorphic type IVB (copper alloy)
    Hawkes and Dunning 1961, no 1, fig 22
18. Buckle plate, type I (copper alloy)
    Hawkes 1974
19. Buckle, zoomorphic type IA (copper alloy)
    Laycock records
20. Strap end, heart-shaped (copper alloy)
    Lentowicz 2002, 64, no 207
Copmanthorpe, North Yorkshire
21. Buckle, zoomorphic type IB (copper alloy)
    PAS YORYM-B47B91
Corbridge, Northumberland
22. Buckle, zoomorphic type IIA (copper alloy)
    Simpson 1976b
23. Buckle plate, probably a non-zoomorphic type (copper alloy)
    Allason-Jones 1989b, 173, no 102
    Note: the plate seems to have been damaged and repaired, but the top plate is offset from its original position
Driffield, East Yorkshire
24. Buckle, zoomorphic type IA (copper alloy)

PAS YORYM1835
Fangfoss, North Yorkshire
25. Buckle, zoomorphic type of the post-Roman period (gilded copper alloy)
    PAS YORYM-364F72
    Note: this buckle is chip-carved and probably imported
Greta Bridge, Durham
26. Buckle plate, zoomorphic type I (copper alloy)
    Hawkes 1974, fig 3.1
Hayton, North Yorkshire
27. Buckle, zoomorphic type IB (copper alloy)
    MacGregor and Bolick 1993, 199–200, no 34.28
28. Strap end, amphora-shaped (copper alloy)
    Leahy records
Langtoft, nr Rudston, North Yorkshire
29. Buckle, zoomorphic type IIA (copper alloy)
    PAS NLM-1278F5
Malton, North Yorkshire
30. Buckle, zoomorphic type IA or IIA (copper alloy)
    Laycock records
31. Buckle, zoomorphic type IA or IIA (copper alloy)
    Laycock records
32. Buckle, zoomorphic type IA (copper alloy)
    Laycock records
33. Belt mount, propeller-shaped stiffener (copper alloy)
    Cool, pers comm
Market Weighton, East Yorkshire
34. Buckle, zoomorphic type IIC (copper alloy)
    Laycock records
Maryport, Cumbria
35. Buckle, Simpson Group III variant (penannular rectangle) (copper alloy)
    Webster 1986, 63–5, fig 7, no 42
36. Belt mount, propeller-shaped stiffener, ribbed (copper alloy)
    Webster 1986, 63–5, fig 7, no 41
37. Belt mount, propeller-shaped stiffener, ribbed (copper alloy)
    Webster 1986, 63–5, fig 7, no 41
38. Belt mount, propeller-shaped stiffener, plain (copper alloy)
    Webster 1986, 63–5, fig 7, no 41
39. Belt mount, propeller-shaped stiffener, plain (copper alloy)
    Webster 1986, 63–5, fig 7, no 41
Newcastle, Tyne and Wear
40. Buckle pin, decorated (copper alloy)
    Allason-Jones 2002, 217, no 23
41. Buckle, Simpson Group II (copper alloy)
    Allason-Jones 2002, 217, no 24
Newton Kyme, West Yorkshire
42. Belt mount, zoomorphic (copper alloy)
    YM YORYM 1984.19.2
    Note: This example is unique in the frontier, with a bird head and a rectangular openwork body with a fan-shaped tail opposite the head
North Dalton, East Yorkshire
43. Buckle, zoomorphic type IB (copper alloy)
    PAS NCL-6AEB17
    Nunburnholme, East Yorkshire
44. Buckle, zoomorphic type IIIB (copper alloy)
    Eagles 1979, fig 116.1
    Overton, North Yorkshire
45. Buckle, possible plate (copper alloy)
    PAS LVPL182
Piercebridge, Durham
46. Strap end, amphora-shaped (copper alloy)
    Cool 2008, no 454
47. Strap end, amphora-shaped (copper alloy)
    Cool 2008, no 668

48. Strap end, amphora-shaped (copper alloy)
    Cool 2008, no 669
49. Buckle pin, chip-carved decoration (copper alloy)
    Cool 2008, no 470
50. Buckle pin, chip-carved decoration (copper alloy)
    Cool 2008, no 471
Pocklington, East Yorkshire
51. Buckle, Simpson Group I with integrally cast plate (copper alloy)
    PAS YORYM1250
Ravenglass, Cumbria
52. Mount, possibly zoomorphic
    Potter 1979, 69, no 15
    Note: from a 4th-century context
Rudston, North Yorkshire
53. Buckle, Simpson Group II (copper alloy)
    Stead and Pacitto 1980, 103, no 44, fig 64
54. Buckle, Simpson Group II (copper alloy)
    Stead and Pacitto 1980, 103, no 45, fig 64
Skirpenbeck, East Yorkshire
55. Buckle, zoomorphic type IA (copper alloy)
    PAS LVPL-FE7C87
South Shields, Tyne and Wear
56. Strap end, Tortworth type with nail-clearer terminal (copper alloy)
    Croom 1994, no 37, fig 7.4
57. Strap end, heart-shaped (copper alloy)
    Allason-Jones and Miket 1984, no 3.610
58. Strap end, amphora-shaped (copper alloy)
    Allason-Jones and Miket 1984, no 3.611
59. Strap end, type VB (copper alloy)
    Allason-Jones and Miket 1984, no 3.613
60. Buckle, zoomorphic type IA (copper alloy)
    Allason-Jones and Miket 1984, no 3.614
61. Buckle, zoomorphic type IA (copper alloy)
    Allason-Jones and Miket 1984, no 3.615
62. Buckle, Simpson Group IV (copper alloy)
    Allason-Jones and Miket 1984, no 3.623
    Note: this example would have had a hinged, probably openwork, plate
63. Belt mount, propeller-shaped stiffener (copper alloy)
    Allason-Jones and Miket 1984, no 3.888
    Stamford Bridge, North Yorkshire
64. Buckle, zoomorphic type IB (copper alloy)
    UKDFD 13087
Stanwick, North Yorkshire
65 Buckle, zoomorphic type IB (copper alloy)
    Hawkes and Dunning 1961, no 49, fig 15m
Stanwix, Cumbria
66. Strap end, amphora-shaped (lead)
    Collingwood 1931a, no 75
Traprain Law, East Lothian
67. Buckle plate, type IIA (copper alloy)
    Curle 1915, no 3
68. Strap end, Tortworth type with nail-cleaner terminal (copper alloy)
    Curle 1915, no 1
69. Buckle, Simpson Group II (silver)
    Painter 2006, 244, no 257
70. Buckle, with ridged bars on plate and belt mounts x5 (silver gilt)
    Painter 2006, 244, no 258
71. Belt mounts, studs x23 on leather strap (silver)
    Painter 2006, 244, no 259
72. Strap end, type VA (silver)
    Painter 2006, 244, no 260
73. Strap end, circular and chip-carved (silver)
    Painter 2006, 245, no 261
Vindolanda, Northumberland
74. Belt mount, propeller-shaped stiffener (copper alloy)
    Bidwell 1985, 122, no 28

75. Strap end or belt mount, rectangular strip (copper alloy)
    Bidwell 1985, 122, no 31
    Note: from 5th-century context
76. Belt mount, quatrefoil stud (copper alloy)
    Bidwell 1985, 122, no 36
    Note: from 4th-century context
77. Belt plate, openwork and enamelled
    Vindolanda Trust 2002, no 7369
    Note: from 4th-century context

Yapham, East Yorkshire
78. Buckle plate, zoomorphic type IIA (copper alloy)
    PAS YORYM-368EF3

York, North Yorkshire
79. Buckle plate, zoomorphic type IIA (copper alloy)
    YM YORYM 1974.4.24
80. Buckle, zoomorphic type IIIB (copper alloy)
    YM YORYM 2001.12530
81. Buckle, possibly zoomorphic IIIB (iron)
    YM YORYM 1974.14.115
    Note: This buckle is unusual, with 2 D-shaped frames set side-by-side with possible confronted animal heads at the base of the frames, and integrally cast on an openwork rectangular frame

'Military' equipment

Beadlam, North Yorkshire
1. Spur, prick type (copper alloy)
   Neal 1996, 49, no 20, fig 32
Catterick, North Yorkshire
2. Spur, prick type (copper alloy)
   Lentowicz 2002, 66, no 213
3. Spur, prick type (copper alloy)
   Lentowicz 2002, 66, no 214
Corbridge, Northumberland
4. Spur, prick type (copper alloy)
   Shortt 1959, 70, no 7, fig 3
5. Spur, prick type (copper alloy)
   Shortt 1959, 70, no 8, fig 3
6. Spur, prick type (copper alloy)
   Shortt 1959, 70, no 9, fig 3
7. Spur, prick type (copper alloy)
   Shortt 1959, 70, no 10, fig 3
Filey, North Yorkshire
8. Spur, prick type (copper alloy)
   Cool 2000b, no 21
Maryport, Cumbria
9. Spur, prick type (copper alloy)
   Brown 1976, 80–1, fig 21
Piercebridge, Durham
10. Spur, prick type (copper alloy)
    Cool 2008, no 501
11. Spur, prick type (copper alloy)
    Cool 2008, no 502
12. Spur, prick type (copper alloy)
    Cool 2008, no 503
13. Spur, prick type (copper alloy)
    Cool 2008, no 504
14. Spur, prick type (copper alloy)
    Cool 2008, no 505
15. Spur, prick type (copper alloy)
    Cool 2008, no 506
16. Spur, prick type (iron)
    Cool 2008, no 120
17. Spur, prick type (iron)
    Cool 2008, no 121
Rudston, North Yorkshire
18. Spur, prick type (copper alloy)

    Stead and Pacitto 1980, 103, no 47, fig 66
South Shields, Tyne and Wear
19. Spur, prick type (copper alloy)
    Allason-Jones and Miket 1984, no 3.685
20. Spur, prick type (copper alloy)
    Allason-Jones and Miket 1984, no 3.686
21. Spur, probable prick (copper alloy)
    Allason-Jones and Miket 1984, no 3.687
22. Spur, probable prick (copper alloy)
    Allason-Jones and Miket 1984, no 3.688

Weaponry

Binchester, Durham
1. Spearhead, barbed (iron)
   Bevan forthcoming b, no 52
Birdoswald, Cumbria
2. Spearhead (iron)
   Summerfield 1997a, 310, no 260
3. Sword, hilt segment (copper alloy)
   Summerfield 1997a, 312, no 275
   Note: dated by context
4. Sword, possible pommel (bone)
   Summerfield 1997a, 312, no 276
   Note: dated by context
Carvoran, Northumberland
5. Spearhead, barbed (iron)
   Manning 1976, no 22
Catterick, North Yorkshire
6. Spearhead (iron)
   Mould *et al* 2002, 82, no 6
   Note: from 4th-century context
7. Spearhead (iron)
   Mould *et al* 2002, 82, no 7
8. Spearhead (iron)
   Mould *et al* 2002, 82, no 8
   Note: from 4th-century context
9. Spearhead, barbed (iron)
   Mould *et al* 2002, 82, no 9
10. Spearhead, barbed (iron)
    Mould *et al* 2002, 82, no 10
11. Spearhead, barbed (iron)
    Mould *et al* 2002, 82, no 11
12. Arrowhead, barbed and socketed (iron)
    Mould *et al* 2002, 83, no 18
    Note: from 4th-century context
Clapham, North Yorkshire
13. Spear, door-knobbed butt (copper alloy)
    Fraser Hunter, pers comm
Goldsborough, North Yorkshire
14. Spearhead (iron)
    Cool 2000a, 59–60, no 27
    Note: 5 heads corroded together
Great Chesters, Northumberland
15. Scabbard slide, possibly (bone)
    Allason-Jones 1996b, no 7
    Note: this form matches that seen on the Venice Tetrarchs statue
Housesteads, Northumberland
16. Arrowhead, triangular and tanged (800+, iron)
    Manning 1976, nos 37–44
    Note: from the last phase of occupation of the *principia*
17. Spearhead, barbed (iron)
    Manning 1976, no 21
18. Axe, possible late type (iron)
    Manning 1976, no 55
Old Penrith, Cumbria
19. Spearhead, barbed (iron)

Austen 1991, 187, no 651

Piercebridge, Durham

20. Spearhead (iron)
   Cool 2008, no 124
21. Spearhead (iron)
   Cool 2008, no 125
22. Spearhead (iron)
   Cool 2008, no 126

Skirpenbeck, East Yorkshire

23. Chape, zoomorphic (copper alloy)
   PAS LVPL-917677

South Shields, Tyne and Wear

24. Spearhead, barbed (iron)
   Manning 1976, no 23

Strensall, North Yorkshire

25. Spear, door-knobbed butt (copper alloy)
   PAS: YORYM-EFBB77

Traprain Law, East Lothian

26. Spear, door-knobbed butt (copper alloy)
   Burley 1956, 203, no 408
27. Spear, door-knobbed butt (copper alloy)
   Burley 1956, 203, no 408

Vindolanda, Northumberland

   Note: All the objects in this listing are from 4th-century contexts

28. Sword (iron)
   Bidwell 1985, 130, no 1
29. Lancehead (iron)
   Bidwell 1985, 130, no 2
30. Shield grip (iron)
   Bidwell 1985, 132, no 2
31. Spearhead, socketed (copper alloy)
   Bidwell 1985, 136, no 23 *addenda*
32. Javelin head (iron)
   Bidwell 1985, 136, no 27
33. Javelin or arrowhead (iron)
   Bidwell 1985, 136, no 29
34. Arrowhead (iron)
   Bidwell 1985, 136, no 30
35. Bolt head, artillery (iron)
   Bidwell 1985, 138, no 34
36. Knife, late type (iron)
   Unpublished, Barbarba Birley, pers comm
37. Spear, door-knobbed butt (copper alloy)
   Bidwell 1985, 126, no 94

Watercrook, Cumbria

38. Knife, probable late type (iron)
   Potter 1979, 224, no 117

7 Brooch use in the 4th- to 5th-century frontier *Rob Collins*

Introduction

Brooches are often separated from other artefacts in finds reports and receive attention as a coherent group of objects for various reasons, despite the fact that they are best classified as a dress accessory. While brooches do contribute to our understanding of personal appearance for past individuals, they have often been used as indicators of ethnic identity (eg 'Romano-British' and 'Anglo-Saxon' brooches). Using brooches to come to an understanding of identity constructs is difficult, perhaps even precarious, but the results of such an exercise can prove interesting.

This paper seeks to examine late brooch use in the frontier zone of Britain with two aims:

1. to identify the extent to which the northern frontier of Britain is comparable to the continental frontiers in the 4th and early 5th century;
2. to determine whether there are any indicators of the late Roman to sub-Roman transition that would further enhance our understanding of this interesting period.

To address the first aim, the use and distribution of the developed crossbow brooch has been considered. Crossbow brooches have been argued to have been part of the uniform of a 4th-century soldier and other state officials (Jobst 1975, 93; Heurgon 1958, 23), and as such can be assumed to indicate the presence of imperial authority and the supply of official items (Swift 2000b, 3–4). Thus, an analysis of the sub-types of developed crossbow brooches can be assessed in terms of their numerical presence and distribution to establish how the northern frontier compares with other regions of the western empire. The second aim can be addressed by considering penannular brooches, a form that was in use from the Iron Age into the Early Medieval period and particularly popular in Britain (Fowler 1960). Certain types of penannular brooches seem to have developed in the 4th century and continued in use into the 5th and 6th centuries, inspiring the further development of new types (eg Fowler 1964, types E, F, G, H, D7, A5, B3, and C; Laing 2007). A consideration of the occurrence and distribution of these types of brooches may indicate both a 'native British' influence or presence and a potential settlement shift between the late Roman and sub-Roman periods.

Given the stated aims, focus has been limited to developed crossbow brooches and only some of the late Roman and Early Medieval types of penannulars. There are other types of brooches in use in the late Roman and Early Medieval periods, for example, plate brooches in the former, and 'Anglo-Saxon' brooches in the latter (eg annular, cruciform, great square-headed, small-long, and supporting arms types). However, not many late plate brooches have been found in the frontier, compared with crossbow and penannular brooches. The Fowler type H penannular is 7th-century and later in date and not necessarily useful in examining the late Roman to Early Medieval transition *per se*, while Fowler type C is more frequently found in the south and east of Britain, notably in Anglo-Saxon graves (White 1988, 9–14), and is not particularly common in the late frontier. Even some variations of type G are known to be later, and so have not been included in this study (Dickinson 1982).

In creating a catalogue of both crossbow and penannular brooches (Appendices 1 and 3), data were gathered from published finds reports and catalogues, unpublished and forthcoming reports, the Portable Antiquities Scheme, and major museum collections in the north of England.[1] The geographical extent of the study was the Humber–Mersey line north to the line of the Antonine Wall, a broad definition of the frontier that sought to determine patterns inside and outside the late Roman diocese of Britannia. In a few cases, outlying crossbow brooches have been included. Where possible (eg from modern excavation reports), full use has been made of contextual information, but in many cases no contextual information has survived and only a very general findspot can be provided. While I have tried to be thorough in the creation of catalogues for both brooch forms, inevitably a few examples will have been missed. It is hoped that any such omissions will not alter significantly the conclusions offered here, but it should be remembered, especially in the case of the distribution maps, that an absence of evidence must not be interpreted as negative evidence.

Crossbow brooches

The fully developed or 'onion-knobbed' crossbow brooch developed in the later 3rd century from the 'light' form crossbow (Bayley and Butcher 2004, 183–4). The developed form is characterised by a P-shaped profile and cruciform plan, with sub-types classified by the detailed shape and proportions of headknobs, arms, bows, and feet. Burial evidence indicates that these brooches were used for the fastening of cloaks or other heavy outer garments, and there is a strong bias in distribution toward military zones, though some examples have been found with women and

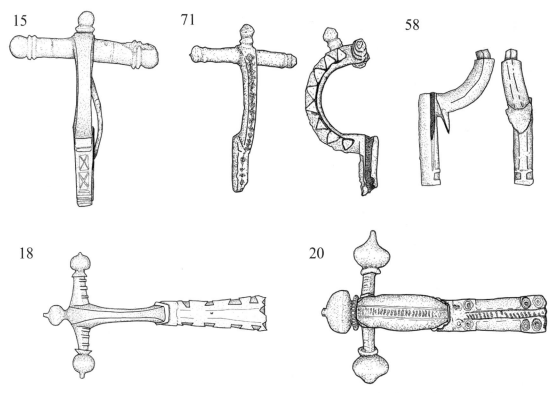

Fig 7.1   A selection of different types of crossbow brooches (scales vary), drawn by the author

children (Swift 2000b, 4). A lack of thorough surveys of provinces distant from the frontiers probably further exacerbates this bias.

Art-historical evidence indicates the brooch was worn on the top or front of the shoulder with the heavy, cruciform head down and the foot up. Heurgon (1958, 24) argued that these brooches were worn by officials of all ranks in conjunction with cloaks, for example, the *magister militum* Stilicho (seen on his famous diptych; see Frontispiece), court officials (as seen on the *Missiorum Theodosius*), clerics/saints (in mosaics), and perhaps 'common' soldiers (seen on the Projecta casket). However, rank may have been indicated by variation in the metal used, gold in rare cases and silver slightly more commonly, but typically in a copper alloy, though some of these were gilded in gold, washed in silver, or even tinned to emulate a silver wash (Keller 1971, 27). These different materials and surface treatments are likely to have distinguished hierarchy in military and civil organisations, but it should not be assumed that every soldier or bureaucrat wore a crossbow brooch. A minimum social, military, or administrative rank or grade may have been necessary before these brooches could be worn.

The established typology for crossbow brooches was developed initially by Keller (1971), with subsequent changes by Pröttel (1988), and the most recent update provided by Swift (2000b). Both Pröttel and Swift have built upon Keller's original typology, and, while the basic framework has been largely retained, some of the changes are significant. Swift's typology has been used for this paper, consisting of types 1 to 7, some of these also containing sub-types (Fig 7.1). Some examples are hybrids of two types, and the type with the most numerous morphological characteristics was favoured in terms of assigning a type for purposes of analysis (see Swift 2000b, 13). It should be noted, however, that the varying quality of the examples in the study area, and the hybrid aspects of some specimens, suggests production in the frontier or elsewhere in Britain, rather than the importation of standardised examples from state-controlled factories on the Continent.

A full catalogue, including findspot, type, and primary material can be found in Appendix 7.1, numbered alphabetically by findspot. Appendix 7.2 lists the brooches by sub-type, and Appendix 7.5 lists the brooches by material (excluding copper alloy).

The catalogue contains 74 examples of crossbow brooches found in the frontier zone, as defined above. Nearly all the types identified by Swift are found in the frontier, with the notable exception of type 5. Comparison of data from the frontier to Swift's (2000b, 29, 31) analysis indicates some interesting patterns. Swift's graph for the diocese of Britannia indicates that types 1 and 3/4 were the most numerous, both at approximately 30% of the total for Britannia. The next most numerous is type 2 at slightly more than 10%, with type 5 under 10% and type 6 at approximately 5%. Compared with the other parts of the empire that Swift surveyed, the type profile for Britain is distinct, as the profile of every other province has type 3/4 as the most numerous, at a minimum of 50%. Interestingly, Swift's profile of Britain is most similar to the Danube provinces of

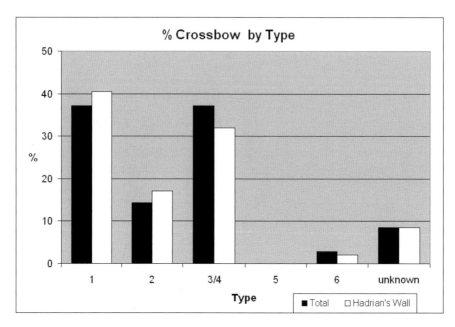

Fig 7.2   The percentage of different types of crossbow brooches in the whole of the study area compared with Hadrian's Wall

Raetia, Noricum, and Pannonia. However, it should be noted that in these latter provinces the relative proportions of each type are different and they are clearly dominated by type 3/4.

A similar graph was created for the frontier (Fig 7.2), depicting the profile of the total frontier assemblage and the profile for brooches from the Hadrian's Wall corridor (which has the greatest concentration of crossbow brooches in the frontier). The frontier profile is in agreement with Swift's profile for Britain, with the exception of a complete lack of type 5 crossbow brooches. The profile for the Hadrian's Wall corridor is somewhat different. Type 1 is the most numerous (slightly over 40%), with type 3/4 the second most numerous category (just over 30%). Other than the dominance of type 1, the profile for Hadrian's Wall agrees with that of the rest of the frontier. A similar pattern is also visible in a distribution map (Fig 7.3), which sees more concentration of the earlier types (1 and 2) along Hadrian's Wall, with type 3/4 found more widely distributed throughout the frontier. Type 1 brooches are not restricted to the Wall, as there are a number found south of the Wall and east of the Pennines. Unfortunately, there are few meaningful distributions that can be seen in Fig 7.3, as there are a number of biases in the distribution, notably the historical focus of antiquaries and archaeologists who excavated along Hadrian's Wall and other Roman forts (to a lesser extent; see Fig 7.4). Despite this, a clear pattern indicates a greater number of crossbow brooches at sites that were probably officially important to frontier administration (South Shields, Corbridge, Vindolanda, Carlisle, and York). A further bias may be attributed to data from the Portable Antiquities Scheme, in which all the examples in the catalogue are from the area

south of the Tees (a favoured search area by hobby metal detectorists) and are usually type 3/4. This suggests that type 3/4 is possibly more numerous than is currently known. In comparison with the Continent, there have been few excavations of late Roman cemeteries in Britain, and late cemeteries have considerably increased the numbers of type 3/4 in the Danube provinces.

Type 3/4 can be further separated into four sub-types based on foot decoration (Swift 2000b, 43, 49): 3/4a is characterised by geometric decoration (including facetted panels; see Fig 7.1 nos 18 and 20); 3/4b is characterised by circle and dot decoration (which can also include facetted panels; see Fig 7.1 no 20); 3/4c is characterised by involuted (C-shaped) decoration along the sides of the foot, which is typically raised from a facetted/bevelled edge; and 3/4d has trapeze decoration along the sides of the foot that is recognised as forming an inset rectangle or trapezoidal shape that can have a regular depth or facetted/bevelled surface angling down from the inside to the outer edge (see Fig 7.1 no 18). Sub-type 3/4b is the most frequent, on the Continent, in Britain, and in the frontier.

Sub-type 3/4b can be further identified by the number and arrangement of circle and dot decoration in various forms, labelled b1 to b30 (see Swift 2000b, 50). It should also be noted that the forms are basic templates, and variants of these were regularly encountered in the frontier crossbows. The frequency and variety of b-forms enables a rate of variability to be calculated (variability = no of patterns/total no of 3/4b brooches). Britannia and Lugdunensis have the highest rates of variability in Swift's (2000b, 32) study, at 0.5 and 0.7, respectively, compared with a rate of 0.2 in the other provinces studied and a rate of 0.75 in the frontier zone of Britain. This rate

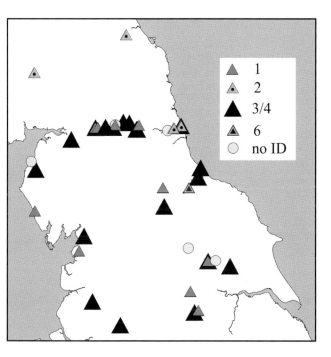

Fig 7.3 *The distribution of crossbow brooch types in the frontier*

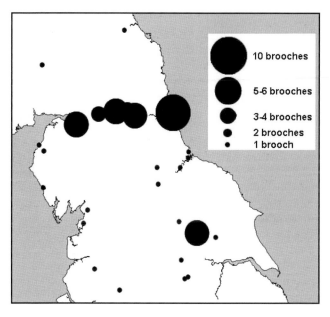

Fig 7.4 *The distribution of crossbow brooches in the frontier, indicating the number of crossbow brooches at each site*

may be superficially high, as there is little repetition of b-forms in the 3/4 brooches from the frontier (for example, only three forms are represented on two brooches while all the other forms were only found on one brooch). Any further discoveries of 3/4b brooches will change the variability rating, with repetition of known forms decreasing the value. In any case, the frontier, Britain, and northern Gaul in general show much higher rates of variability than the rest of the western empire. This suggests that along the Rhine and Danube either there were fewer workshops mass-producing brooches or there was a more restricted repertoire. Given the greater variability of decoration in northern Gaul and Britain, it seems unlikely that there was any state restriction, which means that there may actually have been more centralised production of crossbow brooches on the Rhine and Danube frontiers at the state-controlled *fabricae*.

The b-forms can be considered in more detail, though the small number of 3/4b brooches from the frontier makes any conclusions tentative (Fig 7.5). It is interesting that form b2, generally the most frequently occurring arrangement of circles and dots, is not found in the frontier. According to Swift (2000b, 51), the most frequent forms (in addition to b2) are b4, b5, and b7. All three of these forms are found in the frontier, but only three forms have any repetition on more than one brooch: b5, b7, and b15. B15 is not seen in any quantity outside Britannia and Lugdunensis. Further comparisons can be made, but the small sample from the frontier skews Fig 7.5. Further finds of 3/4b brooches will significantly alter the picture.

Type 6 crossbows have been dated to *c* AD 390–460, with only three examples in the catalogue. Two

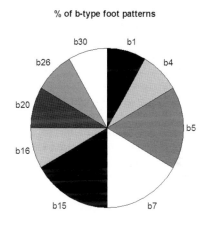

Fig 7.5 *The percentage of b-type foot patterns among type 3/4 crossbow brooches*

of the three are gold (no 41, Moray Firth; no 47, Quarry House Farm, Ingleby Barwick), and there is a bias toward sites with high-status occupants, such as the town at Corbridge and the villa at Quarry House. Swift (2000b, 70) noted a retreat from the frontiers of type 6, and it is possible that the type was limited to only the highest levels of the military or civil servants (for example, on the Stilicho diptych; see Frontispiece). As such, the lack of examples from frontiers may be paralleled by an increase of examples in southern Gaul and Italy, the provinces where the western imperial court resided at this time.

Decorated bows are also a common feature,

occurring on approximately one-third of all the crossbow brooches in the catalogue, across all types. That said, there is little repetition of patterns. The motifs are simple and usually comprise incised lines or hatches, occasionally punched triangles or circles, along the top or sides of the bow. There are some examples of more ornate bow decoration, however. The gold type 2iii from Erickstanebrae (no 29) has an openwork bow, and the copper-alloy type 1 from Adwick le Street (no 1) has highly ornate and elaborate decoration consisting of S-shapes and floral/solar motifs not only on the bow, but across the entire brooch. The copper-alloy type 1 from York (no 71; Fig 7.1) has a series of triangular depressions on each side of the bow, some of which still contain inset pieces of shale, identified by chipping along the edges revealing cleavage typical of shale as well as probable shrinkage of the stone. This brooch may have been gilded as well.

As stated above, nearly all the brooches in the catalogue are from excavations or isolated findspots, rather than cemeteries. The exceptions are no 47 (Quarry House Farm) and no 50 (Shorden Brae), which were from burials, the former associated with a dog burial and the latter with a human body. In the case of the Quarry House Farm brooch, it seems to have been damaged and reused/deposited with the buried dog, which may have been a loved pet or prized hunting dog (Hunter forthcoming b). Where known, contexts for archaeological discoveries tend to be dumps, ditch fills, pits, and other disposal and redeposition features. The dates of these contexts (determined stratigraphically or by other independent dates from artefacts) do not disagree with the different types of crossbow brooch, except that some examples are disposed of considerably later than their presumed production date, between 30 and 100 years later. This sort of 'residuality', however, is common for brooches.

It is significant that the profile for the frontier is different from the diocesan profile determined by Swift, though incorporation of Portable Antiquities Scheme data may further alter the diocesan profile. The lack of type 5 crossbows in the frontier could be significant, though its absence is not related to date of production. Type 3/4 and type 6 overlap in terms of production date, and both types are found in the frontier. Perhaps type 5 was restricted to *comitatensien* officers, or a certain branch of the imperial service. The general lack of crossbow brooches from north of Hadrian's Wall is also telling (see Fig 7.3). Even accepting the less extensive archaeological exploration north of the Wall, some examples would surely be known if there were any 'regular' presence of crossbow brooches. In this light, the examples from Erickstanebrae (no 29; Plate 8), Upsettlington (no 61), and Moray Firth (no 41) are even more exceptional. Further examples may turn up, but the almost complete absence of crossbows in *barbaricum* further reinforces the suggestion these brooches are indicators of time spent in Roman service, probably at a minimum official rank.

Late penannular brooches

The penannular brooch developed in the Iron Age, possibly in Britain, though examples are also found in Scandinavia and the Iberian peninsula (Fowler 1960). Wherever their geographic origins lie, penannular brooches were used throughout the Roman and Early Medieval periods in Britain. The form of the brooch is relatively simple, with a circular or sub-circular hoop, generally circular in section, with two matching terminals keeping the hoop from being truly annular or ring-like. The decoration of the terminals varies considerably, and it is the different forms and decoration of the terminals that are generally used to classify sub-types. Pins on penannular brooches also varied through time, principally in the degree to which a pin was straight or humped, as well as the form of the hinge mechanism. From the late Iron Age until the 5th century, penannular hoops were not very large (generally 40mm or less in diameter) compared with the development of the form in the 6th century and later, when a number of very large and highly decorated examples are known from Ireland in the 7th and 8th centuries. Other examples of late Roman and Early Medieval penannulars are known from Gaul and the Rhine frontier (White 1988, 22).

Penannulars found in furnished graves on the Continent indicate that these brooches were worn singly on the shoulder by males buried with military equipment (Keller 1971, 55–6), suggesting that during the late Roman period penannular brooches were part of the military uniform. Early Medieval art-historical evidence indicates that penannulars were worn by high-status individuals to fasten cloaks or other items of clothing, and Nieke (1993) has argued that this use of brooches as indicators of social status, codified in a 9th-century Irish law, was a practice taken from the Romans. In most cases, penannulars were made in copper alloys, though some examples have been found in iron and silver, and from the 7th century in gold, too (Laing 1993, 5). It is possible that a much higher proportion of brooches was made in iron, but the preservation qualities of iron compared with copper alloys has biased the archaeological record. Generally speaking, the use of iron may also be a feature of Early Medieval brooches rather than those of Roman date, as it is very rare for brooches to have been made in iron, even in the late Roman period. Roman-period brooches also tend to be uniform in their material, with both the body of the brooch and the pin being made from the same material. In comparison, 'Anglo-Saxon' brooches will often have iron pins, even if the main body of the brooch is made in a copper alloy.

The basic typology for late Roman and Early Medieval penannulars was developed by Fowler (1964), and its general simplicity has helped the typology endure, encompassing the considerable variation that can be seen in this form of brooch. Subsequent scholars have attempted to refine the basic

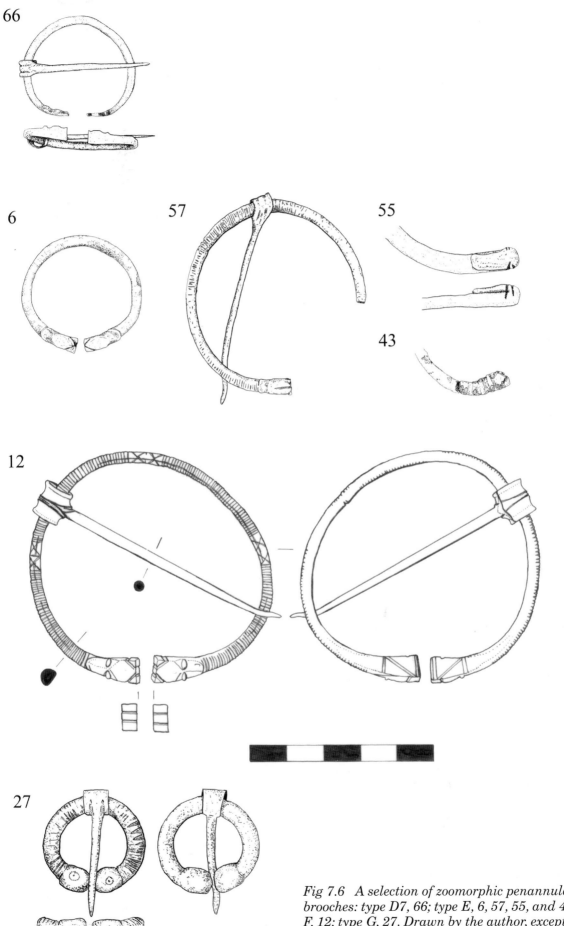

Fig 7.6 A selection of zoomorphic penannular brooches: type D7, 66; type E, 6, 57, 55, and 43; type F, 12; type G, 27. Drawn by the author, except no 12 drawn by Dom Andrews

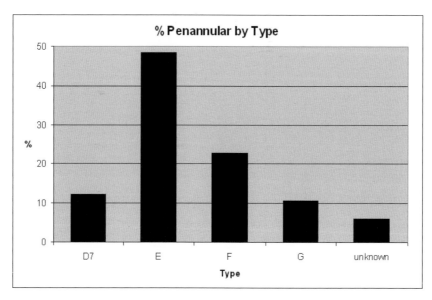

Fig 7.7   The percentage of different types of penannular brooches in the frontier

types into sub-types: Kilbride-Jones (1980) with types E (pseudo-zoomorphic form) and F (zoomorphic initial form); Dickinson (1982) with type G, and Laing (1993) who adopted Dickinson's subdivisions and applied them to all the late Roman and Early Medieval types. There can be clear variation within each type, and it should be noted that the distinction between certain examples of type D penannulars (with folded back terminals) and type E penannulars is not always clear. Type E decoration is said to be zoomorphic, and Laing (1993) includes penannulars with folded back terminals and zoomorphic decoration as type E, rather than a decorated type D. Corrosion or damage may obscure a clear typological identification, and more detailed study is required to clarify the relationship (chronologically and typologically) between penannular types D and E. The matter is probably further complicated by the fact that these brooches were made by craftsmen at sites across Britain, rather than in a few workshops, as attested by the number of recovered moulds (Laing 1993, 11).

A full catalogue of penannular brooches, arranged alphabetically by site, is provided in Appendix 7.3. Appendix 7.4 lists the brooches by type, and examples made from materials other than copper alloy are noted in Appendix 7.5. The types of late Roman and Early Medieval penannulars catalogued from the frontier are D7s, Es, Fs, and Gs (Fig 7.6). Numerically speaking, type E is the most frequent in the frontier, comprising nearly 50% of the total catalogue (Fig 7.7).

In most cases, penannulars conformed to the basic attributes of each type. That said, there were 29 examples of type E, and this has allowed for greater variation to be observed, principally in the terminals but also in other aspects. The majority of examples of type E had the common cast zoomorphic terminal, creating a stylised horse-head consisting of 'ears' as

the outer corners at the end of the terminal, a pseudo-lozengiform 'forehead' leading to 'eye sockets' and a 'snout' with a slight semicircular protrusion (Fig 7.6 no 6). This decoration is typically 'soft', not being in sharp contrast and the animal head is only loosely formed. In contrast, the animal head and its features are more starkly defined in type F (Fig 7.6 no 12). However, a few examples of type E had zoomorphic terminals which had been decorated after being folded back (eg no 5, Birdoswald; no 15, Chesters; and very basically no 55, Vindolanda; Fig 7.6). In some cases (eg no 13, Catterick; no 57, Vindolanda), the terminal is rather different from typical type E decoration, consisting of an incised central line, splitting the 'forehead' into two panels – a feature more common in type F – but in all other aspects a type E terminal. Some examples were more stylised and/or elaborate. The example from Edinburgh (no 17) had cells, which may have taken enamel. The zoomorphic decoration on the type E from Kirkby Thore (no 24) has sharper contrast than is typical, creating a more distinct lozenge shape at the end of the terminal, which was split by a central line. An example from South Shields (no 43; Fig 7.6) also has a more distinct lozenge-shape 'forehead'.

Most of the type E brooches have circular-sectioned hoops, but there were cases of D-sectioned hoops (eg no 58, Vindolanda) and rectangular-sectioned hoops (eg no 59, Vindolanda). Laing (1993, 11) has pointed out that type E brooches with folded over terminals have ribbed hoops, but this is not a strict rule (eg no 55, Vindolanda). Continuous ribbing can be found on examples of both folded and cast terminals (eg no 10, Birdoswald; no 13, Catterick), and discontinuous ribbing is also found (eg no 24, Kirkby Thore). Ribbing, both continuous and discontinuous, can be found on the hoops of types D7, F, and G (eg no 38, Piercebridge; no 12, Catterick; no 31, Newby Wiske).

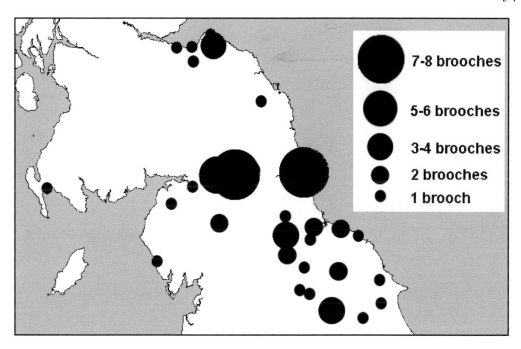

Fig 7.8   The distribution of penannular brooches in the frontier, indicating the number of penannular brooches at each site

Types E and D7 can be further contrasted with types F and G on the basis of the thickness and diameter of the hoop, and the overall strength of the pin, including its hinge. For types E and D7, the diameter is rarely larger than 40mm and the hoop is generally less than 5mm in breadth or thickness. Pins for these types will almost always have a wrap-around hinge, and have been humped either purposely or through use. In contrast, types F and G are almost always more than 50mm in diameter across the hoop, and will be 5mm or greater in thickness (particularly in type G). The pins may have wrap-around hinges, but there are also barrel pins, in which the hinge is formed by a more secure and more decorated cast barrel. Pins on these types also tend to be thicker and more likely to remain straight rather than become humped. These differences may relate to function: the wider and thicker frames of types F and G would be less likely to break from use, as they could handle the stress of bunched cloth more successfully. This also relates to the pins, as the greater internal space within the hoop for bunched cloth meant that a pin could remain straight and would not suffer from as much stress, and a barrel hinge would further strengthen the pin. While these differences are likely to be functional, there are probably implications for dating, which are discussed below.

In terms of the overall distribution (see Fig 7.8), most of the penannulars in the study are from the Hadrian's Wall corridor (28 in total), with other groupings found in Lothian and east of the Pennines. There are occasional 'single finds', but southern Scotland and Lancashire are particularly blank in regard to the penannular types in this study.

When separated by type, the distributions suggest something of more interest (see Fig 7.9).

The D7s form a small group of only eight examples found at just four sites (Birdoswald, South Shields, Piercebridge, and York). These sites were late Roman forts with occupation known to continue into the 5th century. The two specimens from York have no context information, but those from the other three sites are from contexts that date to the late 4th century at the earliest, and possibly the 5th century in some cases. Snape (1992) has argued that the variant of the D7 (with flattened, vertically pinched terminals) is particular to the frontier zone and may be a feature of sites with 5th-century occupation.

All the type Es are from sites inside the frontier, with the exception of one find from Edinburgh (no 17). The distribution is concentrated on Hadrian's Wall, but examples from Kirkby Thore (no 24), Piercebridge (nos 36 and 37), and Catterick (no 13) extend the distribution south. A particularly notable absence in the type E distribution is York, with its legionary fortress (though there are curiously few penannular brooches known from York, given its historical significance in the region). It seems significant that the type E brooches are found on Roman military sites (with the exception of no 17). Where contextual information is available, it confirms that these brooches are found in the mid- to late 4th century, with the notable exception of no 60 from Wallsend, which was found in a context dating to the late 3rd to early 4th century in the alley between two chalet-style barracks (Alex Croom, pers comm). However, it is easy to see a situation where a small discarded brooch of the mid- to late 4th century fell into the gaps formed by large sherds of late 3rd- to early 4th-

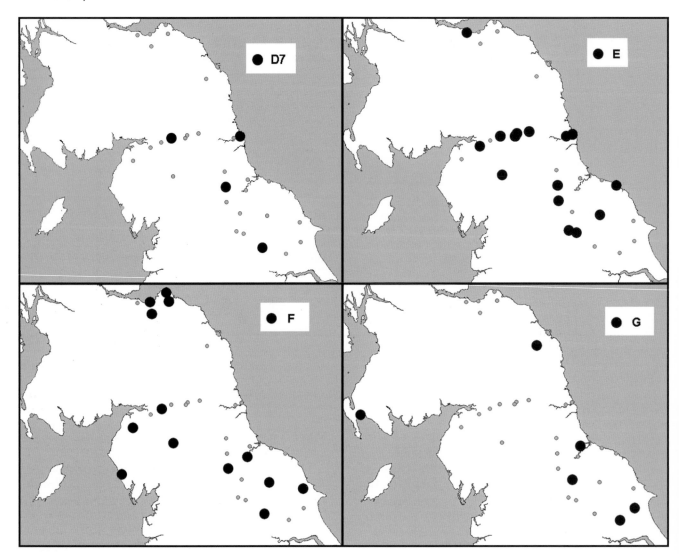

Fig 7.9 The distribution of penannular brooches in the frontier, separated by type

century pottery. The latest brooch is from period 9 at South Shields (no 43), which dates broadly to the 5th–6th centuries. The fact that no type E brooches have been found in the region in 'Anglo-Saxon' cemeteries is telling, and it seems reasonable to suggest a date range of mid-4th to late 5th/early 6th century for the type.

The type F brooches form distinct clusters. The largest concentration is in East Yorkshire and eastern North Yorkshire, with another cluster in Cumbria and another in Lothian. At least two of these brooches, perhaps three, were from burials (no 12, Catterick; no 49, Staxton; possibly no 62, Yarm), while the others are site finds or casual finds. The dating of type F is not certain, with a range of 4th to 7th century common. Laing (1993, 13) suggests that the earliest sub-type (his Fa) should be seen as a larger version of type E, contemporary with it in the late Roman period. Given the possibility of a long 'use-life' for brooches and the clear stylistic links between types E and F, contemporaneity is quite probable. However, it is also possible that

type F developed after type E had already become commonly established. Such a scenario would see type F emerging in the mid- to late 5th century or perhaps later. This later date would help explain why none are found along Hadrian's Wall (though note no 35, Old Church Brampton, immediately south of the Wall), and only three examples are from Roman sites (no 25, Kirkby Thore; no 12, Catterick; and no 64, York). Considered as post-Roman in date, the three distinct clusters of type F in the former Roman frontier correlate to the known areas of the Early Medieval 'kingdoms' of Deira, Rheged, and Gododdin.

The distribution of type G brooches is limited almost exclusively to North and East Yorkshire, with an outlier in Wooler (Northumberland) and Luce Sands (Wigtonshire). Dickinson (1982, 54) has reviewed the dating evidence for type G and has accepted that while the type may have originated in the early 5th century in Wales, it is not a common type in England until the 6th century. The distribution in the frontier further supports Dickinson's dating, as there are no examples from Roman sites and those with known contexts are from 'Anglo-Saxon' burials. The five examples from Yorkshire further reinforce the type F cluster associated with the kingdom of Deira.

The more widely distributed types D7 and E, compared with the more clustered types F and G suggest a different range of dating, and perhaps also political culture. Types D7 and E can be tentatively said to have a 'late Roman' distribution, while F and G have an 'Early Medieval' distribution. Further conclusions can be drawn by comparing the penannular brooches with the crossbow brooches.

Conclusions

Returning to the original aims of the study, the analysis of crossbow brooches in the frontier has provided a comparison of the frontier zone with Britannia at large and other parts of the western empire. Britain is distinct compared with the Continent, and the frontier (accepting the profile from Hadrian's Wall as most representative of the entire frontier) is distinct from the rest of Britain and even more different from the Continent. The differences in the various profiles discussed above suggest changing circumstances in the northern frontier. The dominance of type 1, and secondary presence of type 3/4, suggests differing levels of production of the two types, which may relate to decreasing levels of contact between the frontier and central imperial authorities. The lack of type 5 in the frontier and the few examples of type 6 further reinforce such a conclusion, as does the considerably lower numbers of late Roman belt buckles and accessories relative to the numbers of these objects in southern England (see Coulston, this volume). This is not to say there were no links with continental imperial authorities, but the frequency and nature of such links had become more limited. Decreased levels of contact may correspond to fewer introductions of objects in use in continental frontiers.

The penannular brooches provide an interesting contrast. Dating evidence for these brooches is not as well defined, but on the basis of the discussion in the preceding section, the types that were certainly in production in the late Roman period – types D7 and E – are the most numerous. Perhaps the best dates for these types are from excavated contexts at Birdoswald and South Shields, which place them to between *c* AD 350 and *c* AD 400. Types F and G, where reliable dating evidence is available, are post-Roman in date. Thus, it is suggested that at the same time as contacts with continental authorities and materials were becoming more restricted – notably the second half of the 4th century – there was an opportunity for alternative sources of material, particularly that of the local frontier culture.

Penannular brooches were used throughout the Roman period, but they do not represent any significant proportion of a site brooch assemblage until the late Roman period, when fewer types of brooch were available. Crossbow brooches are arguably confined to an officer class, but the social status of penannular brooches is rarely commented on. Throughout most of the Roman period, penannular brooches may have been available for the 'common' soldier to wear, but this may have changed in the 4th century.

Considered in the *longue durée*, brooches may have become a prestige item over the course of the Roman period, associated with social rank and privilege. By the 4th century, there were very few new and current brooch forms available for use (compared with the 2nd century), and archaeological and art-historical evidence suggests that those available were worn by men and women of a high social status. Such a process may have applied to additional brooch forms, like the zoomorphic penannulars, and the significance of these brooches to social rank is clear in 9th-century Irish law (Nieke 1993). The social codification attached to brooches probably began in the Roman period. As such, the type D7 and E penannular brooches may be local frontier substitutes or alternatives to the developed crossbow brooch, further accounting for the decline in later forms of crossbow brooches. If this proposition can be accepted, then it can also be said that there is an increased incorporation of local or Romano-British expression in the *limitanei*.

Unfortunately, it is not possible to demonstrate 5th-century brooch use with much conviction, but it may be significant that known 5th-century and later deposits at Roman forts have produced type D7 and E penannulars and developed crossbow brooches, but not type F and G penannulars. Furthermore, there are no known crossbow brooches from the sites that produced the type F and G penannulars, suggesting that crossbow brooches had gone out of use. This may have been a simple circumstance of post-Roman fashion choice or loss of the ability to produce such objects, but it is more likely to be a conscious shift away from objects with Roman symbolism to objects with a 'British' association (see Halsall 2007 for further discussion and examples from across the former western empire). Extrapolating from this, the brooches support an interpretation of a transition from a late Roman frontier army to a number of warbands associated with Early Medieval kings in the 5th–6th century (Collins 2007; Wilmott 1997).

It is hoped that future discoveries, both incidental and archaeological, will support the conclusions drawn here, and that future research will considerably reinforce and/or challenge the above conclusions. Targeted excavations of late Roman cemeteries in the frontier, for example, would probably produce a considerable increase in the number of developed crossbow brooches. A cemetery excavation would further test the notion that while crossbow brooches are frequent objects in the frontier, late belt accessories are not. At Lankhills, for example, it is notable that most graves that had a crossbow brooch also had belt remains, including buckles, strap ends, belt stiffeners, and suspension hooks and loops (Clark 1979). Any graves with penannular brooches would be a further bonus, particularly if their discovery refined dating of the D series of penannulars and clarified their typological relationship to type E. Detailed excavation of a cemetery would also contribute to a greater understanding of the role of these brooches in various issues of identity – military, native, gender, and other aspects of social status. Finally, research into the relationships between numerous classes of evidence is the only way in which the late Roman to Early Medieval transition can be studied with any confidence. There has not been scope to do so within this paper, but the data and conclusions provided here may offer a stepping-stone for further research.

Abbreviations

CH   Chesters Museum
CM   Corbridge Museum
HER   Historic Environment Record
PAS   Portable Antiquities Scheme database
       (www.findsdatabase.org.uk)
TH   Tullie House
VM   Vindolanda Museum
YM   Yorkshire Museum

Appendix 7.1: Crossbow brooches by site

Adwick le Street, South Yorkshire
1. Copper-alloy type 1
    PAS SWYOR-19EED2
Barmby Moor, North Yorkshire
2. Copper-alloy type 3/4
    PAS YORYM-21BA04
Birdoswald, Cumbria
3. Copper-alloy type 3/4b
    Summerfield 1997a, no 60
4. Copper-alloy type 3/4d
Summerfield 1997b, no 61
5. Silver type 1
    Summerfield 1997b, no 4
Brigham, Cumbria
6. Copper-alloy type 3/4b
    TH 1909.5.2
Carlisle, Cumbria
7. Copper-alloy type 3/4
    Mackreth 1990, no 19
8. Copper-alloy type 3/4a
    Mackreth 1990, no 20
9. Copper-alloy type 3/4a
    Howard-Davis forthcoming, no 10
10. Copper-alloy type 1
    Howard-Davis forthcoming, no 7
11. Copper-alloy type 1
    Howard-Davis forthcoming, no 8
12. Copper-alloy type 1
    Howard-Davis forthcoming, no 9
Carrawburgh, Northumberland
13. Copper-alloy type 3/4a
    Allason-Jones and McKay 1985, no 48
Castlefield, Greater Manchester
14. Copper-alloy type 3/4

Watkin 1883
Castleford, West Yorkshire
15. Copper-alloy type 1
    Hilary Cool, pers comm
Catterick, North Yorkshire
16. Copper-alloy type 3/4a (site 433)
    Mackreth 2002, no 22
Chesters, Northumberland
17. Copper-alloy type 3/4b
    CH 945
18. Copper-alloy type 3/4d
    CH 946
19. Copper-alloy type 1
    CH 2371
Chorley, Lancashire
20. Copper-alloy type 3/4b
    PAS LANCUM-F1B9A4
Cleveland (no specific findspot)
21. Copper-alloy type 3/4b
    PAS NCL-F43624
Corbridge, Northumberland
22. Copper-alloy type 6i
    Snape 1993, no 83
23. Copper-alloy type 3/4b
    Snape 1993, no 84
24. Copper-alloy type 1
    Snape 1993, no 85
25. Copper-alloy type 3/4d
    Snape 1993, no 86
26. Copper-alloy type 3/4b
    Snape 1993, no 87
Dunnington, North Yorkshire
27. Copper-alloy type unknown
    PAS YORYM-B7DE01
Dunsforths, North Yorkshire
28. Copper-alloy type unknown
    PAS LVPL457
Erickstanebrae, Dumfries and Galloway
29. Gold type 2iii
    Curle 1932
Great Chesters, Northumberland
30. Copper-alloy type 3/4
    Allason-Jones 1996b, no 6
Halton Chesters, Northumberland
31. Copper-alloy type 1
    Allason-Jones forthcoming a, no 13
Hooton Pagnell, South Yorkshire
32. Copper-alloy type 3/4b
    PAS SWYOR-AB7D42
Housesteads, Northumberland
33. Copper-alloy type 1
    Wilkes 1961, no 1
34. Copper-alloy type 1
    Allason-Jones 2009, no 29
35. Copper-alloy type unknown
    Allason-Jones 2009, no 30
36. Copper-alloy type 2iii
    Allason-Jones 2009, no 31
37. Copper-alloy type unknown
    Allason-Jones 2009, no 32
38. Copper-alloy type 1
    Allason-Jones 2009, no 28
Lancaster, Lancashire
39. Copper-alloy type 1
    Webster 1988, no 5
Maryport, Cumbria
40. Copper-alloy type unknown
    Brown 1976
    Note: probably type 2 or 3/4
Moray Firth, Highlands
41. Gold type 6ii

Kent and Painter 1972, no 21
Newcastle, Tyne and Wear
42. Copper-alloy type unknown
Allason-Jones 2002, no 5
Piercebridge, Durham
43. Copper-alloy type 1
Butcher 2008, no 31
Poltross Burn, Cumbria
44. Copper-alloy type 2ii
Gibson and Simpson 1911, no 5
45. Silver type 1
Gibson and Simpson 1911, no 6
Priest Hutton, Lancashire
46. Copper-alloy type 3/4
PAS LVPL761
Quarry House Farm, Stockton-on-Tees
47. Gold type 6ii
Hunter forthcoming b, no 91
Ravenglass, Cumbria
48. Copper-alloy type 1
Olivier 1979, no 10
Seaton Carew, Hartlepool
49. Copper-alloy type 3/4A
Teesside HER no 712
Shorden Brae, Northumberland
50. Copper-alloy type 3/4c
Snape 1993, no 173
South Shields, Tyne and Wear
51. Copper-alloy type 1
Allason-Jones and Miket 1984, no 43
52. Copper-alloy type 3/4b
Allason-Jones and Miket 1984, no 44
53. Copper-alloy type 1
Allason-Jones and Miket 1984, no 45
54. Copper-alloy type 1
Allason-Jones and Miket 1984, no 49
55. Copper-alloy type 2i
Allason-Jones and Miket 1984, no 50
56. Copper-alloy type 1
Allason-Jones and Miket 1984, no 57
57. Copper-alloy type 2iii
Allason-Jones and Miket 1984, no 78
58. Copper-alloy type 2iii
Allason-Jones and Miket 1984, no 86
59. Copper-alloy type 2iii
Croom 1994, no 3
60. Copper-alloy type 2iii
Croom 1994, no 4
Upsettlington, Scottish Borders
61. Copper-alloy type 2i
Miket 2004, no 10
Vindolanda, Northumberland
62. Copper-alloy type 1
Snape 1993, no 209
63. Copper-alloy type 1
VM 788
64. Copper-alloy type 1
Bidwell 1985, VM 2827
65. Copper-alloy type 3/4b
VM 7678
Wallsend, Tyne and Wear
66. Copper-alloy type 1
Allason-Jones forthcoming b, no 30
67. Copper-alloy type 1
Allason-Jones forthcoming b
68. Copper-alloy type 2iii
Allason-Jones forthcoming b
Wincle, Cheshire
69. Gold type 1
Watkin 1886
Note: This brooch was included in the catalogue as a

brooch of interest, but it was found to the south of the
research area of this study.
York, North Yorkshire
70. Copper-alloy type 3/4d
YM YORYM 137.2
71. Copper-alloy type 1
YM YORYM H137.1
72. Copper-alloy type 1
YM YORYM 2003.230
73. Copper-alloy type 3/4b
YM YORYM 1068
74. Copper-alloy type 3/4b
YM YORYM 2001.12531

Appendix 7.2: Crossbow brooches by sub-type

Type 1
Adwick le Street (1)
Birdoswald (5)
Carlisle (10, 11, 12)
Castleford (15)
Chesters (19)
Corbridge (24)
Halton Chesters (31)
Housesteads (33, 34, 38)
Lancaster (39)
Piercebridge (43)
Poltross Burn (45)
Ravenglass (48)
South Shields (51, 53, 54, 56)
Vindolanda (62, 63, 64)
Wallsend (66, 67)
York (71, 72)
Type 2i
South Shields (55)
Type 2ii
Poltross Burn (44)
Type 2iii
Erickstanebrae (29)
Housesteads (36)
South Shields (57, 58, 59, 60)
Wallsend (68)
Type 3/4
Barmby Moor (2)
Birdoswald (3, 4)
Brigham (6)
Carlisle (7, 8, 9)
Carrawburgh (13)
Castlefield (14)
Catterick (16)
Chesters (17, 18)
Chorley (20)
Cleveland (21)
Corbridge (23, 25, 26)
Great Chesters (30)
Hooton Pagnell (32)
Priest Hutton (46)
Seaton Carew (49)
Shorden Brae (50)
South Shields (52)
Vindolanda (65)
York (70, 73, 74)
Type 5
No sites
Type 6i
Corbridge (22)
Type 6ii
Moray Firth (41)
Quarry House Farm (47)

Unknown
>   Dunnington (27)
>   Dunsforths (28)
>   Housesteads (35, 37)
>   Maryport (40)
>   Newcastle (42)

Appendix 7.3: Penannular brooches by site

An * indicates the object was from a furnished 'Anglo-Saxon' grave.

Aldborough, North Yorkshire
1. Copper-alloy type E
    Bishop 1996, no 344
Beadlam, North Yorkshire
2. Copper-alloy type E
    Neal 1996, no 12
3. Copper-alloy type F
    Neal 1996, no 13
Binchester, Durham
4. Copper-alloy type unknown
    Mackreth forthcoming, no 16
Birdoswald, Cumbria
5. Copper-alloy type E
    Summerfield 1997a, no 69
6. Copper-alloy type E
    Summerfield 1997a, no 71
7. Copper-alloy type E
    Summerfield 1997a, no 72
8. Copper-alloy type D7
    Summerfield 1997a, no 73
9. Iron type D7
    Summerfield 1997a, no 74
10. Copper-alloy type E
    Summerfield 1997b, no 2
Carlisle, Cumbria
11. Copper-alloy type E
    Howard-Davis forthcoming, no 9
Catterick, North Yorkshire
12. Copper-alloy type F*
    PAS NCL-A31A61
13. Copper-alloy type E
    Kilbride-Jones 1980, no 14
Chesters, Northumberland
14. Copper-alloy type E
    CH 2051
15. Copper-alloy type E
    Kilbride-Jones 1980, no 16
Driffield, East Yorkshire
16. Copper-alloy type G*
    Dickinson 1982, no 12
Edinburgh, Midlothian
17. Copper-alloy type E
    Kilbride-Jones 1980, no 19
Eskmeals, Cumbria
18. Copper-alloy type F
    TH 1955.15
Goldsborough, North Yorkshire
19. Copper-alloy type E
    Cool 2000a, no 10
Housesteads, Northumberland
20. Copper-alloy type E
    CM 81072078
21. Copper-alloy type E
    Allason-Jones 2009, no 25
Huntcliff, Cleveland
22. Copper-alloy type unknown
    Hornsby and Stanton 1912

23. Copper-alloy type unknown
    Hornsby and Stanton 1912
    Note: Both of the above were unillustrated and there was no detailed description provided. However, their discovery during excavations of the late 4th-century coastal fortlet makes them worth mentioning.
Kirkby Thore, Cumbria
24. Copper-alloy type E
    TH 1951.63.11.1
25. Copper-alloy type F
    Kilbride-Jones 1980, no 24
Littlethorpe, North Yorkshire
26. Silver type E
    Ager 2008, no 99
Londesborough, North Yorkshire
27. Copper-alloy type G*
    Dickinson 1982, no 17
Longfaugh, Midlothian
28. Copper-alloy type F
    Kilbride-Jones 1980, no 2
Luce Sands, Dumfries and Galloway
29. Copper-alloy type G
    Dickinson 1982, no 19
Maelsgate, Cumbria
30. Copper-alloy type F1
    TH 1953.22
Newby Wiske, North Yorkshire
31. Copper-alloy type G
    PAS NCL-030777
North Berwick, East Lothian
32. Copper-alloy type F
    Kilbride-Jones 1980, no 153
Norton, Stockton-on-Tees
33. Copper-alloy type G*
    Sherlock and Welch 1992, no 11
34. Copper-alloy type G*
    Sherlock and Welch 1992, no 2
Old Church Brampton, Cumbria
35. Copper-alloy type F
    TH 2002.1787
Piercebridge, Durham
36. Copper-alloy type E
    Butcher 2008, no 41
37. Silver type E
    Butcher 2008, no 42
38. Copper-alloy type D7
    Butcher 2008, no 46
39. Copper-alloy type D7
    Butcher 2008, no 47
Preston Tower, East Lothian
40. Copper-alloy type F
    Kilbride-Jones 1980, no 151
South Shields, Tyne and Wear
41. Copper-alloy type D7
    Croom 1994, no 9
42. Copper-alloy type D7
    Croom 1994, no 10
43. Copper-alloy type E
    Croom 1994, no 11
44. Copper-alloy type E
    Croom 1994, no 16
45. Copper-alloy type E
    Allason-Jones and Miket 1984, no 115
46. Copper-alloy type E
    Allason-Jones and Miket 1984, no 116
47. Copper-alloy type E
    Allason-Jones and Miket 1984, no 117
48. Copper-alloy type E
    Allason-Jones and Miket 1984, no 118
Staxton, North Yorkshire
49. Copper-alloy type F*

White 1988, no 7
Traprain Law, East Lothian
50. Copper-alloy type F
    Kilbride-Jones 1980, no 1
51. Copper-alloy type F
    Kilbride-Jones 1980, no 4
52. Copper-alloy type F
    Kilbride-Jones 1980, no 5
Vindolanda, Northumberland
53. Copper-alloy type E
    VM 6
54. Copper-alloy type E
    VM 7031
55. Copper-alloy type E
    VM 11756
56. Copper-alloy type E
    Snape 1993, no 231
57. Copper-alloy type E
    VM 7348
58. Copper-alloy type E
    VM 1395
59. Copper-alloy type E
    VM 7046
Wallsend, Tyne and Wear
60. Copper-alloy type E
    Allason-Jones forthcoming b, no 125
Wooler, Northumberland
61. Copper-alloy type G
    Dickinson 1982, no 30
Yarm, Cleveland
62. Copper-alloy type F(*?)
    Brown 1977
York, North Yorkshire
63. Copper-alloy type unknown (terminals missing)
    Butcher 1995: no 6
64. Copper-alloy type F
    Kilbride-Jones 1980, no 7
65. Copper-alloy type D7
    YM YORYM H2060.1
66. Copper-alloy type D7
    YM YORYM H2060.2

Appendix 7.4: Penannular brooches by type

Fowler E
    Aldborough (1)
    Beadlam (2)
    Birdoswald (5, 6, 7, 10)
    Carlisle (11)
    Catterick (13)
    Chesters (14, 15)
    Edinburgh (17)
    Goldsborough (19)
    Housesteads (20, 21)
    Kirkby Thore (24)
    Piercebridge (36, 37)
    South Shields (43, 44, 45, 46, 47, 48)
    Vindolanda (53, 54, 55, 56, 57, 58, 59)
    Wallsend (60)
Fowler F
    Beadlam (3)
    Catterick (12)
    Eskmeals (18)
    Kirby Thore (25)
    Longfaugh (28)

    Maelsgate (30)
    North Berwick (32)
    Old Church Brampton (35)
    Preston Tower (40)
    Staxton (49)
    Traprain Law (50, 51, 52)
    Yarm (62)
    York (64)
Fowler D7
    Birdoswald (8, 9)
    Piercebridge (38, 39)
    South Shields (41, 42)
    York (65, 66)
Fowler G
    Driffield (16)
    Londesborough (27)
    Luce Sands (29)
    Newby Wiske (31)
    Norton (33, 34)
    Wooler (61)
Unknown
    Binchester (4)
    Huntcliff (22, 23)
    York (63)

Appendix 7.5: Brooches by material (other than copper alloy)

Gold
    29. Erickstanebrae Crossbow type 2iii
    41. Moray Firth Crossbow type 6ii
    47. Quarry House Farm Crossbow type 6ii
    69. Wincle Crossbow type 1
Silver
    5. Birdoswald Crossbow type 1
    44. Poltross Burn Crossbow type 1
    26. Littlethorpe Penannular type E
    37. Piercebridge Penannular type E
Iron
    9. Birdoswald Penannular type D7

Notes

1   This paper would not have been possible without the generous information and advice provided by a number of individuals as local experts, collection curators and/or authors of unpublished reports: Lindsay Allason-Jones (Newcastle University); Katherine Bearcock (York Museums Trust, Yorkshire Museum); Barbara Birley (Vindolanda Trust); Hilary Cool (Barbican Research Associates); Alex Croom (Tyne and Wear Museums); Iain Ferris; Chris Howard-Davis (Oxford Archaeology); Fraser Hunter (National Museums of Scotland); David Mason (Durham County Council); Sonja Marzinzik (British Museum); Frances McIntosh (PAS); Tim Padley (Tullie House Museum); Georgina Plowright (Corbridge and Chesters Museums), and Peter Rowe (Tees Archaeology). All mistakes remain my own.

8   Personal appearance   *Lindsay Allason-Jones*

The question that this paper addresses is, at first sight, a simple one: what did people look like in the frontier zone in the 4th and early 5th centuries AD? This question has proved surprisingly difficult to answer, however, as the finds can only provide us with partial evidence and the sources that are used in the earlier centuries to answer a similar question are notable by their absence.

In the 1st century AD there are a few images that provide pictures of individual people. A good example is Flavinus, a cavalryman of the *ala Petriana*, whose tombstone, showing him in the traditional pose of a rider trampling down his enemy, is now in Hexham Abbey (*CSIR* I.1 no 68). These images, however, are invariably of military personnel. In the 2nd and early 3rd century there are some tombstones that depict non-military men, for example Victor, the freedman of Numerianus at South Shields (*CSIR* I.1, no 248), and the anonymous man, now sadly lacking his head, from Housesteads (*CSIR* I.6, no 202), but the majority of the figural tombstones of this period from the Wall area are of women: Regina (*CSIR* I.1, no 247), Aurelia Aureliana (*CSIR* I.6, no 49), and others, and these vary in the level of detail shown.

It is possible that the tombstones were never intended to provide recognisable images of what these people actually looked like, but were stylised, generalised depictions – though in the case of Aurelia Aureliana artistic licence has hardly been applied kindly, to the extent that for some years antiquaries were confused as to whether this depicted a man or a woman and this resulted in her being referred to as the Bearded Lady of Carlisle (Hill 1974, 271–5). Nor are the depictions of children inclined to provide identifiable personal details: both Ertola (*CSIR* I.1, no 71) and Pervica (*CSIR* I.6, no 216), for example, are very stylised in their appearance and even the children of Flavia Augustina at York provide only a few clues as to what the well-dressed child in the North was wearing at the time (*CSIR* I.3, no 39). From these tombstones, however, we can presume that the civilian men in the frontier zone in the 2nd and 3rd centuries wore short tunics with cloaks over them, that children also wore tunics to the knee, and that the women mostly wore longer tunics with over-tunics and shawls. Some of the tombstones show that a wide range of hairstyles was worn and accessories, such as fans, were also used (*CSIR* I.6, no 497).

By the late 3rd and 4th centuries the fashion for pictorial tombstones had been abandoned. In fact, inscribed memorials of all types seem to have fallen out of popularity with only a few, such as the tombstone of Brigomaglos, surviving to give us the names of individuals (*RIB* 1722). Quite why there is this shift from tombstones with pictures to plain ones, and then to an almost complete lack of memorials, is not clear. It may be that when Christianity became the official religion of the empire the concept of a person's existence being recorded on stone lost approval. Certainly the stone remembering Aurelia Aia, wife of Marcus of the century of Obsequens, from Carvoran, has little in the way of embellishments – it is only from the fact that she came from Salonas in modern day Croatia, the first Christian city on mainland Europe, and that the inscription includes the possibly Christian epithet *sine macula*, that is, she lived 'without any blemish', that we can postulate that she was Christian, although the inclusion of the pagan 'DM' *dis manibus* (to the shades) may suggest that her conversion was not wholehearted or that her husband had not converted to Christianity (*RIB* 1828).

It is also possible that this move away from carved stone memorials was a result of the influx of *numeri* and other less regular troops along the frontier. These units, such as the *numerus Hnaudifridi* (*RIB* 1576), do not appear to have been recruited as individuals into the Roman army, but seem to have been brought in from the edge of the empire as groups under their own leaders. Such soldiers do not seem to have worn recognisably Roman armour or been organised according to recognised Roman precepts but to have had their own way of doing things. They also appear to have brought their families, often extended families, with them. When their tour of duty was over it is possible that they would have gone back from whence they came *en masse*. These people probably had no tradition of inscribed memorials and, as they were part of a tribal group, they may not have felt that they needed to leave behind in Britain a reminder of their existence, as within the group they would be remembered.

If there are no surviving portraits in stone to tell us what people looked like in the 4th century, do the small finds provide any clues?

Hairstyles

Throughout Roman history hairstyles were the element of personal appearance that changed the most. Ovid commented, with a slight hint of exasperation, that it would be easier to count the acorns on an oak tree than to list the different hairstyles in fashion in the 1st century AD (*Ars Amatoria* III, 149). He recommended that women should wear hairstyles that best suited the shape of their face (*Ars Amatoria* III, 140), but many women appar-

Fig 8.1 A nummus of Helena, showing the hairstyle of the early 4th century. © PAS, SOM-1B08E4

ently preferred to follow the dictates of fashion. The visit of the empress Julia Domna to Britain in AD 208–11 led to the Syrian style of dressing the hair being adopted throughout Britain. In this style the hair hung in crimped waves down the sides of the face and the back hair was carried up in a large roll, which may have been interlaced with ribbons. In the mid-3rd century a variation on this style called the 'helmet' style was adopted, as can be seen on the tombstone of Aelia Aeliana from York (*CSIR* I.3, no 40) as well as the Fishergate head from York (*CSIR* I.3, no 71). This is the last female hairstyle for which we have sculptural evidence from Britain. So what happened afterwards? Did the women of Roman Britain continue to copy the styles of the reigning empresses, using recently minted coins as their style guides to the latest ideas? If so, we might expect Helena's hairstyle, with a thick plait coiled high on the head (Fig 8.1), to have been common, but this style would have required several hairpins to keep it in position and the bodies of 4th-century date found throughout the province show a remarkable lack of objects associated with them that could have been used to confine or pin the hair. Hilary Cool has pointed out 'the plummeting position of hairpins' in the tables of grave finds through the 4th century (Cool 2000a, 48). She went on to identify hairpins in the mid-4th century as forming 41% of the total assemblages but by the late 4th century they represent only 10%, and this figure includes the pig's fibula pins which are usually dated to the 5th to 7th century AD.

Cool also referred to a pig's fibula pin from Filey, but seemed doubtful as to whether it could be classed as a hairpin (2000a, 48). Alex Croom (pers comm) has recently identified four of these items in the various South Shields assemblages. These would work if a

basic pin were needed to keep the hair up but they are indeed basic; they are not very attractive and it is unlikely that many people would make and use such a pin when it would have taken very little further trouble to produce a more attractive specimen, such as had been used in earlier centuries. It is possible they were used as cloak pins, possibly in association with metal rings, achieving an effect similar to that of penannular brooches (Lovett 1904, 15–23), which, as is discussed by Collins (this volume), were very popular in the 4th and 5th centuries.

The excavations at Catterick provide evidence that there may have been localised fashions in hairstyles as this site produced numerous hairpins, including several examples of composite pins with bone shanks and jet heads (Fig 1.2) (Cool 2002a, 26). These have been found at York and South Shields (Allason-Jones 1996a; Allason-Jones and Miket 1984, Section 7), which suggests that this was a northern style; the examples from Catterick confirm their late 4th-century date. Unusual hairstyles may also have been seen at Brougham (Cool 2004, 466).

Other jet objects that may have been worn in the hair in the 4th century are those which have been designated as 'massive pins'. Two examples were found under the skull of a woman in a stone coffin during the Railway Excavations of 1874 in York (Allason-Jones 1996a, nos 281 and 282). Originally these were identified as spindles, but this is not a convincing identification as one has a deep running cable motif and the other has a decorated octagonal section. Also the shank of no 282 expands away from its head, whilst no 281 has a small hole at its narrow end, which suggests that it had an attached terminal. It is possible that these came from a hairstyle, similar to that seen on coins of the Empress Sabina and her mother Matidia, in which the back hair was rolled round a shank. The early Christian writer Tertullian complained about women who 'add to your weight some kind of rolls or shield bosses to be piled upon your necks' (*On Female Dress* VIII). Sabina and Tertullian were both living in the 2nd century AD and this use of large amounts of jet in York tends to be 4th-century in date so the proof is not positive, but the position in which the two items were found does suggest a hairstyle-related artefact.

To achieve a tidy hairstyle one needs a comb. Recently there has been a lively debate about the use of double-sided antler combs (Cooke and Crummy 2000). Nick Cooke was of the opinion that these can be dated to the late 4th century and has pointed out that if found in burials they are invariably placed by the head and mostly in female graves. Cooke also pointed out that they are more common in Britain than elsewhere in the empire; indeed at Poundbury, after coins, they are the most ubiquitous of the grave-goods (Farwell and Molleson 1993). Giles Clarke, who excavated at Lankhills, Winchester, described these combs under the heading of 'equipment' (Clarke 1979). Nick Cooke believes that they were worn in the hair, but combs designed to be worn in the hair are always curved to fit the shape of the head; if they aren't, they fall out. The combs under discussion are long and straight. They also have teeth of different thicknesses on either side of the central bars, like a modern nit comb, and there would be no reason for this if they were intended to be worn, rather than used to comb the hair. Nina Crummy has also pointed out that there is little point in decorating the central bars at all, and certainly not on both sides, if the main purpose of the combs was to be worn (Cooke and Crummy 2000). Triangular combs, of which there appear to be no examples from the frontier zone, are better designed to be worn in the hair (MacGregor 1985, 83).

The 4th-century double-sided combs have three types of end plate: the simple, plain sort; those which have sinuous ends and can be described as 'slightly elaborate'; and those which have zoomorphic decoration, usually in the form of horses' heads, dolphins and owls. The horses' heads and the dolphins are common zoomorphic decorations throughout the Roman period, particularly on buckles, but the owls are less common. The example of a double-sided comb from South Shields is of Type 2 (Allason-Jones and Miket 1984, no 2.40).

From about AD 326 onwards even the coins fail to give us any clues as to women's appearance as empresses wear diadems and head-dresses in order, as Alex Croom has expressed it, 'to distinguish themselves from ordinary people' (Croom 2000). However, this may not have been as big a blow to the fashion conscious as might at first appear since it became the fashion to cover one's hair, whether in the house or outside, with a veil. This may not have been an entirely voluntary fashion as Christianity was by this time the official religion of the empire and Tertullian was not the only early Christian writer with firm views about women. St Paul in his first letter to the Corinthians (11.1–12) stated that a woman should wear her hair covered as a symbol of her husband's authority over her. In the late 4th century the light veil was often replaced by an enveloping cap. If this was someone's usual day-to-day wear there would be little point in having a complicated hairstyle, with or without decorations, underneath and it is possible that most women's hair was simply coiled under the cap or pinned with very basic pins.

Men were not immune from the vagaries of fashion. Sculpture elsewhere in the empire suggests that by the late 3rd century the most popular haircut was what today would be called a crew cut, with a very short beard, almost designer stubble, which was trimmed on the neck but not shaved away entirely. From the time of Constantine, however, being completely clean shaven seems to have been preferred, with the hairstyles reverting to those of the early empire with short curls brushed forward. In the 4th century the curls disappeared, to be replaced by straight hair worn in what might be described as a 'bowl-cut'; this hairstyle continued for the rest of the period of the Roman occupation of Britain.

These styles, of course, are what would have been worn by those men who followed the Roman, by which is meant the Italian/Mediterranean, fashions. What is unclear is what was being worn by the *limitanei*, who may have preferred the hairstyles of their recent or ancestral homelands. After all, it can be postulated, from the evidence on Trajan's Column, that in the early imperial period Hamian archers preferred wearing their hair long, and it is possible that units, such as the *numerus Hnaudifridi,* may have worn Swabian knots or other styles associated with specific tribes.

Jewellery

Ear-rings have invariably been seen as being worn by women but, as has been discussed elsewhere, there was nothing in the Roman military law manuals to stop serving soldiers from wearing ear-rings, if they came from parts of the empire where men wore such ornaments (Allason-Jones 1995, 25–6). Unfortunately, to know if soldiers on Hadrian's Wall in the later period reflected their tribal origins by wearing ear-rings would require more knowledge about the dress codes of the regions they were recruited from than is currently available.

Certainly for the women, some of the plainer ear-ring types were popular for many generations. Type 3 ear-rings, for example, which have interlocking ends and from which pendants could be hung, start in the Bronze Age, continue through the Iron Age and the Roman period, and are still going strong in the Anglo-Saxon period. During the Roman period they are predominantly 3rd-century in date but examples have been found in 4th-century contexts (Allason-Jones 1989a).

Type 4 ear-rings, that is penannular rings of rectangular-sectioned twisted wire, are of 4th-century date and, as far as can be stated (given the small numbers involved) are confined to the military north. Type 5 ear-rings, made from two strands of twisted wire, are more widely spread, both geographically and chronologically, appearing from the 1st century to the 4th. Type 6, however, which only differs from Type 5 in that it involves three strands of twisted wire rather than two, has a date bias towards the 4th century and is predominantly found in civilian contexts.

More elaborate ear-rings of Types 13 and 14 are known in the region. One variant of Type 13a was found in a 4th-century context at Birdoswald fort (Wilmott 1997, 282, no 77). Several examples of Type 14 have come from the Brougham cemeteries (Fig 8.2) but examples are also known from Brougham, Bewcastle and Vindolanda (Allason-Jones 1989a, nos 4, 10, 11, and 69). These consist of hollow rosettes with pendant leaf-shapes, also hollow. One example from Brougham comes from a 4th-century context; elsewhere in the empire they are almost always from 4th-century contexts (Ergil 1983, no 120).

Beaded necklaces were worn throughout the

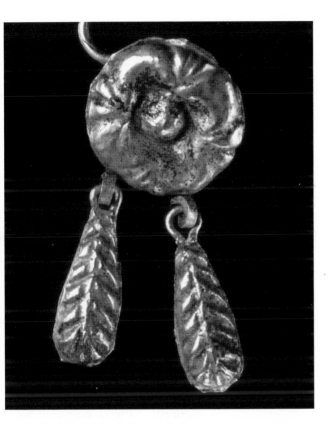

Fig 8.2 A Type 14 gold ear-ring from Brougham.
© *Newcastle University*

Roman period, although we have had to adjust our ideas about who was wearing them following the discovery of the Catterick *gallus* wearing a jet bead necklace (Cool 2002a). The evidence of the finds suggests there was certainly a sharp rise in the use of jet and cannel coal for beads in the 4th century. This is particularly noticeable at York, where it might be linked to the cult of Bacchus. Unfortunately, few of the beaded necklaces or bracelets from York come from good dated contexts so this development may have been earlier.

In Margaret Guido's catalogue it is noticeable that the glass beads she places in later contexts rarely fit into her typology (Guido 1978). This is so noticeable that Hilary Cool has suggested that 'if one has a collection of Roman beads amongst which there are examples that cannot easily be "Guidoised" the possibility that one is dealing with material which comes from a very late site should be considered' (2000a, 50).

Black material was also popular for finger rings in the 4th century. Two examples come from the Wellington Row excavations at York (Allason-Jones 1996a, 36–7, nos 162 and 165). Two are known from the late coastal fortlets at Goldsborough and Filey (Hornsby and Laverick 1932). Goldsborough has also produced several raw lumps of jet, which hint at someone stationed there using his off-duty moments to scavenge for jet on the beach in order to supplement his income; possibly he was saving up until he could afford another finger ring.

Bronze and iron finger rings have been found in 4th-century contexts at Vindolanda but these rarely hold intaglios (Birley and Greene 2006). In fact, of 61 intaglios from Vindolanda only one can be assigned to a 4th-century context. Again this may be because there are fewer people in the area with a Roman understanding of what an intaglio is for or fewer people who were qualified to wear one. This lack may further emphasise how different life had become on the frontier by the 4th century, with less need for sealed documents and letters within the military bureaucracy.

Other types of finger rings are difficult to date with accuracy but a silver ring with a protruding panel, similar at first glance to a key ring which was found at Watercrook (Potter 1979, fig 84, no 1), has been dated to the late 3rd to 4th century on continental parallels. This finger ring, another silver example and a gold example from Corbridge (Charlesworth 1961, 16–17) all have openwork and relief decoration on the panel representing the stylised motif of two squatting felines drinking from a central vessel.

Brooches are considered elsewhere in this volume, with Collins discussing the larger crossbow brooches (Fig 7.1) and small penannulars (Fig 7.6). We might presume that the crossbows were worn to keep cloaks fastened, whilst the penannulars were more probably used to secure tunics. On the whole, late Roman penannulars were not very robust and this, coupled with their small size, would make them less than effective in securing the thick material of the average cloak. Whatever these two sorts of brooches were used for, however, it is noticeable that the more decorative small brooches of previous centuries, such as those in the shape of running animals, shoes, and decorated discs, have disappeared before the 4th century. People do not appear to have been dependent on brooches for securing their clothing, but equally they appear to have been less inclined to use brooches for sheer adornment. It is possible that some of the earlier brooches may have been intended as badges, signifying membership of a cult or a guild; as Christianity became dominant, these may have become increasingly inappropriate.

On the other hand, metal pins do become more evident. Elizabeth Fowler's work on penannular brooches also investigated these pins (1964). Type E pins were considered to have been a combination of the swan's neck pin of the Iron Age and the decoration on D4 and D5 penannular brooches. The majority of these have a simple rounded head, some with a dimple which may or may not have held red enamel. The rest are more angular, with well-engraved zoomorphic heads. The round-headed type E pins appear to have started to be manufactured in the late 2nd or early 3rd century, as at Traprain Law (Fowler 1964, fig 2, no 1). The squarer examples developed in the late 3rd century and early 4th century and carried on into the 5th and 6th centuries; examples have been found at Traprain Law, Chesters, Corbridge, Halton Chesters, and Newstead (Fowler 1964, fig 2). A new type E pin, with a chip-carved head with a dimple drilled into

Fig 8.3   Three views of the head of a silver handpin from Denton. © *Newcastle University*

two faces, has recently been recognised amongst the material excavated at the site of the Roman fort at Newcastle upon Tyne (unpublished), and there is another example from Vindolanda (Bidwell 1985, fig 42, no 44).

The projecting ring-headed pin was a characteristic type in the Scottish Iron Age and carried on through the centuries in a series of developments. Stevenson mentions that the heads of these pins were used to decorate pottery found in both brochs and wheelhead structures in the 3rd to 7th centuries (1955, 293). An example from South Shields fort is less substantial than the ring-headed pins discussed by Stevenson and may not fit into the series (Allason-Jones and Miket 1984, no 3.534).

Halton Chesters has a produced a pin which Fowler (1964, 123) considered to be a 'degeneration from the true bead and corrugated type of pin'. This type was originally dated to the 1st century BC but Stevenson redated them to the 4th century AD (1955). Unfortunately, few have been found in a context which can confirm or deny this dating. Fowler accepted the Halton Chesters pin as being of 4th-century date, on the grounds that 3rd- and 4th-century coins had been found in the same area (1964, 126).

During the excavations at Denton in the 1990s, the head of a silver 'handpin' was discovered (Fig

8.3). Such pins are traditionally dated to the 6th and 7th centuries, but as Colleen Batey has pointed out, a mould for a similar pin was found in a 3rd-century context at North Uist (in Bidwell and Watson 1996, 50–2; see also Gavin and Newman 2007). The Denton example was found in post-Roman ploughsoil, south of Hadrian's Wall.

Fowler's conclusions from her survey of penannular brooches and pins were that 'all the accepted "Dark Age" types of ornament were in existence during the 4th century' (1964, 133). This, coupled with the long survival of some of the 4th-century types of beads, may suggest that our dating presumptions need to be reassessed. What is interesting, however, is that in all the discussions of these pins, there is little reference to what they were used for and by whom. It is unlikely that they were intended to be worn in the hair: although usually decorated on the back, the heads are clearly made to be seen from one direction only. Fowler refers to them as both dress pins and dress ornaments. If it is accepted that a dress pin serves the function of securing cloth, while a dress ornament is simply an item that can be attached anywhere to add a decorative element, then the length of the shanks suggests that these were practical dress pins. What is not clear from the contexts of any of the surviving examples, however,

Fig 8.4 A selection of jet hairpins from South Shields. © Newcastle University

is whether they were worn by men or women or by a particular section of society. Do these reveal what everyone was wearing, or were they the accessories of a limited elite?

Cool has stated that there was a major change in women's appearance during the second half of the 4th century (2000a). She based this conclusion on the proportions of bracelets to hairpins shown in the statistics from Segontium in Wales and Barnsley Park in Gloucestershire, but the small find assemblages from the northern military zone seem to concur with her conclusions.

In the mid-4th century the bracelet assemblages tend to be about 50:50 jet or shale versus bronze. In York this statistic may be biased by the number of black bracelets found in graves but it is noticeable that the number of black bracelets from South Shields is about the same as that from York. On the evidence of half-finished pieces and raw unworked blocks, it does appear that there was a jet/shale workshop at South Shields (Allason-Jones and Miket 1984, Section 7). We have no idea if the bracelets were excavated from this workshop or came from graves or from the *vicus*, but the sheer quantity which has survived makes it clear that the women of the frontier were wearing black bracelets in the mid-4th century. By the end of the 4th century, however, the number of black bracelets drops noticeably whilst the number of copper-alloy examples grows.

Bone bracelets remain rare but are more noticeable in the later 4th century than before. There is one example from Birdoswald and five from Vindolanda, all of which, bar one, come from a 4th-century context (Wilmott 1997, 272; Birley and Greene 2006, 137, 150–1). It is likely that a good trawl through the surviving bone assemblages from older excavations along the Wall would produce quite a few more of these, as fragments can easily be missed. Glass

bracelets had disappeared from the jewellery boxes of the north of England by the late 2nd century.

Cool has remarked that whilst precious metal bracelets had been worn during the early Roman period, 'the habit of wearing copper-alloy bracelets did not spread widely until the 4th century' (2000a, 49). The present writer is of the opinion that copper-alloy bracelets made their appearance on Hadrian's Wall much earlier but it is undeniable that numbers do rise markedly in the later period. So many were found at Piercebridge, for example, that it was postulated that their presence indicated a temple of healing as there was a distinct concentration of their findspots and bracelets were very popular offerings to deities linked to female health (Allason-Jones in Cool and Mason 2008).

Two basic sorts of copper-alloy bracelets can be found in the 4th century: those made of twisted strands of wire and the basic strip bracelets with incised or chip-carved decoration and hook-and-eye fastenings. The cable-twist bracelets are similar to the cable-twist ear-rings mentioned earlier and it is possible that they were worn in sets. Evidence from grave assemblages in York suggests that a woman might own quite a few of these and that they were probably worn in groups; this would, of course, affect the numbers found. Cool has identified a slight change in the proportions of cable-twist bracelets to strip bangles through the 4th century (2000a, 49). In the mid-4th century she found a 1:1 ratio, but by the late 4th century the ratio changes to 1:3. Again, the Catterick assemblage has evidence of localised fashions as the torc twisted bracelets, which elsewhere are quite rare, are at Catterick as common as the cable-twist bracelets in the mid- to late 4th century (Cool 2002a, 26).

So, two major changes might be postulated in the appearance of women in the late 4th century. Firstly, there is an increase in black jewellery, rather than coloured (Fig 8.4). Whether this jewellery was made of jet, shale, cannel coal or detrital coal seems to have been irrelevant, although it is interesting that analysis shows that an appreciable amount of the raw material for these items was coming from north of Hadrian's Wall even at this late period (Allason-Jones and Jones 2001). Clearly a mere military frontier wasn't going to get in the way of trade in the essential ingredients of fashionable jewellery. Secondly, there seems to have been an increase in the amount of cheaper jewellery worn. In the south we may be forgiven for imagining from the famous jewellery hoards such as Hoxne, that everyone was either wearing gold jewellery or hoarding it (Johns 1996). In the north, the singular lack of the precious metal hoards found in the south of the province seems to suggest there was little interest in gold and silver jewellery, but the number of bronze bracelets found may indicate that most women would have been heard coming from some distance – they would have looked different from their mothers and grandmothers but they would also have sounded different, as their bracelets rattled.

Clothing

In the south of Britain wall paintings and mosaics occasionally provide information about the colour of the clothing worn. Wall paintings at Lullingstone villa, in particular, depict men wearing tunics with decorative bands of contrasting colours (Davey and Ling 1981, no 22). Unfortunately, we have no substantial wall paintings surviving in the North; nor was there ever a habit of mosaic flooring in the area, probably because no purchaser was willing to go to the expense and disruption of having a figured mosaic floor laid when there was every likelihood that they might be sent to another posting before the floor was finished or before they had had much use out of it.

Analysis of fragments of cloth found in Carlisle and Vindolanda indicates that a wide range of colours was used (Allason-Jones 2005, 101). At Vindolanda, the local bedstraw produced a good clear red, similar to the madder from Gaul, whilst lichen found in the neighbourhood will provide a purple as good as any derived from the expensive imported orchil. Unfortunately, these textile fragments all come from early contexts and none categorically provides evidence for the use of coloured materials in the 4th century. It might be presumed that, if dyestuffs were available locally, most of the population would have wished to wear coloured clothes but if there were appreciable numbers of Christians in the area that might not necessarily be true. The early Christian fathers were opposed to the wearing of coloured clothing, the colours of wool and linen in their natural state being considered to be quite good enough; Tertullian went so far as to aver that if God had wanted people to wear purple and sky-blue clothes He would have created purple and sky-blue sheep (*On Female Dress* VIII).

The actual garments worn probably didn't change in any particularly noticeable way as both men and women will have continued to wear variations on a tunic. However, there was obviously no need for chained brooches to hold women's tunics together as there had been in the 2nd and 3rd centuries, which suggests that in the 4th century there were slightly different designs. In Rome, the clothing of the emperors and empresses altered to more elaborate dress. For example, a type of decorated toga, called a *trabea*, was worn by the male ruling classes from the mid-4th century onwards but this was to set them apart and would have had little impact on the day-to-day dress of the provincial civilian populations (Croom 2000). There is evidence that men and women from the 3rd century onwards wore a long-sleeved tunic called a *dalmaticus* (Hartley *et al* 2006, 162–5). This often had strips of decoration up the front and down the back. It was worn unbelted and women took advantage of this to wear their skirts shorter than before. Other women wore a girdle high up under the bust. Over this might be worn a new kind of mantle, again with heavily embroidered strips. We are still faced, however, with the problem that all the depictions tend to be far distant from the Wall and if there were large numbers of men, women and children coming to the area from the edges of the north-western provinces would they necessarily be wearing the styles fashionable in the Mediterranean? Throughout Roman history there is a discernible tendency for people to be influenced by their tribal norms when deciding what to wear. German men wore trousers in the 1st century AD and it is likely that they went on wearing trousers. Women wore bonnets if they came from a tribe which wore bonnets and there is no evidence that this changed (Wild 1968).

And here we have the crux of the matter. There is no evidence. Most of the fabric samples from the North are mere scraps and tend to be from early contexts. The sites on the northern frontier have not produced the complete garments found at such sites as Qsar Ibrim in Egypt or even the tunics and socks from Martres-des-Veyre in France. This limited evidence is also to be seen in the shoes. Through her assessment of shoes found across the empire, Carol van Driel-Murray has shown that nailing on the soles of shoes became sparser in the 3rd century and had all but died out in the 4th century (van Driel-Murray 1987). This would have impacted on the sound that people made as they walked around their homes or on the street. A great number of shoes have been found at Vindolanda but, once again, these tend to come from earlier contexts and there is little to show what 4th-century footwear on the Wall looked like.

The famous ivory diptych of Stilicho, a man who had a considerable impact on the garrisoning of Roman Britain at the beginning of the 5th century, shows him with his wife and son (see Frontispiece). Sadly, other than Stilicho's cloak brooch, there is little about his personal appearance that would survive the archaeological process (Fig 1.4). His son, Eucherius, wears a datable brooch but again lacks other accessories which could be dated or even found in excavations. His wife Serena offers a more useful assemblage, although her clothing would have to be found complete in an archaeological context for its pattern to be datable. Her hairstyle is also confusing as it is unclear whether what is visible is a complex hairstyle or a head-dress. She is wearing elaborate ear-rings and a large two-strand necklace, all of which would survive in the ground and be identifiable and datable; none would be out of place on the northern frontier. Her girdle clasp and fittings, however, are particularly interesting as it is quite likely that if these were found at a fort on Hadrian's Wall they would be identified as harness fittings or part of a military assemblage.

Flavius Stilicho was a Vandal by birth who became regent to Theodosius's sons and married Theodosius's niece. His career proves that being a barbarian was no barrier to advancement in the Roman Empire. But when this very detailed, monochrome image is used as evidence for personal appearance in the 5th century AD, can it be said whether it shows a family dressed as any other family would be dressed at this period, anywhere in the empire, or does it show a family whose appearance was influenced by their court role or by their antecedents? In other words, even when a contemporary illustration is available, can it be trusted to tell the whole story?

Conclusion

Whilst the foregoing may indicate that there is little immediate evidence for the personal appearance of the population on Hadrian's Wall in the 4th and 5th centuries, all is not lost. There is the potential to discover more. There is a need for the finds assemblages in the area to be reassessed in terms of their accepted chronologies. For this paper an attempt has been made by starting from the 3rd century and working forwards; what is now required is for an assessment to be made which starts with the Early Medieval material and works backwards. There is also a need to discover more about where the population was coming from in the 4th or 5th centuries. Were they people who were descended from longstanding residents of the area or were they incomers from tribal groups elsewhere in the empire? At Brougham, although the cemetery was mostly earlier than the 4th century, the grave goods provide evidence that incoming troops and their families continued to wear the accessories of their homelands. In the case of Brougham, it has been postulated that the homeland in question was Pannonia and 'the females with their beaded necklaces and possibly unusual hairstyles would have appeared rather alien when stood by the side of a native Romano-British woman living further north' (Cool 2004, 466). It has been pointed out that women tend to follow their traditional fashions longer than their menfolk (Swift 2000a, 11), so it is not unlikely that there would have been a wide range of appearance amongst the women of the military. However, the material culture of some of the areas where troop units were raised to serve in Britain is less well known than Pannonia. Once some assemblages from the putative original homelands of any incomers have been studied as comparanda, archaeologists might be in a position to fill out the picture of what the people of the northern frontier in the 4th and 5th centuries actually looked like.

9 Coins and the frontier troops in the 4th century *Richard J Brickstock*

Many thousand coins have now been recovered from the forts and smaller sites of Hadrian's Wall, the Stanegate, and their hinterland, and a large proportion of these coins relate to 4th-century contexts. This body of data allows numismatists to study the overall distribution of finds from the region in comparison with Roman Britain as a whole; it also enables them to examine the spatial and temporal distribution of finds from individual sites, looking for changes over time and variations from the perceived norm.

These studies, on occasion, yield hints of events on the ground. For example, tabulation of the coin finds from the (limited number of) excavations of Hadrian's Wall milecastles reveals a significantly greater proportion of coins of the Tetrarchic period (AD 294–318) than the 'normal' national profile, perhaps a reflection of reorganisation of the frontier line by Constantius I in the years following his recovery of the province in AD 296 and/or by Constantine during his bid for empire (Brickstock forthcoming).

Coin assemblages can also suggest (or confirm) internal and external changes within the forts and fort garrisons. For example, analysis of the number and denomination of coins recovered from forts on the line of Hadrian's Wall allows numismatists to enter the debate over reduced garrison sizes in the frontier forts of the 4th century, many fort garrisons perhaps being reduced to as little as 20% of previous strength (ie 80–100 strong rather than the nominal 500 of the early imperial quingeniary unit; 160–200 strong rather than the 800 of the milliary unit).

The lack of late coin finds from the *vici* at both Housesteads (on the Wall) and Vindolanda (on the Stanegate) suggests that these *vici* were abandoned in the later 3rd century. In the case of Housesteads, this abandonment may have begun as early as the AD 270s; at Vindolanda, it seems to have been completed by the AD 270s. At Housesteads, only thirteen 4th-century coins derive from contexts in and around the *vicus*, and since virtually all of these were recovered from buildings or other structures adjacent to the fort wall, they may well have been lost or discarded by the inhabitants of the fort rather than of the *vicus*. Additionally, the *vicus* at Housesteads produced a relatively low percentage of copies of coins of the period AD 260–80 in comparison with finds from the fort, suggesting that occupation of the *vicus* came to an end before such copies achieved maximum circulation (Brickstock and Casey 2009):

Coins of AD 260–280	Regular	Copies
Fort	40%	60%
Vicus	80%	20%

Internal modifications within the fort, such as the construction of the so-called 'chalet' buildings in place of the earlier barracks (buildings XIII and XIV), smaller baths, and storehouses (building XV), appear to provide a close match for the date of abandonment of the *vicus*. The numismatic evidence therefore provides initial support for the theory that at this time families took up residence inside the fort alongside the menfolk of a reduced garrison. The temporal match is not hard and fast, however, for although the few stratified coins from the 'chalet' construction are of the Gallic Empire (AD 260–80), all derive from adjacent road surfaces rather than from primary construction levels.

Elsewhere on the frontier line there are other indications of reduced garrison size. At both Newcastle and Wallsend, for example, the quantity and distribution of 4th-century coinage suggest the establishment of markets from about AD 330 onwards in under-used parts of the fort (on the *via praetoria* in front of the *principia* at Newcastle and on the *via quintana* at Wallsend). The number and distribution of coins being recovered from the granaries at Vindolanda in 2008 suggest something similar may be happening there as well.

The above examples all suggest continuity of occupation at the sites concerned, but with significant changes both in the size of the communities and their way of life. In addition to these changes, there are other trends in the coin record of the late Roman period which prompt questions about the wealth of frontier troops at the time and also about their daily lives and general standard of living:

- In 4th-century contexts, there are generally large numbers of coins, but there is a proportionate lack of small change at frontier forts relative to civilian contexts elsewhere in the province. This is attributable, in part at least, to the action of the *annona militaris*, but it may also be that the primary use for small change at this time was in saving up to pay taxes in gold coin, which would make small change more necessary in urban rather than military contexts.
- There is a complete lack of very late 4th-century coin at some frontier sites, eg Housesteads, despite these same sites being listed in the *Notitia Dignitatum* (and therefore clearly still in commission at the time).
- In seeming contrast to the above is the presence of a few sizeable gold hoards from the frontier region, for example the hoard of 48 *solidi* of the House of Valentinian and Magnus Maximus (AD 364–88) discovered at Corbridge in 1908.

Auxiliary pay rates	Upper extreme	Lower extreme
Augustus-Domitian	750 *sestertii* = 187½ den	300 *sest* = 75 den
	(5/6ths of legionary pay)	(1/3rd of legionary pay)
Domitian-Severus	1000 *sest* = 250 den	400 *sest* = 100 den
	(33.3% increase)	(33.3% increase)
Severus-Caracalla	2000 *sest* = 500 den	600 *sest* = 150 den
	(100% increase)	(50% increase)
Caracalla	3000 *sest* = 750 den	900 *sest* = 225 den
	(50% increase)	(50% increase)

Frontier troops in the 4th century (the *limitanei*) are normally presented as the poor relations of the soldiers of the central mobile armies of each province (the *comitatenses*) – inefficient soldiers, poorly paid, and little better than local militia who had to be bailed out when anything serious happened. But were they really poor in monetary terms? Can we measure their wealth?

One way of approaching the problem is to attempt a comparison with the frontier forces of the early empire, virtually all of which were auxiliary units. If we take the example of Housesteads again, we have an imperfect knowledge of which units were in occupation: probably a milliary (800-strong) auxiliary cohort in the Hadrianic period; perhaps a legionary garrison during the Antonine period; the 1st cohort of Tungrians (a milliary auxiliary unit) by AD 200; and one or perhaps two additional units (the Numerus Hnaudifridi; the Cuneus Frisiorum; perhaps a small cavalry contingent) added in the 3rd century. Despite the gaps in our knowledge, however, it is clear that we are mostly dealing with auxiliary infantry forces, at this site and many others.

We have an equally imperfect knowledge, derived from historical sources, of rates of pay, donatives and retirement bonuses in the 1st, 2nd, and early 3rd centuries. Pay rates were fixed by Augustus (Tacitus *Annals* I.17.6); raised by a third by Domitian in AD 83/84 (Suetonius *Domitian* VII.5 and XII.1); increased further by Septimius Severus (Herodian III.8.5; *Historia Augusta, Severus* XVII.1); and raised yet again by Caracalla (Herodian IV.4.7). Legionary infantry pay is thus known to have been established at 225 *denarii* per annum, paid in three equal instalments of 75 *denarii*, from the reign of Augustus; to have been raised to 300 *denarii* under Domitian by the addition of a fourth instalment; to have been increased to 400, 450 or even 600 *denarii* by Severus (various interpretations of the texts are possible); and to have been raised from that figure by a further 50% by his son Caracalla, giving basic legionary pay in the early 3rd century of 600, 675, or 900 *denarii*.

Unfortunately, this level of knowledge does not extend to auxiliary rates of pay. Much of the modern debate revolves around the advisability, or otherwise, of assuming that figures deriving from Eastern, and particularly Egyptian contexts, can be applied empire-wide (something over which many, including the present author, have grave doubts, given the unique nature of the province of Egypt). However, the debate surrounding rates of pay has been well aired elsewhere (eg Speidel 1992; Alston 1994; le Bohec 1994) and need not be continued here. Modern estimates of auxiliary pay range from as little as one-third to as much as five-sixths of legionary rates throughout the period. It is also possible that auxiliary pay gradually caught up with legionary pay (the change mirroring the spread of citizenship to the auxiliary units). The likely extremes are tabulated above.

Thus there is considerable disagreement over auxiliary pay levels at each and every period. In comparison with a living wage in the mid-1st century of perhaps 50/60 *denarii* per annum, auxiliary pay was acceptable (fairly low, but at least steady), even according to the lowest estimates and even taking into account the standard deduction of one-third of annual salary for food and equipment.

At the turn of the 2nd century (around AD 90–120), Vindolanda tablet 184 (and others) makes it fairly clear that ordinary soldiers had some surplus money to spend on items such as cloaks and towels, and were buying such objects from independent traders in (small numbers of) *denarii*. At that stage, it appears that the soldiers' salaries were still adequate for their needs.

This happy situation did not continue indefinitely, however, for the buying power of the *denarius* was being gradually eroded and the periodic pay rises failed to keep pace with the rate of inflation. This assertion can be roughly quantified by analysing the figures above in conjunction with the denominations of the coins recovered from archaeological sites.

Luckily, what is important for our present purposes is not so much the absolute number of *denarii* paid at any given time (over which scholars differ by 300% or more), but the percentage increase in pay levels over the period, over which there is less divergence of opinion. Depending on which scheme you favour, levels of auxiliary pay over the period from Augustus to Caracalla rose either threefold (from 300 to 900 *sestertii*) or fourfold (from 750 to 3000 *sestertii*).

The Augustan system of coinage provided a range of denominations: the gold *aureus* (worth 25 *denarii*); the silver *denarius*; and bronze and copper fractions of the *denarius* – the *sestertius* (¼ of a *denarius*); the *dupondius* (¹/₈); the *as* (¹/₁₆); the *semis* (¹/₃₂); and the *quadrans* (¹/₆₄). Analysis of coinage recovered from sites throughout the province, not just those of the frontier region, indicates that the *semis* and the *quadrans* had virtually vanished from circulation by the Claudian period. The coin record of the 1st century is dominated by the *as* and, increasingly, the *dupondius*; by the mid-2nd century the *sestertius* begins to take over from the *dupondius*; and by the early 3rd century the *denarius* was more common than any of its fractions.

Arriving at this conclusion is, unfortunately, not just a matter of counting the number of coins of each period recovered from a given site and dividing them by denomination. The situation is complicated by the recognition that coins could often remain in circulation for many decades, even a century or more, so we need to include in our calculations an adjustment based on an assessment of circulation wear, in order to gain a more accurate picture of the number and denomination of coins deposited in each archaeological period.

The trick is, of course, to quantify circulation wear, to convert the numismatist's 'slightly worn' or 'very worn' (for an explanation of which see Brickstock 2004) into a number of years of circulation wear. This can done, albeit in a very approximate fashion, through analysis of the circulation wear exhibited by 'residual' coinage from sites with a known foundation date, such as Housesteads, and also through similar analysis of closely datable hoards, such as the Rudchester Hoard (Brickstock unpublished manuscript).

At Housesteads, the various excavations within the fort boundaries have yielded 112 coins of mint-dates up to, and including, the reign of Septimius Severus (AD 193–211). Of these, some 46 (more than 40%) span the period from the late republic through to the first years of Hadrian (AD 117–38) and thus, obviously, must have been minted before the establishment of the fort in the AD 120s – some of them by as much as 150 years. Unsurprisingly, many of these coins, particularly those dating to the reign of Vespasian (AD 69–79) or earlier, exhibit very heavy circulation wear.

If we could be sure that all of these 'residual' coins were deposited at around the same time, ie in the reign of Hadrian, we would be able to quantify the wear shown into a number of years ('extremely worn' = more than 100 years; 'very worn' = 50–100 years, etc). Unfortunately, relatively few of the finds are sufficiently securely stratified to allow of such certainty and some may have continued in circulation long after the Hadrianic period.

We are on safer ground, perhaps, when we turn to hoards. The Rudchester hoard, for instance, consists of 471 *denarii* and 125 *aureii* ranging from Marc Antony (30 BC) to Marcus Aurelius (AD 161–80),

the latest coin being AD 167/168 (Brickstock unpublished manuscript). The *denarii* demonstrate a clear pattern of wear:

Marc Antony	Extremely worn
Vespasian	Very worn
Titus, Domitian	Very worn to worn
Trajan	Worn
Hadrian	Worn to slightly worn
Antoninus Pius	Slightly worn
Marcus Aurelius	Unworn

This gives us a very rough quantifier:

Unworn	up to 10 years
Slightly worn	*c* 10–40 years
Worn	*c* 40–70 years
Very worn	*c* 70–100 years
Extremely worn	more than 100 years

This analysis, of course, needs to be repeated with a large number of hoards before the conclusions can be treated as reliable, but they give a hint, for instance, that some of the very worn coins of Vespasian recovered from Housesteads may in fact have continued in circulation into the reign of Antoninus Pius or even beyond.

Dividing the coinage of Housesteads by period and adjusting according to the wear exhibited, we are able to observe in more detail the distribution of denominations over time, and, indeed, to confirm the general picture outlined above. At Housesteads in the AD 120s Flavian coins, including *asses* and *dupondii,* were still in circulation, but bulk supplies of fractional coinage were of *sestertii* of Trajan and Hadrian. Supplies of fresh *sestertii* were still being received during the reign of Antoninus Pius, at which time the smaller denominations were becoming increasingly rare. From the reign of Commodus (or possibly even Marcus Aurelius), the *denarius* began to dominate the currency, although considerable numbers of old *sestertii* remained in circulation well into the 3rd century alongside the fresher silver.

Analysis of a number of sites in like manner allows us to work out the dominant denomination at any given period:

Reign	**Dominant denomination**	**Fraction of denarius**
Claudius	*As*	¹/₁₆
Domitian	*Dupondius*	¹/₈
Pius	*Sestertius*	¼
Severus	*Denarius*	1

This rough analysis (and it should emphasised once again that it is only rough) suggests that prices rose as much as sixteen-fold over the 140-odd years between the Claudian conquest and the beginning of the 3rd century. Put another way, the *denarius* of AD 200 had a buying power of just 6% relative to its Claudian counterpart. This may sound like an enormous decrease in value, but in reality it represents a compound rate of inflation of only 2% over the period, a rate of which most modern governments would surely be proud.

Even so, if we remember that auxiliary pay rose only three- or four-fold over the same period, it suggests that by AD 200 auxiliary pay rates were very poor indeed, with the basic salary (the *stipendium*) at 25% or less of the mid-1st-century level in real terms. Even a doubling of pay in the AD 230s under Maximinus, an idea now discounted by most scholars, would have left the 3rd-century auxiliary on half pay relative to his 1st-century counterpart. Such a rise would, in any case, have been more than cancelled out in real terms by the increased rates of inflation experienced for much or all of the 3rd century.

The 3rd century, however, saw major changes in the manner in which the armies were remunerated. At an unknown date, perhaps as early as the reign of Septimius Severus, the *annona militaris* was introduced. Deductions for food and equipment ceased and food and equipment were thereafter granted in addition to salary. It is logical to assume that in many instances the troops collected rations from the local populace as a tax in kind, especially in peripheral frontier regions such as northern Britannia, though sometimes demand in grain, etc could be commuted to monetary payment where that was more convenient. Such a change was clearly needed, and the *annona* no doubt became all the more important as monetary crisis gripped the empire in the second and third quarters of the 3rd century.

After the collapse of the Augustan currency system in the AD 260s, if not before, the *annona* would have been much more important to an auxiliary infantryman than his *stipendium*. Indeed, the *stipendium* from this time onwards can have been of little more than nominal value.

The *stipendium* probably remained at the level fixed by Caracalla for much of the 3rd century, but, perhaps in the AD 260s, perhaps not until the reign of Diocletian (AD 284–305), further monetary payments were added in an attempt to keep some cash in the troops' pockets, and the level of stipend was also raised. The Beatty Papyrii suggest that troops (at least those stationed in Egypt) were by AD 299/300 paid a salary (*stipendium*) supplemented by donatives (*donativum*) and ration allowances (*pretium annonae*). There is some doubt about the levels at which these were set, particularly for auxiliaries, though the latter probably received 1200 *denarii* in salary (two-thirds of the legionary rate); and between 200 *denarii* (Jones 1964) and 600 *denarii* (Casey and Davies 1993) as a ration allowance. Donatives were payable annually to legionaries and probably also to auxiliaries (the citizen/non-citizen distinction had, after all, been abolished by Caracalla), marking imperial birthdays, accession days and consulships. Depending on the reading of the text this would further raise an auxiliary's income by between 1250 *denarii* per annum

(Jones 1964) and 2500 *denarii* per annum (Duncan-Jones 1978).

All this means that cash payments to an individual auxiliary infantryman might have reached between 2650 (based on Jones 1964) and 4300 *denarii* per annum by AD 300 (Casey and Davies 1993) in comparison with between 225 and 750 *denarii* under Caracalla – but all these rises were rendered irrelevant by inflation over the same period. In real terms, the soldier's monetary income was now much lower than it had been a century earlier. This is made abundantly clear by Diocletian's Edict of Maximum Prices, in which it is stated that a soldier's *stipendium* and *donativum* might be exhausted in a single purchase; and in which the stated price of corn implies that the annual ration allowance would have purchased only two *modii* of corn (and actual prices were probably already somewhat higher; Jones 1964). These annual payments continued to be made at least until the time of Julian. By this time, however, there was virtually no coin in which such a small sum could be paid (and by then it would have been worth, by my calculations, little more than a *quadrans* per annum at 1st-century rates!).

An auxiliary's monetary income was also much lower than hitherto in purely bullion terms (and remember, there was still supposed to be a direct relationship between a coin's value and its bullion content). Even taking the most generous estimate of the increases awarded to auxiliaries in the course of the 3rd century (ie from 225 *denarii* under Caracalla to 4300 *denarii* in AD 300), the bullion content was reduced by about two-thirds over that period: 225 *denarii* at the time of Caracalla would have contained some 337.5g of silver; 4300 *denarii* paid in the10g coin introduced in the coin reform of AD 294/296 (which contained about 3% silver and was probably tariffed at 10 *denarii*) netted the soldier only 129g of silver (Casey and Davies 1993). If the salary under Caracalla was 750 *denarii*, the percentage reduction in bullion content by AD 300 would be much greater still (close to 90%).

In summary, the frontier soldier's monetary income was low in AD 200 in relation to his Claudian counterpart and pitifully low by AD 300. The introduction of the *annona* (whenever that was) provided at least partial compensation. It ensured that the late 3rd-century soldier was equipped and that he would never starve, and in that respect he was much better off than many free men outside the military. The main difference between him and the soldiers of the 1st and 2nd centuries is that, unless his rank meant that he enjoyed an enhanced ration allowance which could be commuted to coin, he had very little in the way of disposable income. The 'squaddies' were cash poor. They were not in a position to make anything much in the way of luxury purchases, nor to send money away to support extended family, though it may perhaps be supposed that ration allowances were generous enough to provide at least a measure of support for immediate family (a sound investment by the

Accession and quinquennial payments (based on Casey and Davies 1993)

Year	Event	Donative
364	Accession of Valentinian and Valens	5 *solidi* + 1lb silver = 9 *solidi*
367	Accession of Gratian	5 *solidi* + 1lb silver = 9 *solidi*
368	Quinquennalia of Valentinian and Valens	5 *solidi*
372	Quinquennalia of Gratian	5 *solidi*
373	Decennalia of Valentinian and Valens	5 *solidi*
375	Accession of Valentinian II	5 *solidi* + 1lb silver = 9 *solidi*
377	Decennalia of Gratian	5 *solidi*
378	Quindecennalia of Valens	5 *solidi*

authorities since male offspring provided the next generation of recruits into the frontier units).

All this might lead one to expect that coin histograms from frontier sites in the 4th century would demonstrate a dramatic reduction in coin use. Garrisons and associated communities were almost certainly smaller, perhaps much smaller, than those of the 1st and 2nd centuries; food and equipment were being supplied, in most cases, without the necessity for coin changing hands; and individual soldiers had small change sufficient for a game of dice in the bath house, but no money of any real value. To an extent, the coin record supports this picture. Absolute numbers of coins recovered from late 3rd- and 4th-century contexts are high, often extremely high, but their bullion value is very low in comparison with earlier periods. These large quantities of virtually worthless coin generate something of a headache for cataloguers, but they provide no real measure of the standard of living enjoyed by the local population.

In the 4th century, however, yet another element was added to the soldiers' income, and happily this is one which allows a reasonable assessment of their individual wealth, both in absolute terms and in comparison with their predecessors. Papyrological evidence suggests that Constantine I doubled the rates of army pay (*P Oxy* 247; Casey and Davies 1993 suggests *c* AD 330), but the significant change in the 4th century was the addition of a second category of donative, celebrating imperial accessions, every fifth anniversary of the same (*quinquennalia*), and possibly also consulships (though the latter probably followed at a much later date).

Serious sums in gold and silver were distributed, at regular intervals, to the entire army, and we have a reasonable knowledge of the sums involved. The accession donative of 5 *solidi* and a pound of silver is first recorded on Julian's acclamation as Augustus in AD 360 (Ammianus Marcellinus 20.4) and remained at that level at least until the reign of Tiberius Constantine (Jones 1964). The *solidus*, a gold denomination introduced by Constantine, was struck at 72 to the Roman pound, and a pound of silver was worth 4 *solidi*, making the accession donative 9 *solidi* in total.

The quinquennial donative was payable on every fifth anniversary of the accession of every member of the imperial college. The rate, 5 *solidi*, is first recorded under Anastasius and Justinian, but it is reasonable to suppose that it, like the accession donative, was paid at the same rate in the 4th century (Jones 1964).

Donatives on the occasion of the consulships of members of the imperial college were payable to the imperial guard in the 5th century, but probably not to others, and probably not in the 4th century. Even so, frontier troops, and others, could expect to receive a substantial monetary payment at least once in every five years.

Between AD 364 and 378, soldiers of the Roman army, *limitanei* included, perhaps received as many as eight of these payments, amounting to as much as 52 *solidi* over a period of fifteen years, an annual rate of nearly 3.5 *solidi* (see above)

Emperors were not, however, above playing fast and loose with the chronology for their own financial benefit, on frequent occasions moving the anniversaries of senior and junior members of the imperial college into line in order to save money (Kent 1980). Accession donatives had to be paid if the candidate were to be accepted, but it is possible, in the table above, that the quinquennial payments of Gratian might have been amalgamated with those of Valentinian and Valens to remove a payment in AD 372/373 (probably by bringing forward the *decennalia* of Valentinian and his brother rather than delaying a payment due in for Gratian); and likewise in AD 377/378.

These reductions would have saved the treasury 10 *solidi* per man, but even so the payout over fifteen years would still amount to the equivalent of 42 *solidi*, some 2.8 *solidi* per annum. This compares very favourably, for instance, with a civilian tax rate of 1 *solidus* per annum. It should also be remembered that soldiers were still, so far as we know, receiving their food and equipment allowances due under the *annona militaris*. In bullion terms, 42 *solidi* equates to 0.58 of a Roman pound of gold; 52 equates to 0.72 of a pound.

We can compare these figures directly with the auxiliary stipend of earlier times, since we can deal in gold bullion. In AD 100 an auxiliary received a *stipendium* of between 100 *denarii* and 250 *denarii* (according to which scheme you follow; I favour the former). 100 *denarii* was the equivalent of 4 *aureii*, *aureii* being struck at 60 to the Roman pound. This equates to exactly one pound of gold in fifteen years (2.5 pounds if the salary rate was 250 *denarii* pa). Deductions for food and equipment would reduce these figures by a third to 0.67 lb and 1.67 lb respectively.

Thus, if we stick with the 2nd-century salary figure of 100 *denarii*, *limitanei* in the later 4th century appear to have enjoyed a salary roughly equivalent to that of their Hadrianic brethren (though significantly lower if the higher 2nd-century salary estimate proves to be correct). They were paid at about two-thirds the rate in purely cash terms but, unlike their 2nd-century counterparts, with all food and equipment provided on top of that. The later 2nd-century and early 3rd-century soldiers were very badly off (at a period of debasement of the currency and before the introduction of the *annona militaris*), but the 4th-century soldier was probably no worse off than his 2nd-century counterpart. He wasn't rich, but he wasn't that badly off either.

The presence of late 4th-century gold hoards is readily explainable in the light of the donative system, and so is the relative absence of small change, which was less essential than it once had been. The military communities still in place on the direct cessation of Roman rule reaped the benefit of the soldiers' dual system of income (donative and *annona*), for when imperial funds (the donative element) ceased to appear, the mechanism for the gathering and distribution of food was still in place. Military communities could continue to function, albeit at a lower level of wealth, without the necessity for any great social or political upheaval. The garrison could become what, in effect, it already was – a local militia, living off and protecting its own.

10 Can we see a 4th- or 5th-century diet from the plant and animal remains? *Jacqui Huntley and Sue Stallibrass*

Biological materials recovered from excavations can tell us so much more than the types of contemporary plants and animals. However, they have to be preserved in the first place, then excavated, sampled and analysed and that is the 'crunch'. This paper will review briefly two lines of evidence relating to sites around the northern frontier of Roman Britain during the 4th century.

1. Pollen for landscape, or at least vegetation, studies, plus its evidence for arable cultivation.
2. Seeds and bones from excavations used to investigate crop and animal husbandry.

Pollen

It is well recognised that differences in woodland cover to the east and west of the Pennine watershed existed when the Romans arrived in the late 1st century AD (Huntley 1999). In the east there was already an essentially agricultural landscape, with some woodland giving a countryside which was probably not a lot different in appearance from that of today. On the other hand, there was clearly more woodland in the west. This does not necessarily mean that the west was not agricultural, simply that the pollen sites studied have been inappropriate to pick up small-scale farming. For this we need small basins which collect pollen from a few kilometres at most around them; these are better than the large valley mires which are typically used for traditional pollen studies.

Does this picture of the landscape change through the period of Roman occupation? Recent publications have reviewed pollen diagrams with radiocarbon dates around the 3rd/4th–6th centuries in the northern frontier zone (Collins 2007; Dark and Dark 1996; Dark 2006) and these have come to the general conclusion that there are suggestions of increased woodland at some sites during this period, but that at other sites, clearance remained static or even increased. The interpretations offered are that, overall, there probably was less intense agriculture. Cereal pollen continues to be present, however, so at least some farming did still occur. Both Dark and Collins (*op cit*), however, tend to the assumption that changes in vegetation reflect human activity alone or at least to a great extent.

There is very good evidence, from documentary sources as well as other biological proxies, that the climate globally was deteriorating through the 5th

and 6th centuries (Hendon *et al* 2001). There may, therefore, be an argument that trees, or at least some of the more warmth-demanding species, were less favoured. Even today the majority of pollen diagrams have data calculated as percentages (for example, percentage Total Land Pollen or TLP); hence changes have to be 'relative'. An increase in tree pollen, therefore, does not necessarily mean an increase in trees. It could indicate a decrease in grass or herb pollen types, for example. Another possible issue to address in these pollen diagrams is that of the specific tree taxa that increase, even relatively. Hazel often increases – hazel flowers best when it is in open situations, and flowering is suppressed when in woodland. So an increase in hazel could mean a decrease in woodland; but it could equally mean that hazel scrub *per se* was developing on previously cultivated or grazed ground.

Alder is another species that often increases at this time. It is common on wet ground. With other proxy evidence indicating that the climate was becoming wetter during this period (Hughes *et al* 2000), an increase in alder could simply reflect climate change, with more trees growing on the sites that were cored. Thus, more very local pollen was being deposited and the trees were filtering out pollen from further afield. This is considered a highly likely interpretation of, for example, Midgeholme Moss (Innes 1988).

Yet a third issue is that few diagrams have dates around this period. There are often no major changes in pollen, so there is little reason to date the levels from the traditional point of view.

A summary from the pollen evidence, therefore, is that there are suggestions of increased woodland at some sites, although by no means all. At least some of these changes could reflect a climatic change.

Seed evidence

Turning to the more economic aspects of the environment, what was being eaten and how was it produced? When the Romans arrived they found a local population eating a mixture of spelt wheat and hulled six-row barley, having changed from emmer wheat and naked barley some centuries before (Huntley and Stallibrass 1995). Marijke van der Veen's work (1992) indicated that there was a difference between the north and south of the Tyne, with people to the north being dependent upon emmer for longer, which was certainly true when she undertook this work in the 1990s. She suggested social reasons

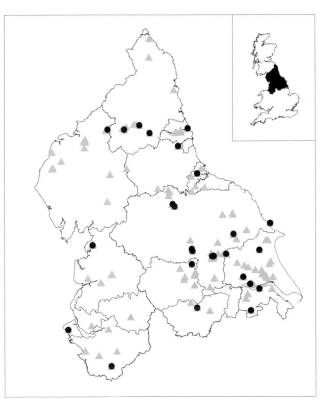

Fig 10.1 The distribution of Roman sites (grey triangles) and those with plant or animal remains (black circles)

for this, basically dismissing environmental parameters as being no more than a minor part of the story, despite the fact that her sites north of the Tyne were mostly upland. This was supported by later experimental work growing emmer and spelt in different parts of the British Isles and investigating their production (van der Veen and Palmer 1997).

More recent developer-funded work, however, in the Tyne and Northumberland lowlands, as at East and West Brunton, Blagdon, and Pegswood, where opencast mining or major urban development have enabled large open-area excavation, is indicating clearly that the story is not that simple. Spelt was being used, almost to the exclusion of emmer, in these lowland areas during the pre-Roman Iron Age and into the period of Roman occupation (Charlotte O'Brien, pers comm). Thus, at this time the situation was more of an upland/lowland divide between species. Unfortunately, many of these sites have been extensively truncated by subsequent ploughing and therefore we know nothing of their occupation, or abandonment, during the later part of the Roman period and/or into the 5th/6th century.

In the west, however, there are slight suggestions that emmer was in use for longer and occasionally even found its way onto the military sites, but data are extremely limited (Huntley 1989a; 1989b). Again these sites date predominantly from the 1st–2nd centuries AD.

In summary, spelt and barley were the dominant cereals being grown in the region when the Romans arrived, and they continued to grow these two cereals throughout the period. Occasionally bread wheat and rye turn up in the first few centuries but in very low numbers and almost certainly as contaminants of seed brought in from elsewhere. Examples include Edderside in Cumbria, a potential Romano-British settlement with possible bread wheat (Huntley 1991b); Annetwell Street, Carlisle, 1st- or 2nd-century deposits within a fort with both bread wheat and rye as well as a little emmer (Huntley 1989a); Birdoswald fort, again, 1st- or 2nd-century, with bread wheat (Huntley 1997); Thornbrough, Northumberland, a Romano-British farmstead with possibly earlier Iron Age occupation, with rye (Huntley 1991a; Huntley 1997; van der Veen 1992); and Scotch Corner, a 1st-century roundhouse with bread wheat and possibly rye (Huntley 1995).

Figure 10.1 presents all sites of Roman date and of any type – military, *vicus*/civilian settlement, native – for the English Heritage Northern Territory (essentially Cheshire to North Lincolnshire through to the Scottish border) with those containing later Roman deposits highlighted. It shows clearly a spread of sites with environmental data but most of these date from either the 1st–2nd centuries AD or are very broadly dated 'Roman' by the presence of a mixed pottery assemblage. Even where there are 3rd- to 4th-century deposits, only a few samples were taken at most so the data are extremely limited. A further issue is that the later deposits tend to have rather poor preservation, especially in the case of animal bones – possibly because of groundwater or possibly because the structures/buildings sampled were generally kept clean and were not used for the disposal of rubbish after they fell into disuse.

Spelt and six-row barley remain dominant throughout these 4th-century samples. A few sites produce the occasional rye and bread wheat, with the catastrophic fire at South Shields demonstrating that at least the granaries there contained abundant bread wheat (van der Veen 1988). More recently, one of the authors of this chapter has recovered bread wheat from excavations within the 3rd- or 4th-century granaries at Vindolanda although insufficient to suggest the storage of pure bread wheat as yet. Oats, interestingly, tend to turn up more frequently in the east in the later Roman period, having always been present in the west probably due to the wetter climate on that side of the Pennines. Although it is not possible to say definitely whether the oats were cultivated or wild, as minimal diagnostic chaff has been recovered, they may reflect horse feed as they tend to be more abundant on forts known to have had cavalry stationed at them.

One local site where we do have continuity of occupation from prehistoric through to Saxon times is at Quarry Farm, a villa site excavated by Durham University Archaeological Services in 2003. Substantial stone buildings were recorded as well as various features interpreted as grain-drying kilns, threshing

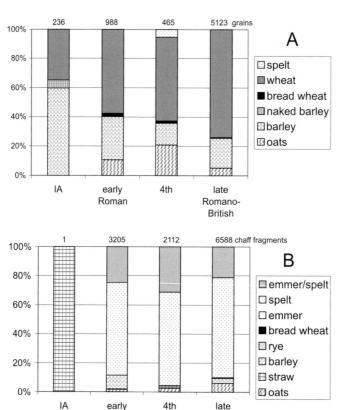

Fig 10.2 Charred plant remains from Quarry Farm, contexts grouped by phase: A, from remains of grains; B, from remains of chaff

floors and so on, which are the types of agricultural features that would be expected at a villa. Some 177 samples were assessed, although only 25 were considered to warrant further analysis (Archaeological Services University of Durham 2006). Full analysis confirmed that very few charred plant remains were present in the Iron Age samples with, disappointingly, even fewer in the Saxon deposits (Huntley 2008). Interestingly, Bronze Age deposits produced the expected emmer and naked barley although radiocarbon was needed to convince the archaeologists of this!

Figure 10.2A shows all cereal grain amalgamated at phase level for the Quarry Farm samples from the Iron Age onwards, demonstrating that there are no major differences through time. Wheat cannot be determined reliably to species from the grain alone (Hillman *et al* 1996 for 1995), hence the 'wheat' category. A few grains were obviously from spelt, and a very few were the rounded compact bread wheat type.

Figure 10.2B presents the data for chaff fragments (ear and straw remains). The Iron Age plot comprised a single fragment of straw only. Roman deposits produced mostly spelt glume bases and spikelet forks typical of processing a home-grown crop. A small amount of emmer chaff was present throughout, with slightly more in the early Roman period, although this can hardly be deemed significant.

Almost 20% of the chaff comprised the fragments of a brittle rachis from either emmer or spelt, but it seems most likely to have been spelt given the abundance of its diagnostic glume bases. Bread wheat and rye chaff was minimal as expected. As free-threshing cereals, these fragments are released without the need of a parching (association with fire) event that is required for the glume wheats (spelt and emmer).

For the cereals, then, there are no major differences in types grown across the whole of the Roman period and indeed back into Iron Age times. Environmental determinism may not be a favourite with theoretical archaeologists, but if the local climate will not support a crop it cannot be grown successfully. An indication that environmental determinism is at least in part at work is the confirmation in 2009 of presence of emmer in the uplands and spelt throughout the lowlands both north and south of the Tyne (see above).

With the arrival of incomers during the 7th, 8th, and 9th centuries, spelt is replaced by a combination of oats, bread wheat, and rye, with barley also decreasing significantly. This might well be a social change but it does not happen through the Roman period. It has to be said that there were major shifts in climate during at least the 7th century and hence climatic or environmental parameters might also have played their part.

Faunal evidence

If cereals do not change, what of animal husbandry? Bones at least are far more collected and studied than plant remains but often preservation is not as good in the 4th or even 3rd century as in the 1st or 2nd century, for reasons of ground chemistry. Relatively few intact bones are recovered; most of the material is poorly preserved and highly fragmentary. Also, species domesticated for food – cow, sheep/goat, pig and possibly horse – are relatively few thus changes in relative proportions are used to indicate differences and these give the same problems as for the relative pollen data. In addition, at many of the older excavations where preservation in these later deposits was quite good, the bone assemblage was interpreted at the site level, and it is not possible to revisit either the bones or the data to record the context or phase level (see Corbridge for example; Hodgson 1967).

Cattle were typically small, and similar in size and mass to modern-day Dexters. Syntheses of cattle sizes from Vindolanda suggest a slight increase through time but as few large animals are represented these might just reflect the need for big white bulls at various religious events (Rayner 1999).

Beef, principally from elderly cows, remains the dominant meat throughout the Roman period, although the occupants of South Shields fort seemed to have preferred mutton/lamb to some extent (Huntley and Stallibrass 1995). As with the plant remains there is little change, in this case in either species' elements or types of butchery. Individual preferences are not observed in the available bone assemblage, though these have been collected almost exclusively from military sites. It could be argued that the 'military way', the provision of butchered meat to soldiers, dictated the diet and might well have overcome any individual preferences. This is not observable, however, with other classes of artefact, such as the North African pottery from early Carlisle, which suggests some level of freedom of choice for members of the military. If soil conditions allowed for the recovery of bone assemblages from native sites, such assemblages might be similar to the military assemblages or might differ. Unfortunately, the current absence of evidence does not allow for comparisions.

What these bones do show is that the pattern of deposition of domestic rubbish is changing in the late Roman period. In later periods, at Wallsend especially, rubbish is deposited within large stone buildings which were interpreted as public places in earlier phases (Hodgson 2003). If the original function was no longer appropriate, the rubbish dumping could be explained as indicating lower levels of occupation or simply lower levels of control and regulation. It would be worth analysing spatial patterns of bone from other forts with large assemblages of bone, for example, South Shields, Vindolanda and Carlisle, irrespective of the period, to determine how widespread this practice was.

Conclusions

So can we see a 4th- or 5th-century diet? The simple answer is no. People ate the same spelt and barley bread with beef stew throughout the Roman period. Any subtleties in terms of herbs and spices cannot be considered because of the lack of samples and poor preservation/lack of waterlogged preservation from the relevant periods. Disposal patterns of bones at least did change and this is perhaps where we should direct future work and questions. It would also undoubtedly be useful to compare the dietary evidence from bones and plant remains with evidence from the other finds, for example ceramics, to consider other questions such as changes in food preparation and rubbish disposal. It is therefore both timely and highly laudable that the conference at which the basics of this paper were presented was organised.

11 Beyond the frontier: interpreting late Roman Iron Age indigenous and imported material culture *Fraser Hunter*

Introduction

The late Roman period beyond Hadrian's Wall has been rather sparsely examined. It is often seen as poor intellectual terrain, with little but a scatter of historical references, mostly to the increasingly troublesome Picts, and a rather evasive archaeological record. The aim of this paper is to consider it anew and see what can be teased from the material culture. Two topics will be tackled: the nature and distribution of late Roman imports, and changes in indigenous material culture. What can these tell us of the inter-relations either side of the late Roman frontier? Key to this is the question of what processes drew northern material south of the Wall, a rarely recognised phenomenon.[1] The chronology used is early (*c* AD 75–160), mid- (*c* AD 160–250) and late Roman Iron Age (*c* AD 250–400), abbreviated to ERIA, MRIA and LRIA, although much indigenous material is less tightly dated, often spanning the 3rd to 6th centuries AD.

Late Roman imports – what and where?

There is a widespread if thin scatter of late Roman material across Scotland. This shows noticeable patterning (Fig 11.1). In particular, the near-total absence of finds from north-east Scotland stands in marked contrast to the abundance of material there in the MRIA, and suggests a deliberate Roman policy of targeting specific areas or groups for diplomatic attention, a policy attested in other areas (Erdrich 2000; Hunter 2007a). Compared with earlier periods, the quantity of late Roman material is markedly less, with only around 40 findspots of LRIA date compared with over 170 of the E–MRIA. This disguises some regional variation: the area south of the Forth-Clyde line shows a dramatic reduction in late Roman material, and the north-east even more so, but the Atlantic zones show much less of a drop, albeit from lower initial levels (Fig 11.2). All such discussions must recognise that some objects may have had long lives after their arrival in the country, but I would argue that the existence of chronologically varied patterns indicates this is a relatively minor concern (Hunter 2007a, 11–12).

In Atlantic Scotland, late Roman material is quite widely distributed, with little sign of concentrations on key sites. In southern Scotland the picture is rather different. There are marked clusters in the Tweed valley and East Lothian,

while much of the material (and the widest range of finds) comes from large hillforts; the wide social spread across the settlement pattern seen in the ERIA is gone, replaced by a concentration on large power centres. This is seen most spectacularly in the case of Traprain Law (E Lothian), the single richest late Roman site in Scotland, but there are similar indications elsewhere, with a range of late Roman finds from hillforts at Eildon Hill (Scottish Borders), Dumbarton Rock (West Dunbartonshire) and Edinburgh Castle. The nature of settlement and society at this archaeologically opaque period is uncertain. It is possible that there was some contraction of settlement onto hillforts, as few other 1st- to 2nd-century sites show 3rd- or 4th-century occupation. However, the pattern of imports most probably highlights the flourishing power centres, with the material (now rather rarer and more exclusive than before) being largely restricted to the social circles on these central sites; indeed, some grew into major elite centres in the Early Historic period, notably Edinburgh and Dumbarton. This ties in with a wider reawakening of hillforts in Scotland (both refortification of old sites and construction of new ones; Alcock 1987b, fig 4), and a more general western British reuse of former hillforts (Arnold and Davies 2000, 87–9; White 2007, 137–43, 158–76).

What of the finds themselves? Ongoing work on the pottery by Colin Wallace will clarify this considerably, as will publication of Dominic Ingemark's (2003) thesis on the glass, but only Traprain shows a broad spectrum of material. Most sites show a focus on pottery (predominantly fine wares) and glass table wares, especially drinking vessels. In contrast to the ERIA, ornaments are few. A more problematic category is coins. While there are some late Roman copper-alloy coins from settlement sites (fourteen coins from nine sites, excluding Traprain), far more stray finds are known, with over 250 recorded. These have been tainted by Casey's observation that most show eastern mint marks, in contrast to the picture on Hadrian's Wall, suggesting modern losses brought in as souvenirs (Casey 1984b). Robertson (1993) has suggested this is too sweeping a dismissal, but the material has been rather ignored. Nevertheless, it has information to yield.

The starting point should be the 37 late Roman coins from Traprain, an unusual assemblage compared with sites within the Roman diocese, but one which may provide a model for late Roman coinage in the north (Sekulla 1982). Its composition can be paralleled by a number of poorly understood

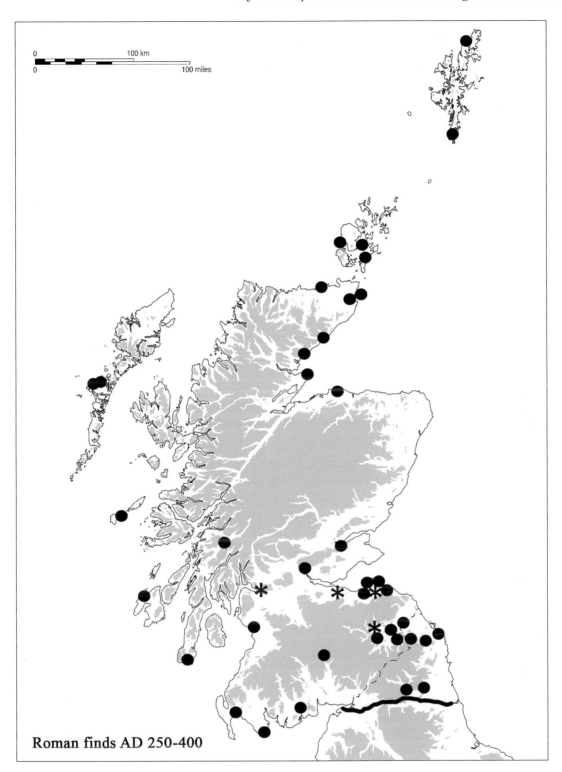

Fig 11.1 Late Roman finds (excluding stray coins) from north of Hadrian's Wall; the gold crossbow brooch 'from the Moray Firth' is not plotted. Stars mark sites with a wider range of finds than normal: Traprain Law, Eildon Hill North, Edinburgh Castle and Dumbarton Rock

scatters of low-value copper-alloy coins, ranging in date from the late 3rd to late 4th century and in number from thirty to several hundred; most are southern Scottish, but a recent find takes the phenomenon much further north, to Girnigoe in Caithness (Fig 11.3; Hunter 2007a, 34; N Holmes, pers comm). The nature of these scatters is not known, but all are either coastal or riverine (on the Tweed); in the case of Springwood, its proximity to the later medieval stronghold of Roxburgh Castle suggests a Traprain-type site may lurk under the later remains. These may be interpreted as accessible or powerful locations which were contact points with the Roman world. The coinage was perhaps

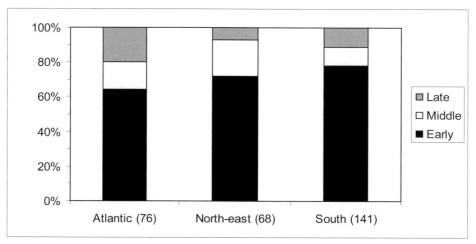

Fig 11.2   Graph comparing quantities of early, middle and late Roman Iron Age finds by area. Northern England is excluded, as are stray finds and those coin concentrations not from a known site

used in transactions at these sites, but then saw little wider dispersal since, unlike other acquired goods (and unlike earlier *denarii* hoards; Hunter 2007b), this base metal coinage had little indigenous value as either status symbol or scrap to recycle.

With this model of late Roman coin use in mind, we can turn again to the stray finds. By taking a slightly less hard-line approach than Casey's, interesting patterns start to emerge. If the corpus is weeded of Alexandrian issues, Greek mints and anything from modern conurbations, a more reliable residue of some 65 coins remains. It is noticeable, for instance, that all eight reliable late Roman coins known from the Western Isles come from North Uist – a pattern hard to explain as repeated modern loss, and suggesting the island was a focus of contact at this time. If we consider only locations with two or more coins (both site and stray finds), this provides striking confirmation of the coastal and riverine distribution (compare the distribution of all late Roman coins in Scotland; Robertson 1970, fig 4). A notable clustering in the catchment of the River Tweed parallels the concentration of other late Roman finds in this area. This supports the argument that clusters of late Roman coins appeared at points of contact with the Roman world, but did not see any significant dispersal. In turn, an acceptance that such coins did have a use in transactions with Rome allows the few late Roman coin hoards from Scotland (Robertson 1978), often treated as anomalies, to be seen as locally useful in some way, as accumulations for trading or votive purposes (as at Covesea, Moray; Shepherd 1993, 80–1).

Contact, conflict, collaboration

It is likely that a range of mechanisms led to movement of material beyond the Wall. The frontier conflicts attested in the literary sources are likely to have led to looting and plunder (Breeze 1982,

144–60). However, the coin nodes highlighted above suggest there was also more directed two-way contact with the Roman world in some form of exchange system, while the marked clusters of finds in south-east Scotland and the quality of certain finds suggest diplomatic links or subsidies were involved. This seems plausible for the magnificent hoard of bronze vessels from Helmsdale (Suther-land), 350km beyond the frontier (Spearman 1990). It probably also lies behind the two remarkable gold crossbow brooches from Erickstanebrae (Dumfries and Galloway; Plate 8) and the Moray Firth, the former an imperial gift on the occasion of Diocle-tian's twentieth anniversary (Curle 1932, 370–1, 392; Noll 1974, 227–30). Of course the history behind any single find is opaque – but the presence of two rare gold brooches in *barbaricum* suggests that dip-lomatic gift-giving or rewards for services rendered to Rome are plausible scenarios.

This leads to the question of other high-value material – notably the *Hacksilber* hoard from Traprain. The interpretation of this has long been contested, whether loot, payment or diplomatic gift (*inter alia* Curle 1923, 108; Birley 1955; Hunter 2006, 142–3). It would be premature to offer further speculations, as a project to reconsider Traprain and other such hoards is currently in progress at the National Museum, but it is worth highlighting that *Hacksilber* is a common phenomenon beyond the northern frontiers, with examples from Ireland, Scotland, the Netherlands, Germany, Denmark, and Poland (Grünhagen 1954, 58–70; Guggisberg 2003, 337, 343, Abb 256; Stupperich 1997, 80–5). It is also, more rarely, attested within the empire, suggesting this was an increasingly accepted way to treat silver in the later 4th and 5th centuries (eg Cahn 1984; Carson and Burnett 1979, 110–17; Burnham *et al* 2002, 346). This and the presence of official ingots in some hoards (Painter 1972, 88–9) suggests these were payments or subsidies to groups beyond the frontier. The clipped coinage

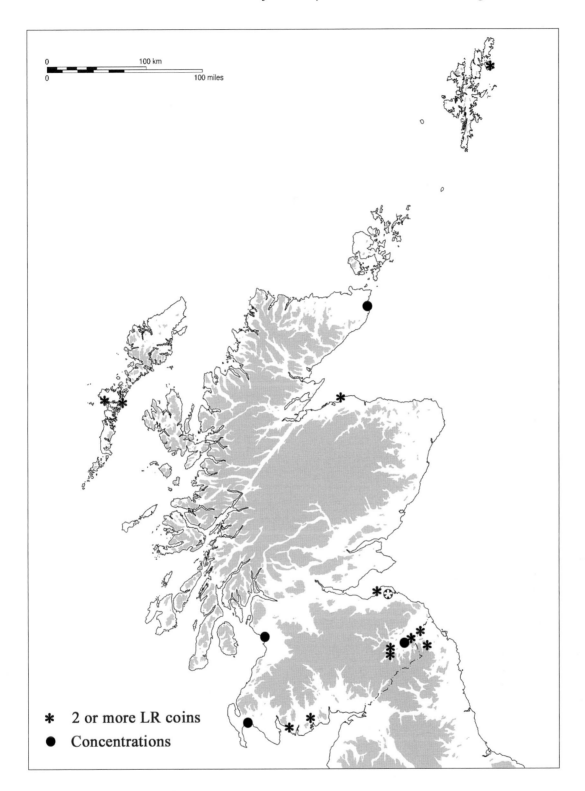

Fig 11.3 Sites producing two or more late Roman coins (excluding eastern and Greek issues, and those from modern conurbations)

and jewellery in Traprain puts this particular example into the mid-5th century (Painter 2006, 229–30). We have of course only a partial picture of such subsidies, as Roman silver was extensively recycled, leading to a burgeoning of indigenous silver jewellery from the 5th century onwards (eg Stevenson 1956).

The late Roman finds from north of the Wall thus highlight a number of themes in relations between Rome and the 'barbarians'. There is evidence of diplomatic targeting of certain areas to the exclusion of others; southern Scotland shows a concentration of finds on focal hillforts, with notable clusters in south-east Scotland suggesting this was seen as a buffer zone. The nature of the material, predominantly tablewares, suggests it had local social value as with earlier Roman finds, while the problematic late Roman coinage is a useful marker of contact nodes with the Roman world. Various processes will have brought material north, but the remarkable quality of some points to diplomatic actions. Overall, we see a picture of interaction driven by Roman concerns with securing the frontier and local (elite) enthusiasm for aspects of Roman material culture. But what of the indigenous material culture?

Defining a new world – changing indigenous material culture

The finds of the LRIA add another angle. The material culture of the northern Iron Age is rarely a focus for study, and much is indeed prosaic and chronologically undiagnostic, but it has untapped potential. The focus here will be on 'signal pieces', more decorative material likely to have played a role in contemporary definitions of status and identity.

To understand the changes, we should briefly review the situation in the 1st and 2nd centuries AD. Key features are the emergence of distinctive regional Celtic art styles in central and north Britain and, linked with this, the development of hybrid Romano-British styles in central Britain. For the former, two styles can be identified in central Britain and another in north-east Scotland; for the latter we can point to types such as glass bangles, dragonesque brooches and certain button-and-loop fasteners which were shared across and beyond the frontier in the Humber-Forth area (MacGregor 1976, 127–33, 184; Stevenson 1976; Price 1988; Wild 1970; Hunter 2008 and forthcoming a).

As far as current dating evidence indicates, these types had died out by the LRIA; their floruit was in the 1st and 2nd centuries AD. Instead, a range of other material came to the fore from the 3rd to the 6th century. This was a time when classic post-Roman 'type-fossils' such as penannular brooches flourished, and when key stages in the development of post-Roman Celtic art occurred; but although such items were made and used in Scotland, they are not specifically a northern phenomenon and will not be considered here (Ó Floinn 2001, 1–7; Laing 2005, 169). Other types are more securely linked to north Britain: variants of projecting ring-headed pins, knobbed spearbutts, massive terrets, and hemispherical 'jet' gaming pieces (Fig 11.4; Laing and Laing 1986). These merit some review and discussion.

The development from the projecting ring-headed pins of the Iron Age to the ornate handpins of the Early Historic period has long been a typological classic. Of concern here are the intermediate types: such variants as proto-handpins, ibex-headed, corrugated and rosette-headed pins (Stevenson 1955, 288–92; Youngs 2005). These lack sustained recent

synthesis, but are well represented in the north, where moulds for all apart from ibex-headed ones are known (Heald 2005). Their typological variety and broad distribution across Britain and Ireland, however, imply multiple inter-related areas of production and development. Some show a northern concentration which suggests they were products of the area, notably beaded and corrugated, rosette, and corrugated pins. These show a thin eastern-biased spread from Orkney to Hadrian's Wall, with outliers in western England and Ireland (Fig 11.5a). They seem to be a mid- to late Roman Iron Age phenomenon.

The dating of the other object types has been more contentious. Knobbed spearbutts were for long considered a classic of the pre-Roman Iron Age, but recent finds and reappraisal strongly indicate a 3rd- to 5th-century AD horizon (Heald 2001). Although the distribution is predominantly Scottish and Irish, they are increasingly found in southern Britain, especially through the Portable Antiquities Scheme; the few from excavations support the northern dating. A series of biases affects interpretation: Ireland has very little settlement evidence of the period (where moulds are most likely to be discovered) but a strong tradition of weaponry deposition; Scotland has the settlements, but not the hoarding habit; while the south has the modern bias of a much more extensive metal-detecting culture. Even so, the southern finds are relatively few and locally unusual; this is best seen as a type common to Scotland and Ireland which was distributed to the south (Fig 11.5b).

Another problematic category is the massive or Donside terrets (Kilbride-Jones 1935; Livens 1976; MacGregor 1976, 47–8). These are usually considered part of the 'massive' metalworking tradition of north-east Scotland, given their size, decoration and traditional distribution (MacGregor 1976, 48). Recent discoveries have raised severe doubts over this, replacing the north-east concentration with a spread over much of northern Britain and a significant number of outliers (Fig 11.5d), similar to the other LRIA material discussed here. The wide technological diversity suggests a number of distinct production centres: some have attachment bars of copper alloy, others use iron, sometimes fixed with lead; some are hollow-cast while others are solid; one is even cast in two halves which are riveted together.

Laing and Laing (1986) suggested a 2nd- to 4th-century AD bracket for the type, but it can be taken even later. There are no secure associations with ERIA material, but one (albeit atypical) comes from an Anglo-Saxon grave at Linton Heath, Cambridgeshire, while the hoard from Crichie, Aberdeenshire, associates massive terrets, knobbed spearbutts and shale gaming pieces (White 1988, 144, fig 88; Laing and Laing 1986, 213–14; Ralston and Inglis 1984, 57–8). Massive terrets do not appear in the sets of five typical of the British Iron Age (Stead 1991, 47–52); of the 44 known to the writer (Appendix

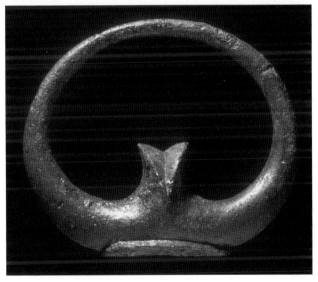

Fig 11.4 Typical late Roman Iron Age material culture: a (top left), variants of projecting ring-headed pins, Covesea, Moray (largest one L 75mm); b (top right), knobbed spearbutt, Crichie, Aberdeenshire (L 51.5mm); c (bottom left), hemispherical gaming pieces, Traprain Law, East Lothian (bottom left, D 30mm); d (bottom right), massive terret, Wheatcroft, Dumfries & Galloway (H 63.5mm). © NMS

11.2), almost all are single finds, with two pairs and one find of three. This suggests a rather different traction system, perhaps a single horse rather than the paired draught of the normal Iron Age cart. Although Livens (1976, 153–6) doubted a role in harness, MacGregor (1976, fig 3.4) proposed a sensible fastening system, and the visible wear is consistent with other terrets.

The complexities are compounded by the close similarities of massive terrets to a continental Roman terret type, often seen as the prototype (Piggott 1955,

63; Piggott 1966, 12; Spratling 1971, 117 n 38), which may have been adopted because of its affinities to local decorative styles. Although not synthesised, their wide distribution suggests they are not solely Gallo-Roman as often stated; they are an infrequent but widespread type, morphologically very similar to the north British style. Some appear indistinguishable from British terrets (eg Bogaers 1952, Afb 3.11), but most have more complex mountings (eg Drexel 1929, 39, fig 3; Palágyi 2000, Abb 6), while the Blerick (Netherlands) ones are flat rather than

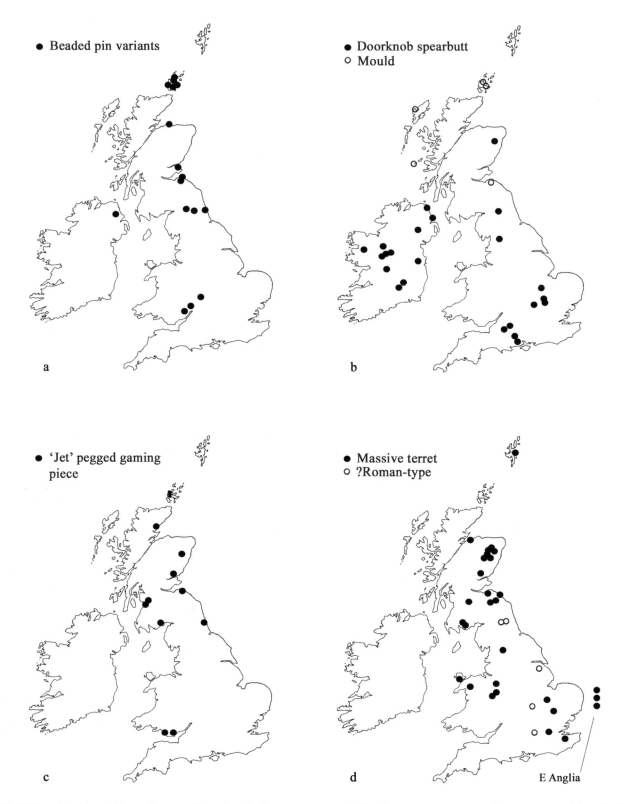

Fig 11.5 Distributions of late Roman Iron Age indigenous material culture: a, corrugated, rosette, and beaded & corrugated pins; b, 'doorknob' spearbutts; c, 'jet' gaming pieces; d, massive terrets (with likely Roman ones differentiated). See Appendices 11.2 and 11.3 for data sources

rounded in section and solid-cast (Gaedechens 1874, 12). I suspect in Britain we are confused by the over-lapping distributions of two different (but visually similar) artefact groups. For instance, the Chesters and Kirmington examples have heavily flared lips

closely paralleled at Blerick; the Billing terret has an unusual central moulding; the Hambleden example has a Roman-type skirt fitting; while the bipartite construction of the Corbridge example is at odds with all other massive terrets (MacGregor

1976, no 113, 115; Leahy 1995; Livens 1976, no 18; Cocks 1921, fig 31.6). These are all likely to be Roman types. The distribution must therefore carry a slight health warning: likely Roman ones are indicated, but others as yet unnoted may be present. With these examples removed, however, it still appears as a northern type with scattered examples to the south.

The final category is 'jet pin-heads' (Figs 11.4c, 11.5c) – an unfortunate term, as they are of black, shiny, organic-rich stone, but rarely if ever of jet, while their flat-based form and (in the Crichie hoard) appearance in quantity makes them more plausibly gaming pieces, related to similar bone items (Close-Brooks 1986, 166). Recent discussion points to a 3rd- to 7th-century bracket (Caldwell *et al* 2006, 78–9).

Patterns and processes

Apart from their dating, these types share a distribution much broader than the central British norm of the late pre-Roman and early Roman Iron Age (Fig 11.5). It covers most of north Britain and in some cases also Ireland, the first substantial sharing of material with Ireland since the late Bronze Age; although there is persistent evidence for Irish-Scottish contacts during the first millennium BC (Raftery 2005), it is small-scale compared to the evidence from the early centuries AD onwards. This group of material is not a 'package': there are marked differences between the distributions. Only spearbutts and pins appear in Ireland, while there is a marked sparsity of all types in northern England apart from Hadrian's Wall and its immediate vicinity. Pins and gaming pieces both show a south Welsh/Severn cluster. In contrast, spearbutts and terrets are found more widely; both occur in eastern England, with butts also in Wessex and an emerging north Welsh/northern Marches cluster of terrets. Of course all such distributions are potentially volatile with low numbers of finds, and may change as the dataset grows, but there is enough to mark suggestions of trends and show a sharing of types over large areas. This is different from the patterns of the ERIA, and suggests new links, perhaps even political alliances – the building of new relationships in the north represented in history by events such as the 'Barbarian Conspiracy' (Laing and Laing 1986).

A key element of these distributions is their significant representation in the southern 'civilian zone' of the province (see above and Fig 11.5). The variety in detail warns against attempts at single interpretations. While interpreting distributions is always hazardous, it is made more so by the small numbers of objects involved: Youngs (2005, 252), discussing proto-handpins, has commented they are 'complex in detail, thinly but very widely spread'; the same could be said of all the material under review. Depositional biases can constrain such distributions, as noted with spearbutts. This is seen even more clearly in hanging bowls, where the existence of an accompanied burial tradition biases distribution maps to south and east England although the only manufacturing evidence is from northern Scotland (Bruce-Mitford 2005, 23–9, 314–16). With the material under study here, there is less obvious bias, as almost all are site or stray finds, less open to distortions from hoarding and burial habits; the distributions are taken as a reasonable basis for initial discussion.

So why are these essentially northern styles found in the south? In contrast to Iron Age metalwork, they cannot readily be seen as prestige imports, and present a puzzling mixture of types, with small ornaments, horse harness, weaponry, and gaming pieces. The pins are best seen as developing and diversifying in multiple centres, but for the others, more firmly northern, some form of contacts must be represented. No single explanation will be convincing for the range of material and geography, but some possibilities should be discussed. Some may be linked to northern raiders, but the broad geographical and chronological spread makes this unlikely as an overarching explanation. It is tempting, however, to see the movement of people in some form. Could some be connected with mercenaries or other forms of barbarian soldier in Rome's service, as the spearbutts might suggest? White (2007, 195–201) has considered the issue of Germanic and Irish mercenaries, arguing that the distribution of distinctive material (brought from the homelands or developed as a 'badge' in new territory) indicates that each late Roman diocese recruited adjacent barbarians as mercenaries – the Irish in western Britain, Germans from the North Sea coast for eastern England. There are indications of Picts and Irish in the south of the province, such as the Irish ogham stone from Silchester (Hants; Fulford *et al* 2000), the Pictish ogham from Weeting (Norfolk; Clarke 1952) and the Latin tombstone of an Irishman from Wroxeter (Shrops; Wright and Jackson 1968), while Rance (2001) has made a convincing case that the Attacotti were an Irish group settling in Wales and recruited into the Roman army in the late 4th century. The material studied here does show a cluster around Hadrian's Wall, although the major concentration is further south; further contacts between Hadrian's Wall and southern Scotland at this date are seen in the movement of black organic-rich stones for jewellery (Allason-Jones and Jones 1994, 271–2). Thus, it is not inconsistent with the patterns White has noted, although less clearly focused on barbarian recruitment to the immediately adjacent frontier.

Another model would be sustained patterns of regional contact, perhaps from kin links. Ó Floinn (2001, 2–7) has suggested this for early penannular brooches and zoomorphic pins, identifying groups which show a strong link between the lower Severn area and northern Leinster. Interestingly, there is little in the current dataset to support the historical or mythical traditions of the migration of a group of *Votadini* under Cunedda to help the north Welsh

(Morris 1993, 66–8); the thin scatter of north Welsh terrets is a poor foundation for a warband. More generally, the material studied here does not show the constrained distributions which would suggest such patterns of kin contact.

Clearly no single interpretation could or should be fitted to all the data. Other finds highlight long-range contacts across Britain and Ireland in the late and immediately post-Roman centuries, such as the (albeit sparse) spread of Mediterranean imports in the 5th and 6th centuries (Campbell 2007a, fig 83) and the development of distinctive Insular art styles (eg Laing 2005). The distribution of pins and gaming pieces could perhaps be fitted into the social ties behind these liaisons. But what makes the terrets and spearbutts unusual is that their distribution goes beyond the 'Celtic west' where imports and Insular art normally reside; the possibility of a connection to mercenary recruitment is a tantalising one.

Discussion

The main aim of this paper has been to show that the under-studied late Roman material culture of northern Britain, both indigenous and imported, can cast new light on our understanding of these complex times. The indigenous use of late Roman imports shows similarities to the 1st and 2nd centuries in its focus on locally useful material such as feasting equipment and its involvement in local social engagements. However, there are also clear differences, notably in the patchy distribution and marked restriction to key sites. Late Roman finds were more exclusive than before. There are also clear signs of high-value material moving beyond the frontier, a phenomenon best connected with diplomatic gifts or payments.

Changes occurred both in Roman policies and local societies. From the later 2nd century onwards, it seems there was more concern with political interference and diplomatic efforts on the part of the Romans, with the targeting (or blackballing) of particular areas and groups (Hunter 2007a).

The local societies were themselves changing, and contacts with Rome must have played a part in this. The renewed interest in hillforts and defended sites probably reflects the increasing dominance of particular powerful groups. Whereas in the ERIA it can be argued that much of Scotland comprised relatively small-scale social units with power-politics at a fairly local scale, the emergence of fewer larger centres probably reflects some form of political consolidation in southern Scotland.

These changing societies are also marked by changes in indigenous material culture. New forms appear and old forms develop, with markedly different, broader distributions from those of the ERIA. This suggests a realignment of political connections, with broader links being forged. It is noteworthy that although Roman diplomatic efforts avoided north-east Scotland, the indigenous finds show that this area was closely connected to this wider picture. The evidence of northern material spreading to the south emphasises that the movement of imports was not simply a one-sided affair from Rome to the 'barbarians'. It stresses the development of extensive connections deep into *Britannia*, and perhaps provides a hint of the involvement of northern groups in southern mercenary activities. These late Roman connections and entanglements ran both ways.

The results of this study are undoubtedly preliminary. Yet I hope they provide steps towards a better understanding of this material, and show that it has much to say. In combination, the thin scatter of late Roman finds and the new forms of indigenous material culture offer ways into the complexities of the late Roman period in the area north of the Wall and its impacts to the south.

Notes

1   I am grateful to the editors for the opportunity to develop these thoughts, to Colin Wallace for very valuable interchanges of opinion and observation, and to David Clarke and Martin Goldberg for comments on an earlier draft.

Appendix 11.1: Late Roman finds from north of Hadrian's Wall – an addendum

Since the last listing of Scottish late Roman finds (Hunter 2007a, appendix 2), further examples have been excavated or identified from museum research. The list has also been expanded to include Northumberland north of Hadrian's Wall. I am grateful to Colin Wallace for his assistance with identifications of the pottery, and for access to his own researches on northern English material. LR = late Roman; C3 = 3rd century; C4 = 4th century.

Two Northumberland finds are omitted because their dating brackets are not primarily late Roman. The glass jug spout from Witchy Neuk, dated in the excavation report to the 3rd century (Wake 1939, 137), is a type now seen as 2nd–3rd century (Ingemark 2003, 134–5; Price and Cottam 1998, 157–61). Likewise, the sherd of colour-coated pottery from West Whelpington cannot be more closely dated than 2nd–3rd century, while the *antoninianus* from there is probably post-medieval (Jarrett and Evans 1989, 131–2; Jarrett 1970, 257).

Girnigoe	Caithness	33 late Roman coins found on a coastal promontory site, dating from *c* 270–370	A Heald and N Holmes, pers comm
Harperdean	E Lothian	*Follis* of Constantius I (recorded as a stray); part of finds cluster in general area of an open settlement	Bateson and Holmes 2006, 165 Hunter 2009
Knowes	E Lothian	Sherd of late Roman glass – too small for detailed identification	Haselgrove 2009
Clatchard Craig	Fife	Sherd published as samian is actually Oxfordshire red slip	Hartley 1986 C Wallace, pers comm
Bamburgh	Northumberland	Oxfordshire red slip	C Wallace, pers comm (from Hope Taylor excavations)
Chatton Sandyford	Northumberland	Mid-C3 flagon sherds deposited in older burial cairn; undiagnostic glass sherd may be related; perhaps disturbed burial or votive offering	Jobey 1968, 19, 24–5
Carry House Camp	Northumberland	LR pot, bronze coin of Victorinus	Rome Hall 1880, 361–2
Huckhoe	Northumberland	Sherds of several C4 pots	Jobey 1959, 256–8
Yeavering Bell	Northumberland	2 LR coins (minimi)	Hope-Taylor 1977, 6
Old Scatness	Shetland	LR folded beaker	C Wallace, pers comm
Sands of Breckon, Yell	Shetland	1 of the 2 sherds of 'samian' is a late Roman colour-coated sherd, probably Oxfordshire red slip	Hunter 2001, 309 C Wallace, pers comm

Appendix 11.2: Massive terrets

This lists details all massive terrets known to the writer as of December 2008. Those which are likely to be Roman in origin are italicised (see text for details). Abbreviations: M = catalogue number in MacGregor 1976; L = Livens 1976. BM British Museum; NMS National Museums Scotland. Fe iron, Pb lead, CuA copper alloy.

Site	County	No	Moulding	Mount	Wear/condition	Notes	Reference	Museum
SCOTLAND								
Rhynie (Tap o'Noth)	Aberdeen	1	Stemmed knob	Integral cast bar	Intact	V small, loop one side, 2-piece casting	M 123 L 6	Marischal 15599
Shellagreen, Culsalmond	Aberdeen	1	Ribbed (two)	Integral cast bar	Wear in 2 areas at top	Repair at top of lips	M 118 L 3	Marischal 15597
Ballestrade, Cromar	Aberdeen	1	Hump	Integral cast bar	Repair on hoop		M 111 L 2	BM 59-12-27-1
Crichie	Aberdeen	1	Hump	Fe bar	Upper loop worn	From hoard	M 116 L 4	BM 56.11-4.6
Clova, Lumsden	Aberdeen	1	Split lip	Missing, thus probably Fe	Section of loop with mortice and tenon join; upper part worn	Cast repair to lip	M 114 L 5	NMS FA 41
Hillock Head, Towie	Aberdeen	2	Ribbed (two)	Fe bar with Pb (on 1 at least)	Upper loop and base hole worn		M 125-6 L 7-8	NMS FA 30-31
Kirriemuir	Angus	1	Ribbed (three)	Integral cast bar	Upper part lost	CuA strip threaded through – to hold upper part?	M 121 L 10	NMS FA 42
Eyemouth	Berwick	1	Ribbed (two)	?Integral cast bar	Worn at two points; repair to lip and ?mount		M 119 L 11	NMS FA 120
Longniddry	East Lothian	2	Ribbed (three, four)	Fe	One with slight base wear, one extensive and upper hoop worn		*DES* 1992, 50	NMS FA 115-6
Cogarth	Kirkcudbright	1	Split lip	Fe?			*DES* 2000, 22	Stewartry
Wheatcroft	Kirkcudbright	1	Split lip	Fe	Wear in upper part	Leaded bronze	*DES* 1999, 23	Stewartry
Cairngryfe	Lanark	1	Ribbed (five)	?Fe with Pb (missing)		Leaded bronze, tinned?; from hillfort	M 112 L 16	NMS HH 464
Culbin Sands	Moray	1	Ribbed (three)	?Integral cast bar	Top lost; lip pierced	Small	M 117 L fig 4	Hunterian B.1951.967
Sorrowlessfield, Oxnam	Roxburgh	1	Split lip	Hollow with Fe bar, held by Pb	Top lost		M 122 L 12	Marischal 15598

Site	County	No	Moulding	Mount	Wear/condition	Notes	Reference	Museum
Springwood Park	Roxburgh	1	Split lip	Fe bar	Broken and distorted at top	Small	*DES* 1996, 88	NMS FA 121
Shetland	Shetland	1	? (damaged)	Integral cast bar	Much of loop lost		M 124	Shetland
Unprov	Scotland	1	Split lip	Integral cast bar, ?later replaced	Upper half lost, tips tapered	No hollow under lip	M 127 L 1	NMS FA 32
WALES								
Y Werthyr	Anglesey	1	Split lip	Fe bar	Part hoop lost	Found on enclosure (?hillfort); brass	L 9	Bangor 48/74
Dinas Emrys	Caernarvon	3	Ribbed (unusual)	Fe bar		Bronze; from hillfort	L 13-15	NMW 37.319
ENGLAND								
Hambleden	*Bucks*	*1*	*Ribbed (?)*	*Flared base and pendant loop*	*Good*	*Roman fitting*	*Cocks 1921, fig 31.6*	
Linton Heath	Cambs	1	Stemmed knob	Integral cast bar		From Anglo-Saxon burial; ring on side, cf Rhynie	Laing and Laing 1986, 212 White 1988, 144	
Nantwich	Cheshire	1	Split lip	?	Poor surface		PAS LVPL2156	
?	E Anglia	1	Split lip	Integral cast bar	Broken; surviving arm thinned from wear, hole worn in lips		R Hurford, pers comm	Private collection
?	E Anglia	1	Ribbed (three)	None visible	Good		R Hurford, pers comm; noted on e-bay	
Godmanchester	Cambs	1	Ribbed (three)	?	Most of hoop lost		R Hurford, pers comm; noted on e-bay	
Dartford	Kent	1	Ribbed (two)	Slot for bar, now lost			*Archaeologia Cantiana* **109** (1991), 350–1; Sotheby's 10.12.92, 47	Private collection
Kirmington	*Lincs*	*1*	*Split lip*	*Skirt and integral cast bar*	*Intact*	*Flat casting; small*	*Leahy 1995*	*Scunthorpe KMAA796*
Moorgate Street, London	Middlesex	1	?	?	?		M 71	Museum of London
Norfolk	Norfolk	1	?	?	?		S Youngs, pers comm	Norwich Castle Museum 1986.252.37

Site	County	No	Moulding	Mount	Wear/condition	Notes	Reference	Museum
Billing	Northants	1	Stemmed knob – open/inlaid?	Socket full of Fe corrosion			L 18	BM WG 2348
Chesters	Northumb	1	Split lip	Fe bar		Roman fort	M 113 L 19	Chesters 1042
Corbridge	Northumb	1	Ribbed (seven)	Missing, thus ?Fe		Cast in 2 halves, riveted together; Roman fort	M 115 L 20	Corbridge
Unprovenanced ('near Scottish border')	Northumb?	1	Ribbed (two)	Fe bar			Bonhams 12.12.95, 339; ? = Sotheby's 8.12.94, 71 'found in Northumberland'	
Shrewsbury	Shrops	1	Split lip	?	Intact, good condition; perhaps slight thinning at top		PAS LANCUM-1F06E0	
Wroxeter	Shrops	1	Split lip	?Fe bar	Intact		White 1994	Shrewsbury A/90/011
High Rigg, Giggleswick	Yorks	1	Ribbed (four)	?	?		M 120 L 21	Tot Lord Museum, Settle
Romford?	Unclear whether Essex, Kent or Dorset	1	Split lip	?	?		R Hurford, pers comm; noted on e-bay	
UNPROVENANCED								
		1	Ribbed (multiple)	Integral cast bar	Hoop worn		L 22	BM 65.12-3.7
		1	Split lip	Fe bar	Most of loop lost		L 23	BM 65.12-3.8
		1	Ribbed (four)	?	Upper part worn		Christie's New York 19.3.97, lot 57	

Appendix 11.3: Source lists for distribution plots in Fig 11.5
(see Appendix 11.2 for massive terrets, and Caldwell *et al* 2006 for 'jet' gaming pieces)

Corrugated, rosette-headed, and beaded and corrugated pins

The terminology of these pins can get confusing. 'Corrugated' is used here (in preference to 'beaded') to refer to pins with small beads all round the head, to differentiate them from those with large beads round the head, normally (but not exclusively) termed rosette-headed. The beaded and corrugated type have large beads in the lower part of the ring and smaller ones around the remainder. They are codified here as C, R and BandC respectively.

Site	County	Type	Reference
Gurness	Orkney	BandC (moulds)	Close-Brooks 1987
Howe	Orkney	C, BandC	Ballin Smith 1994, illus 133 nos 7097, 1729
Mine Howe	Orkney	B (moulds)	A Heald, pers comm
Swandale, Rousay	Orkney	BandC	Stevenson 1955, 290, n 4
Covesea	Moray	R, BandC	Benton 1931, 194–6
Tentsmuir	Fife	C	Stevenson 1955, 290, n 1
North Berwick	East Lothian	BandC	Richardson 1907, fig 4
Traprain Law	East Lothian	C, R (some moulds)	Burley 1956, nos 110–17
Corbridge	Northumberland	BandC	Stevenson 1955, 290, n 4
South Shields	Co Durham	C	Allason-Jones and Miket 1984, no 3.536
Gloucester	Gloucs	BandC	Heighway and Bryant 1999, fig 3.15 no 47
Lydney	Gloucs	BandC	Wheeler and Wheeler 1932, fig 18.63
Ulster	Ulster	BandC	Ulster Museum, unpublished
Whitchurch	Warwicks	R	N Sharples, pers comm
Great Chesters	Northumberland	R	Allason-Jones 1996b, fig 4.14
Lingrow	Orkney	C?	Stevenson 1955, 290 n 1

Doorknob spearbutts
(excluding Irish finds, for which see Raftery 1982 and 1998; Hunter 1994)

Site	County	Notes	Reference
Gurness	Orkney	Iron Age site (moulds)	Close-Brooks 1987
Mine Howe	Orkney	Iron Age site (moulds)	Heald 2001, 691
Loch na Beirgh	Lewis	Iron Age site (moulds)	Heald 2001, 689–90
Crichie	Aberdeen	2, from a hoard	Raftery 1982, fig 10; *DES* 2001, 11
Dun Mor Vaul	Argyll	Iron Age site (moulds)	Heald 2001, 691
Traprain	E Lothian	Iron Age site (moulds)	Raftery 1982, fig 11
Vindolanda	Northumberland	Roman fort (unstratified)	Bidwell 1985, fig 44 no 94
Clapham, Ingleborough	N Yorkshire	Stray find	*The Searcher* October 1995, 42; Val Rigby, pers comm
Dropshort, Little Brickhill	Northants	Roman small town	Neal 1987, fig 24 no 39
Titchmarsh	Northants	Stray find	PAS NARC 1664 *Britannia* **36** (2005), 468
Warren Villa	Beds	Roman villa	Heald 2001, 690–1 *Roman Finds Group Newsletter* **2** (1990), 1
Sandy	Beds	Roman small town	Heald 2001, fig 2
Calne	Wilts	Stray find	D Boughton, pers comm
Rushall Down	Wilts	Romano-British open settlement	Raftery 1982, fig 10
Aldershot	Hants	Stray find	*The Searcher* December 1995, 46; Val Rigby, pers comm
Ellingham Harbridge and Ibsley	Hants	Stray find	PAS HAMP-EFC828 *Britannia* **36** (2005), 468

12 The emergence of Northumbria: artefacts, archaeology, and models *Colm O'Brien*

Introduction

The archaeology of Northumbria, if viewed from the standpoint of a review of Anglo-Saxon England, has a feel of ambiguity about it. Although Bede wrote (*HE* 1.15) of the *tota Nordanhymbrorum progenies* as numbering among the *Anglorum populi* who came from *Angulus*, the country of the Angles, one would be hard-pressed to make a case for a close affinity between the Early Medieval archaeology of, say, Northumberland and Nottinghamshire. The Yorkshire Wolds has a sense of a continuum across the Humber from Lincolnshire and Nottinghamshire, and burial archaeology in particular would suggest this; but in the area considered in this review, broadly from the Yorkshire Derwent northwards to the modern Scottish border, this is hardly the case. This could be a question of drawing a line between the two constituent kingdoms which at the beginning of the 7th century were brought together to form Northumbria, Deira to the south and Bernicia to the north (Fig 12.1). Even at a political level, the unity of Northumbria was not a given; as late as the AD 660s King Oswiu was ruling Deira at one remove, through devolved government, and three of his sub-kings attempted rebellion. But scholars have struggled to find an archeologically convincing boundary. Brian Roberts' exposition of cultural corelands, presented in Chapter 13 of this volume, now enables us to see why this has been so and explains why a Bernician-Deiran duality will not serve as a model for investigating Northumbrian origins.

The *villa regia* of Yeavering, north of the Cheviots and within the River Tweed catchment zone, is the element above all others in Northumbria which features in the broad-based accounts of Anglo-Saxon archaeology; it provides the definitive archaeological expression of the feasting-hall of the Germanic kings. In this respect, it might be seen as a counterpart to Sutton Hoo which supplies the definitive expression of kingly burial. But to say this is to step right into the centre of the ambiguity: the Yeavering cemeteries are not as Sutton Hoo, and it is by no means clearly the case that Bernician kings saw a need to dramatise kingship in funerary architecture and practice in the ways of the Wuffingas kings of East Anglia. Yeavering, in its burials, shows a profound rootedness in place and past in a north British cultural milieu, a point taken up below. As well as the geography which Roberts elucidates, there is also a chronology to consider here. The standard model of a previous generation of scholarship (Stenton 1971, 74–6) held that the Bernician kings in the line of Ida did not break out from their coastal rock-bound enclave at Bamburgh to dominate the wider hinterland before the accession of Aethelfrith in AD 592. Brian Hope-Taylor's (1977) archaeological study of Yeavering, however, convinced him that its complex stratification could not be compressed into the 7th century, and that a long timescale was represented here. This led him to the radical conclusion that Yeavering was a place of contact between a native society and an incoming Anglian elite at which a hybrid culture was forged. Although there are new understandings of Early Medieval ethnicity since Hope-Taylor wrote (discussed below in relation to burial archaeology), Yeavering still leads us to a sense of cultural syncretism (O'Brien forthcoming).

So the sense of depth in time which Hope-Taylor introduced invites reflection on this question: out of what did Roberts's cultural corelands emerge? It may well be that the factor which most deeply influenced the entities and material cultures which eventually emerged as Northumbria is the fact that

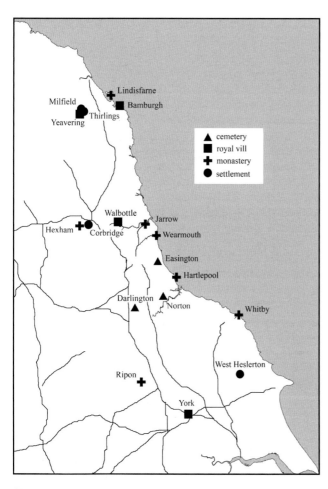

Fig 12.1 The location of important archaeological sites in the kingdom of Northumbria (map: Rob Collins)

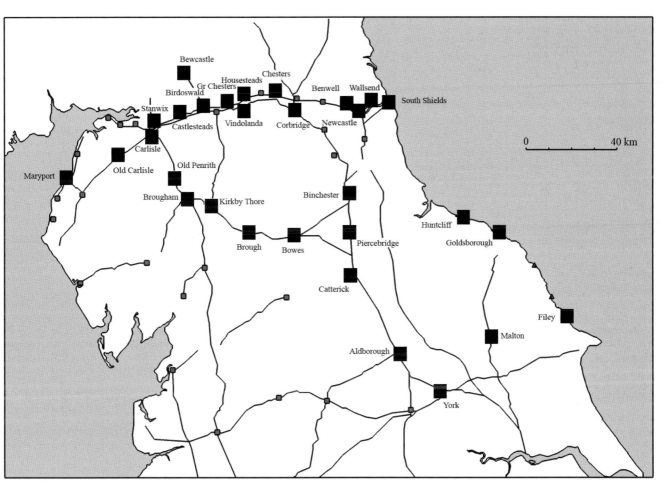

Fig 12.2   A map of Roman military and town sites with evidence for occupation in the 5th–8th centuries (map: Rob Collins)

in the 2nd, 3rd and 4th centuries AD the area considered here was politically and culturally liminal; it spanned the Tyne-Solway frontier zone, with a hinterland of support systems to the south, less strongly asserted outposts to the north, and a road system to enable coherence. The point which stands out most clearly from a review of artefacts from the post-Roman period, even, perhaps, into the 8th century, is the continued use of fort sites of the Wall corridor and, to a lesser extent, the hinterland (Fig 12.2). The second point of note is a predominance of objects which were certainly or probably deposited in burials. The rest of this paper goes on to discuss these two points.

Forts and the wall corridor and the emergence of cultural corelands

Artefacts found within and near to the Roman forts can be considered in two groups: stones with Latin inscriptions, which are likely to have been set up in the late Roman or early post-Roman period and which complement the evidence of some late episodes of building construction and penannular brooch-types; and items of the 6th to 8th centuries, many of which

may have come from burials and whose cultural references are broadly 'Germanic' (Tables 12.1 and 12.2). In the Wall corridor, inscriptions are found at Castlesteads and Vindolanda, while Maryport, Old Carlisle, and Brougham in the hinterland have also produced probable post-Roman inscriptions. All are memorials: to Pluma from his wife Lunaris (*RIB* 786); to Tancorix, a lady of 60 years (*RIB* 908); to Rianorix whose age is now missing from the stone (*RIB* 862); to Spurcio who was 60 or 61 (the text is uncertain) years old (*RIB* 863). The Vindolanda memorial to Brigomaglos (Fig 12.3; *RIB* 1722) has the verb *iacit*; often, though not in this case, the expression is *hic iacit* (here lies), widely used in Christian memorials. These monuments appear long after formal consular inscriptions had ceased to be carved and displayed. As Mark Hassall notes in this volume, the latest date for a consular inscription in the Wall zone is AD 297–305. Questions to consider are: whether these inscriptions are evidence of an unbroken tradition of the use of Latin or whether the language was reintroduced from elsewhere; the chronology of such inscriptions – and this connects with the first question; and why our known examples are at fort sites.

Our inscriptions are perhaps best considered as

Fig 12.3   The Brigomaglos stone (RIB 1722) from Vindolanda. © English Heritage

outliers to a larger group with a distribution centred in southern Scotland. Charles Thomas (1992) discussed the Brigomaglos stone from Vindolanda in these terms and we can extend his analysis to these other northern English stones. In a wider setting, these sit within a corpus of some 250 inscriptions, mostly epigraphs, from a period before AD 700 from western Britain, in the Scilly Islands, the peninsula of Cornwall and Devon, Wales, and the Isle of Man.

Thomas's (1992) southern Scottish group comprises six stones in Galloway, in the extreme south-west, and another seven in the interior of the country from Kirkliston, Midlothian, in the north to the Northumbrian example at Vindolanda. Five more are considered here. For his group, Thomas commented on the breadth of the Latinity, in contrast to a more restricted vocabulary in Cornwall-Devon. But there is an even richer vocabulary in North Wales, with evidence of 'a continuing Roman civil organisation and formal monasticism, for neither of which is there any direct evidence north of Hadrian's Wall' (Thomas 1992, 7). To Thomas's list of 40 Latin words on the Scottish inscriptions, we can add from Cumbria the words *carissima*, *coniux*, *mulier*, *titulum*, *vixit*.

Thomas (1992, 7–8) allowed the Latinus stone from Whithorn as evidence of an offshoot of local Christianity brought from (say) late 4th-century Carlisle; other Galloway stones, however, represented 'entirely intrusive Christian activity'. He sees the Brigomaglos stone as native sub-Roman, from the late 5th or early 6th centuries. Use of the verb *iacit* derives from its use on Christian memorials in Atlantic Gaul in the second quarter of the 5th century. As long ago as 1950, V E Nash-Williams linked the British inscriptions, through the formula *hic iacit*, with funerary practice in Gaul in the first half of the 5th century and, beyond that, to Italy

in the late 4th century. Both Thomas and Jeremy Knight have developed this line of thought to the point that Christian commemoration of this kind is understood to be a post-Roman introduction into Britain, beginning about AD 420–40, derived from exemplars in Gaul (Handley 2001, fn 3 for bibliography on this point.).

Mark Handley (2001) has challenged this orthodoxy. The overall decline in numbers of inscriptions in late Roman Britain is not evidence of Britain becoming excluded from the Roman world, and the Christian commemoration here did not need to be introduced anew from outside. The pattern through time of inscriptions in Britain, with a sharp fall-off after AD 200 and a late 4th- to 5th-century rise in memorial inscriptions matches the pattern for the western empire as a whole. He argues (Handley 2001, 183–4) there are Christian inscriptions in Britain in the 4th century; the expression *titulum posuit* is one such indicator and this occurs in the dative case *titulo posuit* (as a memorial) at Brougham amongst our set. He shows (*ibid*, 186–9) that *hic iacet* (or, the form normal on the British inscriptions, *iacit*) is widely used in the late Roman West and North Africa from the late 4th century onwards. Nash-Williams inexplicably derived its use in Britain from two inscriptions in Lyon of AD 447 and 449, and others have followed this uncritically. In summary, Handley concludes (*ibid*, 195) that the Christian inscriptions of western Britain share many features with those of much of western Europe and North Africa and with those of Roman Britain. There is little reason to believe that they were a Gallic introduction of the 5th century.

Whatever else they tell us, these inscriptions speak of knowledge and use of the Latin language and a tradition of announcements in stone extending into the 5th century. The fact that fort sites have been the main focus of excavation in northern England over the years may have introduced a bias into the record, but the presence of such memorials here is more than simple coincidence, for there is good structural evidence of the continuing occupation of forts into the 5th century and evidence for Christian observance within forts. Housesteads, Birdoswald, Vindolanda, and South Shields all have small buildings interpreted as churches fitted at a late stage into the *praetorium* or the *principia* or elsewhere in the fort (Collins forthcoming). The *principia* at Carlisle saw rebuilding in the 5th century and the nearby fort at Stanwix also may have seen activity (McCarthy 2002). At Birdoswald, a timber building, possibly of cruck construction, was built on the ruins of the fort granaries and may have remained in use beyond AD 500 (Wilmott 1997, 202–32). Ideas have been developed to explain why forts remained in use. Tony Wilmott, from his excavations at Birdoswald, suggested (1997, 228) that the occupants of the fort, continuing to extract customary tax levies for their maintenance, could have entered into alliance with tribal leaders or might themselves have become a self-sustaining community based around a hereditary commander (cf Casey 1993a; 1993b). Rob Collins (2004), noting that the number of crossing points through the Wall had been reduced during the late Roman period, suggests control of movement through these points as a mechanism for the development of a sub-Roman military elite. He has subsequently (Collins forthcoming) invoked Occupational Community Theory, which looks at ways in which a group of people sharing an occupation and common life can develop a sense of identity separate from the rest of society. This idea suggests that a martial tradition underlying a soldierly identity developed by the *limitanei*, the garrison troops of the late Roman frontier, allows for their evolution into an elite warband forming around the figure of a leader.

Complementing the inscriptional and structural evidence for continuing use of frontier and hinterland forts into the 5th century is that of the penannular brooches reviewed by Collins in this volume. Types D7 and E, taken together, occur in eleven wall-zone and hinterland forts in a distribution pattern which is markedly different from that of the later Types F and G in which Catterick and Kirkby Thore alone among the fort sites feature (see Collins, Appendix 7.4).

The models which Wilmott and Collins have proposed for the evolution of 5th-century leaders and warrior elites emerging around Roman forts bring process to the geography of Roberts's cultural corelands and these models can be applied to the Bernician cultural core of the eastern half of the Wall corridor, to Rheged in the western end of the corridor and the valley of Eden, and to the unit of *Catraeth* around Teesside and North Yorkshire. But there is no evidence to suggest that such models should apply in the northern coastal zone of Bamburgh or around the Tees Basin; the outpost forts in Northumberland, north of the Wall, are notable for an absence of artefactual or structural evidence suggestive of their continuing relevance in the late 4th century, let alone in the 5th or 6th centuries. The driving forces here must have been different. I have referred above to Hope-Taylor's idea of Yeavering as a place of contact where influences from a British cultural milieu came forward into the Northumbria of the 7th century. The burial evidence, reviewed below, is part of that argument. Leslie Alcock (1988) established a wider interpretative framework for this idea when he brought forward evidence to show that a number of places, known from writings of the 8th century to have kingly associations, had high status at a time before they came under the influence of English speakers. The evidence is in part linguistic. Yeavering and Milfield have carried forward Brittonic names, *Gefrin* and *Maelmin*, into the English language. The name Bamburgh is a coinage of King Aethelfrith late in the 6th century; previously it was Brittonic *Din Guoaroy* in which the element *din-*, which became translated into English as -burgh, indicated a fortified stronghold. Dunbar brings though Brittonic *Dynbaer*, again

the *din-* element. Coldingham carries the Britonnic *Colud* and there is the unidentified *Broninis*, possibly somewhere in Northumberland. The territorial basis of Northumbrian-Bernician kingship here, 60km and more north of the Wall corridor, is built on a geography of British power centres.

By the time we come to the 6th century, the artefacts in circulation and being deposited show Anglo-Saxon cultural affiliations. The point which emerges most strongly from the artefact record is that there is again, or perhaps still, interest in the former fort sites as late as the 6th, 7th, and even 8th centuries. If this is a real phenomenon and not simply an effect of a concentration of archaeological work at these sites, it prompts us to ask what is the basis for this interest. The grounds for caution here are that a long history of investigations at the Roman fort sites could have biased recovery of objects of any period in favour of these sites. However, the findings of the Portable Antiquities Scheme, which are not subject to such a bias, tend to suggest that observed distributions are valid. As shown in Table 12.1, forts sited in the tidal reaches of the Tyne valley, South Shields, Wallsend, and Newcastle, all have finds from this period, as does Benwell, just west of Newcastle. We might note also the cruciform brooch of mid- to late 6th century from Whitehill Point, the next riverbank headland east from Wallsend, and the small-long brooches of 6th-century date from Cleadon, in the hinterland of South Shields, and Hylton, near Sunderland. The precise contexts for these three brooches are not known but they are likely to have come from burials (discussed below). Anglian finds from further afield are largely confined to north Northumberland in the Tweed and Till valleys and the area south of the Tees valley.

Ian Wood (2008a, 2008b) suggests that by the middle of the 7th century, the mouth of the Tyne had become a centre for kingship in Northumbria, with the kings placing monasteries along this routeway. At the river mouth on the south side stands the former fort of *Arbeia*, claimed as the birthplace of King Oswine, with a monastery directly across the river at Tynemouth (Jobey 1967). Some 2km upstream from *Arbeia* stood the nunnery and former monastery of *Donemuthe*, known as Ecgferthes mynster; 2km from here, on the opposite edge of the mudflats of Jarrow Slake, King Ecgfrith is known to have endowed the monastic house of Jarrow in AD 681 and the estates which he provided in the neck of land between the Rivers Tyne and Wear for the joint houses of Wearmouth and Jarrow may have been taken from what was once the *territorium* associated with the fort of *Arbeia* (Roberts 2008b). The Slake, which Symeon of Durham calls *Portus Ecgfridi*, is possibly a royal harbour. A connection of some sort between Jarrow and Wallsend is suggested by the fact that Wallsend, though on the north bank, was part of the parish of Jarrow. Some 15km upstream of the estuary, a monastery stood at Gateshead. The status of Newcastle, immediately across the river,

Table 12.1 Type of evidence for occupation and activity at sites in the Wall corridor in the 5th–8th centuries

Along the Wall	Earthen defences with stone/timber revetment	Structural or Occupational Evidence	Class I Inscribed Stone	'British' type Artefacts	'Anglo-Saxon' type Artefacts	Evidence for Christianity	Burial Evidence
South Shields	■	■		■	■	■	■
Wallsend					■		□
Newcastle	□	■			■		■
Benwell					■		□
Corbridge		□		■	■		
Chesters				■	■		□
Housesteads	■	■		■	□	□	□
Vindolanda	■	■	■	■	■	■	□
Great Chesters					□		
Birdoswald	■	■		■	■	□	□
Castlesteads			□				
Stanwix		□					
Carlisle		■		■	■	■	

A solid square indicates definite evidence, while an open square indicates probable or possible evidence. For references see Appendix 12.1

is not known at this time but archaeological excavations revealed a cemetery in use from the 7th century within the former fort. And we can extend this interest another 10km upstream, beyond the former fort of Benwell, to Wallbottle, the site in the mid-7th century of King Oswiu's villa of *Ad Murum* (*vicus regis* and *villa regia* are Bede's terms for this place: *HE* 3.21 and 22).

This Lower Tyne test case gives good reason to believe that the prominence of the former Roman fort sites in the artefact record genuinely reflects the use of these sites by the royal elites. The finds themselves indicate that, while the texts which describe monastic endowments give us a window of around the mid-7th century, use of the fort sites has a longer duration, reaching back into the 6th century.

Extending from the Lower Tyne case, we might note a royal interest in a nunnery in Carlisle, for it was to there, among the visible ruins of the Roman town, that Queen Iurmenburh travelled in AD 685, in company with Cuthbert, then Bishop of Lindisfarne, to visit her sister while King Ecgfrith was in Pictland (Bede *VCP*). How early the western end of the wall corridor began to come under the influence of an Anglian culture zone is not well understood. A small-long brooch of early to mid-6th-century date is thought to have come from Birdoswald (Fig 12.4). This provenance has been questioned on the grounds

that it is well outside the distribution range for such an object, but that begs the question. Birdoswald's most recent excavator (Wilmott 1997, 218) thinks that the case against is not proven and that the possibility that this brooch did come from here should remain open. Although the pin is missing and the catchplate damaged, the brooch is well enough preserved to serve as a good example of the type, 68mm long with a trefoil head, the top and bottom of the convex bow articulated with horizontal grooves, and the foot having a raised panel from which the apex of a V extends downwards as the edges splay slightly outwards.

South of the Wall corridor, the town of Aldborough takes us to the centre of an estate in which Bishop Wilfrid had interests in the AD 670s (Jones 1971). The hinterland forts of Binchester, Piercebridge, and Catterick all have artefacts of this period (Table 12.2). Bede writes (*HE* 2.14) of the River Swale by Catterick as being a place at which Bishop Paulinus conducted baptisms while visiting in the entourage of King Edwin. In this text, the Swale is juxtaposed as a baptismal place with the River Glen by Edwin's *villa regia* of Yeavering, and this is surely an indication that within or close to the former fort of Catterick stood another *villa regia*. York, the centre of late Roman military command in the north, was the place where Edwin himself received baptism

Fig 12.4 The cruciform (right) and square-headed (left) brooches from Benwell, and the small-long brooch (centre) from Birdoswald. © Newcastle University

and where he commissioned construction of first a temporary wooden church and then a successor in stone (*HE* 2.14).

Another element of Roman frontier infrastructure to have survived was Dere Street, and possibly other parts of the road network. Rosemary Cramp observed (1983, 267) how both *Ceaster* names, which came through into place-names in the English language from a late Latin form of *castrum*, and Germanic *burh* names aligned themselves along Dere Street. If the heroic verse of the *Gododdin* can be read as evidence of an historical event, it seems that warriors marched to death and poetic immortality along this road; or, to take a more securely sourced event, King Oswald could well have raised the sign of the cross at Heavenfield in AD 635 having marched his army south along that road. As late as the 10th century, the monastic community of St Cuthbert used this road as a boundary marker (*HSC* 12 and 24).

In summary, when all sources of evidence are combined, we have strong indications that along the Wall corridor and in the hinterland new identities and forms of leadership developed from former Roman forts as a set of cultural corelands emerged,

while beyond the Wall zone an infrastructure of native British organisation formed the underlay. Places and structures of these corelands continued to support the functioning of kingship during the 6th–8th centuries, in part through strategic partnerships which, from the mid-7th century, kings forged with monks.

'Anglo-Saxon' burials in Northumbria

There have been several region-wide reviews of burial evidence, from Roger Miket's (1980) restatement and catalogue of the Bernician evidence, Rosemary Cramp's (1983) discussion which takes in an area from southern Scotland to the Humber in which burial is considered along with settlement, place-name, and monastic evidence, Sam Lucy's (1998) monograph on the burials of East Yorkshire, and Helen Geake's (1997) study on a national scale of the burials of the conversion period. Sam Lucy's (1999) catalogue of Northumberland, Durham, and Yorkshire (the historic county areas) is now the best standard reference for the data set. The area of the former East Riding stands out for its great con-

**Table 12.2 Type of evidence for occupation and activity
at former Roman sites in Northumbria in the 5th–8th centuries**

	Earthen defences with stone/timber revetment	Structural or Occupational Evidence	Class I Inscribed Stone	'British' type Artefacts	'Anglo-Saxon' type Artefacts	Evidence for Christianity	Burial Evidence
South of the Wall							
York		■		■	■	■	■
Malton	■				■		■
Filey	■						
Goldsborough				■			
Huntcliff				□			
Aldborough	■				■		
Catterick		■		■	■		■
Piercebridge	■			■	■		
Binchester		■			■		■
Bowes	■						
Brough under Stainmore					■		
Brougham			□				
Old Carlisle			□				
Old Penrith					■		
Kirkby Thore				■	■		
Maryport			□				
Manchester					■		■
North of the Wall							
Bewcastle					■	■	

A solid square indicates definite evidence, while an open square indicates probable or possible evidence. For references see Appendix 12.1

centration of burial sites, with present-day North Yorkshire and the northern counties having a total of 63 sites. Bamburgh Bole Hole (Northumberland) and Street House (Cleveland), investigated since 1999, can be added to the catalogue. Inhumation of a single body, often, though not always, with a range of dress-fittings and accompanying goods, in its own grave is the normal burial rite; cremations, though present, are not numerous in Northumbria north of the Yorkshire Wolds. Normally the body was laid out supine, face-up and fully extended, or side-facing and crouched, with the legs flexed. Very occasionally, a body is prone, face-down, with limbs splayed as if the body had been thrown into the grave. As in the case at Sewerby in east Yorkshire (Hirst 1985), this is sometimes thought to indicate the burial, possibly while still alive, of a criminal.

Miket pointed out (1980, 289–90) a factor which severely limits the quality of the archaeological evidence, that most of the finds have been made by chance, usually in quarrying, 'leaving a deficient record that admits neither a contemporary sketch of the position of the body and related objects nor the survival of one undeniably Anglo-Saxon skeleton'. Only three sites, he suggested, had been excavated to modern standards (a figure which has to be revised since 1980) and this calculation led him to lament what he called the 'unhappy practice' of inferring burials solely from objects at Barrasford, Benwell, Capheaton, and Corbridge; and, he might have added, Whitehill Point, where the square-headed brooch was dredged up from the River Tyne. Despite this severe critique, it is reasonable to observe that the artefact record is dominated by objects from burials or which are likely to have come from burials.

Taken overall, the artefacts show the characteristics of an Anglian cultural assemblage. The brooches from Benwell, for example, are of the cruciform and square-headed types, both in bronze (Fig 12.4; Cramp and Miket 1982, nos 6 and 7). Both are decorated with Salin Style I animal ornament. The cruciform brooch has on the lower part of its foot an elongated horse's head with protruding eyes and widely flared nostrils. At the top of the foot, just below the convex bow which allows access to the pin at the back, is a pair of stylised bird-heads, one on each side. The cross-arms at the top are damaged. The headplate of the square-headed brooch has a border in the form of masks in high relief with protruding eyes and ears. The central panel, beneath the convex bow has bird-heads, more elaborate in form than those in the equivalent position on the cruciform brooch. Immediately below, the foot of the brooch begins in a mask with a prominent brow-ridge, round bulging eyes and curling moustache. Set at the mouth is the apex of a tongue formed in six concentric triangles outlined in high relief and filling the space of the wide-splayed footplate which ends in a pair of bird-heads looping around beyond and back into the line of the plate. The whole composition is symmetrical on either side of the long axis of the brooch. The square-headed brooch recovered from the River Tyne by Whitehill Point (Cramp and Miket 1982, no 10), though now corroded, shows much the same characteristics as the Benwell brooch: masks forming the headplate border; side-features below the convex bow, too damaged to see their original decoration; a mask at the top of the foot, lacking the moustache of Benwell brooch but with a similar triangular tongue on the flaring plate; a pelta (shield) shape rounds off the foot of the brooch.

Stray finds are of limited value in defining an assemblage; this is better characterised from objects recorded in the context of the grave itself. In this way, we may say that a female might during the 6th century have been buried dressed with some or all of the following items: a pair of annular brooches to fasten a tubular dress at the shoulders; a set of beads suspended across the chest from the two brooches; a single brooch at the throat or the chest to fasten an outer cloak or shawl. The latter is of the safety-pin type, in which the pin at the back engages in a curved metal plate. It may be of cruciform or square-headed shape, some 110–140mm long, with cross-form or rectangular plate at the top, a convex bow and a long shaft, the surfaces decorated with Style I animal ornament, or the shorter and usually less elaborately ornamented small-long brooch which is also cruciform at its head. At the wrists is a pair of metal fasteners, stitched on to the cuffs of a chemise worn under the dress, in which a small curved plate on one side engages in a slot on the other. Mineralised textile fragments sometimes found adhering to the metal of the brooches may give evidence of weave patterns in the clothing which the brooches fastened. Hanging from a girdle there may be a chatelaine set with one or more iron keys or latchlifters, simple bars of metal up to *c* 200mm long with one end hooked round both sides of the bar to engage in two slots of a sliding lock or bent into a U-shape to lift a latch. The set could also include a small iron-bladed knife, copper-alloy tweezers, and pendants of various types.

The cemetery at Norton on Tees (Sherlock and Welch 1992) can serve as an example to illustrate something of both the common characteristics and the range of variability within a set of graves. This cemetery of 117 inhumations and three cremations is judged to have been the burial ground of a small community of three or four households over three or four generations during much of the 6th and into the early 7th century. Grave 35, of a female aged 25–35 buried crouched on her side, had a pair of annular brooches and a set of beads around the shoulders and neck, sleeve clasps on both wrists, a small bronze buckle in the area of the pelvis, and below the pelvis a knife blade, a set of latch lifters, pendants and a strap end. Grave 30, another female in the same age bracket and also buried crouched, has a set of beads, a pair of annular brooches and a highly decorated cruciform brooch about the area of the shoulders and neck, and two fragments of pins. A young adult female in grave 87 was buried with some beads but no brooches. She had a knife about her and two small metal rings of uncertain use. Best-furnished of all was the female of 20–30 years who was buried in Gravel 40 with her body fully extended. She had the full set of beads, brooches, and sleeve clasps, as well as a knife and latch lifter. She also wore a pair of bracelets, each formed from a strip of silver twisted into a spiral. An unusual feature in this case was that the single brooch at the neck, accompanying the pair of annular brooches at the shoulder, was penannular. Male burials may contain a small belt-buckle and a knife. Some have a spear, of which the iron head and ferrule may have survived, or a shield, of which the iron parts are all that are likely to have survived, the central boss, the strip of metal for the grip and perhaps some rivets. In addition to the dress fittings and elements of personal weaponry, a grave may be furnished with such items as an iron-bound wooden bucket or a wooden bowl or a glass claw-beaker, such as that found at Castle Eden in County Durham.

In the later stages of this burial tradition, the 'final phase' graves of the late 7th to 8th centuries, burials may be completely unfurnished, or the individual might have been buried with just a few dress fittings. The Milfield North and South cemeteries in Northumberland (Scull and Harding 1990; Geake 1997, 172) are a case in point. Grave 1 in Milfield North, thought to be that of a female, contained a pair of small annular brooches, a buckle of copper alloy, a fragment of an iron knife, and a small wheel-shaped ornament, possibly a girdle pendant. Knife blades are the most commonly occurring item and there is also a chatelaine set and a fragment of a sword blade.

The two penannular brooches from Norton, in graves 40 and 65, stand out as being exotic in this assemblage, as do two from the cemetery at West Heslerton, on the north edge of the Yorkshire Wolds (Haughton and Powlesland 1999, 102). Brooches of this type are cast as a ring of metal, some 40–45mm in diameter, broken by a narrow gap, with the terminals on either side of the gap usually broadened and ornamented in some way. The fastening pin is at one end looped around the metal of the ring. In use, the pin is held secure in the gap between the terminals, with its point projecting some way beyond. This type has been identified also at Catterick and in the Yorkshire Wolds at Londesborough and Driffield (Cessford 1999). They are known to have been made in southern Scotland – there is a casting mould from the Mote of Mark on the Dumfriesshire coast – and as such they suggest a strand of western influence in the Anglian culture zone. Exotic also are the hanging bowls of the 7th century and these too appear to come from Scotland, possibly from within the Pictish lands (Brenan 1991). In Northumbria they have been found at Capheaton, Northumberland, in North Yorkshire at the monastery of Whitby and in York, and also at Hawnby and Garton Slack on the Yorkshire Wolds. The Capheaton bowl came into the possession of the Society of Antiquaries of Newcastle upon Tyne in 1813 (Cramp and Miket 1982, no 12) after it was recovered from a tumulus along with 'several pieces of copper, two fibulae, a finger ring and a great quantity of bones'. Of this material, the bowl alone survives. It is formed from a bronze sheet beaten paper-thin. The bowl, 193mm in diameter at its shoulder and 64mm at the base, is joined to a rim, giving it a height of 87mm. The base is slightly concave in profile and has four small rivet holes, presumably for attaching a footstand. Within, the base is decorated with concentric circles finely incised with a compass and a compass-traced design of a six-petalled flower. Three escutcheons are soldered on to the bowl, each a flat ring of metal inscribed with a simple key pattern. Immediately below each, an enamel disc is held between two scrolls. The suspension loops, rising from the escutcheons to the top of the rim, are each formed as animal heads, resting their snouts on the rim as if peering into the bowl.

Settlement excavation in the north of the region has yielded little in the way of artefacts: loom-weights and occasional fragments of pottery, and some small glass fragments from Thirlings. Perhaps the area was largely aceramic at this time, with materials such as wood, skins, and leather used where otherwise pottery might have been employed. However, current work at Cheviot Quarry, close to both Yeavering and Thirlings, is yielding numerous pottery vessels (Clive Waddington, pers comm) and so for the time being it is best to reserve judgement as to the use of ceramics in the Early Medieval material culture.

Studies of the burials of this era have considered both typological aspects of the artefacts, in particular the brooch forms and their ornamentation, and the mode of burial to debate three topics: the status of incoming Anglo-Saxons; their relationships with the indigenous populations; and the location of the boundary between Bernicia and Deira. Sam Lucy (1999, 22–3; 2000, 174–86) doubts that mortuary evidence can contribute usefully to such questions. Her approach is informed by the appreciation developed in archaeological thinking during the 1980s that the actions of using material items in societal contexts are in themselves a con-stituting process of culture and that the objects cannot be taken as an extrinsic by-product; and her approach to burials of this era, in particular, acknowledges a fundamental reappraisal of the concept of ethnicity which argues that 'peoples' of late and post-Roman Europe were not fixed entities defined by their DNA. As Patrick Geary (2002, 155–6) expressed it, 'the names of peoples were less descriptions than claims' for unity under leaders 'who appropriated disparate traditions and invented new ones'. Or to put it another way, a community's decision to bury one of their dead in a particular place, according to particular rites and with brooches having particular forms and orna-mental styles, has little to do with any legendary ancestor having stepped off a boat from somewhere in north Germany or the Low Countries and every-thing to do with that community's development of its own sense of identity in its own place and in its own time. The different features of burial practice can, suggests Lucy (1999, 22–3), be interrogated to see how local identities were being developed. Her review of the Northumbrian burials brings forward some of the features of local variability: the use of former Roman fort sites in the Wall corridor and its hinterland, prominent in the 6th century, less so in the 7th. Benwell, Chesters, Corbridge, Newcastle, and Vindolanda all feature. South Shields also must be included in this list as a place in use, possibly as late as the 8th century; and in the hinterland, Aldborough, Binchester, Catterick, and Piercebridge. 'Community'-type cemeteries are frequent in Yorkshire and on the north side of the River Tees at Norton, Darlington, and Easington. Cist burials occur between the Rivers Tyne and Tees at Blackhall, Castle Eden, Cornforth, and Houghton-le-Spring. Cremation is rare north of the Tees. Different traditions seem to mingle in the area between the Tees and the Yorkshire Derwent: cist graves, burials in Roman forts and burials in or clustering around prehistoric burial mounds, as at West Heslerton. A tradition of barrow burial is strong on the Yorkshire Wolds, but in the far north of the region also; two prehistoric ring-ditches were foci for graves at Yeavering and the two Milfield cemeteries use small henge-type monuments from the Neolithic or Bronze Ages. Examination of local context is a wide-ranging agenda for future study of burials and in her own reappraisal of the problematic burial record at Yeavering, Lucy (2005) shows how it sits within a north British cultural context and within ide-ologies of syncretism. In this respect, the burial rites contribute to a deep engagement with place as a liminal setting in which ancestry and totemic power are embodied (O'Brien forthcoming).

By the 8th century, new elements of material culture were coming into being: the furnished-burial tradition was fading; a new way of commemorating individuals through name stones began to emerge in the monasteries; and a new artistic repertoire was developed in the medium of stone crosses to promulgate Christian ideologies. These are the signifiers of a world changing from old ways.

Appendix 12.1

References for Table 12.1

Archaeologia Aeliana 3, **5**, 342, 405, 406–07; *Archaeologia Aeliana* 3, **6**, 270; *Archaeologia Aeliana* 5, **6**, 177; Bidwell and Speak 1994; Collins, this volume, Appendix 7.4; Collins forthcoming; Cramp and Miket 1982; Dark 1992; Dark and Dark 1996; Dore and Gillam 1979; McCarthy 1990; *Med Arch* **21**, 214; PAS: NCL-230C84; *RIB* 1722; Summerfield 1997b; Vindolanda Museum.

References for Table 12.2

Austen 1991; Bevan forthcoming c; Bryant *et al* 1986; Collingwood 1931b; Collins, this volume, Appendix 7.4; Collins forthcoming; Dark 1992; Dark and Dark 1996; Gillam *et al* 1993; Malton Museum; PAS: NCL-29FAA7; NCL-D93A01; *RIB* 786; *RIB* 908; *RIB* 862 and 863; Wilson *et al* 1996; Yorkshire Museum.

13 Northumbrian origins and post-Roman continuity: an exploration *Brian K Roberts*

I must admit, as a geographer, that I approach this problem with a strong perception of the *longue durée*. In my view no consideration of post-Roman conditions along the *lineam valli* from the 4th century to the 'end of Roman Britain' can side step the origins of Northumbria. Further, to quote from an altar to Silvanus from Weardale (*RIB* 1041), I owe a vast debt to many 'illustrious predecessors in the chase'; to name only a few, Peter Hunter-Blair (1947; 1949), Rosemary Cramp (1988b), David Dumville (1993), and more recently, Ian Wood (2007), as well as the scholars who have contributed to this volume, not least Rob Collins. To me, the discussions of the collapse of the 'full Roman order by the later third century' heard in the conference were revelatory and thought-provoking. They made clear to me the fact that the northern frontier was no longer as central to imperial thinking as it had been in the 1st and 2nd centuries AD, when much of the material and administrative substance of the Roman north was brought into being. The changes over the remaining two centuries fashioned local, regional, and provincial characteristics to replace the earlier, more cosmopolitan imperial focus. Of course, the period involved is one of great complexity and vast literature, and here, in order to steer a course through the many quicksands, I am consciously following the footsteps of Ian Wood (2007). His study of the 'Fragments of Northumbria' provides a perceptive and synoptic view, a powerful synthesis of the work of many scholars, fully documented and with every word chosen with care. Further, it is usefully supported by his concurrent study of the origins of Jarrow (Wood 2008b).

From Ian Wood's (2007) analyses the following points are germane to the theme of this present study:

- In a discussion of the *Bernicii* and the Wall he notes, citing Dominic Powlesland's work, that even in a core region occupied by the *Deiri* only one in six of the buried population at West Heslerton in the Vale of Pickering and the Yorkshire Wolds appear to have been continental immigrants from either eastern Europe or, more likely, Scandinavia. In contrast, a high proportion of the buried were first generation immigrants from further west in Britain. Wood concludes (2007, 111), '[t]his is not proof that the dynasties of Ida and Aella had been in Britain long before their emergence in the historical narrative. But it does mean that one should think carefully about the fact that those dynasties [ie those of Bernicia and Deira] and indeed the Northumbrian peoples in general did not present themselves as incomers with origins on the Continent.' Later he asks (2007, 111), 'Were the *Bernicii* in some manner heirs to the Wall and the zone to the north and south of it?'

- Discussing the nature of the late Roman military occupation of the Wall zone, Ian Wood (2007, 112–14) notes that 'from the early fourth century onwards it is important to distinguish between Roman frontier troops, *limitanei*, and more crack troops, *comitatenses*, which were held in reserve'. While the withdrawal of the latter mobile units was easy, the former were settled in the region they were supposed to defend, and were well-entrenched, often being veterans, who were likely to have possessed wives and families. He asks if the descendants of the frontier troops on the Wall might have come to see themselves as members of the *gens Berniciorum* – 'the people of the mountain passes' (Jackson 2000, 701–5) – and subsequently as part of the 'Anglian' people of Northumbria?

- Further, Germanic units and religious dedications are found on the Wall in the 3rd century, and although an inscriptional darkness then descends (see Hassall, this volume), it is likely that the population of the military zone was of mixed geographic origins. Thus 'already in the third and fourth centuries [they] might have been speaking a Germanic language in their everyday exchanges with comrades – and this may have been a factor in the emergence of Old English as the dominant language of the region' (Salway 1967, 17–18).

- Finally, to justify this plundering of Ian Wood's materials, I return to an almost plaintive comment embedded in his arguments (2008b, 113): 'While it has become increasingly likely that there was a survival of a sort into the sixth century, there is little evidence, as yet, to suggest further continuity into the Anglo-Saxon period. To date Birdoswald has produced a single Saxon pin, though rather more has now been identified at South Shields – the Roman *Arbeia* and Saxon *Urfa* and the birthplace of Oswine', and indeed Jarrow, with Ecgfrith's harbour, if we are to accept Symeon's identification of the latter place as Jarrow Slake.

Though elusive, there may be evidence to suggest the existence of a bridge between the Roman past and the Early Medieval period. This view generates the thrust of the following argument.

Northern landscapes

The way I perceive northern landscapes is encapsulated in Figure 13.1. The eminent economic historian Joan Thirsk (1967) has demonstrated that

120

all English, indeed all British, cultural landscapes result from different balances in three basic ingredients. First, there are open pastures, ranging from the grazings of the wet and windy uplands or lowland pastures of fen, marsh and salt marsh. Second are wood pastures and surviving woodlands. These latter are sometimes in large woods, but are more often smaller groves, spinneys, copses, hangers, and parks, together with the shrubs and timber trees of enclosing live hedges. The haphazard bushes and trees serve to give a 'woodland' image, to which the French term *bocage* can be applied. Finally, there is productive land, namely that land that has experienced the plough, perhaps for many centuries, where the soils have been cleared of timber and shrubs, stone-picked, manured, drained by ditches, ploughed, harrowed, cropped, and effectively warmed by human care – all activities subsumed under the beautiful term 'husbanded'. Two points are germane to what follows. First, while Britain can be divided into large tracts where one of these types predominates and defines macro-regional cultural landscapes, in detail each local region, parish, township, and indeed, each farm-hold, will contain its own particular assemblage drawn from each landscape type. It is thus today and it was thus in Roman and Iron Age times, although prehistory is the saga of the fashioning of these cultural patterns from nature and the wild wood. Second, it follows that variations in scale, from the national scene down through the macro-regional scales to wholly local regions, are fundamental to all landscape thinking. At each of these scales continuity and change spiral around each other in the matrix of time and space, creating unimaginable complexities that our reconstructions and models can only simulate darkly. When writing of the transition period between 'Roman Britain' and 'Anglo-Saxon England' all scholars wrestle with challenging, limited, yet spatially and temporally diffuse evidence. Nevertheless, at root the research problems are identical with those found, for instance, when considering the Industrial Revolution; different events occurred at different times and in different localities and yet were interconnected by flows of people, materials, and ideas.

Figure 13.1 shows northern England, and incorporates four data sets. The base comprises the distribution of moorland, heath, rough pasture and woodland (excluding plantations) as recorded in the Land Utilisation Survey of the later 1930s and 1940s. This is merely a surrogate, because the northern late 18th-century county maps, particularly those for Durham, Northumberland, Cumberland and Westmorland, are too imperfect to be relied upon. Nevertheless, specific local studies in Durham and Cumbria show that these are no more than the survivors of former even greater areas, vast tracts, forming 'temperate savannas' (Roberts and Wrathmell 2002; Roberts *et al* 2005). Next, for the counties where a record survives, all the woodlands documented in Domesday Book of 1086 are shown, derived from the work of Sir Clifford Darby and

his co-workers (1977). To these distributions Old English and Scandinavian place-names indicative of woodland have been added, and although adumbrated are ultimately sourced from work by Oliver Rackham (1986). In spite of the many caveats and qualifications that must be entered, in broad terms where the distributions overlap, the place-names and the Domesday record tell the same story, of wood-pastures, while in Durham exceedingly detailed local mapping has served to confirm the usefulness of this national generalised map (Dunsford and Harris 2003). The final element is an outlining of the lands with only very small areas of recorded woodlands, namely, the longstanding tracts of cultivated land. Let us be clear: the outlining is subjective. There are peculiarities, such as that seen in the long corridor of such land along the Vale of York, where the recorded woodland of 1086 has been plotted at each manorial locus, although in practice the woodland and wood-pastures lay further west along the sides of the foothills and dales. The evidence for Northumberland and Cumbria, lacking Domesday Book, is less substantial and is wholly place-name based. Nevertheless, the map defines a series of cultural cores, *zones of essentially cleared land*, which contrast with the open pastures, woodlands, and wood-pastures. The pattern that emerges is hardly surprising, but two points must be emphasised. First, we have here an essentially base-stable distribution, although undoubtedly 'capable of improvement' in detail. Second, this experiment in positive and negative mapping, subject to the limitation of scale, embraces the whole land surface. More detailed local mapping and small region mapping will produce local variations, of course, but this is a challenge rather than a dead end.

The documented names of early polities have been added to the distinctive patches present in north-eastern England, from Yorkshire to the Tweed. Following Nick Higham (1986, fig 6.2), I have separated Bamburgh/*Dinguaroy* and Catterick/*Catraeth* from Bernicia and Deira. These identifications, of the two well-known polities Bernicia and Deira, are locations on scholarly maps that flutter from place to place like sparrows in a hedge (and here no criticism is implied of many valiant efforts), while the two other polities, perhaps mere postulations, negate any simple definition of the boundary between Bernicia and Deira (Hunter Blair 1949, 50; Cramp 1988b, 74; Loveluck 2003). In my view the frontier between the two main entities, variously united amid the course of time, is to be sought in the less fertile woodland tract across northern Durham. This conclusion rejects both the Tees and the Tyne as polity boundaries and explains Reginald of Durham's statement that the land between the Tyne and the Tees was a wilderness inhabited only by wild beasts (Hunter Blair 1949, 50). The documentary record clearly reveals, in the life trajectories of individuals, that the Old English nobility of the early northern polities were the subject of constantly shifting alliances and power foci. The Viking incursions and

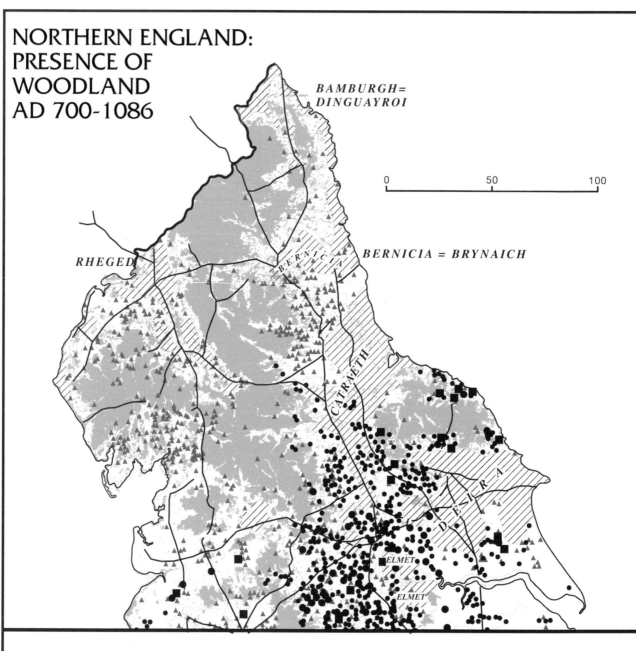

NORTHERN ENGLAND: PRESENCE OF WOODLAND AD 700-1086

BAMBURGH= DINGUAYROI

BERNICIA = BRYNAICH

RHEGED

BERNICIA

CATRAETH

DEIRA

ELMET

ELMET

0   50   100

1086: woodland recorded in Domesday Book

■   Very large areas of woodland

●   Large areas of woodland

•   All other references, woodland, underwood and miscellaneous

Pre-1086: woodland implied by place-names

▲   Place-name evidence *-leah, -hyrst, -feld* and *-thveit*

Common lands and woodlands in 1930s *(after Stamp 1937-46)*

Fig 13.1   Map showing presence of woodland

the formation of County Durham – perhaps the cuckoo in the nest – destroyed any antecedent polity and ecclesiastical boundaries (Hunter Blair 1949, 51; Aird 1998; Harvey 1994).

Cultural cores and cultural distributions

Figures 13.2 and 13.3 show how this concept of cultural cores can be used. The first, Figure 13.2, uses them as a base to record all the pre-AD 950 sculptural remains and the monasteries recorded in documents (Cramp 1984, fig 2; 1988a, fig 2; Lang 1991, fig 3; 2001, fig 4; Wood 2008a). In this case it is striking how the evidences are peripheral in two senses: first, a liminal distribution of the monasteries between the land and the sea is well known, but second, it can be seen that the inland sites lay in the borderlands between the tracts of most cultivated land and the great savannah-like areas of waste to the west and north. All substantive sites lie in these two peripheral zones. Again, let us be clear: the cultural cores were in no way wholly cultivated, but within them cultivated and improved lands were present in far greater concentrations than in the vast cattle-grazed wastes which surrounded them. It is distinctly possible that in this distribution we are seeing zones within which it was more possible for generous royal donators to alienate lands and use grants to the church as colonising ventures. Of course, this is not to say that within the two types of countryside defined here there were no local anomalies such as common grazings resulting from the retreat from former cultivated land. We cannot create more than a generalised picture at this scale. Nevertheless, colonisation and recession are a normal part of all cultural landscapes. Such cycles can be annual, or in the case of the cultivation of outfields, decennial, in the form of local misfortunes and over-optimistic ventures, perhaps linked to climatic variations, or longer term, in the form of major regional social and economic dislocations or climatic change. Nevertheless, this nested hierarchy of changes must and will always take place within a broader framework of terrains, soils and climate, latitude, longitude, and altitude. The potentials for local variations are vast, but the macro-picture given here has a ring of truth. Furthermore, in this an important point is concealed. Underlying the author's mode of thought is a view that all archaeological evidence, essential as it is, only touches a very small portion of the conceptual but intangible total 'real' image. Fragmentary materials must be used and interpreted, not only in their own terms, but to nourish what we can imagine of each successive real world total picture, the *longue durée* of my introduction. In this circumstance, as the volume of archaeological material increases, trans-temporal questions and interpretations become increasingly important, so that bringing 20th-century evidence and an interpretation of landscape types into a single map (Fig 13.2) with an 11th-century documentary record and the hard-won evidence of early sculpture is a useful exercise. Thus a third map, Figure 13.3, integrates work by many scholars to create an overview of 'evidences' – to use this succinct 17th-century term – pertaining to the 4th, 5th, and 6th centuries. Following Barri Jones and David Mattingly (1990), the map divides the evidence from the *Notitia Dignitatum* into two groups, superimposed upon which is a vertical bar, using work by Ken Dark (1992; 2000a). The 5th- to 6th-century material is from an analysis by Sam Lucy (1999). In this complex map much-debated documentary evidence (eg the *Notitia, Y Gododdin*; Koch 1997) is placed alongside patiently culled archaeological recovery from several time periods, analyses of onomastic material from place-names still in use (Coates *et al* 2000), and my own mapping (Roberts 2007). Of course, this data could be presented in several individual maps, perhaps even attempting a time series, but the massed material represents an element of historical truth: 'this happens, in these places, within a period of three crucial centuries'. No short analysis can do justice to this map's rich content.

How can Figure 13.3 be interpreted? One thing is wholly clear: the experiences of each of the cultural cores and their immediate peripheries differed. Deira, with 5th- and 6th-century burials and finds rooted deeply in a prehistoric past (note the downward-pointing black triangles) and a well-farmed and populated Roman antecedent landscape bears traces of a markedly different post-Roman trajectory to that of the lower Tyne valley (ie the land east of the confluence of the North and South Tyne). The putative core of Bernicia, *Dinguaroy/Bamburgh*, is another story, inevitably overshadowed by the Yeavering excavations and the *Anglo-Saxon Chronicle* reference to the founding of Bamburgh in AD 547 by Ida, while between Bernicia and Deira the substantive but shadowy tract here named *Catraeth*, raises echoes of Aneirin's *Gododdin*. Within this tract 5th- and 6th-century burials and finds fill niches peripheral to core lands in the Tees valley, and with the 'Derian-Bernician' boundary set amid the wedge of wood-pasture and open pastures around the former Roman sites of Binchester and Chester-le-Street, and eventually, Wearmouth and Jarrow. In fact this boundary is sustained as a cultural break until the advent of industrialisation (Roberts *et al* 2005, 232–5). Of course, as Sam Lucy stressed, this map cannot reveal ethnicity. Nevertheless, artefacts of Germanic type are effectively the markers for late 5th- and 6th-century archaeological evidences, while the *Notitia* hints – and no more – at the presence of 4th-century activity in the forts once in the command of the *dux Britanniarum*, notably those along the line of the Wall. Reassessments of older finds and new excavations will surely reveal more. Thus, Bernician origins are surely not only to be sought in the Bamburgh-based 'Woden-born' figure of Ida (*Anglo-Saxon Chronicle* [E], *sub an.* 449 and 547) but in the rich grain lands of the

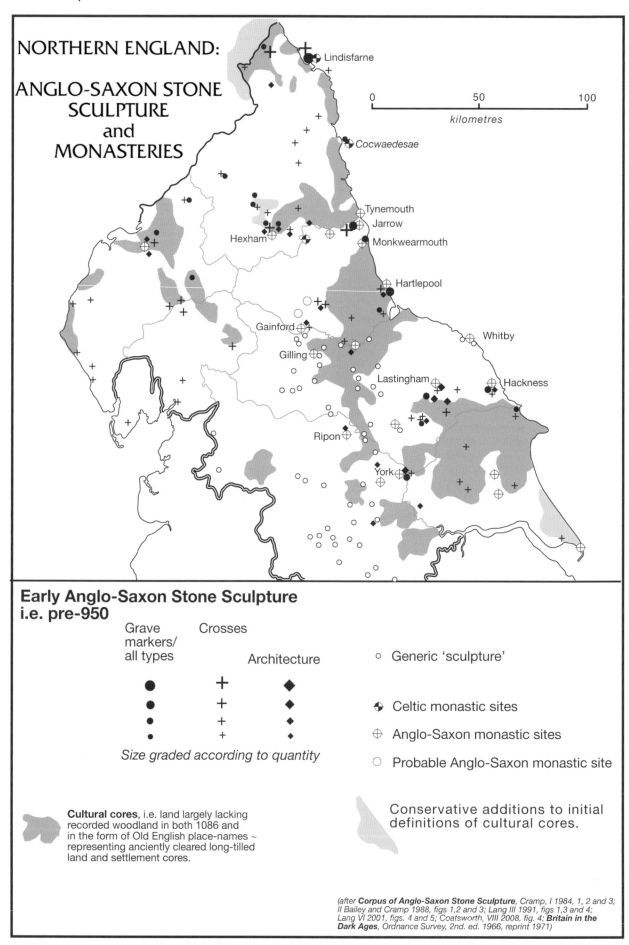

NORTHERN ENGLAND:

ANGLO-SAXON STONE
SCULPTURE
and
MONASTERIES

0   50   100
kilometres

Lindisfarne

Cocwaedesae

Tynemouth
Jarrow
Hexham
Monkwearmouth

Hartlepool

Gainford
Whitby

Gilling

Lastingham
Hackness

Ripon

York

**Early Anglo-Saxon Stone Sculpture
i.e. pre-950**

Grave   Crosses
markers/
all types
                 Architecture   ○ Generic 'sculpture'

●   +   ◆

●   +   ◆   ✦ Celtic monastic sites

●   +   ◆
                                      ⊕ Anglo-Saxon monastic sites
•   +   ◆

Size graded according to quantity   ○ Probable Anglo-Saxon monastic site

Cultural cores, i.e. land largely lacking   Conservative additions to initial
recorded woodland in both 1086 and   definitions of cultural cores.
in the form of Old English place-names ~
representing anciently cleared long-tilled
land and settlement cores.

*(after **Corpus of Anglo-Saxon Stone Sculpture**, Cramp, I 1984, 1, 2 and 3;
II Bailey and Cramp 1988, figs 1,2 and 3; Lang III 1991, figs 1,3 and 4;
Lang VI 2001, figs. 4 and 5; Coatsworth, VIII 2008, fig. 4; **Britain in the
Dark Ages**, Ordnance Survey, 2nd. ed. 1966, reprint 1971)*

Fig 13.2   Map showing Anglo-Saxon sculpture or monasteries

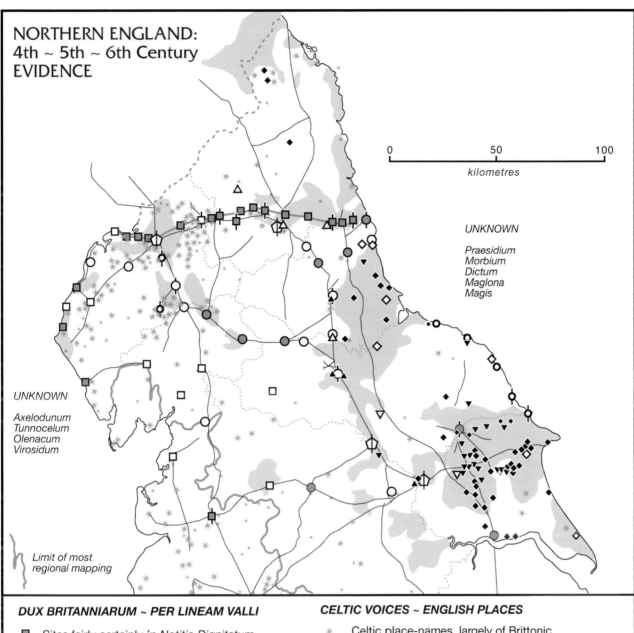

NORTHERN ENGLAND: 4th ~ 5th ~ 6th Century EVIDENCE

0   50   100

kilometres

UNKNOWN

Praesidium
Morbium
Dictum
Maglona
Magis

UNKNOWN

Axelodunum
Tunnocelum
Olenacum
Virosidum

Limit of most regional mapping

DUX BRITANNIARUM ~ PER LINEAM VALLI

■ Sites fairly certainly *in Notitia Dignitatum*

□ Sites **NOT** in *Notitia Dignitatum* but with 4th C. occupation

DUX BRITANNIARUM

● Sites fairly certainly *in Notitia Dignitatum*

○ Sites **NOT** in *Notitia Dignitatum* but with 4th C. occupation

(after Jones and Mattingley 1990, map 4:70)

POSSIBLE 5th and 6th C. activity

⬠ Towns

| Forts

♀ o Coastal fortlets, with and without 5th/6th C. evidence

(after Dark 2000a, fig. 56)

CELTIC VOICES ~ ENGLISH PLACES

* Celtic place-names, largely of Brittonic origin, a few are Goidelic or very ancient; large symbol = 'wholly', small symbol = 'partly'

(after Coates, Breeze and Horovitz, 2000)

5th - 6th CENTURY BURIALS / FINDS

Chance find	Known burial	
▽	▼	with prehistoric associations
△	▲	with Roman associations
◇	◆	with no such associations

(after Lucy 1999, figs. 2.2, 2.3 and 2.4)

✂ Battle of Catraeth, A.D. 570
(after Koch 1997, xli)

▨ Cultural cores, i.e. land largely lacking recorded woodland in both 1086 and in the form of Old English place-names ~ representing anciently cleared, long-tilled land and settlement cores.

County and riding boundaries

Fig 13.3 Map showing 4th- to 6th-century sites / evidence

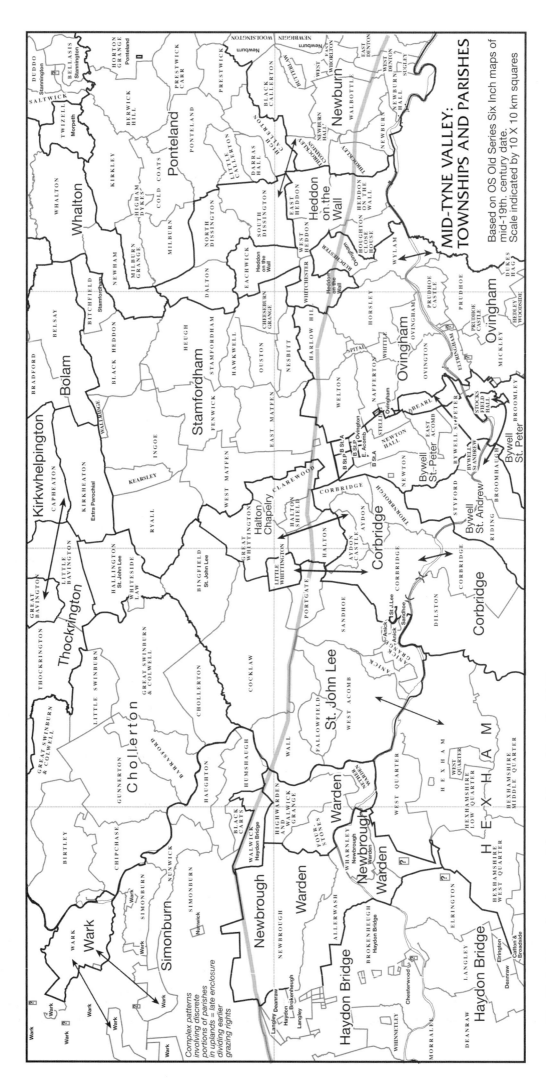

Fig 13.4 Map showing parishes and townships of mid-Tyne

middle and lower Tyne, although no doubt dynastic power was transmitted via the swords and spears of undocumented warlords and aristocratic clans of which Ida was but a successful part. As Ian Wood implies, these people originated in a mixture of Celtic/British, Roman, and Germanic 'North Sea' stock.

From this short analysis we have created a shadowy picture of cultural landscape patterns in northern England in the period during and after the 4th, 5th, and 6th centuries, a broad-brush image that begs many questions. There can be no doubt that the eastern sector of Hadrian's great wall, beginning at Wallsend, ran initially though a zone of better agricultural soils, with sloping south-facing land possessing sufficient post-glacial stream channels to afford easy natural drainage. In short, this was a productive zone. We may indeed ask questions about precise boundaries, if indeed these have any real meaning, and the answers to these will lie in a planned more extensive, more embracing, study than is possible here.

Bernician corelands: around the Wall

Figure 13.4 shows the parishes and townships of a section of the Tyne valley and it is noteworthy that the line of the Wall forms neither a parish nor a township boundary except in two cases. In this matter we must recall two things: first, that the parish and township boundaries seen in the map are derived from the First Edition Six Inch Ordnance Survey maps of the middle decades of the 19th century. Units of civil administration, townships in the north of England, are the building blocks of the large parishes, and their roots are both complex and normally lost in time. Second, most townships originate as units of agricultural production, and in 99% of cases they centre, or have once been centred, upon local communities, a village, a hamlet, a lordly hall, a group of farmsteads or even a single farmstead (Winchester 1990 and 2000). Only between Walwick and Black Carts and between Wall township and Cocklaw does a township boundary follow the line of the Roman wall, while the stretch between Newbrough and Simonside is probably no more than a 'late' division of former common pastures. In the former case not only do small angles and kinks suggest that a fine-grained landscape, involving cultivation, was subdivided to create the two small territories, but the two townships lie in separate parishes. The overall pattern of townships is a reflection of land-exploitation and stands as a surrogate for the density of local small communities. This pattern can be 'read', analysed, and used as a historical source, while these *tegulae* were assembled to create the church-supporting territories, parishes. As with so much of this evidence, no firm chronology can be defined, so that townships are apt to float in time: they mean what we can interpret them to mean. Thus, the Wall townships could be pre-Roman in origin, for the

Wall cuts across them like a railway line, although this is perhaps not a potentially fruitful pressure point. Nevertheless, a strong and useful presumption must be that the townships along the Wall developed to serve small communities living on or very near its line, and this observation touches the core of our enquiry.

Of place-names, Germans, and the Wall

Figure 13.5 shows the place-name evidence for the same area as Figure 13.4. The smallest symbols, deliberately recessive, are names indicative of woodlands and largely open cattle pastures – the summering grounds or shielings. No further comment on these is needed. However, the vast majority of place-names are Old English and topographic in character, referring to landscape features. Such names appeared while Old English was spoken, and there is a broad scholarly consensus that topographic names originate *earlier* than habitative forms, ie those names ending in -*ham*, -*tun* (-*ton*) and the like. When these are added to the distribution in Figure 13.5, the remarkable thing is that the two categories 'infill' most of the terrain north of the main Tyne and east of the North Tyne. There are indeed gaps, where careful observation and a rough and ready method of mapping suggests the presence of tracts of common grazing, but essentially the landscape is replete, with name forms generally considered to appear after AD 730 largely absent (Cameron 1996, 66–72; Gelling 1978; 2000). A few names, those with the elements *burh* (= 'a fortification') or *geweorc* (= 'fortifications') and *warden* (*weard-dun* = 'watch hill') are scattered strategically. Of course, much of this evidence needs re-evaluation, for the maps have been assembled from varied sources using work undertaken at varied dates, for which I form a rather uncertain filter. There is no up-to-date analysis of the place-names of Northumberland, and we are reliant on Mawer (1920) and a broader view given in Eckwall (1960). Nevertheless, there are important questions here, for Old English place-names dominate this section of the Wall landscape, and this is why I have recorded in Figure 13.3 all of the Celtic names identified in a recent magisterial study (Coates *et al* 2000). The bulk of these lie further west, with only a thin scatter in this Tyne valley zone. Old English names such as Heddon, 'the hill where the heather grew', Thornborough, 'thorn-*burh*', and Whitchester, 'the white Roman fort', predominate. In this matter Horsley (Eckwall 1960, 252) is pure speculation: generally the -*leah* suffix is normally seen as 'later' in the temporal sequence. Nevertheless in this case there must be a suspicion that this isolated 'woodland' indicator could indeed be early, and, to leap to unsubstantiated assumption, that it subtly recognises the use of land near Rudchester, originally (under

Fig 13.5 Map showing mid-Tyne place-names

The content within the figure:

**MID-TYNE VALLEY:
ANALYSIS OF
PLACE-NAMES**

*Based on OS Old Series Six Inch maps of
mid-19th. century date.
Scale indicated by 10 X 10 km squares*

Place labels: Rudchester, Horsley, Stamfordham, Corbridge, Hexham, Walwick, Warden Law, Wark

*To west of North Tyne
extensive late enclosure
shows that vast areas were
once grazing lands, commons,
wastes, fells, subjected to usage
by surrounding communities.*

Legend:
- Old English topographic names.
- Old English habitative names with the suffix -wic.
- Old English habitative names: usually in -tun, Stamfordham being an exception.
- Old English place-names indicative of fortification.
- Old English place-names with composite information, e.g. -leah, -feld, -wudu.
- Old English place-names indicative of woodland, e.g. Stamfordham and Horsley.

**Evidence for wastes and
common pastures, etc.**
- Shield names, summer pastures
- Presence of fell, commons,bogs, moor, carrs and whins indicated on OS First Ed. 6 Inch map.
- Areas of 'late enclosure' based on author's professional experience,

Hadrian) housing a *cohors quingenaria equitata*, and by the 4th century the *cohors prima Frixagorum* (presumably Frisiavonum).

The presence of so many 'early' Old English name forms in the vicinity of this section of the Wall brings us to a large question: when were the topographic elements of the language of the place-names introduced? If the forms are indeed 'early', and we have no reasons for assuming them to be 'late', we touch the possibility that Old English was first found amongst some of the Wall soldiers and the merchants and seafarers using the port of Tyne, so that this locality presents a picture of continuity rather than dislocation. Proving this is near impossible, but let the case of Stamfordham serve to illustrate the issues. First documented in AD 1188, the name means the *'ham* at the stony ford'. The first element *stan* broadly implies what it says, 'stone', and 'the stony ford' tells of a water passage, in fact where a road crosses the River Pont. Nationally the word *ford* is often adumbrated by appellatives describing the material of the track. The *-ham* element, implying an estate, a village community, a homestead of some status, derives from deep Germanic roots. It is often considered broadly 'early' yet surely in this case represents a sequentially 'later' habitative addition to an even earlier topographic name-form? In the Lindisfarne gospels *In hus fadres mines hamas meniga sint*, the word *hamas* glosses the Latin *mansiones* of *In my father's house...* (Smith 1956, 181, 226). Stamfordham is not, of course, on the Wall, although the parish just touches its line, but this illustrates something of the real issues of interpretation for each and every place-name. The linguistic origins are not in doubt, in spite of the first reference being in the 12th century. The interpretation is clear, but establishing a precise contextual chronology is difficult. Stamfordham is not on any known Roman road, but nevertheless, it must often have been visited by cavalry patrols.

Stephen Oppenheimer (2006) has postulated, convincingly, that post-Neolithic genetic inputs to the British population were very small, say 5% and below, and, in the north at least, infiltration over time appears more likely than any catastrophic invasion and take-over by exotic heroic war bands. In the formulation of local cultural identities in this port zone, sea traffic was important.[1] Continental scholars recognise in the post-Roman period the existence of a North Sea interaction zone, not a North Sea culture, but linkages sustained by ships, namely the carvel-built vessels of the Channel and Germanic coasts, the clinker-built vessels of the German coasts and Scandinavia, and the skin boats of Pictland to the north. To appreciate the effect of time we must take account of all that this involved: trading and army supply, joining the (paid) Roman army and eventually warband recruits, marriage and political alliances, couriers and emissaries, and eventually missionary-work, piracy, and exile. Not least there was slaving. These forces swilled people around the edges of the North Sea basin, sustaining

contacts that may have roots deep in prehistory, and while they varied in intensity from decade to decade and century to century, the links were sustained from generation to generation. The results from West Heslerton cited earlier suggest a very complex model indeed. That Celtic/British was spoken is not in doubt; that Latin was spoken is not in doubt; but it is my suspicion that the 'Angles and Saxons' are a figment of royal heroic eulogies brought to history via Bede's need for a tidy beginning and used by him, very effectively, to enliven his abstract of Gildas's polemical arguments. In short, Old English first emerged as a minority language amongst soldiers – for many of the units attached to the Wall forts had links with the lower Rhine – and as a *lingua franca* of sea-farers around the North Sea basin, opening Britain to varied contacts of varying intensity throughout a long period of time (Bibre 2001, 91–100; Cunliffe 2001, 296, 558–60, 565–7; Pentz *et al* 2000; TeBrake 1985, 96–103, 117–32). The emergence of powerful Old English-speaking aristocracies, successful in war and polity formation and perhaps rich *because* of North Sea trading links, served to draw eastern Britain, with its inherently greater agricultural potential, away from any trading nexus of the Irish Sea province and place it securely within the North Sea cultural zone. In this context, however, we are left to explain why the Germanic artefacts found in Deiran graves are so rarely recovered in this potentially rich Bernician core, with its access to sea-borne trade. This is no easy task. The relative absence of British place-name survival is no different in both polities yet the contrast in the presences of 5th- to 6th-century burials is striking, with Catraeth, also lacking British onomastic survivals, forming an intermediary zone in terms of 'Germanic' artefacts. One possible explanation is that Germanic incomers, and their varied followers, were quite simply not invited into the Tyne valley where a mixed population was already concentrated and deeply integrated. Nevertheless, even if these spatial variations cannot yet be understood and explained, their existence is a challenge.

The Wall townships

Finally, Figure 13.6 places the Roman Wall and its forts and milecastles upon a background of those townships that centre upon the Wall line (ie excluding Matfen and Sandhoe, Acomb and Cocklaw). Again, let us be clear what is being said: the Wall townships are ***not*** simple survivals of earlier territories attached to Wall communities. Their nibbled edges suggest a much, much more complex situation. What can be seen are residuals, survivals after earlier administrative territories have been reduced and reconstituted, whose place-names raise important questions about their chronological context. All could represent sections carved from larger territories, perhaps in measure those represented by the parishes, and we may note

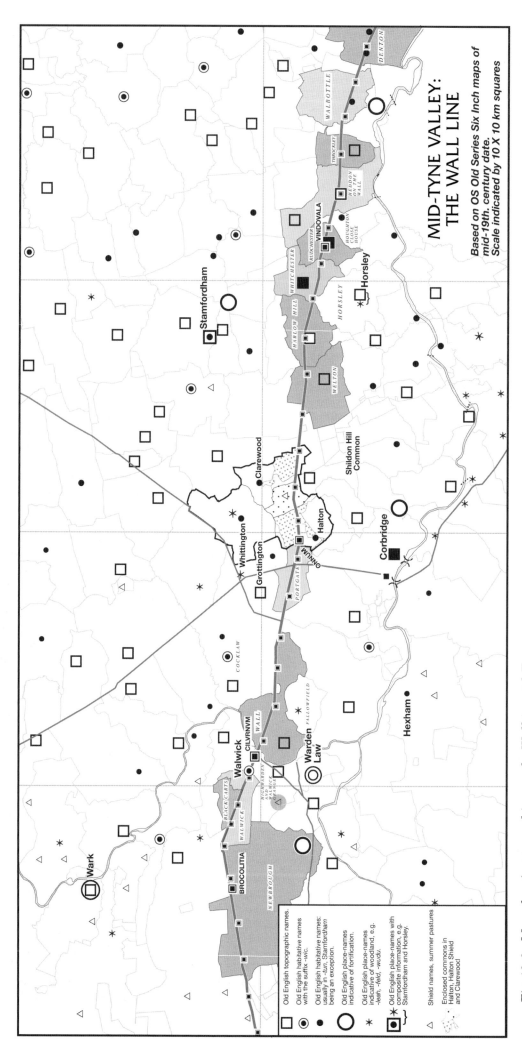

Fig 13.6 Map showing townships on the Wall in mid-Tyne

that Corbridge, along with others, actually spans the river Tyne, for *Coria*, with its important bridge, must surely have had a territory associated with it. Nevertheless, this observation embodies a research theme worthy of pursuit, and what follows merely touches on some of the possibilities. The detail of the maps may appear daunting, indeed they are a challenge to create and reproduce, but they carry the reader from the on-ground topographic complexities of the First Edition Ordnance Survey Six Inch to the mile maps to the superimposed plotting of many other forms of evidence. With the detail my mistakes can be isolated and new material integrated.

It is inevitable that each Wall township tends to contain either a fort or a milecastle. This would be the same were the Wall a railway line with a close succession of halts and stations. In other words, there need be no significance in any such correlation. Here, it must be admitted that archaeology poses a problem. It is a simple fact, as Wilmott's (2001) recent work at Birdoswald shows, that earlier excavations have missed much of the ephemeral post-Roman evidence, while the stratigraphy at Sewingshields milecastle is our only guide to the deep-time complexities (Breeze 2006, 232). To this must be added another factor: even if we exclude the turrets (signal boxes in our model) then the enclosed milecastles must have been ideal for cattle pens (crew yards) or even farmsteads, and any regular post-Roman scouring of accreted manure would have worn away the uppermost stratigraphy along with the urine- and dung-sodden muds. Soil phosphate levels need testing, while in this matter, the precise location of any coin hoards and/or coin finds in such contexts emerges as crucial to all post-Roman interpretation. That is to say, why do these coins survive to be found in milecastle interiors if these were well used in post-Roman times and even scoured for manure? However, wholly central to my thinking about the Roman to post-Roman transition is Rob Collins's (2009) summary of the changes in the usage of Roman forts. This involves the narrowing of entrances by blocking walls, repairs taking the form of earthen ramparts and the scouring of only a single ditch, all pointers to new military practices. More importantly, the conversion of the *principia* buildings to occupation, storage and industrial use, and the introduction of chalet-style barrack arrangements, point to a swing away from a long-standing Hadrianic orthodoxy. Informality appears, with even encroachment upon roadways, and while baths and *principia* survived, their forms and usage were frequently modified. Above all, the *horrea*, the great military granaries, experienced demolition or conversion, raising crucial issues of supply and storage (Wilmott, this volume).

In all this there can be no clear glimpse of the real nature of the later garrisons. The desertion of earlier *vici* by the AD 250s–270s and critical declines in the arrival of continental and Mediterranean imports after AD 200, and, by the later 4th century, the end of Roman pottery traditions and

other imports, all point towards complex social and economic changes (Bidwell and Croom, this volume). While it is tempting to suggest that a withdrawal of non-military persons into the protection of the forts, a more realistic scenario would be to envisage the contemporary rise of local farming communities in more favourable locations. If we accept that we are seeing a transition from a 3rd-century imperial military community (*techno-complex* comes to mind here), the 4th century saw the appearance of a regional military control. By the 5th century this led to purely local military communities, with no withdrawal of the Wall *limitanei*, and this sets the scene for assessing the nature of the 'Dark Age' communities that emerged within and around the antecedent Roman structures and their territories. All the Western imperial mints stop producing small change/copper-based coins shortly after AD 400. It is possible that gold and silver continued to be shipped to Britain, but these are very rare coins to find north of the Tees in general. In this circumstance, it may be that the lower numbers of Valentinianic and later coinage in the frontier compared with 'lowland' Britain are indicative of more largely and locally based supply and subsistence economies in the 'military' zone (Rob Collins, pers comm). Such changes thrust local communities into a largely subsistence-based agricultural economy in which the support of the 'garrisons' rested wholly on local farmers, while high-status prestige and luxury items were bartered by gift and exchange. Emergent local political and economic power resided in the control of this exchange (Ward-Perkins 2005, 40–3; Millett 1992, 212–30; Casey 1994, 4–51; Dark 1996, 63–5; Swift 2000a). Thus, even when trade declined – and it did – coastal locations and inland foci and roads remained important. Imperial taxation was replaced by renders of cattle and grains, honey and ale, and with military and perhaps even ship-service rendered to local 'big-men' of varied origins and pretensions (Bannerman 1974, 107–56). Internecine polity-building warfare provided a steady flow of the most important items of trade: youths and girls for slave-trading. Thus it is that *Cobrig*, the Roman *Coria*, appears as a slave market in the early Middle Ages, with North Shields as the focus of a royal palace and, perhaps, a royal harbour (Wood 2008b; Pelteret 1995, 76).

We are left with many questions. To take only Halton Chapelry: it contains the fort of Halton Chesters (*Onnum*) and three milecastles. The place-name contains large ambiguities, either being the OE 'farm on the *healh*', or perhaps 'nook, corner, angle, somewhere secluded', although Ekwall interprets it as *haw-hyll* = 'look-out hill'. It could even be *halig(a)tun*, 'holy farm'! A modern view is not available, but I note the 'persistent early *w*' and tend to favour 'look-out hill' (Gelling 2000, 124). Today Halton is a small hamlet a little to the south of the fort, but joined to it by the trackway leading through the former *vicus*. The name of Halton Shields, which is associated with MC 20 and sits on higher land to the east, implies grazing lands with seasonal occupation, although by the 16th century even this township was almost wholly arable and possessed a three-field system (*NCH* **10**, 389; Roberts and Wrathmell 2002, 86–7). Surely a move from the fort site to a more sheltered south-facing valley was sensible for a farming community, whilst it preserved grazing rights along the line of the Wall. In this case, we have little more than a small shift in the focus of settlement.

Clarewood does not possess the obvious meaning: it derives from the OE *clæfre-weorth* = 'clover enclosure', the suffix being a habitative indicator, but here conceivably applied in a pastoral context. Great Whittington, and the nearby Grottington, are exceptional within the compass of the data mapped in Figures 13.4–13.6; both are habitative forms perhaps incorporating a possessive Old English personal name. This grouping of four townships was, by the mid-13th century, a thanage, ie under the control of an individual, and paid the cattle rent of cornage, considered by many authorities to be a very ancient cattle render (Roberts 2008a). Halton, however, was part of the parish of Corbridge, the centre of a great royal estate once 'covering the whole of middle Tyneside' (Fraser 1968, 47). It should be noted that this fort, formerly possessing a substantial *vicus* sprawling to the south and east, was engaged in 'elaborate jewellery manufacture', probably in the 3rd century, including the use of gold (Breeze 2006, 183). It was, furthermore, set alongside the major routeway through the Wall line, at Portgate, but then the relationship between this locus and the great stock trading nexus at Stagshaw – avoiding the terms 'market' and 'fair' – is another lead to be pursued, for Portgate township does not encompass the traditional site of the stockmart at Stagshaw Bank! The Old English root may have been *æt port* – 'at the gate', but the Old English term *port* is also strongly linked with places possessing a trading function. Portgate township is special. It contains no more than a farmstead of that name, and was part of the parish of St John Lee in the 12th century, itself a part of the great church estate of Hexhamshire and the focus of an Old English bishopric on land granted to Wilfred by Queen Æthelthryth, the wife of King Ecgfrith (Kirby 1974, 45–6). How she obtained it is unknown, but like Corbridge it was surely once part of royal lands. This split, between Corbridge and Hexham, may explain why the fort at *Onnum* lies on the edge of the territory of Halton Chapelry, and may hint that we are seeing an echo of the former large Roman administrative unit based on *Coria,* part of a nascent Bernicia, and including a putative sub-unit based on the fort at *Onnum.*

To conclude, our understanding of all Roman sites and landscape fragments can be greatly enhanced when these are set within a framework provided by reconstructions of the post-Roman activity superimposed upon them. This step forces new questions to be confronted concerning survival and destruction, continuity and discontinuity, and more importantly, the reasons for these. Ultimately this approach leads towards some understanding of Roman features within the *longue durée.* Here, indeed, be shadows, but they need chasing.

Note

1   Note Oppenheimer's (2006) fig 7.1a. When this map, showing the tribes of northern Gaul, is set against the regiments of the Roman army levied in Lower Germany, the Morini, Menapii, Frisiavones, Nervii, Tungri, Vangiones, and the Lingones appear in the army of northern Britain, and, with the exception of the last, all are likely to have been speakers of a Germanic dialect.

14 Material culture at the end of empire
Rob Collins and Lindsay Allason-Jones

Introduction

The initial inspiration for the present volume came from a sense of frustration on the part of the editors. Material from 4th- and 5th-century contexts was known from a number of excavations along the frontier, but detailed treatment of the material was limited to a single article (Cool 2000a). The editors felt that, despite the merits and originality of Cool's contribution, a fuller treatment of the material culture was needed to take the discussion and interpretation of life in the late frontier zone further. This was particularly necessary given the tendency of many Roman specialists to perceive the 4th century from a 2nd-century perspective, as Cool has noted (Chapter 1, this volume). The time also seemed right to reassess the artefact assemblages, given that excavations over the past 30 years have revealed numerous sequences of continuous late to post-Roman activity, summarised in Chapter 2 (Wilmott, this volume; Wilmott and Wilson 2000; Collins 2007). For this reassessment to be useful it needed to be tackled not by a single author but by a range of contributors, all of whom have considerable experience in their specialist field. The results have exceeded even some of the contributors' expectations as to the quality and quantity of the material to be found in the frontier zone and what it can tell us about life in the 4th and 5th centuries AD.

Artefacts from 4th-century Britain have previously been most often thought of in terms of the large precious metal hoards found in the south of England, for example Hoxne or Mildenhall, both in Suffolk. Of course, there are extraordinary discoveries from 4th-century northern Britain too, the Corbridge lanx and Traprain Law hoard being the two most prominent examples. The more mundane, everyday objects, however, are generally divided into classes with little attempt at generalising or synthesising either by period or function (but note the exceptions of Cool 2006; Croom 2000; Eckhardt and Crummy 2008; Swift 2000a and 2000b). The preceding papers in this volume remedy this situation by offering an overview of the materials and artefacts found in the late Roman frontier zone; the current chapter simply teases out some of the implications of the discussions in the individual papers.

Topics not covered

There are a number of topics that have not been discussed, despite an attempt to offer a comprehensive consideration of the material culture of the period. The manufacture and production of many of these objects is one such topic. It is clear that many artefacts were made locally or within the region at several locations, as yet unidentified, including some elements of a soldier's equipment The lead strap end from Stanwix noted in Chapter 6 is one example of the local production of military belt fittings (Collingwood 1931a, 79; Coulston, this volume), and an examination of crossbow brooches has concluded that they also were produced at one or more locations around the frontier (Collins, Chapter 7 this volume). Evidence for glass vessel production is only known as yet at Binchester, but it is uncertain how far these products travelled. In contrast, evidence for ceramic production, specifically the Crambeck industry, is known from excavations of kilns in East Yorkshire and the examples of their products, found distributed throughout northern England. Some objects, however, are more likely to have been made at some distance and transported to the frontier. Coins, for example, were sent from the official imperial mints, and, for most of the 4th century, the closest of these were in Gaul. Some prestige objects, such as silver and some glass vessels, also came from further afield, for example the polychrome glass found at the villa at Ingleby Barwick (Archaeological Services University of Durham forthcoming). Other imported goods, like wine and olive oil, were brought to the frontier in amphorae, but there are relatively limited numbers of imported ceramics in the region, either as items in their own right or as containers.

This volume has included no discussion of tools, despite the frequent comments on decoration and the methods of production of the artefacts in each paper. Each class of artefact, and each type of craft worker, would have had a number of tools for the execution of their specific art. There would also have been the day-to-day tools typical of rural, urban, and military life. Some of these, like wooden mallets, rarely leave any archaeological trace unless found in the extreme environmental conditions that favour such preservation. Other tools, like iron hammers, are likely to have been recycled once damaged to utilise the metal or other recyclable material which made up the object. Tools also tend to be very conservative in their design, which makes it difficult to date individual types unless they are found in very securely dated contexts. It is, therefore, unsurprising that few tools have been positively identified as surviving into the late Roman period, though the recent discovery of a tool hoard from Ingleby Barwick is a notable exception (Hunter forthcoming b).

In addition to tools, there is a range of domestic equipment and objects that have not received adequate attention, including keys and locks, furnishings, and objects related to food processing and production. There is some evidence for domestic objects; for example, keys or suspected keys have been found in late strata at Vindolanda (Birley 1997), and an escutcheon from a late cauldron or hanging bowl was found at Wallsend (unpubl E14 19 1311). Recent work on the 4th-century stone querns from South Shields has emphasised the extent to which they contrast with earlier querns (Rory O'Neill, unpubl). On the whole, they tend to be made with local sandstones and gritstones that wear more rapidly and generally provide a coarser flour than the earlier imported querns, which has further implications for bread quality and the health of the consumers.

Readers may notice the absence of other categories. These have invariably not been covered due to their paucity in the region (eg mosaics) or because of the lack of modern research into the specific topic. However, the lack of *hacksilber* in the region, in comparison with the situation found north of the frontier, as, for example, in the Traprain Law hoard, is noticeable and would profit from further study.

Interpretation

Throughout the volume a number of sites have provided key assemblages for interpretation, usually those that have been the focus of modern excavation or assessment. Along the Wall corridor, these sites are South Shields, Housesteads, Vindolanda, Birdoswald, and Carlisle; to the south of the Wall are Binchester, Piercebridge, Catterick, and York. The most important aspect of these key sites, other than the fact that they are all fort sites, is that a clear understanding of the stratigraphy, with generally clear dating evidence provided for phases of structural activity, has unequivocally identified the later material, some of which would have passed for 2nd- or 3rd-century material if found or discussed without context. It is significant that the sites with late artefacts are nearly all forts, with one buckle of possible late date from Banks East turret (52a), two crossbow brooches from Poltross Burn milecastle, and single, unstratified coins of Valens found at Turret 44b and Milecastle 52. In contrast to this handful of artefacts, there is ceramic evidence from a number of turrets and milecastles that is suggestive of occupation into the late 4th century (Breeze and Dobson 2000, 237).

There is a noticeable absence of sites from the west of the Pennines mentioned in this volume, though this is largely a result of a bias in recent excavation history and a lack of modern assessment of materials from excavations. However, there is also a noticeable geographical bias when casual discoveries of artefacts are considered, as seen in those papers including Portable Antiquities Scheme data. In fact, a general assessment of PAS data from the 4th century (using coins and diagnostic 4th-century artefacts) demonstrates a number of 'blanks' in England and Wales (Fig 14.1, from data compiled January 2009). To some extent, this reflects real differences in historic settlement, for example, in the Wash or on the Weald. But there are also biases in modern settlement, for example the urban sprawl of Greater London or the eastern bias of modern population density. The map also reflects search biases, in that the North-East and the North-West are less extensively or intensively searched by metal-detectorists, who approximate 70% of the people recording with the PAS. Yet there are further real differences that are not apparent from the map; if 2nd- and 3rd-century artefacts and coins were assessed, the North-East and North-West would be better represented. Thus, the PAS does offer some insight into the frontier, with an observable restriction of 4th-century material. Within the frontier zone, the North and East Ridings of Yorkshire are the best represented by public finds, and this area also has more villas and a greater density of non-military settlement in the 4th century.

Dating can still be difficult with certain types of artefacts. Ultimately, date ranges associated with any particular form or type can be traced back to its association with ceramics and/or coins from excavated strata. Coins are very well dated, in terms of their production date. This also extends to ceramics, as reviewed by Bidwell and Croom (Chapter 4, this volume). However, there is always a tension between the production date and use-life of an artefact, and many artefacts have a less specific date range associated with their use. Through much of the 4th century, dating is rarely an issue when artefacts are found in context, as coins and ceramics provide secure dating associations. The later 4th century saw a reduction in the number of coins in the frontier zone (Brickstock 2000a), but Crambeck parchment ware and Huntcliff-type wares occur, acting as a signal for the last 30 years of the 4th century (Bidwell 2005). In the 5th century dating becomes more problematic, as the latest coins to arrive in any quantity were minted around AD 402, and ceramic vessel forms appear to continue unchanged. Significantly, Bidwell and Croom (Chapter 4, this volume) have demonstrated a change in the proportions between Crambeck grey wares and Huntcliff-type wares that is associated with the latest Theodosian coinage (AD 388–402), and Cool (2000a) has identified changes in proportions between different classes of artefacts as 'signals' of 5th-century activity. This comparative and 'layered' approach has yielded positive results, enabling archaeologists to distinguish the late 4th century from the early 5th century. The next challenge is to refine dating in the 5th and 6th centuries, before the occurrence of the earliest identifiable Anglo-Saxon material culture in the frontier, as reviewed in Chapter 12 (O'Brien, this volume). There is also the potential that comparative analysis of site assemblages can determine inter-site associations that can supplement and

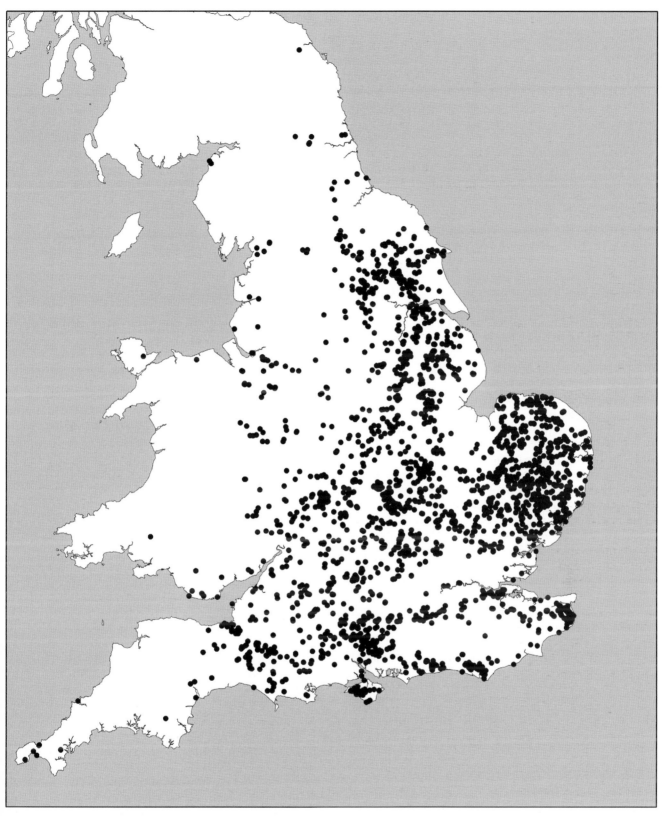

Fig 14.1   A distribution of 4th-century artefacts recorded with the Portable Antiquities Scheme, from data compiled January 2009 (map: Rob Collins)

reinforce landscape analyses, such as that offered by Roberts (Chapter 13, this volume).

In addition to Cool's layered approach, there are a number of types of artefact, notably dress acces-

sories, that provide a strong indication of a 5th- or 6th-century date. Zoomorphic penannular brooches are one example (Chapter 7, this volume), but Allason-Jones also adds zoomorphic pins, handpins, and pig's fibula pins (Chapter 8, this volume), while Hunter demonstrates a spread of 'native' types of artefacts like door-knobbed spearbutts and massive terrets from *barbaricum* into the Roman provinces of Britain (Chapter 11, this volume). For some of these artefacts, their likely origins and initial appearance in the archaeological record are dated to the 3rd century. However, these artefacts are significant due to their presence in deposits in post-Roman contexts and from non-Roman sites.

As the dating of artefacts favours the 4th century, and the distribution is concentrated on some categories of military and urban sites, this limits our interpretation of frontier economy and society primarily to the military community. Some of the papers in this volume have addressed logistical aspects of the military economy. Ceramics and environmental evidence, for example, indicate a shift in the supply and dietary economy in the late frontier. These shifts must be considered in reference to the geographic origins of objects and aspects of cultural practice. As noted in Chapter 4, ceramics throughout the northern frontier were dominated by East Yorkshire products by the second half of the 4th century, with occasional vessels from further afield being imported. In terms of ceramic supply and the products contained by the ceramics, this suggests that frontier supplies were largely drawn from northern England. The forms of the various vessels provide an understanding of cultural culinary economy. The dominance of jar forms and other coarse wares in forts (rather than tablewares) has been taken to mean a 'reversion' to native Iron Age styles of cooking and eating (Evans 2000). Such an interpretation cannot be wholly accepted, as ceramic assemblages in the late 4th/early 5th century are still more diverse in terms of vessel forms and fabric than in the late pre-Roman Iron Age. However, it is interesting that Huntley and Stallibrass (Chapter 10, this volume) have stated that plant macrofossil and zooarchaeological evidence is generally the same from the late Iron Age throughout the Roman period and into the Early Medieval period, though there was an increase in diversity with the introduction of further sources of food, both plant and meat. Cups, beakers, bowls, and mortaria are still present in the culinary culture of the late frontier, but whether and how these are related to the increased 'native' culinary traditions is unclear. Perhaps this is an indication of an increasingly northern British population rather than a population from outside the region. On the other hand, it may be that fort populations, regardless of their geographical origins, were incorporating local culinary traditions into everyday military practices. Given the long-term continuity of staples in the diet over the centuries, it seems that culinary traditions were not directly related to the provisions supplied.

At the level of the individual soldier, Brickstock (Chapter 9, this volume) has argued that the *limitanei* were paid at roughly equivalent levels to soldiers in the early 2nd century. In contrast to his 2nd-century counterpart, however, the 4th-century soldier had his food and equipment provided at no additional charge, and the majority of his salary was provided in kind; yet this volume has shown that this is not always apparent from the excavated assemblages and non-coin data. Most cash probably came in the form of imperial donatives. Depending on the regularity of delivery of such gifts from the emperor to his soldiers, this possibly limited the spending-power of the soldier to short bursts of consumerism. In conjunction with pay-in-kind, this perhaps explains declining numbers of low denomination coinage in the last half of the 4th century across much of the frontier, in contrast to areas of Yorkshire and southern and eastern Britain. Military communities may have been participating in multiple types of economies in parallel. High-denomination coins of precious metal would have retained a bullion value regardless of their function as coins. So finds of high-denomination coins, for example the gold *solidus* found at Scotch Street in Carlisle (Keevill *et al* 1989), cannot always be understood to represent a cash economy when found in 5th-century contexts (Abdy 2006; Moorhead 2006). Cash exchange was still practised when cash was available in sufficient quantities, perhaps periodically, for example during regular markets and fairs of which we have evidence at the forts of Newcastle (Bidwell and Snape 2002) and Carlisle (Zant 2009), and on a smaller scale at Wallsend (Hodgson 2003). There are tentative hints of continued low-denomination coin use at some settlements in Britain in post-Roman occupation levels (Abdy 2006; Moorhead 2006), but only two 5th-century coins post-dating AD 402 are known from the frontier (Collins 2008) and coin use in post-Roman occupation levels is as yet unproven at any frontier site. On a more daily basis, military communities were probably engaged in a barter-exchange economy from the mid- to late 4th century. Soldiers, in particular, were probably accustomed to a more socially embedded economy, in which the commanding officer acted as a patron, distributing supplies and goods as needed. This role as a provider would have enhanced the status of the commanding officer, increasing the economic and social ties of the soldiers and their dependants to the *praepositus*.

There are few examples of artefacts that serve as markers of elite status or military status during this period. Crossbow brooches must have been relatively common, and perhaps also the distinctive 'late' belt equipment discussed by Coulston (Chapter 6, this volume), though these occur in lower numbers in the frontier zone than other regions of Britain. 'Military' artefacts, including weapons, are regular finds at forts – even if rarely in large quantities – but there are relatively few artefacts that serve as status distinctions within the military community. Glass vessels may be one of these, and Price has noted the relatively low levels of glass vessels from forts and more notably towns (Chapter 5, this volume). Even accounting for recycling, glass vessels should perhaps be associated with an officer class rather than the common soldier. Another aspect of elite culture, though one poorly represented in the late frontier, is literacy. Hassall (Chapter 3, this volume) has reviewed the evidence for late epigraphy. The dedication inscription from Ravenscar (*RIB* 721) is exceptional for the entirety of Britannia and it is perhaps significant that there are more sub-Roman inscriptions from the frontier zone than have emerged from the whole of Britain in the 3rd and 4th centuries (O'Brien, this volume). Even given the small numbers of stones under consideration, this disparity has yet to be addressed or convincingly explained. Of course, the late military would have had an extensive documentary archive for recording the *minutiae* of military life, but unfortunately there is no British companion to the Abinnaeus archive (Bell *et al* 1962), nor a 4th-century counterpart to the famous Vindolanda letters.

Broader patterns are discernible. Bearing in mind the difficulty of sexing artefacts (Allason-Jones 1995), female artefacts, namely bracelets/armlets and hairpins, are also present in significant numbers inside the forts. This indicates a mixed-gender community, which is hardly surprising as the evidence suggests that many soldiers will have had wives/partners and other family members with them. The difficulty is demonstrating where these women and children lived, as *vici* seem to have been abandoned by the early 4th century at the latest. The limited *vicus* excavations undertaken in the area so far, eg Vindolanda and Housesteads, have all been conducted very close to the walls of their adjacent forts and it is possible that the later *vicus* buildings might be found further away; however, the coin data seem to support the theory that the *vici* were abandoned before the mid-4th century. In view of the lack of contradictory evidence, however, it must be presumed that the soldiers' dependants lived inside the forts in the late period, and recent research has emphasised that the fort wall cannot be seen as a demarcation of 'men only' (Andrew Birley, pers comm; Elizabeth Greene, pers comm). Unfortunately, no structures have been identified as married or mixed-gender accommodation, though the possibility that some normal barrack accommodation may have served such a purpose should not be precluded. The probability that forts housed the entire military community and not just the unit in residence may explain why 4th-century forts seem to be so full of buildings, many of which infringe on former road space. This would also help explain why late forts seem to be 'busy' with activity when the size of the unit may have decreased by some 50–70% from the size of its 2nd-century ancestor.

Unfortunately, there are few 4th-century non-military sites in the region which can be compared with military sites, the majority of the rural settlement sites having been apparently abandoned by the mid-2nd century AD, with very limited exceptions. In terms of rural settlement in the North, villas have the largest artefact assemblages, but these are generally found south of the Tees and east of the Pennines. Other rural settlements, the so-called 'native' farmsteads, that have late assemblages are rare and typically dated to the 4th century by ceramic assemblages only, other late artefacts, including coins, being relatively atypical. One can argue that the lack of late material in these assemblages may be heavily biased by past excavation methods, in which entrances, gates, and ditch terminals were favoured for excavation rather than total open-area excavation; however, recent excavations on Bollihope Common in County Durham, which have used open-area excavation and scientific dating methods, have failed to produce any diagnostic 4th- or 5th-century artefacts despite evidence for probable Early Medieval occupation of the site (J Webster, pers comm).

Conclusions and future research

As acknowledged above, there are gaps in coverage, and interpretation is hampered by a number of factors. That said, the excellent contributions in the volume have provided a benchmark and a useful reference for comparison with other parts of Britain as well as other Roman frontiers. The contributions also go some way to brighten a period that is often called the 'twilight' of the Roman Empire.

Despite the expertise and insight each author has contributed, however, there is always room for further research. Undoubtedly, new excavations will generate important data, which will further refine our knowledge. Excavations focused on forts west of the Pennines, smaller military structures like milecastles, and any rural sites with 4th- and 5th-century occupation would be particularly helpful, redressing some of the imbalance of current datasets.

It has also been noted, particularly in Coulston's paper, that there is a conservative stylistic aspect to some of the military metalwork; this may be a more general feature of the frontier that needs to be explored further. Key to this is a reconsideration of artefacts by context. One of the key findings of this volume is that there is more late material than has been previously appreciated; an examination of assemblages by context rather than form or class would, no doubt, further increase the amount of material under consideration. Changing disposal practices and/or taphonomic processes must always be considered, and these aspects may account for the presence of 2nd- and 3rd-century artefacts in 4th-century contexts. However, this contextual analysis will also further elucidate any conservative aspects of material culture, particularly if preconceptions and preoccupations with the early frontier are discarded. As Cool stated at the beginning of this volume, the 4th century is not poorer, just different. The challenge is to be able to quantitatively and qualitatively demonstrate and explain that difference.

More than one contributor has noted that particular changes in the various classes of artefact occur in the second half of the 4th century, many of them in the last quarter of the 4th century. Why? Are we witnessing a revolution in material culture in the late Roman frontier that can be associated with the 'end' of Roman Britain? Or is there a transformation over time with no clear connection to the political history of Britain? The more comprehensive and statistical analyses that Cool has employed have yielded positive results (eg Cool and Baxter 1999; 2005), and further methodological developments are likely to refine dating of different classes of artefacts, which will further enhance site interpretation. The papers in this volume provide a useful starting point, but it is hoped that future research can make useful advances based on the information provided, not only to increase our understanding of the late frontier, but of the rest of Roman Britain and the later Roman Empire in general.

Bibliography

Classical Works and Abbreviations

Ammianus Marcellinus *The Surviving Books of the History*, trans J C Rolfe, 1963, Loeb edition. Cambridge, Mass

Codex Theodosianus: The Theodosian Code and Novels and the Sirmondian Constitutions, trans C Pharr, 1969. New York

CSIR Corpus Signorum Imperii Romani. Vol I: E J Phillips 1977; *Vol 1.6*: J N C Coulston & E J Phillips 1988. Oxford

DES *Discovery and Excavation in Scotland*. Council for Scottish Archaeology. Edinburgh

Digest Justinian *The Digest of Roman Law*, trans C F Kolbert, 1979. Penguin edition. London

HBMCE Historic Buildings and Monuments Commission for England

HE Bede's *Ecclesiastical History of the English People*, ed B Colgrave and R A B Mynors, 1969. Oxford

Herodian *Histories,* trans C Whittaker, 1969, Loeb edition. Cambridge, Mass

HSC Historia de Sancto Cuthberto: A History of Saint Cuthbert and a Record of his Patrimony, ed T Johnson South, 2002. Woodbridge

ILS (cited by item number), H Dessau (ed), 1892–1916 *Inscriptiones latinae selectae*. Berlin

NCH A History of Northumberland (Volume 10 The Parish of Corbridge), ed H H E Craster, 1914. Newcastle upon Tyne

Notitia Dignitatum, O Seeck (ed), 1962 (reprint of the 1876 edition). Frankfurt am Main

Ovid *Ars Amatoria*, trans F J Miller, 1916, Loeb edition. Cambridge, Mass

PAS Portable Antiquities Scheme

Petronius *The Satyricon*, E H Warrington (ed), W H D Rouse & M Hesletine (trans), 1989, Loeb. Cambridge, Mass

Polybius *The Histories*, trans W R Paton, 1989, Loeb edition. Cambridge, Mass

P.Oxy, Papyri Oxyrhynchus, http://www.papyrology.ox.ac.uk/

RIB (cited by item number) R G Collingwood & R P Wright, 1965, *The Roman Inscriptions of Britain, Volume 1*. Oxford

Scriptores Historiae Augustae trans D Magie, 1921–32, Loeb edition. Cambridge, Mass

Suetonius *Lives of the Caesars,* trans R Graves, 1957. London

Tacitus *Annals,* trans M Grant, 1985. London

Tertullian *On Female Dress,* trans C Dodgson, 1842, A Library of Fathers of the Holy Catholic Church. London

VCP Bede, *Life of Cuthbert in Prose*, in B Colgrave (ed), 1940 *Two Lives of Saint Cuthbert*. Cambridge

Vegetius *Epitoma Rei Militaris*, M D Reeve (ed), 2004. Oxford

Modern Works

Abdy, R, 2006 After Patching: Imported and Recycled Coinage in Fifth- and Sixth-Century Britain, in B Cook & G Williams (eds), *Coinage and History in the North Sea World, c AD 500–1250: Essays in Honour of Marion Archibald*. Boston, 75–98

Abramson, P, Berg, D S, & Fossick, M R, 1999 *Roman Castleford. Volume II: The structural and environmental evidence*. Yorks Archaeol **5**. Wakefield

Ager, B, 2007 Appendix: A Note on the Continental Background to Late Romano-British Belt Fittings with Zoomorphic Features, in M Henig & T J Smith (eds), *Collectanea Antiqua. Essays in Memory of Sonia Chadwick Hawkes*, BAR Int Series **1673**. Oxford: British Archaeological Reports, 141–3

Ager, B, 2008 Littlethorpe, North Yorkshire: Late Roman silver penannular brooch, *Treasure Annual Report 2005/6*, 253

Aillagon, J-J (ed), 2008 *Roma e i Barbari*. Venezia/Milano

Aird, W, 1998 The foundations of power: the Church of St Cuthburt, in W Aird, *St Cuthbert and the Normans: the Church of Durham, 1071–1153*. Woodbridge, 635–1065

Alcock, L, 1987a *Economy, Society and Warfare among the Britons and Saxons*. Cardiff

Alcock, L, 1987b Pictish studies: present and future, in A Small (ed), *The Picts: a new look at old problems*. Dundee, 80–92

Alcock, L, 1988 *Bede, Eddius and the forts of the North Britons*, Jarrow Lecture. Jarrow

Alcock, L, 1995 *Cadbury Castle, Somerset: the early medieval archaeology*. Cardiff

Allason-Jones, L, 1988 'Small Finds' from Turrets on Hadrian's Wall, in J C Coulston (ed), *Military Equipment and the Identity of Roman Soldiers: Proceedings of the Fourth Roman Military Equipment Conference*, BAR Int Series **394**. Oxford: British Archaeological Reports, 197–233

Allason-Jones, L, 1989a *Ear-rings in Roman Britain*, BAR Brit Series **201**. Oxford: British Archaeological Reports

Allason-Jones, L, 1989b The Small Finds, in M C Bishop and J N Dore, *Corbridge: Excavations of the Roman Fort and Town, 1947–80*. London, 159–218

Allason-Jones, L, 1995 'Sexing' small finds, in P Rush (ed), *Theoretical Roman Archaeology: Second Conference Proceedings*. Aldershot, 22–32

Allason-Jones, L, 1996a *Roman Jet in the Yorkshire Museum*. York

Allason-Jones, L, 1996b Roman military and domestic artefacts from Great Chesters, *Archaeol Aeliana* 5th series **24**, 187–24

Allason-Jones, L, 2002 Small Finds, in Snape & Bidwell 2002, 211–33

Allason-Jones, L, 2005 *Women in Roman Britain*. York

Allason-Jones, L, 2009 The small finds, in Rushworth 2009, 430–87

Allason-Jones, L, forthcoming a The Finds, in J Dore 2009, *Excavations directed by J P Gillam at the Roman Fort of Halton Chesters, 1960–61*. Oxford

Allason-Jones, L forthcoming b The Finds from *Wallsend (Segedunum Roman Fort)*

Allason-Jones, L, & Jones, J M, 1994 Jet and other materials in Roman artefact studies, *Archaeol Aeliana* 5th series **22**, 265–72

Allason-Jones, L, & Jones, J M, 2001 Identification of 'jet' artefacts by reflected light microscopy, in *European J Archaeol* **4** (2), 233–51

Allason-Jones, L, & McKay, B, 1985 *Coventina's Well*. Chollerford

Allason-Jones, L, & Miket, R, 1984 *The Catalogue of Small Finds from South Shields Roman Fort*. Newcastle upon Tyne

Allen, D, 1988 Roman glass from Corbridge, in M C Bishop & J N Dore, *Corbridge. Excavations of the Roman fort and town, 1947–80*. HBMCE Archaeol Rep **8**. London, 287–93

Allen, D, 1991 The Glass, in N Holbrook & P T Bidwell *Roman Finds from Exeter*. Exeter Archaeol Rep **4**. Exeter, 220–9

Allen, D, 1993 Roman glass, in Casey & Davies 1993, 219–228

Alston, R, 1994 Roman Military Pay from Caesar to Diocletian, *J Roman Stud* **84**, 113–23

Alston, R, 1995 *Soldier and Society in Roman Egypt*. London/New York

Anderson, A C, 1980 *A Guide to Roman Fine Wares*. Highworth

Appels, A, & Laycock, S, 2007 *Roman Buckles and Military Fittings*. Witham

Archaeological Services University of Durham, 2006 A Roman villa and settlement at Ingleby Barwick, Stockton-on-Tees. Revised assessment report and updated project design, ASUD Rep **1174**. Durham

Archaeological Services University of Durham, forthcoming *Excavations at the Roman villa at Quarry Farm, Ingleby Barwick, Stockton on Tees*

Arnold, C J, & Davies, J L, 2000 *Roman and Early Medieval Wales*. Stroud

Austen, P S, 1991 *Bewcastle and Old Penrith: a Roman outpost fort and a frontier vicus*, Cumb West Antiq & Archaeol Soc Res Series **6**. Kendal

Ballin Smith, B, 1994 *Howe: four millennia of Orkney prehistory*, Soc Antiq Scot Monogr **9**. Edinburgh

Bannerman, J, 1974 *Studies in the History of Dalriada*. Edinburgh

Barag, D, 1987 Recent important epigraphic discoveries related to the history of glassmaking in the Roman period. 3. Glass in Diocletian's list of maximum prices, *Annales du 10e Congrès de l'Association Internationale pour l'Histoire du Verre*. Madrid-Segovie, 113–16

Barag, D, 2005 Alexandrian and Judaean glass in the Price Edict of Diocletian, *J Glass Studies* **47**, 184–6

Barber, B, & Bowsher, B, (eds) 2000 *The Eastern Cemetery of Roman London. Excavations 1983–1990*. London

Barker, P, 1979 'The *plumbatae* from Wroxeter', in Hassall & Ireland 1979, 97–9

Bateson, J D, & Holmes, N M McQ, 2006 Roman and medieval coins found in Scotland, 2001–2005, *Proc Soc Antiq Scot* **136**, 161–98

Bayley, J, & Butcher, S, 2004 *Roman Brooches in Britain: A Technological and Typological Study based on the Richborough Collection*. London

Bell, A, & Evans, J, 2002 Pottery from the CfA excavations, in Wilson 2002, 352–496

Bell, H I, Martin, V, Turner, E G, & van Berchem, D, 1962 *The Abinnaeus Archive: papers of a Roman officer in the reign of Constantius II*. Oxford

Benton, S, 1931 The excavation of the Sculptor's Cave, Covesea, Morayshire, *Proc Soc Antiq Scot* **65**, 177–216

Berger, P C, 1981 *The Insignia of the Notitia Dignitatum*. London

Bevan, L, forthcoming a Copper alloy objects, in Ferris & Jones forthcoming

Bevan, L, forthcoming b Iron objects, in Ferris & Jones forthcoming

Bevan, L, forthcoming c The Anglo-Saxon female burial and grave-goods and other Anglo-Saxon objects, in Ferris & Jones forthcoming

Bibre, P, 2001 North Sea language contacts in the Early Middle Ages, in T Liszka & L Walker (eds), *The North Sea World in the Middle Ages*. Dublin, 88–107

Biddulph, E, 2008 Form and function: the experimental use of Roman samian ware cups, *Oxford J Archaeol* **27**, 73–89

Bidwell, P T, 1985 *The Roman fort of Vindolanda at Chesterholm, Northumberland*, HBMCE Archaeol Rep **1**. London

Bidwell, P T, 1991 Later Roman barracks in Britain, in Maxfield & Dobson (eds) 1991, 9–15

Bidwell, P, 1999 *Hadrian's Wall 1989–1999*. Kendal

Bidwell, P, 2005 The dating of Crambeck parchment ware, *J Roman Pottery Stud,* **12**, 15–21

Bidwell, P, & Croom, A, 1997 The coarse wares, in Wenham & Heywood (eds) 1997, 61–103

Bidwell, P, & Croom, A, 2002 The Roman pottery, in Snape & Bidwell 2002, 139–72

Bidwell, P, & Snape, M, 2002 The history and setting of the Roman fort at Newcastle upon Tyne, in Snape & Bidwell 2002, 251–83

Bidwell, P, & Speak, S, 1994 *Excavations at South Shields Roman Fort, I*, Soc Antiq Newcastle Monogr Series **4**. Newcastle upon Tyne

Bidwell, P, & Watson, M, 1996 Excavations on Hadrian's Wall at Denton, *Archaeol Aeliana* 5th series **24**, 50–2

Birley, A, 1997 *Security: The Locks and Keys*, Vindolanda Research Reports, New Series vol 4 The Small Finds. Fasc **2**. Greenhead

Birley, B, & Greene, E, 2006 *The Roman Jewellery from Vindolanda: the beads, intaglios, finger rings, bracelets and ear-rings*. Vindolanda

Birley, E B, 1930a The pottery, in Richmond & Birley 1930, 175–98

Birley, E B, 1930b Excavations on Hadrian's Wall west of Newcastle upon Tyne in 1929, *Archaeol Aeliana* 4th series **7**, 143–74

Birley, E, 1955 Review of Grünhagen 1954, *Antiquity*, **29**, 246

Bishop, M C, 1991 Soldiers and military equipment in the towns of Roman Britain, in Maxfield & Dobson (eds) 1991, 21–8

Bishop, M C, 1992 The early imperial 'apron', *J Roman Military Equip Stud* **3**, 81–104

Bishop, M C (ed), 1993 Excavations in the Roman fort at Chester-le-Street (Concangis), Church Chare 1990–91, *Archaeol Aeliana* 5th series **21**, 32–85

Bishop, M C, 1996 *Finds from Roman Aldborough: a catalogue of small finds from the Romano-British town of* Isurium Brigantium. Oxford

Bishop, M C, 2002 *Lorica Segmentata. Vol 1: a handbook of articulated Roman plate armour.* Duns

Bishop, M C, & Coulston, J C N, 2006 *Roman Military Equipment from the Punic Wars to the Fall of Rome*, 2nd edn. Oxford

Blagg, T F C, 2000 The architecture of the legionary *principia*, in Brewer (ed) 2000, 139–47

Bogaers, J, 1952 Bewoning uit de Romeinse tijd: 2e helft van de 2e en 1e helft van de 3e eeuw na Chr. Rockanje (Prov. Zuid-Holland), *Berichten van de Rijksdienst voor het Oudheidkundig Bodemonderzoek*, **3**, 4–8

Böhme, H W, 1986 Das Ende der Römerherrschaft in Britannien und die angelsächsische Besiedlung Englands im 5 Jahrhundert, *Jahrbuch des Römisch-Germanischen Zentralmuseums Mainz* **33**, 469–574

Böhner, K, 1963 Zur historischen Interpretation der sogenannten Laetengräber, *Jahrbuch des Römisch-Germanischen Zentralmuseums Mainz* **10**, 139–67

Booth, P, 2007 Lankhills, Winchester, Hampshire: two Roman grave assemblages, in *Treasure Annual Report 2004*. London, 58

Boppert, W, 1992 *Corpus Signorum Imperii Romani, Deutschland* II.5. *Militärische Grabdenkmäler aus Mainz und Umgebung*. Mainz

Bosanquet, R C, 1904 Excavations along the line of the Roman Wall in Northumberland: the Roman camp at Housesteads, *Archaeol Aeliana* 2nd series **25**, 193–300

Braithwaite, G, 1997 Face pots, in Wenham & Heywood 1997, 103–6

Breeze, D J, 1972 Excavations at the Roman fort of Carrawburgh, 1967–1969, *Archaeol Aeliana* 4th series **50**, 81–144

Breeze, D J, 1982 *The Northern Frontiers of Roman Britain*. London

Breeze, D J, 2006 *J Collingwood Bruce's Handbook to the Roman Wall*, 14th edn. Newcastle on Tyne

Breeze, D, & Dobson, B, 1985 Roman military deployment in North England, *Britannia* **16**, 1–19

Breeze, D J, & Dobson, B, 1987 *Hadrian's Wall*, 3rd edition. London

Breeze, D J, & Dobson, B, 2000 *Hadrian's Wall*, 4th edition. London

Brenan J 1991 *Hanging Bowls and their Contexts*. BAR Brit Series **220**. Oxford: British Archaeological Reports

Brewer, R, 1986 The beads and glass counters, in Zienkiewicz 1986, 147–56

Brewer, R J (ed), 2000 *Roman Fortresses and their Legions*. London

Brickstock, R J, 2000a Coin Supply in the North in the Roman period, in Wilmott & Wilson (eds) 2000, 33–8

Brickstock, R J, 2000b The coins, in Ottaway 2000, 131–40

Brickstock, R J, 2004 *The Production, Analysis and Standardisation of Romano-British Coin Reports*. London

Brickstock, R J, forthcoming, The Coins, in Crow forthcoming, Steel Rigg excavation report

Brickstock, R J, unpublished, *The Rudchester hoard rediscovered*

Brickstock, R J, & Casey, J, 2009 The Coins, in Rushworth 2009

Brown, D, 1976 Fourth-century bronzework, in M Jarrett, *Maryport, Cumbria: a Roman fort and its garrison*. Kendal

Brown, M, 1977 Yarm (NZ 421117), *Yorks Archaeol J* **49**, 8

Bruce-Mitford, R, 2005 *A Corpus of Late Celtic Hanging Bowls*. Oxford

Brüggler, M, 2006 Spätrömischer Glasherstellung im Hambacher Forst, in G Cereemers, B Demarsin & P Cosyns (eds), *Roman Glass in Germania Inferior. Interregional Comparisons and Recent Results*. Atuatuca I. Tongeren, 86–90

Bryant, S, Morris, M, & Walker, J S F, 1986 *Roman Manchester: A Frontier Settlement*, Archaeology of Manchester **3**. Manchester

Buckland, P, & Dolby, M, 1971 Doncaster, *Current Archaeol* **3**, 273–7

Budge, A E W, 1907 *An Account of the Roman Antiq-*

uities preserved in the Museum at Chesters, Northumberland. London

Bullinger, H, 1969 *Spätantike Gürtelbeschläge. Typen, Herstellung, Tragweise und Datierung*. Brugge

Burley, E, 1956 A catalogue and survey of the metalwork from Traprain Law, *Proc Soc Antiq Scot* **89**, 118–226

Burnham, B C, Hunter, F, Fitzpatrick, A P, Hassall M W C, & Tomlin, R S O, 2002 Roman Britain in 2001, *Britannia* **33**, 275–371

Busby, P A, Evans, J, Huntley, J P, & Wilson, P R, 1996 A pottery kiln at Catterick, *Britannia* **27**, 283–97

Bushe-Fox, J P, 1949 *Fourth Report on the Excavations of the Roman Fort at Richborough, Kent*. Oxford

Butcher, S, 1995 Roman Brooches, in D Phillips & B Heywood *Excavations at York Minster*. London, 391–3

Butcher, S, 2008 The Romano-British brooches and enamelled objects, in Cool & Mason (eds) 2008, Ch 11, D11.105–22

Cabart, H, 2008 Une production originale du Nord de la France au IVe siècle: les verres à décor de serpents, *J Glass Stud* **50**, 31–50

Cagnat, R, 1913 *L'armée romaine d'Afrique et l'occupation militaire de l'Afrique sous les empereurs*. Paris

Cahn, H A, 1984 Hacksilber mit Mainz Offizinstempel, in H A Cahn & A Kaufmann-Heinimann (eds), *Der spätrömische Silberschatz von Kaiseraugst*. Augst, 322–3

Caldwell, D H, Holmes, N, & Hunter, F, 2006 Dundonald Castle excavations: further information on the finds, *Scot Archaeol J*, **28(1)**, 75–80

Cameron, A, 2006 Constantius and Constantine: an exercise in publicity, in Hartley *et al* (eds) 2006, 18–30

Cameron, K, 1996 *English Place Names*. London

Campbell, E, 1997 Early medieval vessel glass, in P Hill (ed), *Whithorn and St Ninian*. Whithorn/Gloucester, 297–314

Campbell, E, 2007a *Continental and Mediterranean Imports to Atlantic Britain and Ireland, AD 400–800*. CBA Res Rep **157**. York: Council for British Archaeology

Campbell, E, 2007b Glass, in R C Barrowman *et al, Excavations at Tintagel Castle, Cornwall, 1990–1999*. Rep Res Comm Soc Antiq London **74**. London, 222–9

Carson, R A G, & Burnett, A M, 1979 *Recent Coin Hoards from Roman Britain*. British Museum Occ Paper **5**. London

Casey, P J (ed), 1979, *The End of Roman Britain: papers arising from a conference, Durham 1978*, BAR Brit Series 71. Oxford: British Archaeological Reports

Casey, P J, 1984a The coins, in Haigh & Savage 1984, 33–47

Casey, J, 1984b Roman coinage of the fourth century in Scotland, in R Miket & C Burgess (eds), *Between and Beyond the Walls*. Edinburgh, 295–304

Casey, P J, 1985 The Coins, in Bidwell 1985, 103–16

Casey, P J, 1991a *The Legions in the Later Roman Empire*. Caerleon

Casey, P J, 1991b Coins, in Austen 1991, 34–40

Casey, P J, 1993a The end of the fort garrisons on Hadrian's Wall: a hypothetical model, in Vallet & Kazanski 1993, 259–68

Casey, P J, 1993b The End of Garrisons on Hadrian's Wall: An Historico-Environmental Model, in D Clark, M Roxan & J Wilkes (eds), *The Later Roman Empire Today*. London, 69–80

Casey, P J, 1994 *Roman Coinage in Britain*. Princes Risborough

Casey, P J, & Davies, J L, 1993 *Excavations at Segontium (Caernarfon) Roman Fort, 1975–1979*, CBA Res Rep **90**. London: Council for British Archaeology

Casey, P J, & Savage, M, 1980 The coins from the excavations at High Rochester in 1852 and 1855, *Archaeol Aeliana* 5th series **8**, 75–87

Cessford, C, 1999 Relations between the Britons of Southern Scotland and Anglo-Saxon Northumbria, in J Hawkes & S Mills (eds), *Northumbria's Golden Age*. Stroud, 150–60

Chapman, E M, 2005 *A Catalogue of Roman Military Equipment in the National Museum of Wales*, BAR Brit Series **388**. Oxford: British Archaeological Reports

Charlesworth, D, 1959 Roman glass in northern Britain, *Archaeol Aeliana* 4th series **37**, 33–58

Charlesworth, D, 1961 Roman jewellery found in Northumberland and Durham, in *Archaeol Aeliana* 4th series **39**, 1–36

Charlesworth, D, 1979 Glass, in P T Bidwell, *The Legionary Bath-house and Basilica and Forum at Exeter*. Exeter Archaeol Rep **1**. Exeter, 222–31

Clarke, G, 1979 *The Roman Cemetery at Lankhills*. Oxford

Clarke, R R, 1952 An ogham inscribed knife-handle from south-west Norfolk, *Antiq J*, **32**, 71–4

Close-Brooks, J, 1986 Excavations at Clatchard Craig, Fife, *Proc Soc Antiq Scot*, **116**, 117–84

Close-Brooks, J, 1987 The clay moulds, in J W Hedges, *Bu, Gurness and the Brochs of Orkney. Part II: Gurness*, BAR Brit Series **164**. Oxford: British Archaeological Reports, 303–5

Coates, R, Breeze, A, & Horovitz, D, 2000 *Celtic Voices English Places*. Stamford

Cocks, A H, 1921 A Romano-British homestead in the Hambleden Valley, Bucks, *Archaeologia* **71** (1920–21), 141–98

Coello, T, 1996 *Unit Sizes in the Late Roman Army*, BAR Int Series **645**. Oxford: British Archaeological Reports

Collingwood, R G, 1931a Roman Objects from Stanwix, *Trans Cumb West Antiq & Archaeol Soc* **31**, 71–80

Collingwood, R G, 1931b Objects from Brough-under-Stainmore in the Craven Museum, Skipton, *Trans Cumb West Antiq & Archaeol Soc* **31**, 81–6

Collins, R, 2004 Before the End: Hadrian's Wall in the Fourth Century and after, in R Collins & J Gerrard (eds), *Debating Late Antiquity in Britain AD 350–700*, BAR Brit Series **364**. Oxford: British Archaeological Reports, 123–32

Collins, R, 2007 Decline, Collapse, or Transformation: the 4th and 5th centuries on Hadrian's Wall. Unpubl PhD thesis, University of York

Collins, R, 2008 The Latest Roman Coin from Hadrian's Wall: a Small Fifth-Century Purse Group, *Britannia* **39**, 256–61

Collins, R, 2009 Hadrian's Wall and the Collapse of Roman Frontiers, in A Morillo, N Hanel & E Martín Hernádez (eds), *Limes XX: Actax XX Congreso Int. de Esudios sobre la Frontera Romana (León)*, Anejos de Gladius **13**. Madrid

Collins, R, forthcoming, Military Communities and the Transformation of the Frontier from the 4th–6th Centuries, in D Petts & S Turner (eds), *Early Medieval Northumbria: New Visions and New Directions*, Studies in the Early Middle Ages **24**. Turnhout

Cooke, N, & Crummy, N, 2000 Antler combs, big hair and the mafia in Late Roman Britain; an e-mail correspondence reported in *Roman Finds Group Newsletter* **30**, 3–7

Cool, H E M, 1995 Glass vessels of the fourth and early fifth century in Roman Britain, in Foy (ed), 1995, 11–23

Cool, H E M, 2000a The parts left over: material culture into the fifth century, in Wilmott & Wilson (eds) 2000, 47–65

Cool, H E M, 2000b The Roman Finds, in P Ottaway, Excavations on the site of the Roman signal station at Carr Naze, Filey, 1993–94, *Archaeol J* **157**, 122–31

Cool, H E M, 2002a An overview of the small finds from Catterick, in Wilson 2002, 24–43

Cool, H E M, 2002b Bottles for Bacchus?, in M Aldhouse-Green & P Webster (eds), *Artefacts and Archaeology: Aspects of the Celtic and Roman World*. Cardiff, 132–51

Cool, H E M, 2003 Local production and trade in glass vessels in the British Isles in the first to seventh centuries AD, in Foy & Nenna (eds) 2003, 139–43

Cool, H E M, 2004 *The Roman Cemetery at Brougham, Cumbria. Excavations 1966–67*, Britannia Monogr **21**. London

Cool, H E M, 2006 *Eating and Drinking in Roman Britain*. Cambridge

Cool, H E M, 2007 The small finds in their regional context, in Miles *et al* 2007, 342–50

Cool, H, 2008 The Small Finds, in Cool & Mason (eds) 2008, 241–69

Cool, H E M, & Baxter, M J, 1999 Peeling the onion: an approach to comparing vessel glass assemblages, *J Roman Archaeol* **12**, 72–100

Cool, H E M, & Baxter, M J, 2005 Cemeteries and significance tests, *J Roman Archaeol* **18**, 397–404

Cool, H E M, & Mason, D J P (eds), 2008 *Roman Piercebridge: Excavations by D W Harding and Peter Scott, 1969–1981*, Architect Archaeol Soc Durham Northumberland Rep **7**

Cool, H E M, & Philo, C (eds), 1998 *Roman Castleford. Volume I: the small finds*, Yorks Archaeol **4**. Wakefield

Cool, H E M, & Price, J, 1991 The Roman vessel and window glass, in M R McCarthy, *Roman waterlogged remains at Castle Street Carlisle*, Cumb West Antiq & Archaeol Soc Res Series **3**, mf2/165–76

Cool, H E M, & Price, J, 1993 Roman Glass, in P J Woodward, S M Davies, & A H Graham, *Excavations at the Old Methodist Chapel and Greyhound Yard, Dorchester*. Dorset Nat Hist Archaeol Soc Monogr Series **12**. Dorchester, 150–67

Cool, H E M, & Price, J, 1995 *Roman Vessel Glass from Excavations in Colchester, 1971–85*. Colchester Archaeol Rep **8**. Colchester

Cool H E M, & Price, J, 2008 The glass vessels, in Cool and Mason (eds) 2008, 235–40, D10.1–29

Cool H E M, Price, J, & Cottam, S, 2002 The glass from Catterick, in Wilson 2002, 212–58

Cooper, N J, 2002 Group 5 (434, R II 7, Phase 4b, c AD 340–50/5), in Wilson 2002, 259–60

Corder, P, 1928 *The Roman Pottery at Crambeck, Castle Howard*, Roman Malton and District Rep **1**. York (reprinted in Wilson 1989)

Corder, P, & Birley, M, 1937 A pair of fourth-century Romano-British kilns near Crambeck, *Antiq J* **17**, 392–413 (reprinted in Wilson 1989)

Corder, P, & Kirk, J L, 1932 *A Roman Villa at Langton, near Malton, E Yorkshire*, Roman Malton & District Rep 4. Leeds

Coulston, J C, 1985 Roman Archery Equipment, in M C Bishop (ed), *The Production and Distribution of Roman Military Equipment. Proceedings of the Second Roman Military Equipment Seminar*, BAR Int Series **275**. Oxford: British Archaeological Reports, 220–366

Coulston, J C N, 1990 Later Roman armour, 3rd–6th centuries AD, *J Roman Military Equip Stud* **1**, 139–60

Coulston, J, 2002 Arms and armour of the Late Roman army, in D Nicolle (ed), *A Companion to Medieval Arms and Armour*. Woodbridge, 3–24

Coulston, J C N, 2004 Military identity and personal self-identity in the Roman army, in L de Licht, E L Hemelrijk, & H W Sengor (eds), *Impact of Empire IV. The Empire at the Lower Level: Effects of Roman Rule on Life in Italy and the Provinces*. Amsterdam, 133–52

Cowan, J D, 1948 The Carvoran spear-head again, *Archaeol Aeliana* 4th series **26**, 142–4

Cramp, R, 1983 Anglo-Saxon Settlement, in J C Chapman & H C Mytum (eds), *Settlement in North Britain 1000 BC–AD 1000*, BAR Brit Series **118**. Oxford: British Archaeological Reports, 263–98

Cramp, R, 1984 *Corpus of Anglo-Saxon Stone Sculpture* I. Oxford

Cramp, R, 1988a *Corpus of Anglo-Saxon Stone Sculpture* II. Oxford

Cramp, R, 1988b Northumbria: the archaeological evidence, in S Driscoll & M Nieke (eds), *Power and Politics in Early Medieval Britain and Ireland*. Edinburgh, 69–78

Cramp, R, & Miket, R, 1982 *Catalogue of the Anglo-Saxon and Viking Antiquities in the Museum of Antiquities, Newcastle upon Tyne*. Newcastle upon Tyne

Craster, H H E, 1932 The coin-evidence from the signal-stations, in Hull 1932, 251–3

Cree, J E, 1923 Account of the excavations on Traprain Law ... in 1922, *Proc Soc Antiq Scot* **57**, 180–226

Creighton, J, 1999 The pottery, in P Halkon & M Millett (eds), *Rural Settlement and Industry: studies in the Iron Age and Roman archaeology of lowland East Yorkshire,* Yorks Archaeol Rep **4**. Leeds, 141–64

Croom, A, 1994 Small Finds, in Bidwell & Speak 1994, 177–205

Croom, A, 2000 *Roman Clothing and Fashion*. Stroud

Croom, A T, McBride, R M, & Bidwell, P T, 2008 The coarse pottery, in Cool and Mason (eds) 2008, 208–30

Crummy, N, 1983 *The Roman Small Finds from Excavations in Colchester, 1971–9,* Colchester Archaeol Rep **2**. Colchester

Cunliffe, B, 1975 *Excavations at Portchester Volume I: Roman,* Rep Res Comm Soc Antiq London **32**. London

Cunliffe, B, 2001 *Facing the Ocean: The Atlantic and its Peoples 8000 BC–AD 1500*. Oxford

Curle, A O, 1915 Account of excavations on Traprain Law, *Proc Soc Antiq Scot* **49**, 139–202

Curle, A O, 1923 *The Treasure of Traprain*. Glasgow

Curle, A O, & Cree, J E, 1916 Account of the excavations on Traprain Law... in 1915, *Proc Soc Antiq Scot* **50**, 64–144

Curle, J, 1932 An inventory of objects of Roman and provincial Roman origin found on sites in Scotland not definitely associated with Roman constructions, *Proc Soc Antiq Scot* **66**, 277–397

Dahlmos, U, 1977 Francisca-bipennis-securis. Bemerkungen zu archäologischen Befund und schriftlicher Uberlieferung, *Germania* **55**, 141–65

Daniels, C M, 1980 Excavation at Wallsend and the Fourth Century barracks on Hadrian's Wall, in Hanson & Keppie (eds) 1980, 173–200

Darby, H C, 1977 *Domesday England*. Cambridge

Dark, K, 1992 A sub-Roman re-defence of Hadrian's Wall? *Britannia* **23**, 111–20

Dark, K R, 1994 *Civitas to Kingdom; British political continuity 300–800*. Leicester

Dark, K, 1996 *External Contacts and the Economy of Late Roman Britain*. Woodbridge

Dark, K, 2000a *Britain and the End of the Roman Empire*. Stroud

Dark, K R, 2000b The late Roman transition in the North: a discussion, in Wilmott & Wilson (eds) 2000, 81–8

Dark, K R, & Dark, S P, 1996 New archaeological and palynological evidence for a sub-Roman reoccupation of Hadrian's Wall, *Archaeol Aeliana* 5th series **24**, 57–72

Dark, P, 2006 Climate deterioration and land-use change in the first millennium BC: perspectives from the British palynological record, *J Archaeol Sci* **33**, 1381–95

Darling, M J, & Gurney, D, 1993 *Caister-on-Sea Excavations by Charles Green 1951–55*, East Anglian Archaeol Rep **60**. Dereham

Davey, N, & Ling, R, 1981 *Wall Painting in Roman Britain*, Britannia Monogr **3**. London

De Tommaso, G, 2000 *Alcuni vetri incise dalle collezioni de Museo Nazionale Romano*. Annales du 14e Congrès de l'Association Internationale pour l'Histoire du Verre (Venezia-Milano 1998), 113–16

Dickinson, T, 1982 Fowler's Type G penannular brooches reconsidered, *Medieval Archaeol* **26**, 41–68

Dilly, G, & Mahéo, N, 1997 *Verreries antiques du Musée de Picardie*. Picardie/Amiens

DES. Discovery and Excavation in Scotland. Edinburgh: Council for Scottish Archaeology

Dobson, B, & Mann, J C, 1973 The Roman army in Britain and Britons in the Roman army, *Britannia* **4**, 191–205

Dore, J N, 1983 The coarseware, in R Miket, *The Roman Fort at South Shields: excavation of the defences 1977–1981*. Newcastle upon Tyne, 61–107

Dore, J N, 1984 The coarseware, in Haigh & Savage 1984, 33–47

Dore, J N, & Gillam, J P, 1979 *The Roman Fort at South Shields,* Soc Antiq Newcastle upon Tyne Monogr Series **1**. Newcastle upon Tyne

Drew, C D, & Selby, K C C, 1939 The excavations at Colliton Park, Dorchester, carried out in 1938, *Proc Dorset Nat Hist Archaeol Soc* **60**, 1–15

Drexel, F, 1929 Das Kastell Faimingen, *Das Obergermanisch-Raetische Limes des Roemerreiches*, Abteilung B, Band VI, no 66c. Berlin & Leipzig

Dumville, D, 1993 The origins of Northumbria: some aspects of the British background, in *Britons and Anglo-Saxons in the Early Middle Ages*. Aldershot, 2–16

Duncan-Jones, R P, 1978 Pay and numbers in Diocletian's army, *Chiron* **8**, 541–60

Dunsford, H, & Harris, S, 2003 Colonisation of the wasteland in County Durham, 1100–1400, *Economic History Review* **56**, no 1, 34–56

Eagle, J, 1989 Testing *plumbatae*, in C van Driel-Murray (ed), *Roman Military Equipment: the sources of evidence. Proceedings of the Fifth Roman Military Equipment Conference,* BAR Int Series **476**. Oxford: British Archaeological Reports, 247–53

Eagles, B, 1979 *The Anglo-Saxon Settlement of Humberside*, BAR Brit Series **68**. Oxford: British Archaeological Reports

Eckhardt, H, & Crummy, N, 2008 *Styling the Body*

in Late Iron Age and Roman Britain, Monographies Instrumentum **36**. Montagnac

Eckwall, E, 1960 *English Place-Names*. Oxford

Edwards, B J N, & Webster, P V, 1985 *Ribchester Excavations, Part 1: excavations within the Roman fort, 1970–1980*. Cardiff

Elsner, J, 1998 *Imperial Rome and the Christian Triumph*. Oxford

Elton, H, 1996 *Warfare in Roman Europe, AD 350–425*. Oxford

Engelhardt, C, 1867 *Kragehul Mosefund*. København

Erdrich, M, 2000 *Rom und die Barbaren: Das Verhältnis zwischen dem Imperium Romanum und den Germanischen Stämmen vor seiner Nordwestgrenze von der späten römischen Republik bis zum Galischen Sonderreich*. Mainz

Ergil, T, 1983 *Ear-rings: the catalogue of the Istanbul Museum*. Istanbul

Erim, K T, & Reynolds, J, 1973 The Aphrodisias copy of Diocletian's Edict on Maximum Prices, *J Roman Stud* **63**, 99–100

Esmonde-Cleary, A S, 1989 *The Ending of Roman Britain*. London

Esmonde-Cleary, A S, 2000 Summing up, in Wilmott & Wilson (eds) 2000, 89–94

Ésperandieu, E, 1907–66 *Recueil General des Bas-reliefs, Statues et Bustes de la Gaule Romaine*. Paris

Evans, D R, & Metcalf, V M, 1992 *Roman Gates Caerleon*, Oxbow Monogr **15**. Oxford

Evans, J, 1989 Crambeck; the development of a major northern pottery industry, in Wilson (ed) 1989, 43–90

Evans, J, 1993 Pottery function and finewares in the Roman north, *J Roman Pottery Stud* **6**, 95–118

Evans, J, 2000 The end of Roman pottery in the North, in Wilmott & Wilson (eds) 2000, 39–46

Evans, J, 2002 Pottery from Catterick Bypass excavations and Catterick 1972 (Sites 433 and 434), in Wilson 2002, 250–80

Evans, J, Stroodley, N, & Chenery, C, 2006 A strontium and oxygen isotope assessment of a possible 4th century immigrant population in a Hampshire cemetery, southern England, *J Archaeol Sci* **33**, 265–72

Evison, V I, 2008 *Catalogue of Anglo-Saxon Glass in the British Museum*. British Museum Res Pub **167**. London

Farwell, D E, & Molleson, T I, 1993 *Excavations at Poundbury 1966–80 Vol 2: the cemeteries,* Dorset Nat Hist & Archaeol Soc Monogr Series **11**. Dorchester

Ferris, I, & Jones, R, 2000 Transforming an elite: reinterpreting Roman Binchester, in Wilmott & Wilson (eds) 2000, 1–12

Ferris, I, & Jones, R, forthcoming *Excavations at Roman Binchester*

Follman-Schultz, A-B, 1995 A propos des précurseurs romains du *Rüsselbecher*, in Foy (ed) 1995, 85–92

Fowler, E, 1960 The origin and development of the penannular brooch in Europe, *Proc Prehist Soc* **26**, 149–77

Fowler, E, 1964 Celtic metalwork of the fifth and sixth centuries AD, *Archaeol J*, **120**, 98–160

Fowler, P J, 2000 *Landscape Plotted and Pierced. Landscape history and local archaeology in Fyfield and Overton, Wiltshire*. London

Foy, D (ed), 1995 *Le Verre d'Antiquité Tardive et du Haut Moyen Age. Typologie-chronologie-diffusion*. Guiry-en-Vexin

Foy, D, & Nenna, M-D, 2001 *Tout Feu, Tout Sable. Mille ans de verre antique dans le Midi de la France*. Marseille

Foy, D, & Nenna, M-D (eds), 2003 *Échanges et Commerce du Verre dans le Monde Antique*, Monographies Instrumentum **24**. Montagnac

Franzoni, C, 1987 *Habitus Atque Habitudo Militis. Monumenti funerari di militari nella Cisalpina Romana*. Roma

Fraser, C, 1968 *The Northumberland Lay Subsidy Roll of 1296*. Newcastle on Tyne

Fremersdorf, F, 1967 *Die römischen Gläser mit Schliff, Bemalung und Goldauflagen aus Köln*. Köln

Frere, S S, 1967 *Britannia: a history of Roman Britain*. London

Frere, S S, & Tomlin, R S O (eds), 1991 *R G Collingwood and R P Wright, The Roman Inscriptions of Britain, volume II: Instrumentum Domesticum, fascicule 2; weights, gold vessel, silver vessels, bronze vessels, lead vessels, pewter vessels, shale vessels, glass vessels, spoons (RIB 2412–2420)*. Stroud

Fulford, M, 2006 Corvées and civitates, in Wilson (ed) 2006, 65–71

Fulford, M, Handley, M, & Clarke, A, 2000 An early date for ogham: the Silchester ogham stone rehabilitated, *Medieval Archaeol*, **44**, 1–23

Gaedechens, R, 1874 *Das Medusenhaupt von Blariacum*. Vorstande des Vereins von Alterthumsfreunden im Rheinlande (Fest-Programm zu Winckelmanns Begurtstage am 9. December 1874). Bonn

Gardner, A, 2007 *An Archaeology of Identity: soldiers and society in Late Roman Britain*. California

Gavin, F, & Newman, C, 2007 Notes on insular silver in the 'Military Style', *J Irish Archaeol* **16**, 1–10

Geake, H, 1997 *The use of grave-goods in conversion-period England c 600–c 850*, BAR Brit Series **261**. Oxford: British Archaeological Reports

Geary, P, 2002 *The Myth of Nations: the medieval origins of Europe*. Oxford

Gelling, M, 1978 *Signposts to the Past*. London

Gelling, M, 2000 *The Landscape of Place Names*. Stamford

Giacchero, M, 1974 *Edictum Diocletiani et Collegarum de pretiis rerum venalium*. Genova

Gibson, J P, & Simpson, F G, 1911 The milecastle on the Wall of Hadrian at the Poltross Burn, *Trans Cumb West Antiq & Archaeol Soc*, new series **11**, 390–461

Gillam, J P, 1957a Types of Roman coarse pottery

vessels in northern Britain, *Archaeol Aeliana,* 4th series **35**, 180–251

Gillam, J P, 1957b The coarse pottery, in E J W Hildyard (ed), Cataractonium, fort and town, *Yorks Archaeol J* **39**, 224–65

Gillam, J P, 1970 *Types of Roman Coarse Pottery in Northern Britain* (3rd edn). Newcastle upon Tyne

Gillam, J P, 1973 Sources of pottery found on northern military sites, in A Detsicas (ed), *Current Research into Romano-British Coarse Pottery,* CBA Res Rep **10**. London: Council for British Archaeology, 53–62

Gillam, J P, Jobey, I M, & Welsby, D A, 1993 *The Roman bath-house at Bewcastle, Cumbria,* Cumb West Antiq & Archaeol Soc Res Series **7**. Kendal

Goodburn, R, & Bartholemew, P, 1976 *Aspects of the Notitia Dignitatum,* BAR Int Series **15**. Oxford: British Archaeological Reports

Greep, S, 1987 Lead sling-shot from Windridge Farm, St Albans, and the use of the sling by the Roman army in Britain, *Britannia* **18**, 183–200

Grigg, R, 1983 Inconsistancy and lassitude: the shield emblems of the *Notitia Dignitatum, J Roman Stud* **73**, 132–42

Grose, D F, 1989 *Early Ancient Glass.* New York

Grünhagen, W, 1954 *Der Schatzfund von Groß Bodungen.* Römisch-Germanisch Forschungen **21**. Berlin

Gudea, N, & Baatz, D, 1974 Teile spätrömischer Ballisten aus Gornea und Orsova (Rumänien), *Saalburg Jahrbuch* **31**, 50–72

Guest, P S W, 2005 *The Late Roman Gold and Silver Coins from the Hoxne Treasure.* London

Guggisberg, M A, 2003 Katalog der Hortfunde aus Edelmetall des 4. und frühen 5. Jahrhunderts, in M A Guggisberg & A Kaufmann-Heinimann (eds), *Der Spätrömische Silberschatz von Kaiseraugst: die neuen Funde.* Forschungen in Augst **34**, 333–46. Augst

Guido, M, 1978 *The Glass Beads of the Prehistoric and Roman Periods in Britain and Ireland.* London

Haigh, D, & Savage, M, 1984 Sewingshields, *Archaeol Aeliana* 5th series **12**, 33–148

Halsall, G, 2007 *Barbarian Migrations and the Roman West 376–568.* Cambridge

Handley, M A, 2001 The Origins of Christian Commemoration in Late Antique Britain, *Early Medieval Europe* **10**, pt 1, 177–99

Hanson, W S, & Keppie, L J F (eds), 1980 *Roman Frontier Studies 1979,* BAR Int Series **71**. Oxford: British Archaeological Reports

Hanson, W S, Speller, K, Yeoman, P A, & Terry, J (eds), 2007 *Elginhaugh: A Flavian Fort and its Annexe* 2, Britannia Monogr **23**. London

Harden, D B, 1958 The glass objects, in M A Cotton and P W Gathercole, *Excavations at Clausentum, Southampton, 1951–1954.* London, 48–9

Harden, D B, 1960 The Wint Hill hunting bowl and related glasses, *J Glass Stud* **2**, 45–81

Harden, D B, 1962 Glass in Roman York, in *Eburacum, An Inventory of the Historical Monuments in the City of York, 1*. London: HMSO, 136–41

Harden, D B, 1969 Ancient Glass, II: Roman, *Archaeol J* **126**, 44–77

Harden, D B, 1975 Glass jug, in S A Castle, Excavations in Pear Wood, Brockley Hill, Middlesex, *Trans London Middlesex Archaeol Soc* **26**, 273

Harden, D B, Hellenkemper, H, Painter, K, & Whitehouse, D, 1987 *Glass of the Caesars.* Milan

Hartley, B R, 1986 Roman pottery, in Close-Brooks 1986, 155

Hartley, E, Hawkes, J, Henig, M, & Mee, F (eds), 2006 *Constantine the Great: York's Roman Emperor*

Hartley, K, 1995 Mortaria, in D Phillips & B Heywood, *Excavations at York Minster vol I: from Roman fortress to Norman cathedral: part 2 the finds*. York, 304–23

Harvey, P, 1994 Boldon Book and the wards between Tyne and Tees, in D Rollason, M Harvey & M Prestwick (eds), *Anglo-Norman Durham 1093–1193*. Woodbridge, 399–405

Haselgrove, C, 2009 *The Traprain Law Environs Project: fieldwork and excavations 2000–2004.* Edinburgh: Soc Antiq Scot

Hassall, M W C, 1976 Britain in the *Notitia,* in Goodburn & Bartholemew 1976, 103–17

Hassall, M W C, 1984 The date of the rebuilding of Hadrian's Turf Wall in stone, *Britannia* **15**, 242–4

Hassall, M W C, 2004 The defence of Britain in the 4th century, in Le Bohec & Wolff (eds) 2004, 178–89

Hassall, M W C, & Ireland, R I, 1979 *De Rebus Bellicis,* BAR Int Series **63**. Oxford: British Archaeological Reports

Haughton, C, & Powlesland, D, 1999 *West Heslerton: The Anglian Cemetery,* Vols 1 and 2. Yedingham

Hawkes, S, 1974 Some recent finds of late Roman buckles, *Britannia* **5**, 386–93

Hawkes, S, & Dunning, G C, 1961 Soldiers and settlers in Britain, fourth to fifth century, *Medieval Archaeol* **5**, 1–70

Heald, A, 2001 Knobbed spearbutts of the British and Irish Iron Age: new examples and new thoughts, *Antiquity* **75**, 689–96

Heald, A, 2005 Non-ferrous metalworking in Iron Age Scotland c 700 BC–AD 800. Unpublished PhD thesis, University of Edinburgh

Heighway, C, & Bryant, R, 1999 *The Golden Minster: the Anglo-Saxon minster and late medieval priory of St Oswald at Gloucester.* CBA Res Rep **117**. York: Council for British Archaeology York

Hendon, D, Charman, D J, & Kent, M, 2001 Palaeohydrological records derived from testate amoebae analysis from peatlands in northern England: within-site variability, between-site comparability and palaeoclimatic implications, *The Holocene* **11**, 127–48

Heurgon, J, 1958 *Le Trésor de Ténès.* Paris

Higham, N, 1986 *The Northern Counties to AD 1000.* London

Hill, M, & Nenna, M-D, 2003 Ain et-Turba and Bagawat necropolis in the Kharga oasis, Egypt, *Annales du 15e Congrès de l'Association Internationale pour l'Histoire du Verre (New York 2001)*, 88–92

Hill, S, 1974 The bearded lady of Carlisle, *Archaeol Aeliana* 5th series **2**, 271–5

Hillman, G, Mason, S, de Moulins, D, & Nesbitt, M, 1996 for 1995 Identification of archaeological remains of wheat: the 1992 London workshop, *Circaea* **12**, 195–209

Hird, L, 1997 The coarse pottery, in Wilmott 1997, 233–56

Hird, L, 2008 The type series, in Cool & Mason (eds) 2008, D9.188

Hirst, S, 1985 *An Anglo-Saxon inhumation cemetery at Sewerby, East Yorkshire,* University of York Archaeology Publications **4**. York

Hodgson, G W I, 1967 A Comparative Analysis of Faunal Remains from Some Roman and Native Sites in Northern England. Unpublished MSc thesis, University of Durham

Hodgson, K S, & Richmond, I A, 1938 Coarse pottery from Bewcastle, *Trans Cumb West Antiq & Archaeol Soc,* new series **38**, 219–29

Hodgson, N, 1996 A late Roman courtyard house at South Shields and its parallels, in P Johnson (ed), *Architecture in Roman Britain.* CBA Res Rep **94**. York: Council for British Archaeology, 135–51

Hodgson, N, 1999 South Shields – *Arbeia*, in P Bidwell (ed) *Hadrian's Wall, 1989–1999*. Kendal, 73–82

Hodgson, N, 2003 *The Roman fort at Wallsend (Segedunum). Excavations in 1997–98,* Tyne Wear Archaeol Monogr **2**. Newcastle upon Tyne

Hodgson, N, & Bidwell, P T, 2004 Auxiliary barracks in a new light: recent discoveries on Hadrian's Wall, *Britannia* **35**, 121–57

Holbrook, N (ed), 1998 *Cirencester: the Roman Town Defences, Public Buildings and Shops,* Cirencester Excavations **5**. Cirencester

Holbrook, N, & Bidwell, P T, 1991 *Roman finds from Exeter,* Exeter Archaeol Rep **4**. Exeter

Holder, P A, 1982 *The Roman Army in Britain.* London

Holmes, N, Collard, M, & Lawson, J A, 2003 *Excavations of Roman sites at Cramond, Edinburgh,* Soc Antiq Scot Monogr **23**. Edinburgh

Hooley, D, Mould, Q, & Tomlin, R S O, 2002 Leather, in Wilson 2002, 318–80

Hope-Taylor, B, 1977 *Yeavering: an Anglo-British centre of early Northumbria.* London

Hornsby, W, & Laverick, J D, 1932 The Roman signal station at Goldsborough, Whitby, *Archaeol J* **90**, 203–53

Hornsby, W, & Stanton, R, 1912 The Roman fort at Huncliffe, near Saltburn, in *J Roman Stud* **2**, 215–32

Howard-Davis, C, forthcoming The brooches, in R Newman & J Zant (eds), *The Carlisle Millennium Excavations*

Hughes, P D M, Mauquoy, D, Barber, K E, & Langdon,

P G, 2000 Mire-development pathways and palaeoclimatic records from a full Holocene peat archive at Walton Moss, Cumbria, England, *Holocene* **10**, 465–79

Hull, M R, 1932 The pottery from the Roman signal-stations on the Yorkshire coast, *Archaeol J* **89**, 220–53

Hunter, F, 1994 An unpublished Irish doorknob spearbutt, *Ulster J Archaeol* **57**, 185–6

Hunter, F, 2001 Roman and native in Scotland: new approaches, *J Roman Archaeol* **14**, 289–309

Hunter, F, 2006 Traprain Law, Reallexikon der Germanischen Altertumskunde **31**, 139–44. Berlin

Hunter, F, 2007a *Beyond the Edge of the empire – Caledonians, Picts and Romans.* Rosemarkie

Hunter, F, 2007b Silver for the barbarians: interpreting denarii hoards in north Britain and beyond, in R Hingley & S Willis (eds), *Roman Finds: context and theory.* Oxford, 214–24

Hunter, F, 2008 Celtic art in Roman Britain, in C Gosden, J D Hill, & D Garrow (eds), *Rethinking Celtic Art.* Oxford, 129–45

Hunter, F, 2009 Recent work on 'stray finds' of Roman objects in East Lothian, in Haselgrove 2009, 259–65

Hunter, F, forthcoming a Changing objects in changing worlds – dragonesque brooches and beaded torcs, in M Lewis, S Worrell & H Geake (eds), *Proc Portable Antiquities Scheme Conference.* Oxford

Hunter, F, forthcoming b The finds, in Archaeological Services University of Durham forthcoming

Hunter Blair, P, 1947 The origins of Northumbria, *Archaeol Aeliana* 4th series **25**, 1–51

Hunter Blair, P, 1949 The boundary between Bernicia and Deira, *Archaeol Aeliana* 4th series **27**, 46–59

Huntley, J P, 1989a Plant remains from Annetwell Street, Carlisle, Cumbria: the bulk samples, *Ancient Monuments Laboratory Rep* **1/89**. London, 103

Huntley, J P, 1989b Plant remains from Annetwell Street, Carlisle: a synthesis, *Ancient Monuments Laboratory Rep* **107/89**. London, 32

Huntley, J P, 1991a Macrobotanical remains from the Roman fort of Banna (Birdoswald, Cumbria), *Ancient Monuments Laboratory Rep* **104/91**. London, 33

Huntley, J P, 1991b Plant remains from Edderside, Cumbria, 1989 and 1990: EDD90, *Durham Environmental Archaeol Rep* **3/91**. Durham

Huntley, J P, 1995 Scotch Corner: SC95. An evaluation and assessment of the environmental samples, *Durham Environmental Archaeol Rep* **12/95**. Durham, 5

Huntley, J P, 1997 Macrobotanical evidence from the *horrea*, in Wilmott 1997, 141–4, 461

Huntley, J P, 1999 Environmental evidence from Hadrian's Wall, in Bidwell 1999, 224

Huntley, J P, 2008 Quarry Farm QF03: analysis of charred plant remains from a Roman Villa and

148   *Finds from the Frontier*

settlement in the Tees Valley, North Yorkshire, *Durham Environmental Archaeol Rep* **3/2008**. Durham

Huntley, J P, & Stallibrass S M, 1995 *Plant and Vertebrate Remains from Archaeological Sites in Northern England: data reviews and future directions*, Architect Archaeol Soc Durham & Northumberland Res Rep **4**. Durham

Ilkjær, J, 1990 *Illerup Ådel 2. Die Lanzen und Speere*, Jutland Archaeol Soc Publications **225.2**. Aarhus

Ingemark, D, 2003 Glass, alcohol and power in Roman Iron Age Scotland. Unpublished PhD thesis, Lund University

Innes, J B, 1988 (unpublished) Report on Pollen Analysis, from Midgeholme Moss, Birdoswald, Cumbria, Institute Prehistoric Science & Archaeology, University of Liverpool

Isaac, B, 1988 The meaning of the terms *limes* and *limitanei*, *J Rom Studies* **78**, 125–47

Jackson, K, 2000 *Language and History in Early Britain*. Dublin

James, S, 1984 Britain and the late Roman army, in T F C Blagg & A King, *Military and Civilian in Roman Britain*, BAR Brit Series **136**. Oxford: British Archaeological Reports, 161–87

James, S, 1988 The *fabricae*: state arms factories of the Later Roman empire, in Coulston, J C (ed), *Military Equipment and the Identity of Roman Soldiers. Proceedings of the Fourth Roman Military Equipment Conference*, BAR Int Series **394**. Oxford: British Archaeological Reports, 257–331

James, S, 2000 The community of the soldiers: a major identity and centre of power in the Roman empire, in P Baker, C Forcey, S Jundi, S & B Witcher (eds), *Proceedings of the Eighth Annual Theoretical Roman Archaeology Conference, Leicester, 1998*. Oxford, 14–25

James, S, 2004 *The Excavations at Dura-Europos Conducted by Yale University and the French Academy of Inscriptions and Letters, 1928–1937. Final Report VII. The Arms and Armour and Other Military Equipment*. London

Jarrett, M G, 1970 The deserted village of West Whelpington, Northumberland: second report, *Archaeol Aeliana* 4th series **48**, 183–302

Jarrett, M G, & Evans, D H, 1989 Excavation of two palisaded enclosures at West Whelpington, Northumberland, *Archaeol Aeliana* 5th series **17**, 117–39

Jobey, G, 1959 Excavations at the native settlement at Huckhoe, Northumberland, 1955–57, *Archaeol Aeliana* 4th series **37**, 217–78

Jobey G, 1967 Excavations at Tynemouth Priory and Castle, *Archaeol Aeliana* 4th series **45**, 33–104

Jobey, G, 1968 Excavations of cairns at Chatton Sandyford, Northumberland, *Archaeol Aeliana* 4th series **46,** 5–50

Jobey, I, 1979 Housesteads ware – a Frisian tradition on Hadrian's Wall, *Archaeol Aeliana* 5th series **7**, 127–43

Jobst, W, 1975 *Die Römischen Fibeln aus Lauriacum*, Forschungen in Lauriacum **10**. Linz

Johns, C, 1996 *The Jewellery of Roman Britain: Celtic and Classical Traditions*. London

Johnson, S, 1980a *Late Roman Britain*. London

Johnson, S, 1980b A late Roman helmet from Burgh Castle, *Britannia* **11**, 303–12

Jones, A H M, 1964 *The Later Roman Empire*. Oxford

Jones, B, & Mattingly, D, 1990 *An Atlas of Roman Britain*. Oxford

Jones, G R J, 1971 The Multiple Estate as a model framework for tracing stages in the evolution of rural settlement, in F Dussart (ed), *L'Habitat et les Paysages Ruraux d'Europe*. Liège, 251–64

Jørgensen, E, & Vang Petersen, P, 2003 Nydam Bog – new finds and observations, in E Jørgensen, B Storgaard & L Gebauer Thomsen (eds), *The Spoils of Victory. The North in the Shadow of the Roman Empire*. København, 258–85

Junkelmann, M, 1992 *Die Reiter Roms III: Zubehör, Reitweise, Bewaffnung*. Mainz

Keevill, G, Shotter, D, & McCarthy, M, 1989 A Solidus of Valentinian II from Scotch Street, Carlisle, *Britannia* **20**, 254–5

Keller, E, 1971 *Die Spätrömische Grabfunde in Südbayern*. Münchner Beiträge zur Vor- und Frühgeschichte **14**. München

Kent, J P C, 1980 The Imperial *Vota* of the House of Constantine, *Roman Imperial Coinage* **8**, 50–4

Kent, J P C, & Painter, K S, 1972 *Wealth of the Roman World AD 300–700*. London

Kieferling, G, 1994 Bemerkungen zu Äxten der römischen Kaiserzeit und der frühen Völkerwanderungszeit im mitteleuropäischer Barbarikum, in C von Karnapp-Bornheim (ed), *Beiträge zu Römischer und Barbarischer Bewaffnung in den ersten vier Nachchristlichen Jahrhunderten*. Lublin & Marburg, 335–56

Kilbride-Jones, H E, 1935 An Aberdeenshire Iron Age miscellany, *Proc Soc Antiq Scot* **69**, 445–54

Kilbride-Jones, H E, 1980 *Zoomorphic Penannular Brooches*, Rep Res Comm Soc Antiq London **39**. London

King, E M, & Moore, M, 1989 The Romano-British settlement at Crambeck, North Yorkshire, in Wilson 1989, 105–7

Kirby, D, 1974 *Saint Wilfrid at Hexham*. Newcastle upon Tyne

Klumbach, H, 1973, *Spätrömische Gardehelme*. München

Koch, J 1997, *The* Gododdin *of Aneirin: text and context from Dark-Age north Britain*. Cardiff

Laing, L, 1993 *A Catalogue of Celtic Ornamental Metalwork in the British Isles c AD 400–1200*, BAR Brit Series **229**. Oxford: British Archaeological Reports

Laing, L, 2005 The Roman origins of Celtic Christian Art, *Archaeol J* **162**, 146–76

Laing, L, 2007 Romano-British metalworking and the Anglo-Saxons, in N Higham (ed), *Britons in Anglo-Saxon England*. Woodbridge, 42–56

Laing, L, & Laing, J, 1986 Scottish and Irish metalwork and the *'conspiratio barbarica'*, *Proc Soc Antiq Scot* **116**, 211–21

Lang, J, 1991 *Corpus of Anglo-Saxon Stone Sculpture* III. Oxford

Lang, J, 2001 *Corpus of Anglo-Saxon Stone Sculpture* IV. Oxford

Laycock, S, 2008 *Britannia, The Failed State. Tribal Conflicts and the End of Roman Britain*. Stroud

Leahy, K, 1995 Some recent finds of Celtic-type vehicle fittings from Lincolnshire, *Lincs Hist Archaeol* **30**, 7–11

Leahy, K, 1996 Three Roman rivet spurs from Lincolnshire, *Antiq J* **76**, 237–40

Leahy, K, 2007 Soldiers and settlers in Britain, fourth to fifth century – revisited, in M Henig & T J Smith (eds), *Collectanea Antiqua. Essays in Memory of Sonia Chadwick Hawkes*, BAR Int Series **1673**. Oxford: British Archaeological Reports, 133–43

Le Bohec, Y, 1994 *The Imperial Roman Army*. London

Le Bohec, Y, & Wolff, C, 2004 *L'Armée Romaine de Dioclétien a Valentinien I: Troisieme Congres de Lyons sur l'armée romaine*. Lyon

Leech, R, 1982 *Excavations at Catsgore 1970–1973*, Western Archaeol Trust Monogr **2**. Bristol

Lentowicz, I J, 2002 Copper-alloy objects from Catterick Bypass and Catterick 1972, in Wilson 2002, 46–78

Liebeschuetz, J H W G, 1986 Generals, federates and bucellarii in Roman armies around AD 400, in P Freeman & D Kennedy (eds), *The Defence of the Roman and Byzantine East*, BAR Int Series **297**. Oxford: British Archaeological Reports, 463–74

Livens, R G, 1976 A Don terret from Anglesey, with a discussion of the type, in G Boon & J M Lewis (eds), *Welsh Antiquity*. Cardiff, 149–62

Lockwood, H, 1979 Coarse pottery, in Potter 1979, 106–20

Loveluck, C, 2003 The archaeology of post-Roman Yorkshire, in T Manby, S Moorhouse & P Ottaway (eds), *The Archaeology of Yorkshire*, Yorks Archaeol Soc Occ Paper **3**. Leeds, 155–66

Lovett, E, 1904 Some suggestions as to the origin of the penannular brooch, *The Reliquary and Illustrated Archaeologist* **10**, 5–23

Lucy, S, 1998 *The Early Anglo-Saxon Cemeteries of Eastern Yorkshire*, BAR Brit Series **272**. Oxford: British Archaeological Reports

Lucy, S, 1999 Changing burial rites in Northumbria AD 500–750, in J Hawkes & S Mills (eds), *Northumbria's Golden Age*. Stroud, 12–43

Lucy, S, 2000 *The Anglo-Saxon Way of Death*. Stroud

Lucy, S, 2005 Early Medieval Burial at Yeavering: a retrospective, in P Frodsham & C O'Brien (eds), *Yeavering: people, power, place*. Stroud, 127–44

Luttwak, E, 1976 *The Grand Strategy of the Roman Empire*. Pennsylvania

Lyne, M, 1994 Late Roman helmet fragments from Richborough, *J Roman Military Equip Stud* **5**, 97–105

Lyne, M, 1999 Fourth century belt fittings from Richborough, *J Roman Military Equip Stud* **10**, 103–13

MacGregor, A, 1985 *Bone, Antler, Ivory and Horn*. London

MacGregor, A, & Bolick, E, 1993 *A Summary Catalogue of the Anglo-Saxon Collections (Non-Ferrous Metals), Ashmolean Museum*, BAR Brit Series **230**. Oxford: British Archaeological Reports

MacGregor, M, 1976 *Early Celtic Art in North Britain*. Leicester

Mackreth, D, 1990 Brooches, in McCarthy 1990, 105–13

Mackreth, D, 2002 Brooches from Catterick Bypass and Catterick 1972 (Sites 433 and 434), in Wilson 2002, 149–57

Mackreth, D, forthcoming The brooches, in I Ferris & R Jones, *Excavations at Binchester Roman Fort*

MacMullen, R, 1963 *Soldier and Civilian in the Later Roman Empire*. Cambridge, Mass

MacMullen, R, 1980 How big was the Roman imperial army?, *Klio* **62**, 451–60

Mann, J C, 1974 The northern frontier after AD 369, *Glasgow Archaeol J* **3**, 40–2

Mann, J C, 1991 The *Notitia Dignitatum* – dating and survival, *Britannia* **22**, 215–19

Mann, J C, 1992 *Armamentaria*, *Archaeol Aeliana* 5th series **20**, 157–8

Manning, W H, 1976 *Catalogue of Romano-British Ironwork in the Museum of Antiquities, Newcastle upon Tyne*. Newcastle upon Tyne

Mattingly, D, 2006 *An Imperial Possession, Britain in the Roman Empire*. London

Mawer, A, 1920 *The Place-Names of Northumberland and Durham*. Cambridge

Maxfield, V A, & Dobson, M J (eds), 1991 *Roman Frontier Studies. Proceedings XVth International Congress Roman Frontier Studies 1989*. Exeter

McCarthy, M, 1990 *A Roman, Anglian and Medieval Site at Blackfriars Street, Carlisle: Excavations 1977–79*. Kendal

McCarthy, M, 2002 *Roman Carlisle and the Lands of the Solway*. Stroud

Miket, R, 1980 A restatement of evidence from Bernician Anglo-Saxon burials, in P Rahtz, T Dickinson & L Watts (eds), *Anglo-Saxon Cemeteries 1979*, BAR Brit Series **82**. Oxford: British Archaeological Reports, 289–305

Miket, R, 2004 Archaeological finds from the Tweed Valley in 2002–2003, *Archaeol Aeliana* 5th series **33**, 175–81

Miks, C, 2007 *Studien zur römischen Schwertbewaffnung in der Kaiserzeit*, Kölner Studien zur Archäologie und Römischen Provinzen **8**. Rahden

Miks, C, 2008 *Vom Prunkstück zum Altmetall. Ein Depot Spätrömischer Helmteile aus Koblenz*. Mainz

Miles, D, Palmer, S, Smith A, & Jones, G P, 2007 *Iron Age and Roman Settlement in the Upper Thames Valley*, Thames Valley Landscape Monogr **26**. Oxford

Millett, M, 1992 *The Romanization of Britain*. Cambridge

Mitchelson, N, 1951 A late fourth-century occupation site at Seamer near Scarborough, *Yorks Archaeol J* **37**, 420–9

Monaghan, J, 1997 *Roman Pottery from York*, The Archaeology of York **16/8**. York

Moorhead, T S N, 2006 Roman Bronze Coinage in Sub-Roman and Early Anglo-Saxon England, in B Cook & G Williams (eds), *Coinage and History in the North Sea World, c AD 500–1250: Essays in Honour of Marion Archibald*. Boston, 99–109

Morris, J, 1993 *The Age of Arthur: a history of the British Isles from 350 to 650*. London

Mould, Q, Anderson, A, & Isaac, A, 2002 The iron objects from Catterick Bypass (Site 433), in Wilson 2002, 82–99

Nash-Williams, V E, 1932 The Roman legionary fortress at Caerleon II, *Archaeol Cambrensis* **87**, 48–104

Nash-Williams, V E, 1950 *The Early Christian Monuments of Wales*. Cardiff

Neal, D S, 1987 Excavations at Magiovinium, Buckinghamshire, 1978–80, *Records of Bucks* **29**, 1–24

Neal, D, 1996 *Excavations at the Roman Villa at Beadlam, Yorkshire*, Yorks Archaeol Rep **2**. Leeds

Nenna, M-D, 2002 New research on mosaic glass: preliminary results, in G Kordas (ed), *Hyalos-Vitrum-Glass*. Athens, 153–8

Nenna, M-D, 2003 Verreries de luxe de l'antiquité tardive découvertes à Douch, Oasis de Kharga, Égypte, *Annales du 15e Congrès de l'Association Internationale pour l'Histoire du Verre*. New York, 93–7

Nicasie, M J, 1998 *Twilight of Empire. The Roman army from the reign of Diocletian until the Battle of Adrianople*, Dutch Monographs Ancient Hist Archaeol **19**. Amsterdam

Nieke, M, 1993 Penannular and related brooches: secular ornament or symbol in action, in R Spearman & J Higgitt (eds), *The Age of Migrating Ideas: early medieval art in Northern Britain and Ireland*. Edinburgh

Noll, R, 1974 Eine goldene 'Kaiserfibel' aus Niederemmel vom Jahre 316, *Bonner Jahrbücher* **174**, 221–44

O'Brien, C, forthcoming Yeavering and Bernician Kingship: a review of debate on the hybrid culture thesis, in D Petts and S Turner (eds), *Early Medieval Northumbria: New Visions and New Directions*, Studies in the Early Middle Ages **24**. Turnhout

Ó Floinn, R, 2001 Patrons and politics: art, artefact and methodology', in M Redknap, N Edwards, S Youngs, A Lane & J Knight (eds), *Pattern and Purpose in Insular Art*. Oxford

Oldenstein, J, 1976 Zur Ausrüstung römischer Auxiliareinheiten, *Bericht der Römisch-Germanischen Kommission* **57**, 49–284

Oldenstein, J, 1986 Neue Forschungen im spätrömischen Kastell von Alzey; Vorbericht über die Ausgrabungen 1981–85, *Bericht der Romisch-Germanischen Kommission* **67**, 289–356

Oliver, A, 2005 Late Roman engraved glass, *J Roman Archaeol* **18**, 747–53

Olivier, A C H, 1979 Brooches, in Potter 1979, 65–9

Oppenheimer, S, 2006 *Origins of the British*. London

Ottaway, P, 2000 Excavations on the site of the Roman signal station at Carr Naze, Filey, 1993–94, *Archaeol J* **157**, 79–199

Paddock, J M, 1998 Military equipment, in Holbrook 1998, 305–7

Painter, K S, 1971 Six Roman glasses with cut decoration from Amiens, *British Museum Quarterly* **36** i–ii, 41–50

Painter, K, 1972 A late-Roman silver ingot from Kent, *Antiq J* **52**, 84–92

Painter, K, 1989 A fragment of a glass dish in the Antiquarium Comunale, Rome, *Kölner Jahrbuch* **22**, 87–98

Painter, K, 1993 Late-Roman silver plate: a reply to Alan Cameron, *J Roman Archaeol* **6**, 109–15

Painter, K, 2006 Traprain Law treasure, in Hartley *et al* (eds) 2006, 229–46

Palágyi, S K, 2000 Joche aus Pannonien, *Kölner Jahrbuch* **33**, 535–44

Paolucci, F, 2002 *L'arte del Vetro Inciso a Roma nel IV secolo dC*. Firenze

Pauli, L, 1980 *The Alps: Archaeology and Early History*. London

Pauli-Jensen, X, 2007 The use of archers in the northern Germanic armies. Evidence from the Danish war booty sacrifices, in T Grane (ed), *Beyond the Roman Frontier. Roman Influences on the Northern Barbaricum*. Rome, 143–51

Pelteret, D, 1995 *Slavery in Early Medieval England*. Woodbridge

Pentz, P, *et al*, 2000 *Kings of the North Sea AD 250–850*. Newcastle upon Tyne

Perrin, J R, 1999 Roman pottery from excavations at and near to the Roman small town of Durobrivae, Water Newton, Cambridgeshire, 1956–58, *J Roman Pottery Stud* **8**, 1–141

Philpott, R, 1991 *Burial Practices in Roman Britain*, BAR Brit Series **219**. Oxford: British Archaeological Reports

Piggott, S, 1955 The archaeological background, in F T Wainwright (ed), *The Problem of the Picts*. Edinburgh, 54–65

Piggott, S, 1966 A scheme for the Scottish Iron Age, in A L F Rivet (ed), *The Iron Age in North Britain*. Edinburgh: Edinburgh University Press, 1–15

Pirie, E, 1968 A Constantinian coin hoard from Womersley, W R, *Yorks Archaeol J* **42**, 127–9

Potter, T W, 1976 Excavations at Watercrook 1974: an interim report, *Trans Cumb West Antiq & Archaeol Soc* **76**, new series, 6–66

Potter, T W, 1979 *Romans in North-west England; excavations at the Roman forts of Ravenglass, Watercrook and Bowness on Solway,* Cumb West Antiq & Archaeol Soc Res Series **1**. Kendal

Potter, T W, 1983 *Roman Britain*. London

Price, J, 1982 The glass, in G Webster & L Smith, The excavation of a Romano-British establishment at Barnsley Park, Gloucestershire, 1961–1979. Part II c AD 360–400+, *Trans Bristol Glos Archaeol Soc* **100**, 174–85

Price, J, 1983 The Roman vessel glass, in C Heighway, *The East and North Gates of Gloucester,* Western Archaeol Trust Monogr **4**. Bristol, 168–70

Price, J, 1985 The glass, in Bidwell 1985, 206–14

Price, J, 1988 Romano-British glass bangles from East Yorkshire, in J Price, P R Wilson, C S Briggs & S J Hardman (eds), *Recent Research in Roman Yorkshire,* BAR Brit Series **193**. Oxford: British Archaeological Reports, 339–66

Price, J, 1990 Roman vessel and window glass, in McCarthy 1990, 163–79, microfiche 2/64–2/80

Price, J, 1991 The glass, in B Rawes, A prehistoric and Romano-British settlement at Vineyards Farm, Charlton Kings, Gloucestershire, *Trans Bristol Glos Archaeol Soc* **109**, 70–3

Price, J, 1992 Glass, in Rahtz P *et al, Cadbury Congresbury 1968–73. A late/post-Roman hilltop settlement in Somerset,* BAR Brit Series **223**. Oxford: British Archaeological Reports, 131–43

Price, J, 1993 Vessel glass, in A Woodward & P Leach, *The Uley Shrines. Excavation of a ritual complex on West Hill, Uley, Gloucestershire, 1977–79,* English Heritage Archaeol Rep **17**. London, 210–15

Price, J, 1995 Glass tablewares with wheel-cut, engraved and abraded decoration in Britain in the fourth century AD, in Foy (ed) 1995, 25–33

Price, J, 2000a Glass vessels, objects and window glass, in E Price, *Frocester: a Romano-British settlement, its antecedents and successors,* Vol 2: *The finds.* Glos District Archaeol Res Group. Stonehouse, 103–22

Price, J, 2000b Late Roman glass vessels in Britain, from AD 350 to 410 and beyond, in J Price (ed) 2000, *Glass in Britain and Ireland AD 350–1100,* British Museum Occ Paper **127**. London, 1–31

Price, J, 2004 Romano-British and early Post-Roman glass vessels, in H Quinnell, *Trethurgy. Excavations at Trethurgy Round, St Austell.* Cornwall County Council, 85–92

Price, J, 2005 'A glass vessel of peculiar form': a late Roman mould-blown bottle found with a burial at Milton-next-Sittingbourne in Kent, *J Roman Pottery Stud* **12**, 155–63

Price, J, & Cool, H E M, 1983 Glass from the excavations of 1974–76, in A E Brown & C Woodfield, Excavations at Towcester, Northamptonshire: the Alchester Road Suburb, *Northampton Archaeol* **18**, 115–24

Price, J, & Cool, H E M, 1993 The Vessel Glass, in M J Darling & D Gurney, *Caister-on-Sea. Excavations by Charles Green, 1951–55,* East Anglian Archaeol Rep **60**, 141–52

Price, J, & Cottam, S, 1995 Late Roman glass bowls from Beadlam villa, North Yorkshire, in B Vyner (ed), *Moorland Monuments: studies in the archaeology of north-east Yorkshire in honour of Raymond Hayes and Don Spratt,* CBA Res Rep **101**. York: Council for British Archaeology, 235–42

Price, J, & Cottam, S, 1996 The glass, in D S Neal, *Excavations on the Roman Villa at Beadlam, North Yorkshire,* Yorks Archaeol Rep **2**. Leeds, 93–108

Price, J, & Cottam, S, 1997 Roman glass in Wilmott 1997, 341–55

Price, J, & Cottam, S, 1998 *Romano-British Glass Vessels: a Handbook,* CBA Practical Handbook in Archaeology **14**. York: Council for British Archaeology

Price, J, & Worrell, S, forthcoming Report on the Roman glass from Binchester in Ferris and Jones forthcoming

Pröttel, P, 1988 Zur Chronologie der Zwiebelknopffibeln, *Jahrbuch des Römisch-Germanischen Zentralmuseum Mainz* **35**, 347–72

Rackham, O, 1986 *The History of the Countryside.* London

Raftery, B, 1982 Knobbed spearbutts of the Irish Iron Age, in B G Scott (ed), *Studies on Early Ireland: essays in honour of M V Duignan.* Dublin, 72–92

Raftery, B, 1998 Knobbed spearbutts revisited, in M Ryan (ed), *Irish Antiquities: essays in memory of Joseph Raftery.* Dublin, 97–110

Raftery, B, 2005 Ireland and Scotland in the Iron Age, in W Gillies & D W Harding (eds), *Celtic Connections Volume 2: archaeology, numismatics and historical linguistics.* Edinburgh, 181–9

Ralston, I, & Inglis, J, 1984 *Foul Hordes: the Picts in the North-East and their Background.* Aberdeen

Rance, P, 2001 Attacotti, Déisi and Magnus Maximus: the case for Irish federates in late Roman Britain, *Britannia* **32**, 243–70

Rayner, L J, 1999 An examination of the cattle metapodials from the Roman fort at Vindolanda to identify the possibility of breed improvement over time. Unpublished undergraduate dissertation, Durham University.

Richardson, J S, 1907 Notice of kitchen-midden deposits on North Berwick Law, and other antiquities in the vicinity of North Berwick; with a note of an undescribed sculptured stone, with symbols, on the island of Raasay, *Proc Soc Antiq Scot* **41**, 424–36

Richmond, I A, 1940 The barbaric spear from Carvoran, *Proc Soc Antiq Newcastle* 4th series, 136–8

Richmond, I A, & Birley, E B, 1930 Excavations on Hadrian's Wall, in the Birdoswald-Pike Hill Sector, 1929, *Trans Cumb West Antiq & Archaeol Soc* new series **30**, 169–205

Richmond, I A, & Gillam, J P, 1951 The Temple of Mithras at Carrawburgh, *Archaeol Aeliana* 4th series **29**, 1–92

Richmond, I A, Hodgson, K S, & St Joseph, K, 1938 The Roman fort at Bewcastle, *Trans Cumb West Antiq & Archaeol Soc* new series **38**, 195–237

Rigby, V, 1980 Coarse pottery, in I M Stead, *Rudston Roman Villa*. Leeds, 45–94

Roberts, B K, 2007 Between the brine and the high ground: the roots of Northumbria, in R Collis (ed), *Northumbria: history and identity 547–2000*. Chichester, 12–32

Roberts, B K, 2008a *Documents and Maps*. Oxford

Roberts, B K, 2008b The Land of Werhale – Landscapes of Bede, *Archaeol Aeliana* 5th series **37**, 27–159

Roberts, B K, & Wrathmell, S, 2002 *Region and Place: a study of English rural settlement*. London

Roberts, B K, Dunsford, H, & Harris, S, 2005 Framing Medieval landscapes: region and place in County Durham, in C Liddy & R Britnell (eds), *North-East England in the Later Middle Ages*. London, 221–37

Robertson, A, 1970 Roman finds from non-Roman sites in Scotland, *Britannia* **1**, 198–226

Robertson, A S, 1978 The circulation of Roman coins in north Britain: the evidence of hoards and site-finds from Scotland, in R A G Carson & C M Kraay (eds), *Scripta Nummaria Romana: essays presented to Humphrey Sutherland*. London, 186–216

Robertson, A S, 1993 Finds of Imperial Roman coins in Britain from Near-Eastern and Eastern mints: the evidence of Romano-British coin hoards, in M Price, A Burnett & R Bland (eds), *Essays in honour of Robert Carson and Kenneth Jenkins*. London, 229–40

Rome Hall, G, 1880 An account of researches in ancient circular dwellings near Birtley, Northumberland, *Archaeologia* **45**, 355–74

Rushworth, A (ed), 2009 *Housesteads Roman Fort – the grandest station: Excavation and survey at Housesteads, 1954–95, by Charles Daniels, John Gillam, James Crow, and others*. London

Sagui, L, 1996 Un piatto di vetri inciso da Roma; contibuto ad uninquadramento delle officine vetrarie tardoantiche, *Studi Miscellanei* **30**, 337–58

Salway, P, 1967 *The Frontier People of Roman Britain*. Cambridge

Salway, P, 1981 *Roman Britain*. Oxford

Sarnowski, T, 1985 Bronzefunde aus dem Stabsgebäude in Novae und Altmetalldepots in den römischen Kastellen und Legionslagern, *Germania* **63**, 521–40

Sauer, E, 2007 Milestones: misunderstood stone monuments? Paper delivered at the British Epigraphic Society Spring Colloquium in Edinburgh, *British Epigraphy Soc Newsletter* new series **17** (spring 2007), 13–14 http://www.csad.ox.ac.uk/BES/Newsletter.htm

Schulze-Dörlamm, M, 1985 Germanische Krieg-ergräber mit Schwertbeigabe in Mitteleuropa aus dem späten 3 Jahrhundert und der ersten Hälfte des 4 Jahhunderts n Chr, *Jahrbuch der Römisch-Germanischen Museums Mainz* **32**, 509–69

Scott, I R, 1980 Spearheads on the British *limes*, in Hanson & Keppie (eds) 1980, 333–43

Scull, C, & Harding, A, 1990 Two Early Medieval Cemeteries at Milfield, Northumberland, *Durham Archaeol J* **6**, 1–29

Sekulla, M F, 1982 The Roman coins from Traprain Law, *Proc Soc Antiq Scot* **112**, 285–94

Sennequier, G, 1985 *Verrerie d'Époque Romaine*. Rouen

Shepherd, I A G, 1993 The Picts in Moray, in W D H Sellar (ed), *Moray: province and people*. Edinburgh, 75–90

Shepherd, J, 2000 Glass, in B Barber & D Bowsher, *The Eastern Cemetery of Roman London*, MoLAS Monogr **4**. London, 125–30

Sherlock, D, 1979 *Plumbatae* – a note on the methods of manufacture, in Hassall & Ireland 1979, 101–2

Sherlock, S, & Welch, M, 1992 *An Anglo-Saxon Cemetery at Norton, Cleveland*, CBA Res Rep **82**. London: Council for British Archaeology

Shortt, H de S, 1959 A provincial Roman spur from Longstock, Hants and other spurs from Roman Britain, *Antiq J* **39**, 61–76

Shotter, D C A, 1993 The coins from Ambleside, in R H Leech, The Roman fort and *vicus* at Ambleside: archaeological research in 1982, *Trans Cumb West Antiq & Archaeol Soc* new series **93**, 66–8

Simpson, C, 1976a Belt-buckles and strap-ends of the Later Roman Empire: A preliminary survey of several new groups, *Britannia* **7**, 192–223

Simpson, C, 1976b A Late Roman belt buckle from Corbridge, Northumberland, *Britannia* **7**, 285–6

Simpson, F G, 1913 Excavations on the line of the Roman Wall in Cumberland during the years 1909–12, *Trans Cumb West Antiq & Archaeol Soc* new series **13**, 297–397

Simpson, F G, & Hodgson, K S, 1947 The coastal milefortlet at Cardurnock, *Trans Cumb West Antiq & Archaeol Soc* new series **47**, 78–127

Smith, A, 1956 *English Place-Name Elements*. Cambridge, 25–27

Snape, M, 1992 Sub-Roman brooches from Roman sites on the northern frontier, *Archaeol Aeliana* 5th series **20**, 158–60

Snape, M, 1993 *Roman Brooches from North Britain: a classification and a catalogue of brooches from sites on the Stanegate*, BAR Brit Series **235**. Oxford: British Archaeological Reports

Snape, M, & Bidwell, P, 2002 Excavations at Castle Garth, Newcastle upon Tyne, 1976–92 and 1995–6: the excavation of the Roman fort, *Archaeol Aeliana* 5th series **31** (special edition)

Sommer, M, 1984 *Die Gürtel und Gürtelbeschläge des 4 und 5 Jahrhunderts im römischen Reich*, Bonner Hefte zur Vorgeschichte **22**. Bonn

Spearman, R M, 1990 The Helmsdale bowls, a re-assessment, *Proc Soc Antiq Scot* **120**, 63–77

Speed, G, forthcoming *Excavations at Hollow Bank Quarry Scorton, North Yorkshire. Volume 2: the Romano-British and Anglian cemeteries*

Speidel, M A, 1992 Roman army pay scales, *J Roman Stud* **82**, 87–106

Speidel, M P, 2000 Who fought in the front? in G Alföldy, B Dobson & W Eck (eds), *Kaiser, Heer und Gesellschaft in der römische Kaiserzeit: Gedenkschrift für Eric Birley*, Heidelberger Althistorische Beiträge und Epigraphische Studien **31**. Stuttgart, 473–82

Spratling, M G, 1971 Bronze terret, in P V Webster, Melandra Castle Roman fort: excavations in the civil settlement 1966–1969, *Derbyshire Archaeol J* **91**, 113–15

Stallibrass, S, 2000 How little we know and how much there is to learn: what can animal and human bones tell us about the late Roman transition in northern England, in Wilmott & Wilson (eds) 2000, 73–9

Stamp, L D (ed), 1937–46 *The Land of Britain*, County Fasicles. Royal Geographical Society and Geographical Publications Ltd

Stead, I M, 1991 *Iron Age Cemeteries in East Yorkshire*. London

Stead, I M, & Pacitto, A L, 1980 Small Finds, in I M Stead, *Rudston Roman Villa*. Leeds, 95–123

Stenton, F M, 1971 *Anglo-Saxon England*. Oxford

Stern, E M, 1999 Roman glassblowing in a cultural context, *American J Archaeol* **103**, 441–84

Stevens, C E, 1940 The British sections of the *Notitia Dignitatum*, *Archaeol J* **97**, 125–54

Stevens, C E, 1941 Gildas Sapiens, *English Hist Review* **56**, 353–73

Stevenson, R B K, 1955 Pins and the chronology of the brochs, *Proc Prehist Soc* **21**, 282–94

Stevenson, R B K, 1956, Pictish chain, Roman silver and bauxite beads, *Proc Soc Antiq Scot* **88**, 228–30

Stevenson, R B K, 1976 Romano-British glass bangles, *Glasgow Archaeol J* **4**, 45–54

Stupperich, R, 1997 Römisches Silbergeschirr der mittleren bis späten Kaiserzeit in Germanien, in H-H von Prittwitz und Gaffron & H Mielsch (eds), *Das Haus lacht vor Silber*. Köln, 71–80

Summerfield, J, 1997a The small finds, in Wilmott 1997, 269–321

Summerfield, J, 1997b Appendix 2: Other small finds from Birdoswald, in Wilmott 1997, 412–15

Sumpter, A B, 1990 Pottery from well 1, in S Wrathmell & A Nicholson (eds), *Dalton Parlours Iron Age Settlement and Roman Villa,* Yorks Archaeol **3**. Wakefield, 235–45

Swan, V G, 2002 The Roman pottery of Yorkshire in its wider historical context, in P Wilson & J Price (eds), *Aspects of Industry in Roman Yorkshire and the North*. Oxford, 35–79

Swanton, M J, 1973 *The Spear-heads of the Anglo-Saxon Settlements*. Leeds

Swift, E, 2000a *The End of the Western Roman Empire. An Archaeological Investigation*. Stroud

Swift, E, 2000b *Regionality in Dress Accessories in the late Roman West*, Monographies Instrumentum **11**. Montagnac

Symonds, R, & Tomber, R, 1991 Late Roman pottery: an assessment of the ceramic evidence from the city of London, *Trans London Middlesex Archaeol Soc* **42**, 59–99

Tainter, J A, 1988 *The Collapse of Complex Societies*. Cambridge

TeBrake, W, 1985 *Medieval Frontier: culture and ecology in Rijnland*. College Station, Texas

Thirsk, J, 1967 The farming regions of England, in J Thirsk (ed), *The Agrarian History of England and Wales, IV, 1500–1640*. Cambridge, 1–112

Thomas C 1992 The Early Christian Inscriptions of Southern Scotland, *Glasgow Archaeol J* **17**, 1–10

Timby, J R, 1998 *Excavations at Kingscote and Wycomb, Gloucestershire*. Cirencester

Tomlin, R S O, 2000 The legions of the Late Empire, in Brewer 2000, 159–81

Tomlin, R S O, & Hassall, M W C, 2004 Roman Britain in 2003. III. Inscriptions, *Britannia* **35**, 335–49

Tomlin, R S O, & Hassall, M W C, 2005 Roman Britain in 2004. III. Inscriptions, *Britannia* **36**, 473–97

Tomlin, R S O, Wright, R P, & Hassall, M W C, forthcoming *The Roman Inscriptions of Britain* Vol 3

Treadgold, W, 1995 *Byzantium and its Army, 284–1081*. Stanford

Trowbridge, M L, 1928 *Philological Studies in Ancient Glass,* University of Illinois Studies in Language and Literature **13**, nos 3–4. Urbana: University of Illionois Press

Tyers, P, 1996 *Roman Pottery in Britain*. London

Vallet, F, & Kazanski, M (ed), 1993 *L'armée romaine et les barbares du IIIe au VIIe siècle*. Rouen

van der Veen, M, 1988 Carbonised grain from a Roman granary at South Shields, North-east England, *Der Prahistorische Mensch und Seine Umwelt* **31**, 353–65

van der Veen, M, 1992 *Crop Husbandry Regimes: an archaeobotanical study of farming in northern England 1000 BC–AD 500*. Sheffield

van der Veen, M, & Palmer, C, 1997 Environmental factors and the yield potential of ancient wheat crops, *J Archaeol Sci* **24**, 163–82

van Driel-Murray, C, 1987 Roman footwear: a mirror of fashion and society, *Recent Research in Archaeological Footwear*, Assoc Archaeol Illustrators and Surveyors Technical Paper **8**. London

van Driel-Murray, C, 1990 New light on old tents, *J Roman Military Equip Stud* **1**, 109–38

Vindolanda Trust, 2002 *All Vindolanda Excavation Reports 1997–2000*, cd-rom produced December 2002

Viner, L, 1998 Kingscote field-walking finds, in Timby 1998, 206–16

von Schnurbein, S, 1974 Zum ango, in G Kossack & G Ulbert (eds), *Studien zur Vor- und Frühgeschichtlichen Archäologie. Festschrift für Joachim Werner zum 65 Geburtstag*. München, 411–33

Wacher, J S, 1969 *Excavations at Brough-on-Humber, 1958–61*, Rep Res Comm Soc Antiq London **25**. London

Wacher, J S, 1971 Yorkshire towns in the fourth century, in R M Butler (ed), *Soldier and Civilian in Roman Yorkshire*. Leicester, 156–77

Wake, T, 1939 Excavations at Witchy Neuk, Hepple, *Archaeol Aeliana* 4th series **16**, 129–39

Ward-Perkins, B, 2005 *The Fall of Rome and the End of Civilisation*. Oxford

Watkin, W T, 1883 *Roman Lancashire*. Liverpool

Watkin, W T, 1886 *Roman Cheshire*. Liverpool

Webster, J, 1986 Roman bronzes from Maryport in the Netherhall Collection, *Trans Cumb West Antiq & Archaeol Soc* new series **86**, 49–70

Webster, J, 1988 Bronze Objects: Brooches, in G D B Jones & D Shotter, *Roman Lancaster: rescue archaeology in an historic city 1970–75*. Manchester, 146

Welch, M G, 1993 The archaeological evidence for federate settlement in Britain within the fifth century, in Vallet & Kazanski 1993, 269–78

Welsby, D A, 1982 *The Roman Military Defence of the British Provinces in its Later Phases*, BAR Brit Series **101**. Oxford: British Archaeological Reports

Wenham, L P, & Heywood, B, 1997 *The 1968 to 1970 Excavations in the* Vicus *at Malton, North Yorkshire*, Yorkshire Archaeol Rep **3**. Leeds

Wheeler, R E M, & Wheeler, T V, 1932, *Report on the Excavation of the Prehistoric, Roman and Post-Roman Site at Lydney Park, Gloucestershire*. Oxford

White, R H, 1988 *Roman and Celtic Objects from Anglo-Saxon graves* BAR Brit Series **191**. Oxford: British Archaeological Reports

White, R H 1994 A massive (Donside) terret found near Wroxeter, Shropshire, *Trans Shropshire Arch Hist Soc* **69**, 129–31

White, R, 2007 *Britannia Prima: Britain's last Roman province*. Stroud

Whittaker, D, 1993 Landlords and warlords in the Later Roman Empire, in J Rich & G Shipley (eds), *War and Society in the Roman World*. London, 277–303

Wild, J P, 1968 Clothing in the north-west provinces of the Roman Empire, *Bonner Jahrbucher* **168**, 166–240

Wild, J P, 1970 Button-and-loop fasteners in the Roman provinces, *Britannia* **1**, 137–55

Wilkes, J, 1961 Excavations in Housesteads fort, 1960, *Archaeol Aeliana* 4th series **39**, 279–99

Williams, D F, 1994 Campanian amphorae, in Bidwell & Speak 1994, 217–19

Wilmott, T, 1997 *Birdoswald: Excavations of a Roman Fort on Hadrian's Wall and its Successor Settlements: 1987–92*, English Heritage Archaeol Rep **14**. London

Wilmott, T, 2000 The late Roman transition at Birdoswald and on Hadrian's Wall, in T Wilmott & P Wilson (eds) 2000, 13–23

Wilmott, T, 2001 *Birdoswald Roman Fort*. Stroud

Wilmott, T, & Wilson, P (eds), 2000 *The Late Roman Transition in the North*, BAR Brit Series **299**. Oxford: British Archaeological Reports

Wilson, P R, 1989 *Crambeck Roman Pottery Industry*. Leeds

Wilson, P R, 2002 *Cataractonium: Roman Catterick and its hinterland. Excavations and research, 1958–1997, Part 1*, CBA Res Rep **128**. York: Council for British Archaeology

Wilson, P, 2003 The Roman towns of Yorkshire; 30 years on, in P Wilson (ed), *The Archaeology of Roman Towns: studies in honour of John S Wacher*. Oxford, 258–69

Wilson, P R, Cardwell, P, Cramp, R J, Evans, J, Taylor-Wilson, R H, Thompson, A, & Wacher, J S, 1996 Early Anglian Catterick and *Catraeth*, *Medieval Archaeol* **39**, 1–61

Wilson, R J A (ed), 2006 *Romanitas: Essays on Roman archaeology in honour of Sheppard Frere on the occasion of his Ninetieth Birthday*. Oxbow

Winchester, A, 1990 *Discovering Parish Boundaries*. Princes Risborough

Winchester, A, 2000 *Discovering Parish Boundaries*, 2nd edn. Princes Risborough

Wood, I, 2007 Fragments of Northumbria, in F Orton, I Wood & C Lees (eds), *Fragments of History: rethinking the Ruthwell and Bewcastle Monuments*. Manchester

Wood, I, 2008a, Monasteries and the geography of power in the age of Bede, *Northern History* **XLV** (1), 11–25

Wood, I, 2008b *The Origins of Jarrow: the monastery, the slake and Ecgfrith's minster*. Jarrow

Worrell, S, 2003, The glass, in N Hodgson 2003, 195–20

Worrell, S, 2004a Roman Britain in 2003, II. Finds reported under the Portable Antiquities Scheme, *Britannia* **35**, 317–34 and frontispiece

Worrell, S, 2004b Some new late Roman rivet spurs, *Lucerna* **28**, 20–2

Wright, R P, 1960 Roman Britain in 1959. II. Inscriptions, *J Rom Stud* **50**, 236–42

Wright, RP, 1965 Roman Britain in 1964. II. Inscriptions, *J Rom Stud* **55**, 220–8

Wright, R P, & Jackson, K H, 1968 A late inscription from Wroxeter, *Antiq J* **48**, 296–300

Young, C J, 1977 *Oxfordshire Roman pottery*, BAR Brit Series **43**. Oxford: British Archaeological Reports

Youngs, S, 2005 After Oldcroft: a British silver pin from Welton le Wold, Lincolnshire, in N Crummy (ed), *Image, Craft and the Classical World*. Montagnac, 249–54

Zanier, W, 1988 Römische dreiflügelige Pfeilspitzen, *Saalburg Jahrbuch* **44**, 5–27

Zant, J, 2009 *The Carlisle Millennium Project, Excavations in Carlisle 1998–2001: Volume I, the Stratigraphy*, Lancaster Imprints **14**. Lancaster

Zienkiewicz, J D, 1986 *The Legionary Fortress Baths at Caerleon. 2, The Finds*. Cardiff

Index

Page numbers in *italics* denote illustrations; plates are shown with *pl* before the number; page numbers with 't' are tables.